Prostitution and Victorian society
Women, class, and the state

Prostitution and Victorian society
Women, class, and the state

JUDITH R. WALKOWITZ
Department of History, Rutgers University

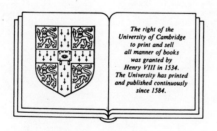

The right of the
University of Cambridge
to print and sell
all manner of books
was granted by
Henry VIII in 1534.
The University has printed
and published continuously
since 1584.

Cambridge University Press

CAMBRIDGE
NEW YORK   PORT CHESTER
MELBOURNE   SYDNEY

Published by the Press Syndicate of the University of Cambridge
The Pitt Building, Trumpington Street, Cambridge CB2 1RP
40 West 20th Street, New York, NY 10011, USA
10 Stamford Road, Oakleigh, Melbourne 3166, Australia

First Published 1980
First paperback edition 1982
Reprinted 1983, 1986, 1988, 1989, 1991

Printed in the United States of America

Library of Congress Cataloging in Publication Data
Walkowitz, Judith R.
Prostitution and Victorian society.
1. Prostitution – Great Britain –
History – 19th century.
2. Venereal diseases – Great Britain –
History – 19th century.
3. Venereal disease – Law and legislation –
Great Britain – History – 19th century.
I. Title.
HQ185 A5W34 301.41′54′0941 79 – 21050

ISBN 0 521 27064 2 paperback

I wish to express my gratitude toward Indiana University Press for permission
to reprint "The Making of an Outcast Group," which appears in revised form
as Chapter 10. It was originally published as "The Making of an Outcast
Group: Prostitutes and Working Women in Nineteenth-Century Plymouth and
Southampton," in *A Widening Sphere: Changing Roles of Victorian Women,*
ed. Martha Vicinus (Bloomington, 1977), pp. 72–93.

Contents

Contents

Preface

When I began research on this project in 1970, sexuality and prostitution were only just emerging as legitimate subjects for historical inquiry. Two influential works, Steven Marcus's *The Other Victorians* (1966), and a 1963 essay by Peter Cominos, had already begun to explore the relationship between sexual ideology and social structures and to identify prostitution as a fundamental aspect of social life in Victorian Britain.

Since that time, the study of Victorian sexuality has been refined in a number of ways. Critics have challenged the assumption of a unitary, Victorian culture and single, repressive standard of sexuality. Others have questioned how precisely sexual prescription translated into behavior. Historians of women, in particular, have taken exception to the exclusively negative image of women—as subordinated, silent victims of male sexual abuse—that emerged from the study of prescriptive and pornographic literature. Instead Mary Ryan, Carroll Smith-Rosenberg, and Linda Gordon have focused on the efforts of female moral reformers in America to dictate sexual standards and to carve out a moral territory for themselves in the public world. Although the argument for women's power and autonomy can be carried too far—female moral reformers sometimes reinforced rather than challenged modes of class and gender domination—the story of women's resistance to the dominant forces of society needs to be told.

The Contagious Diseases Acts present a particularly good opportunity to study class and gender relations in mid-Victorian Britain. Both the acts and the public controversy surrounding them generated a massive documentation about the lives and actions of people such as prostitutes, who are usually missing from historical accounts. The acts also provide insight into important social and political developments in the mid-Victorian period: the rise of the institutional state; the emergence of the women's movement; changing social and sexual mores; and the problems of state intervention and deviance.

Research for this book was supported in part by the Rutgers Research Council and the National Library of Medicine, under grants PHS-LM. 2574-01 and 2574-02. I should like to thank the staff of the following libraries for their assistance: the Bodleian Library, British Library, Fawcett Library, Friends Library, Harvard University Libraries, Oxford University, Princeton University Library, the Public Record Office, Royal College of Surgeons, Rutgers University Library, the Wellcome Library, and Dr. Williams' Library. My thanks also to the archivists and local-history librarians at the Aldershot, Belfast, Birmingham, Bristol, Chatham, Greenwich, Manchester, Newcastle-on-Tyne, Plymouth, Portsmouth, Southampton, and the Woolwich public libraries.

Many friends and comrades on both sides of the Atlantic read all or part of this manuscript. My thanks to the following for their critical suggestions and encouragement: Barbara Abrash, Rudolph Bell, Marcia Carlisle, Lenore Davidoff, Anna Davin, Alan Dawley, John Gillis, Deborah Gorham, Mary Hartman, Angus McLaren, Phyllis Mack, Charles Rosenberg, Ellen Ross, Raphael Samuels, Carrol Smith-Rosenberg, Barbara Taylor, and Martha Vicinus. I should also like to express my appreciation to Drs. Sol Jarcho, William Liefer, and Michael Waugh for their technical assistance on the history of medicine. The Reverend J. Vaughan-Jones kindly provided me with information relating to Mrs. Steward of Ongar from his parish records.

I should also like to thank the editors and staff of Cambridge University Press, especially Steven Fraser, for his support and encouragement, and Robert Ackerman, who edited the manuscript with care and intelligence.

Rachel Bernstein, Ellen Holtzman, Waverly Lowell, and Susan Tracy assisted me in my research and in the preparation of the manuscript. My undergraduate and graduate students at Rutgers University served as an intelligent sounding board for my ideas and arguments over the past eight years.

Esther Breisacher typed many drafts of this book. My thanks to her and also to June Johnson, who also typed parts of the final manuscript.

I am especially indebted to Daniel J. Walkowitz for his careful reading, criticism, and editing of the entire book. Much of the research on Southampton and the Portsmouth Hospital was originally his, which he generously passed on to me. I should also like to thank my daughter, Rebecca Walkowitz, for her encouragement and patience while this long project underwent completion. Finally I should like to thank the women of the women's liberation movement, for inspiring this project and giving me the courage to persevere.

J.R.W.

Rutgers, The State University
New Brunswick, New Jersey

Introduction: The revolt of the women

In 1864, Parliament passed the first of three statutes providing for the sanitary inspection of prostitutes in specific military depots in southern England and Ireland. Initially this first Contagious Diseases Act, as it was obliquely entitled, aroused little attention inside or outside governmental circles. Florence Nightingale had objected to its passage, on the grounds that it officially sanctioned "vice," but she failed to convince politicians like William Gladstone that a standing army could be a "moral institution."[1] Public opposition to regulation did, however, surface in the 1870s, when a coalition of middle-class nonconformists, feminists, and radical workingmen challenged the acts as immoral and unconstitutional, and called for their repeal. The participation of middle-class women in repeal efforts fascinated and shocked many contemporary observers, who regarded this female rebellion as an ominous sign of the times. One troubled member of Parliament was moved to remark to Josephine Butler, the feminist repeal leader, "We know how to manage any other opposition in the House or in the country, but this is very awkward for us—this revolt of the women. It is quite a new thing; what are we to do with such an opposition as this?"[2]

The public controversy surrounding the Contagious Diseases Acts constitutes a fascinating chapter in the history of class and gender relations in mid-Victorian Britain. This book looks at the origins of these acts, the successful feminist campaign to repeal them, and their impact on registered prostitutes and their community. As a social experiment in the custodial treatment of poor "outcast" women, the acts provide a framework for examining some connections between ideology, public policy, and social change.

The Contagious Diseases Acts of 1864, 1866, and 1869 were introduced as exceptional legislation to control the spread of venereal disease among enlisted men in garrison towns and ports.[3] By 1869, they were in operation in eighteen "subjected districts." Under the acts, a woman could be identified as a "common prostitute" by a special plainclothes policeman and then subjected to a fortnightly internal examination. If found suffering from gonorrhea or syphilis, she would be interned in a certified lock hospital (a hospital containing venereal wards) for a period not to exceed nine months. The definition of common prostitute was vague, and consequently the metropolitan police employed under the acts had broad discretionary powers. When accosted by the police, a woman was expected to submit voluntarily to the medical and police registration system or else be brought before the local magistrates. If brought to trial for refusing to comply, the woman bore the burden of proving that she was virtuous – that she did not go with men, whether for money or not.

The administration of the acts was extraordinarily complex, a testimony to the chaotic state of government expansion in the middle of the century. These were pieces of national legislation, officially overseen by the Admiralty and the War Office, employing metropolitan police under the Home Office; yet they had to rely on provincial magistrates, doctors, and hospital authorities to enforce the sanitary and penal requirements. Not surprisingly, the opportunities for bureaucratic and jurisdictional conflicts were great.

Organized public agitation against the regulations first mounted in 1869, in response to the aggressive efforts of civilian doctors and authorities to extend the acts to the north. In December 1869 the National Association was formed, which excluded women from its first meeting, but soon opened its membership to them. This resulted in the formation of a parallel but separatist female organization, the Ladies' National Association (LNA).

Under the leadership of Josephine Butler, the LNA issued a sharply worded Ladies' Manifesto denouncing the acts as a blatant example of class and sex discrimination. The manifesto argued that the acts not only deprived poor women of their constitutional rights and forced them to submit to a degrading internal examination, but they officially sanctioned male vice. In the years to come, various repeal organizations proliferated, reflecting the ideological, class, regional, and gender divisions within the repeal camp.

Between 1870 and 1886, when the acts were repealed, repealers sustained an impressive public campaign that sought both to educate public opinion about repeal and to influence elite political circles in Parliament. As part of their political agitation, repeal leaders and their paid agents descended upon the subjected districts, agitated among registered prostitutes, and encouraged them to resist the legal requirements of the acts. The subsequent controversy over the C.D. acts, as they were called in the nineteenth century, encouraged public discus-

2

sion on a wide range of social, medical, and political questions. The double standard of sexual morality; the participation of women in political activity; the control of women by male doctors; and the role of the state in enforcing sexual and social discipline among the poor were all subjected to public scrutiny and debate.

Both the acts and the repeal campaign are familiar aspects of Victorian history that have never been adequately studied in their broad social context. Military historians and others have regarded the acts as a pragmatic response to a pressing social problem.[4] From their perspective the acts were a realistic attempt to control prostitution and venereal disease in disorderly garrison towns and ports. However, the practical medical goals that underlay the C.D. acts were in fact fused with, and at the same time undermined by, a set of moral and ideological assumptions. In pressuring for the medical inspection of prostitutes without imposing periodic genital examination on the enlisted men who were their clients, architects of the acts obliterated from the start whatever effectiveness as sanitary measures the acts might have had. Just as important, regulationists reinforced a double standard of sexual morality, which justified male sexual access to a class of "fallen" women and penalized women for engaging in the same vice as men.[5] Indeed, an earlier attempt to institute periodic examination among soldiers had failed because enlisted men violently objected and officers feared that compulsory examination would lead to the demoralization of their men. It was contended that such objections could not apply to prostitutes, who were presumably bereft of "self-respect" and more powerless to protest this intrusion.

This cultural interpretation, although important, does not explain, among other things, the timing of the acts. Why were they introduced in the 1860s, and why, from a European standpoint, so late? However blatant the sex prejudice, the acts were not simply a sign of the relative strength of the double standard in the mid-Victorian period. A casual acceptance of male sexual license was traditional among the British upper classes and continued to be upheld by aristocratic "reprobates" in parliamentary debates throughout the Victorian period. What may have changed was the increased official concern over prostitution as a dangerous form of sexual activity, whose boundaries had to be controlled and defined by the state.

The concern with prostitutes reflects another important ideological component of the regulationist position – a new enthusiasm for state intervention into the lives of the unrespectable poor. Both prostitutes and enlisted men were members of the social "residuum," the casual laboring poor who inhabited the "nether regions" of society.[6] A

state intervent

3

source of cheap labor and illicit pleasures for middle-class Victorians, this social underworld was also the focus of deep-seated social fears and insecurities, most vividly expressed in the images of filth and contagion associated with the "Great Unwashed." Pollution became the governing metaphor for the perils of social intercourse between the "Two Nations"; it assumed heightened scatological significance in a society where the poor seemed to be living in their own excrement, and where the first programmatic attempt to deal with urban social problems was in the realm of sanitary engineering. Literally and figuratively, the prostitute was the conduit of infection to respectable society. She was nonetheless an object of class guilt as well as fear, a powerful symbol of sexual and economic exploitation under industrial capitalism.

The C.D. acts reflect this view of the social underclass as degraded and powerless, yet potentially threatening and disloyal.[7] As military reforms, the acts were linked to a conscious policy to create a professional bachelor army and navy without family ties or local identities; military authorities additionally hoped that, by offering enlisted men controlled outlets for heterosexual activity, they could curb homosexuality in the ranks as well.[8] For their part, local civilian officials warmly endorsed the acts as a means of curtailing street disorders and disciplining the unrespectable civilian poor in their community.

Through the control of sexuality, the acts reinforced existing patterns of class and gender domination. They illustrate the obsessive preoccupation with and codification of sex that, according to Michel Foucault, distinguished Victorian sexuality from the official sexual code of earlier epochs. The modern debate over sex, Foucault argues, was a strategy for exercising power in society. By ferreting out new areas of illicit sexual activity, a new "technology of power" and "science of sexuality" were created that facilitated control of an ever-widening circle of human activity. The new "science of sexuality" identified sex as a public issue; rigidly differentiated male from female sexuality; focused attention on extramarital sexuality as the primary area of dangerous sexual activity; and "incorporated" perversions in individuals who, like the homosexual, were now accorded an exclusive and distinct sexual identity.[9]

These shifts in focus and concern were embodied in and reinforced by the C.D. acts. Under the acts, extramarital sex became a question of state policy, a matter of vital national importance. A complicated "technology of power" was established to oversee and manipulate the social lives of the unrespectable poor. Special controls were placed on the female body in that prostitutes, not their male clients, were identi-

4

fied as the primary source of disease and pollution. This medical and police supervision in turn created an outcast class of "sexually deviant" females, forcing prostitutes to acknowledge their status as "public" women and destroying their private associations with the general community of the laboring poor.

The study of the acts that follows begins where Foucault's schematization leaves off; it will examine how sexual and social ideology became embedded in laws, institutions, and social policy. This study treats ideology as a "child of social experience";[10] not as an abstract static system, but something more fluid, reflective of the power dynamics of Victorian society and responsive to changing historical circumstances. The acts were not simply the expression of a programmatic and coherent social policy toward "fallen women" and the residuum; they were instrumental in crystallizing and shaping many of these social views. The acts were, in fact, introduced piecemeal, over a five-year period; their limits were constantly extended, as government officials, doctors, and local authorities devised a new purpose and function for the regulation system. Many of the social and political assumptions underlying their operation were initially implicit and undefined, and only later consciously formulated and defended by regulationists when confronted with organized resistance.

Most studies of Victorian sexuality have focused on one single code of sexuality, expressive of the "world view of those persons in positions of power" – namely adult middle-class males.[11] In so doing, they have assumed the existence of a unitary Victorian culture. In fact, several Victorian subcultures existed at the same time, each with distinct prescriptions about sex.[12] This pluralistic model, however, can also be misleading; these subcultures were not equally powerful nor were they fully autonomous within the dominant culture. But as Raymond Williams has noted, the "reality of any hegemony, in the extended political and cultural sense, is that while by definition is always dominant, it is never either total or exclusive."[13]

Thus, although the C.D. acts created a "technology of power," they also generated a formidable social and political resistance. The acts became a battleground where diverse and competing groups vied with each other for social and political power. The repeal campaign reveals how social groups mobilized over sex, how they articulated their demands, and how they impressed their views on a popular audience.

The repeal campaign has occupied an important niche in the history of nineteenth-century feminism, although its contribution to the emerging feminist movement has never been satisfactorily explored.[14] As conventionally depicted in the historiography of feminism, the Ladies

Introduction

National Association's attack on male vice and the double standard is made to seem out of place next to the more decorous struggles for the franchise, property rights, and access to higher education. British historians have only recently begun to relate the public struggles for women's rights to the private lives of middle-class feminists, and more generally to the social relations between the sexes in the nineteenth century.

Traditionally, feminist repeal efforts have been entirely subsumed under the charismatic personality of Josephine Butler—so much so that the campaign has commonly been labeled "Josephine Butler's campaign."[15] The exclusive focus on Butler does a disservice to male and female repealers alike. It ignores the role of male leaders, notably Henry J. Wilson and James Stansfeld, who directed the political strategy of the campaign at certain stages, and it fails to examine the repeal campaign as an organized movement.

Brian Harrison has done much to redress this latter shortcoming in the historical literature.[16] In *Drink and the Victorians*, his classic study of the temperance movement, and in a more recent essay on moral reform movements, he has identified the repeal campaign as a key mid-Victorian pressure group, whose leaders were prominent in other moral and social reform activity. Although a useful beginning, this effort to fit the repeal movement into a model of liberal nonconformist reform has serious drawbacks. It obscures the conflicts between factions within the repeal camp, so that the significance of the campaign as a distinct moment in moral reform, one in which feminism and class consciousness came to the fore, is lost.[17]

For instance, one of the most striking developments of the repeal campaign was the interclass alliance between workingmen and middle-class feminists. This alliance was initiated by feminist leaders of the Ladies' National Association to protect their own rights and authority within the repeal camp from the encroachments of middle-class male leaders. These behind-the-scenes struggles reveal as much about the pervasive character of class and gender divisions in Victorian society as the frequent public denunciation of "aristocratic doctors" and male vice found in repeal literature.

Female and male repealers had different attitudes and emotional commitments toward the issues raised by the campaign. Women often expressed an identity of interest with inscribed prostitutes and intense anger at the police and medical domination of their "fallen sisters." They perceived the acts as a direct threat to their own status and self-respect, whereas most male repealers tended to view repeal as only one of a series of "anti-causes" they espoused.

6

The struggle for female power and autonomy was not without historical ironies. In their defense of prostitutes, feminist repealers were still limited by their own class bias and by their continued adherence to a separate-sphere ideology that stressed women's purity, moral supremacy, and domestic virtue.[18] Thus they became indignant when confronted with an unrepentant prostitute who refused to be reformed or rescued. Moreover, they lacked the cultural and political power to shape the world according to their own image. Although they tried to set the standards of sexual conduct, they did not control the instruments of state that would ultimately enforce these norms. Through the repeal campaign, they were able, for a time, to dominate and structure the "public discourse" on sex, and to arouse popular female anger at male sexual license. Yet this anger was easily coopted and rechanneled into repressive antivice campaigns. The history of the repeal campaign does not end triumphantly with the removal of the C.D. acts from the statute books in 1886, but more ominously, with the rise of social-purity crusades and with police crackdowns on streetwalkers and brothel keepers.

A study that encompasses regulationists, repealers, and prostitutes requires a complex strategy. A simple chronological narrative of the rise and fall of the Contagious Diseases Acts is insufficient because it is my intention to use the acts as an occasion to explore a series of social, institutional, medical, and political developments in the mid-Victorian period. The operation of the regulation system needs to be examined from both a national and local perspective, as the acts were the dual product of state policy and the social and political environment of garrison towns and ports. Local study also makes it possible to examine how feminists, prostitutes, magistrates, doctors, and police experienced this historical moment, and how they mediated each other's response to the acts.

Plymouth and Southampton, two subjected districts where the acts aroused substantial local opposition, form the basis of a local study. Both were southern dock towns in similar stages of economic development, although Plymouth had substantial naval installations, whereas Southampton was exclusively a commercial port. The political economy of prostitution in these urban centers as well as the network of control and confinement that loomed over the lives of the unrespectable poor were also comparable. In both districts, a band of Liberal nonconformists readily committed themselves to repeal and successfully galvanized registered prostitutes to resist the acts. This public agitation generated a wealth of information about local regulationists, repealers, and the subject working-class population – thus making it

7

possible to examine the lives and actions of people usually missing from the historical record.

A study of garrison towns brought under the acts might well have yielded different results. In places like Aldershot and Colchester, government influence was far greater and local opposition to the acts less sustained.[19] Aldershot, to use an extreme example, was described by one observer as a "town of yesterday," a town without a history, which sprang up as a garrison camp in the early nineteenth century with inadequate accommodations and meager employment opportunities for a civilian population.[20] Many Aldershot prostitutes appeared to have been impoverished, transient camp followers, with a large number coming from London and Ireland. In contrast, prostitutes residing in Greater Plymouth and Southampton had predominantly migrated from the surrounding countryside and encountered a more complex and established community life.

The C.D. acts present a special opportunity to explore the lives and self-perception of working-class prostitutes at a moment of intense political crisis.[21] Until recently historians have not regarded prostitution as a serious subject for examination, choosing instead to treat it with coy facetiousness or to ignore it altogether. The problematic nature of traditional sources has further hampered a more searching inquiry: most of the surviving testimony comes from evangelical reformers or officials with a decidedly moral and social bias against the "residuum"; the numbers of prostitutes have been difficult to assess; and prostitutes themselves were understandably anxious to preserve their anonymity against prying investigators. However, local sources, such as the manuscript census, police columns of local newspapers, and institutional records, provide a solid foundation upon which to reconstruct the social profile of Victorian prostitutes. By using these sources, it is possible to outline the age of streetwalkers, their social background, length of stay on the streets, clientele, and residential patterns – always recognizing that this is just a beginning and not a full and authentic representation of prostitutes' social experience, as they may have interpreted it themselves.

Although useful, these sources still have to be translated and decoded by the historian. One must keep in mind, for example, that a woman's appearance at police court was a "staged event," a social drama largely manipulated by police and judicial authorities. Only a select number of streetwalkers were ever brought before the magistrates, and the criminal record of those arrested by no means constituted the sum total of their life experience.[22]

Fortunately the controversy over the Contagious Diseases Acts opens up a small window into these women's private lives. In the 1870s, Plymouth and Southampton prostitutes left an impressive record of protest against the regulation system that revealed their involvement in a set of informal female networks. In their struggle against the acts, they were able to call upon female relatives, neighbors, and male lovers for support. Prostitutes thus emerge as important historical actors, as women who made their own history, albeit under very restrictive conditions. They were not rootless social outcasts but poor working women trying to survive in towns that offered them few employment opportunities and that were hostile to young women living alone. Their move into prostitution was not pathological; it was in many ways a rational choice, given the limited alternatives open to them. Moreover, their "sexually deviant" behavior must be measured against the standards of their own social class, whose norms were often distinct, if not fully autonomous, from the values of the dominant culture. Nonetheless, by the 1880s, external forces, in particular the acts themselves, may have disrupted the normal pattern of these women's lives and effectively isolated them from the general laboring-poor community.

Because reformers and authorities drew upon older modes of social explanation in their response to regulation, it is important to place a discussion of the public debate over the acts along the continuum of social attitudes on prostitution in nineteenth-century Britain. In addition, the history of registered women under the Contagious Diseases Acts needs to be seen within the context of the general social and political economy of Victorian prostitution. We turn first, then, to an historical assessment of the "great social evil" and to Victorian programs for its amelioration.

PART I
*Prostitution, social science,
and venereal disease*

PART 1

Prostitution, social science
and venereal disease

1 *The common prostitute in Victorian Britain*

> I was a servant gal away down in Birmingham. I got tired of
> workin' and slavin' to make a living, and getting a——— bad one
> at that; what o' five pun' a year and yer grub, I'd sooner starve, I
> would. After a bit I went to Coventry, cut brummagem, as we
> calls it in those parts, and took up with soldiers as was quartered
> there. I soon got tired of them. Soldiers is good – soldiers is – to
> walk with and that, but they don't pay; cos why they ain't got no
> money; so I says to myself, I'll go to Lunnon and I did. I soon
> found my level there.
> —"Swindling Sal," quoted in Bracebridge Hemyng, "Prostitution
> in London," in *London Labour and the London Poor*, ed. Henry
> Mayhew (rpt., New York, 1968), IV, 223.

This East End prostitute was a member of the proletariat of prostitution – part of the vast numbers of working-class women who plied
their trade on the streets or in the pubs and music halls of working-
class districts of mid-Victorian Britain. In this brief autobiographical
sketch, she demonstrates a fine gift for storytelling as well as a secular
and materialist understanding of her situation worthy of Defoe. She
defies the social and sexual stereotypes of fallen women that pervaded
mid-Victorian literature. She was not an elegantly attired Haymarket
streetwalker, one of those dressy "somebodies whom nobody knows,"
"who elbow ... wives and daughters in the parks and promenades
and rendez-vous of fashion."[1] Nor was she simply a pathetic embodiment of social injustice – a "miserable creature" "ill-fed, ill-clothed,
uncared for, from whose misery the eye recoils, cowering under dark
arches and among bye lanes."[2] A boisterous woman, she lacked the
melodramatic flair of the depraved, degraded temptress who figured
so importantly in evangelical tracts against the "great social evil."[3]

Her move into prostitution further challenges a whole series of conventional assumptions about prostitutes handed down to us from the
Victorian period. She was not the innocent victim of middle-class
seduction and betrayal; nor was she a mere child drugged and en-
trapped into prostitution by white slavers. Instead, her entry into prostitution seems to have been voluntary and gradual. As she told her

13

story, she first left her position as an underpaid, overworked slavey in Birmingham to take up with soldiers in Coventry, and only subsequently wended her way to London. In London, she "found her level" in the East End rather than the West End, and continued to service transient working-class men. In her case, then, prostitution was not a question of middle-class demand and working-class supply, but rather involved a social and sexual relationship between men and women of the same social class.

Yet in a number of ways this woman was exceptional. Few prostitutes in the nineteenth century were as self-possessed as she. Most were more ambivalent and defensive about their occupation. Moreover, their move into prostitution was not as clearcut and intentional as her personal account would suggest. Rather, most women's entry into prostitution appears to have been circumstantial rather than premeditated – less frequently a result of deliberate migration to specific centers of "gay life" than a response to local conditions of the urban job market. Placed in a vulnerable economic and social position, some women may have found the shorter hours and better pay of prostitution a temporary solution to their immediate difficulties.

This chapter will outline a social profile of the common prostitute in the Victorian period and locate her place in the prostitution market of various urban centers. Prostitution will be treated as an occupation – one that involved casual sexual encounters with men for "cash payment." It was also an activity structured and defined by the law. "Common prostitute" was an exceptionally vague legal category generally meant to designate women who solicited men in public thoroughfares. During the nineteenth century, solicitation was not illegal, and the constable's formal control over streetwalkers was limited. Authorities were mainly concerned to impose a certain level of public decorum on prostitutes, to contain them within certain areas, and to break up collusions between prostitutes and thieves. To do so, they entered into some accommodation with streetwalkers, permitting them to ply their trade as long as they were not public nuisances.[4]

The focus of attention will be on those women who earned their living principally from prostitution. Unfortunately, it is impossible to estimate the number of clandestine prostitutes, or "dollymops," who supplemented their meager earnings as dressmakers, milliners, and the like, by occasional prostitution. Some nineteenth-century observers argued that casual prostitutes greatly exceeded the more visible, full-time streetwalkers.[5] Precise information on these clandestines is unavailable, but the likelihood is that their numbers have been exaggerated. Experts doubted that working women could maintain a dual

14

identity over any extended period–slaving away fourteen hours a day at dressmaking or launderessing and then going on the streets in the evening.[6] Moreover, in the case of "sly" prostitutes, it becomes even more problematic to define their sexual activity as prostitution. Frequently it is difficult to distinguish what may have been a traditional bartering of goods in exchange for sexual favors from an obvious violation of traditional sexual mores.[7] In contrast, among full-time prostitutes the departure from traditional norms was more clearcut; their life-style and participation in a distinctive female subculture set them apart from the rest of the laboring-poor community. But, as we shall see, prostitutes' exclusion from a general working-class life was never complete in the nineteenth century. Moreover, even for the more notorious prostitutes who came under police surveillance, streetwalking was a transitional stage that they would pass through.

The harlot's progress

Available nineteenth-century sources provide a fairly precise social profile of the working-class women who moved into prostitution. On the whole, there is little to distinguish these women from the large body of poor women who had to eke out a precarious living in the urban job market. Their migration patterns appear to be no different from the general population: most prostitutes were either natives of the city or recent migrants from the local countryside.[8] In terms of religious preference, Sunday-school attendance, and even conservative politics, they shared many of the cultural values of their class.[9] Some changes occurred in the composition of prostitutes over the course of the nineteenth century and early twentieth century that reflected their increased social marginality; these changes were gradual, and they chiefly affected age, education (after 1870), and occupation.[10] However, seen in context, the modest character of these variations suggests that the economic horizons of poor working-class women had not changed dramatically over this period, nor had the more general political economy of the casual laboring poor.

Throughout the Victorian period, most prostitutes remained, in Abraham Flexner's phrase, the "unskilled daughters of the unskilled classes."[11] In one late-Victorian study of London prostitutes interned in Millbank prison, the fathers of over 90 percent of the sample were unskilled and semiskilled workingmen.[12] Over 50 percent of these women had been servants, largely general servants; the rest had worked in equally dead-end jobs, such as laundering, charing, and

15

street selling. A high preponderance of servants were also found among mid- and late-Victorian inmates of London rescue homes and lock (venereal disease) hospitals.[13] Some variation in prior work experience seems to have occurred on a regional basis; in Liverpool, there was a greater concentration of street sellers, whereas in Glasgow former millworkers entered lock hospitals at the same rate as servants.[14] An only slightly altered recruitment pattern seems to have developed in the last decades of the nineteenth century: shopgirls, waitresses, and barmaids entered the ranks of prostitutes, reflecting the new but equally low-grade and unskilled female occupations in the tertiary sector of the economy.[15]

Being poor, these young women had left home for economic reasons; hence, on a daily basis they were expected to survive on their own resources. The degree to which working-class women were expected to shift for themselves without depending on their parents shocked middle-class commentators. When "Marion," one of A. J. Munby's London workingwomen, found herself in desperate need of money and thought she might have to resort to the streets, Munby asked her, "Why didn't you tell your mother?" "Oh what could she have done for me? Father couldn't afford to keep me at home; and I was ashamed for mother to know I was so bad off." In his diary, Munby complained of the "utter want of mutual intercourse, and even interest between the members of a family; and especially between mothers and daughters."[16]

Marion's response did not necessarily represent a break with traditional working-class expectations. As Louise Tilly and Joan Scott have noted, young women's entrance into the urban job market represented a continuation of long-held values that prescribed that women work to support themselves and contribute to the family income. Because of declining employment opportunities for women in the countryside as well as changes in production, young single women were increasingly required to seek work outside the home and sometimes to migrate to nearby urban areas to find alternative employment. There, they were expected to fend for themselves, and not burden their family for support.[17]

Despite some evidence of continued family connections, the family background of these women seems to have been unusually disrupted. An extraordinarily high percentage of prostitutes had lost one or both parents during the Victorian and Edwardian period; rescue homes and lock hospitals consistently reported that fewer than one-third of the young women interviewed had both parents living.[18] This constituted about twice the proportion of half or full orphans estimated by

16

Michael Anderson for young women and men in Preston in 1851.[19] It may be, as Bracebridge Hemyng suggested, that "loose women generally throw a veil over their early life,"[20] and calling oneself an orphan was a way of eliciting sympathy as well as closing off one's past to unwelcome middle-class scrutiny. However, rescue workers regularly declared that they further investigated women's histories, besides relying on the prostitutes' own declarations. In addition, rescue-home reports indicated that many of the nonorphans came from broken homes where the father had deserted the family or where the parents were separated.[21]

Another characteristic of prostitutes that appears to have remained constant was their age of sexual initiation. Sixteen seems to have been the most common age when, as the prostitutes interviewed described it, they "first went wrong."[22] It is impossible to determine to what degree sexual initiation at sixteen corresponded to the sexual experience of working-class girls generally because information for the general case is not available. This question puzzled Victorians as well. Daniel Cooper, secretary of the Rescue Society of London, wrote that prostitutes often "fell at a young age; and having actually fallen they become the victims of occasional temptation, and in the course of years, lapse into a life of open shame."[23] Yet he acknowledged that not "all women who have thus been led early astray give themselves up subsequently to an abandoned life. Probably a majority of them never enter such a course."[24]

If most prostitutes had their first sexual encounter at or around the age of sixteen, then the throngs of child prostitutes so highly advertised during the white-slavery campaign of 1885 must be dismissed as imaginary products of sensational journalism intended to capture the attention of a prurient Victorian public.[25] Police hardly ever arrested a girl under sixteen for prostitution; also, metropolitan and provincial police reported the virtual absence of known prostitutes under sixteen – a statement so categorical that it deserves to be treated with some suspicion.[26] Nonetheless, judicial statistics were consistent with the returns on female lock patients: between 1849 and 1856 the proportion of female inmates under sixteen at the London Lock Hospital was only 6.5 percent; this declined to 2.3 percent between 1857 and 1863.[27] Furthermore, the Rescue Society of London, which specialized in rescuing young girls and women, vigorously denied the existence of child prostitutes under sixteen in London, which was supposedly the mecca for child prostitution and "five pound virgins."[28]

In addition, the entrapment of innocent working-class girls by middle-class rakes does not fit the circumstances of these women's

17

first sexual experience, although a substantial minority of former servants seem to have been seduced by their masters.[29] Most appear to have had their first relationship on a noncommercial basis with a man of similar social status. In a late-nineteenth-century survey, 2,836 out of 16,000 prostitutes gave "seduction" as the immediate cause for their going on the streets; of this number only 659 said they had been seduced by a gentleman. And, as the author remarked, these women had a "broad" understanding of the term "gentleman," which included travelers, clerks, and shop assistants.[30]

According to authorities, early sexual experience was only the first stage in these women's decline; it was not coincident with their move into prostitution.[31] The abstract from the Rescue Society's register for 1877 shows a one-to-two year interval between sexual initiation and the move into prostitution, a time span confirmed by other studies.[32] These records would suggest that women most frequently entered prostitution in their late teens. Of course, women in rescue homes tended to be the most youthful prostitutes, as most homes restricted admission to relatively inexperienced "fallen" women who were considered to be most amenable to reformation. Still, lock hospitals reported a similar age concentration, with eighteen and nineteen being the most common ages of female inmates.[33] Most of these women had been on the streets less than a year, and had soon contracted syphilis, chancroid, and/or gonorrhea.[34] Only a small proportion of inmates were past their mid-twenties, the age at which, according to commentators like Acton, women left the streets to resume respectable employment or to settle down with a man.[35]

The stereotyped sequence of girls seduced, pregnant, and abandoned to the streets fitted only a small minority of women who ultimately moved into prostitution. In general illegitimacy seems to have been a social problem distinct from prostitution. According to the testimonies before the Infant Life Protection Commission, most unwed mothers were servants who were not prostitutes.[36] Moreover, from the limited historical evidence available, unwed mothers were in their early and mid-twenties, hence several years older than newly initiated prostitutes.[37] It is possible that a late age of menarche among poor working-class girls accounted for the small numbers of teenage pregnancies, even among young females who were sexually active.[38]

Of course, some women had children after they entered prostitution, and older women in their mid-twenties – often deserted wives or widows – were known to go on the streets to support their children. But such women were a minority.[39] Doctors and local-government-board inspectors were adamant in their belief that very few children of

18

prostitutes survived.[40] The presumed infertility of prostitutes and the low survival rate of their offspring were ascribed to two causes: high incidence of venereal disease that caused sterility, miscarriages, and sickly children who died in infancy; promiscuous sexual intercourse with numerous men that "produced in the female an imperfect elaboration of secretion necessary for impregnation."[41] The second argument, although suiting Victorian sexual ideology, has no scientific foundation. There is more medical evidence to support the first argument on venereal disease.[42] In addition, prostitutes boarded their children out, left them in the workhouse, or employed contraception, abortion, and infanticide to control their fertility.[43]

On the basis of the above information, it is possible to identify the dominant social characteristics of women who moved into prostitution in the second half of the nineteenth century. It is important to acknowledge, however, that the noninstitutionalized and fluid character of nineteenth-century prostitution permitted a wide variation of social types and recruitment patterns. Still, most prostitutes seem to have moved onto the streets in their late teens and remained there for no more than a few years.[44] Most were single, and more often than not their previous occupation had been as casual maids of all work. They were local girls, indigenous to the region. They overwhelmingly lived outside the family—indeed, they would most likely have been half or full orphan. Before going onto the streets, they had already had sexual relations of a noncommercial sort with a man of their social class.

Parts of this portrait would apply to many women who did not move into prostitution as well as to the numbers who did. The problem still remains to identify the factors that predisposed women to prostitution. Poverty seems to have been a principal cause for women's move into prostitution, but most women were not driven to prostitution from "sheer want," at the point of actual starvation.

Difficult circumstances precipitated the move into prostitution, but for many, that move still constituted a choice among a series of unpleasant alternatives. Why did some women choose this option and others not? Historical inquiry is hampered here by the limited information available on certain aspects of these women's family life and prior sexual experience, as well as their personality development. We know very little about their socialization and interpersonal relations and less about the character of their early sexual experience: whether, for example, they were grossly mistreated by their parents, or whether their sexual initiation was voluntary or involuntary, a consequence of rape or incest.[45]

19

Still, it might be helpful to focus on the one striking feature of these women's social background, their orphaned status. Late-nineteenth-century commentators laid great stress on the broken family background of many prostitutes, which they felt rendered the women economically vulnerable, and unable to cope with the circumstances of life, and therefore likely to run adrift and to get into trouble.[46] Without discounting the likelihood that many women drifted into prostitution without much forethought about their future, one must challenge the simple interpretation of the prostitute as passive victim. An alternative interpretation is possible, one that takes into consideration the extremely limited opportunities open to working-class women. It is important to consider the absolute level of subordination and acquiescence required of working-class girls. This condition of dependency and self-effacement was the normal behavior expected of them in their work situation as well as at home, but it was the family that functioned as the principal socializing agency in this regard.

In the late nineteenth and early twentieth centuries, girls were taken out of school to care for the younger children when mothers had to go out to work; they were given less free time at home than their brothers; they had less choice about their occupation; they were fed worse than their brothers, not to speak of their fathers. All this reflects a consistent social undervaluing of daughters, their financial exploitation, and the constraints placed upon them in hard-pressed working-class families.[47]

In contrast, a broken family background or strained family relations may have released these women from the stranglehold of standard female socialization. Without an emotional attachment to a mother and/or father, it may have been easier for a young woman to act against conventional norms. Mrs. Layton, a working woman growing up in the late nineteenth century, recalled the time when a "gentleman" offered her ten shillings to go "with him into a house for a short time. I thought of what I would buy and how long I had to work for ten/. And then I thought of my dear mother. Her poor tired face came into my mind and I felt that if I had been tempted to do wrong with the promise of £10,000 I would not for my mother's sake."[48]

Without these emotional constraints, women may have more openly resisted the conditions of subordination and dependency traditionally expected of them. According to rescue workers and others, a wild impulsive nature, a restlessness, and a desire for independence frequently characterized the young women who moved into prostitution.[49] Moreover, seasoned prostitutes were capable of independent and assertive behavior rarely found among women of their own social class.

20

Higher expectations may have been another factor that distinguished these women from their contemporaries. In the Millbank prison sample, for example, 14,000 out of 16,000 prostitutes indicated they were led away by such allurements as "nothing to do; plenty of money; your own mistress; perfect liberty; being a lady."[50] Living in a society where status was demonstrated by material possessions, women sold themselves in order to gain the accoutrements that would afford them "self-respect." One brothel keeper remarked to W. T. Stead: " . . . at fourteen and fifteen they begin to get more liberty without getting much more sense; they begin to want clothes and things which money can bring, and they do not understand the value of what they are parting with in order to get it."[51]   However calamitous the results, sexual activity was one of the few avenues of revolt open to a working-class girl: "The boy who runs away to sea is in comparatively little danger. His feminine equivalent is in great danger. There are few openings in life for her, and the very qualities of vitality and enterprise which make her run away render her perilously attractive."[52]

This form of rebellion could be contradictory and self-defeating. Poor working women often drifted into prostitution because they felt powerless to assert themselves and alter their lives in any other way. Even those young women who were positively attracted to prostitution soon discovered that streetwalking was a more hazardous and precarious occupation than they had anticipated. As we shall see, streetwalking may have afforded poor women a certain degree of autonomy, but it did not liberate them from a life of poverty and insecurity.

Although the specific circumstances of these women's lives are illuminating, their personal history needs to be placed in a larger social and economic framework in order to understand the operation of the prostitute market as a dynamic of supply and demand. Hence one needs to look at the various urban environments that were more or less likely to trigger a woman's move into prostitution, as well as the hierarchical structure of prostitution within those centers.

Modern Babylon

Police returns on "known" prostitutes and brothels provide an overview of the general geographic distribution of prostitutes and of their relative concentration in different kinds of cities—although such records are unreliable as indicators of the actual numbers of prostitutes in any specific locale. Between 1857 and 1869, when such returns were discontinued, the relative concentration of known prostitutes was

21

highest in commercial ports and pleasure resorts and lowest in hard-ware towns, cotton and linen manufacturing centers, and woolen and worsted centers.[53] This pattern is supported by early-twentieth-century data on death rates from syphilis and parasyphilitic diseases: the high-est death rates occurred among men of the unskilled laboring class, followed by men of the middle and professional classes, whereas the incidence of syphilis-related deaths was significantly lower among miners and textile and agricultural workers.[54]

Both sets of statistics raise rather than answer a whole series of questions about class and sexual mores, the political economy of ur-ban populations, and their influence on prostitution. The relatively high concentration of prostitutes in ports and pleasure towns could have reflected the uneven sex ratios, the limited employment opportu-nities open to women, as well as the presence of a transient male population that formed a ready clientele for the prostitutes. Likewise, the relatively lower concentration of prostitutes in textile and hard-ware areas probably reflected the particular character of working-class social life there: in those areas stable employment for men and (in the case of textile centers) women may have permitted the continuation of traditional courting practices, so that premarital sexuality with steady lovers culminated in marriage.[55] Furthermore, the venereal-disease sta-tistics cited above suggest that rural and industrial male workers were least likely to engage in promiscuous sexual intercourse or to rely on prostitutes.

In view of the limited geographic mobility of prostitutes, how does one explain the differential concentration of prostitutes in various urban areas? Taken together, it would appear that women's move into prostitution was circumstantial, not premeditated—less a result of de-liberate migration to specific centers of "gay life" for the purposes of prostitution than a response to local conditions of the urban job mar-ket. There are, of course, important individual exceptions to this gen-eral pattern, one being the former servant girl from Birmingham in the opening quotation. Munby and Hemyng interviewed West End and East End prostitutes who said they had come to London expressly to go on the streets. One fashionable Haymarket prostitute told Munby "she was a farmer's daughter from near Chesterfield; and came nomi-nally to be a draper's assistant, but really to become of her own accord what she is. N.B. *After nine months*, her family still think she is at the shop."[56]

The lure of London was apparently strong among seasoned prosti-tutes from the provinces, as a haven from police harassment and as the place where more money could be made.[57] Oxford, with its large pool of affluent male students, was another magnet for experienced street-walkers.[58] Certain categories of prostitutes were more mobile than others. Some soldiers' and sailors' prostitutes followed regiments and fleets to different military depots and ports throughout Britain.[59] None-theless, even among these women, those who made the move were exceptional. And they could often find themselves lonely and deserted "amongst strangers," like the soldiers' prostitute interviewed by Hemyng who fell in love with a private and "left my old friends and went to live in a new locality."[60]

Within cities, the hierarchy of prostitutes mirrored the class struc-ture of those centers. Police returns available on the various ranks of prostitutes challenge the conventional assumptions held by both Vic-torians and modern commentators that the demand for prostitution largely emanated from middle-class men. Although the precise pro-portion of prostitutes known to the police who catered to middle-class customers varied according to locality, the returns available indicate that a substantial majority of prostitutes catered to a work-ing-class clientele. As one might expect, this is particularly true of garrison towns and ports. But it also applies to certain centers with a substantial residential and transient middle class, like Edinburgh and London.[61]

The "wages of sin" varied according to one's place in the social hierarchy of prostitutes.[62] Possibilities for savings certainly existed for West End prostitutes, who even as streetwalkers could expect upwards of a pound from a well-heeled customer. Sarah Tanner, as described by Munby, was a living testimony to prudential individualism:

> Now here is a handsome young woman of twenty-six, who, having begun life as a servant of all work, and then spent three years in *voluntary* prostitution amongst men of a class much above her own, retires with a little competence, and invests the earnings of her infamous trade in a respectable coffee house ... Surely then this story is a singular contribution to the statistics of the "Social Evil" and of female character and society in the lower classes.[63]

For her East End sister, however, income could be measured in shillings and pence rather than pounds. For poor prostitutes, street-walking was a highly casual and seasonal occupation – much like the alternative legitimate occupations open to the class of women who moved into prostitution. Like alcoholic consumption, prostitution was linked to male leisure patterns, and therefore responded to fluctua-tions in the trade cycle as well as to the economic rhythms of the week.[64] Hence, income varied according to the means and availability of ready customers, who in the case of laboring men were also casu-

23

ally employed. Women adjusted their prices accordingly: "Sometimes I get three shillings, half a crown, five shillings often occasionally, according to the sort of man."[65] Some women had such difficulty living on the proceeds of prostitution that they had to resort to the workhouse and to other forms of casual employment in off-seasons. A soldier's woman, past her prime, but still tied to the "gay life," explained: "I don't get much, very little, hardly enough to live upon. I've done a little needlework in the day-time. I don't now, although I do some washing and mangling now and then to help it out."[66]

But even this woman, although very hard up, refused to enter a house as a kept prostitute: "Some of the girls about here live in houses. I don't; I never could bear it. You ain't your own master, and I always like my freedom."[67] Only a minority of prostitutes ever resided in formal brothels, and the reported number of brothels in London rapidly declined from 933 in 1841 to 410 in 1857.[68] In the late sixties, the numbers of public houses letting out rooms to prostitutes also experienced a significant decline throughout the country, owing to the enforcement of the new licensing laws.[69] While the connection between the drink trade and prostitution continued after the 1860s, especially in garrison towns where "pot house" girls were encouraged to frequent pubs to attract male customers, women largely *resorted to* rather than *resided in* these houses. They moved into private lodgings, where they were more likely self-employed and less physically segregated from a general poor working-class neighborhood. Licensing laws were also employed to crack down on casinos, pleasure gardens, and music halls, thus requiring prostitutes to solicit customers on the streets.[70]

Because of these developments, one could argue that the 1860s and 1870s represented the high point for the prostitute as an independent operator, relatively unencumbered by third parties who had a vested interest in keeping her in prostitution. It should be remembered, however, that British prostitution was always less institutionalized than prostitution on the Continent, where the regulation system fostered police corruption, women's dependence on pimps, and on organized brothel systems. In contrast, numerous observers, police officials, and rescue workers denied the existence of English brothels that at all resembled the continental model. Prostitutes tended to reside in dwellings with two or three other women that were "scarcely distinguishable" from "low class lodging houses," or sometimes in "externally respectable establishments," where the inmates had achieved a "quiet" truce with the police.[71]

Most Victorian cities had at least one notorious district where pub-

red light districts

lic women lived and plied their trade among a heterogeneous population of the laboring poor. Some districts were traditional centers of prostitution, like the narrow streets around the Water Lanes of York; others were of more recent origin. Whether old or new, they early acquired derogatory popular names, such as "Grapecunt Lane," York, the "Dust-Hole," Greenwich, and "Damnation Alley," Plymouth. Changes in urban geography and periodic police crackdowns on solicitation and brothel keeping often forced the "supply" to move from one part of town to another. In Victorian Manchester, for example, poor prostitutes congregated in Angel Meadow, once a "carriage parish," that, lacking good approaches to the new commercial district, had become the abode of hawkers, laborers, vagrants, prostitutes, and the Irish poor.

Prostitutes did not always reside in the least desirable quarters, however: they were often attracted to neighborhoods where male customers could be found. Hence, the emergence of a new pub and entertainment center, like Wellclose Square, Stepney, or the building of a railroad terminus could prove a strong magnet for public women. In addition to these large-scale movements, there was a constant flow of individuals in and out of the notorious streets, as women left the lodging-house brothels to take up a more respectable life elsewhere or simply to carry on their trade more discreetly in quieter working-class districts.[72]

During most of the nineteenth century, British prostitutes appear to be relatively independent of the control of pimps. William Tait found very few pimps resident among Edinburgh prostitutes in the 1840s; Acton made similar observations for Aldershot in the 1850s and 1860s.[73] There were exceptions, of course. East End bullies, for example, were a traditional feature of the low brothels on the Ratcliff Highway.[74] A number of prostitutes in this area had "fancy men," often casually employed waiters and laborers who resided nearby, whereas some others lived with thieves and were part of a professional criminal underworld.[75] This was a world organized and dominated by men – where the women lived under the control of flashmen, magsmen, and corrupt police – the world of Fagin, Bill Sikes, and Nancy in Dickens's *Oliver Twist*. On the whole, however, prostitution in Victorian Britain was a trade largely organized by women rather than men.[76] Moreover, although prostitutes generally maintained connections with a criminal society of petty thieves, fences, and runaway sailors, they were not cut off from general working-class life, nor were they mere creatures of the male criminal element, as Dickens's portrait of Nancy in *Oliver Twist* would suggest.[77]

In fact, a strong female subculture was a distinguishing feature of

25

nineteenth-century prostitution. As "outcast women," prostitutes banded together and adopted an outward appearance and a more affluent style of life that distinguished them from other working-class women. The most visible symbol of the prostitute's relative affluence was her dress. Middle-class commentators repeatedly complained that the "painted dressy women flaunting along the streets" in "dirty white muslin and greasy cheap blue silk"[78] exercised a pernicious influence on the impressionable servant girls in the neighborhood. The dress code of prostitutes also served as a way of advertising themselves and attracting male customers. Bonnetless, without shawls, they presented themselves "in their figure" to passersby.[79]

Their costume was also a badge of membership in a special female peer group, one that bore a peculiar relationship to the values of the dominant culture. In their dress, prostitutes emulated the conspicuous display of Victorian ladies. This effort to ape ladies was usually lost on self-righteous middle-class observers. For example, in a letter to the Home Office in 1858, one gentleman denounced the "outrageous style of dress" and the "revolting language and manners" of sailors' prostitutes who frequented the pubs of Wellclose Square, Stepney. His complaints were refuted point by point by the commander of the "K" division of the metropolitan police for Stepney. The officer explained that the women endeavored only "to imitate the style of ladies at evening parties and the theatre."[80] To these women, flaunting it "first rate" undoubtedly signified status, autonomy, and freedom from the workaday world of their respectable sisters.

Upon closer inspection, however, this showy affluence sometimes proved to be illusory. James Greenwood, for example, examined the parcels of clothing of prostitutes interned in the Westminster House of Correction. He observed that

> nothing is more common that for these poor creatures to be found wearing a gaudy hat and feather and a fashionably made skirt and jacket of some cheap and flashy material and nothing besides in the way of under-garments but a few tattered rags that a professional beggar would despise.

Thus attired, these "gay women" would saunter the pavements on bitter cold wintry nights, "with their wretchedly thin shoes soaking in the mud and their ill-clad limbs aching with cold."[81]

While in the "life," prostitutes seem to have been most tied to the other women living in lodging houses and to the lodging-house keeper. Mary Higgs, a turn-of-the-century "explorer" into the social abyss, gave the following description of the female fellowship and high sociability among prostitutes in a female lodging house in Oldham:

26

> Round the fire was a group of girls far gone in dissipation, good-looking girls most of them, but shameless; smoking cigarettes, boasting of drinks or drinkers, using foul language, singing music-hall songs, or talking vileness. The room grew full and breakfasts were about . . . a girl called "Dot" danced the "cake-walk" in the middle of the room.[82]

Higgs, like earlier social observers, was both horrified and fascinated by the scene. Although she could view the "promiscuous congregation" of women in the kitchen only as leading to general demoralization, she also understood that prostitutes viewed this female companionship as a positive feature of their situation. Speaking of one "good-natured affectionate girl" whom she was trying to "save," she remarked, "On her soul lay the knowledge of the *horror* of respectable society towards what she had become and the *attraction* of the fellowship of those who would receive her freely."[83]

Numerous commentators remarked on the frequent acts of generosity between members of the "fallen sisterhood."[84] Prostitutes were well known to aid each other in times of distress, to "club together" to pay for a proper funeral or to raise money for bail or for a doctor's fees.[85] The "wrens" of Curragh, observed James Greenwood, organized their "nests" along "communistic" principles: "None of the women have any money of their own; what each company get is thrown into a common purse and the nest [household] is provisioned out of it."[86] Group solidarity was also expressed in more ritualized fashion. Victorian prostitutes engaged in collective action rooted in preindustrial traditions of protest, such as the use of charivari against public authorities intent on repressing their trade.[87]

Yet the support system was an unstable one, caught up as many of these women were in an elementary struggle for survival. Higgs remarked that any article of clothing left in the lodging house would be pinched: "Here it was impossible for a girl even to keep her own property; there was not a locker or any place to put anything away. Girls slept with their hats on their beds for security. Everything was 'borrowed' or 'made off with.' "[88] Violent drunken brawls and conflict between women over "pitch," or territory, were not uncommon. This last form of disagreement, however, suggests as well that prostitution was a self-regulating industry. When asked about juvenile prostitutes in 1881, police officers in Liverpool explained that prostitutes strictly excluded young girls from streetwalking:

> For instance, round about the Sailors' Home, and about the Central Station in Liverpool, if any of the older prostitutes find any of these young girls, they hunt them and treat them very roughly as soon as

27

they find them on their walk. In the same way if there is any particular house in the neighborhood which receives very young girls information is given.[89]

Prostitutes' relationship with their female lodging-house keeper was more ambivalent. Most of these older women did not operate an explicit brothel, but it was nonetheless in their interest that their "girls" go out and seek male clients. Despite this mercenary outlook, lodging-house keepers also assisted prostitutes when they were down on their luck. Acton interviewed a woman who ran a house on the Ratcliff Highway who entered into a rambling statement

> as to the care and leniency with which she treated her lodgers when they were "out of luck." She asserted and the statement was corroborated by the girls, that they kept themselves; two may chum, or sleep together when disengaged; but they receive the money they earn, and are not farmed out.[90]

Besides housing single women, the brothel operated as a family industry, run by women who needed to support their dependents. Most of the men and the children in the brothel were attached to the brothel-keeper's family, often living in a separate residence in the house.[91] Although the children of some brothel keepers were "religiously" excluded from interaction with resident prostitutes, older girls were sometimes employed in domestic duties around the house — fetching beer, opening the door, or looking out for the police. When queried in 1885, local-government-board inspectors noted that very few girls were actually trained up to prostitution, although other officials warned against the "constant familiarity in immoral surroundings" that could "end in disaster" if adolescent daughters were allowed to remain in brothels.[92]

Moral reformers, preferring to see brothel keepers as hardened professionals rather than as hard-pressed working-class women, were frequently shocked at the respectable pretensions of these women. Sarah Robinson commented on the attempts of Portsmouth brothel keepers to join her newly established temperance organization in the 1860s:

> When we started a "Helping Hand Temperance Society" at the institute, several of these women came forward to join it; I called on them, to explain privately that they could not be admitted; and found texts hanging on their walls, and really superior books lying about.[93]

The women were "highly indignant" at their rejection. "You see, Mrs. Robinson, you get your living in one way and I in another. I pay my tradesman's bills the same as yourself, and I do not see why I should be excluded."[94]

28

Prostitutes' relationship with their customers was marred by similar tensions. The police columns of local newspapers were filled with accounts of drunken brawls and acts of petty theft between prostitutes and their clients. Frequently, women worked together in pairs, both to protect themselves from abusive men and to overpower and rob tipsy customers. Still, the fact that these women principally catered to single men of the same social class, even for "cash payment," also shaped the encounter. With working-class customers, there always existed the possibility of establishing a more intimate and enduring connection. Indeed, it would appear that many prostitutes had regular customers at pubs they would frequent and some settled down with men who had been their clients.[95] This pattern was institutionalized among sailors' prostitutes, who tended to form a more permanent relationship with one or more sailors, living with them when they were in port and drawing their half pay in their absence. These women provided a whole series of social as well as sexual services to sailors in port, housing them, holding their money, and protecting them from being skinned by unscrupulous lodging-house keepers and thief-prostitutes. One German prostitute in Stepney explained to Bracebridge Hemyng: "I know very many sailors – six, eight, ten, oh! more than that. They are my husbands. I am not married, of course not, but they think me their wife while they are on shore."[96] According to the police, these women readily integrated themselves into the social life of the Stepney neighborhood.

Clearly the notions of respectability among the poor did not completely mirror those of the middle class. In this regard, it is particularly difficult to discern precisely what "respectable" neighbors thought of prostitutes and brothel keepers, given the limited historical sources available. The social integration of prostitutes in the working-class community largely depended on the specific character of the local neighborhood. Artisans were generally quite hostile to the presence of prostitutes in their neighborhood. In Plymouth and York, the Irish also kept their distance from prostitutes in their midst, whereas the indigenous laboring poor were more likely to tolerate public women on an informal basis.[97] Yet this toleration could easily wear thin if official pressure was brought to bear on neighbors who led economically fragile lives.

Certain institutions in the working-class neighborhood, like music halls and pubs, provided a common meeting ground for prostitutes and their more respectable neighbors. Acton, while visiting an East End music hall in 1868, was shocked at the "elbowing of virtue and vice there."

29

Prostitution, social science, and venereal disease

My first interest lay in considering the effect produced upon married women by becoming accustomed at these *réunions* to witness the vicious and profligate sisterhood flaunting it gaily, or "first-rate" in their language – accepting all the attention of men, freely plied with liquor, sitting in the best places, dressed far above their station, with plenty of money to spend and denying themselves no amusement or enjoyment, encumbered with no domestic ties and burdened with no children.[98]

An explanation for the apparent toleration of "fallen" women by the respectable wives of operatives was offered by the accompanying police officer who argued that

> the mechanic and the mechanic's wife have their troubles and very serious ones, in providing for their mutual wants, and any persons connected with them whom they see well-dressed, and with money in their pockets, command a kind of respect, although the source from whence the means are obtained may be a disreputable one.[99]

Similarly, the camaraderie of the pub was demonstrated at the funeral of one of the Whitechapel murder victims in 1888. The casket of Marie Jean Kelly was covered with wreaths from friends "using certain public houses in common with the murdered woman."[100]

But outside the pub, not all respectable women responded as kindly. Frederick Rogers, reminiscing about his childhood in the East End in the late 1860s, remembered a prostitute's funeral at Mile End, where her "comrades," "clad in old hideous black hoods and scarves" followed the hearse to the grave, while a "guard of men of the kind who were called 'bullies' walked on either side of the women, to prevent – it was said – any hooting or stone throwing on the part of the virtuous matrons of the neighborhood through which the procession passed."[101] As we shall see in Plymouth and Southampton, local "matriarchs" acted as the voice of righteous indignation in the neighborhoods, objecting to the presence of "bad" women as well as the scandal of an examination house, where prostitutes registered under the Contagious Diseases Acts were brought for regular fortnightly examinations.

Community toleration of prostitutes also depended on the amount of external pressure placed upon the poor to adhere to a more stringent standard of sexual respectability. In the last decades of the nineteenth century, the legal repression of streetwalking and brothels intensified. This external intervention would directly affect the structure of the market for prostitution as well as the character of the women's social relationship with the laboring poor community. These developments will be considered in subsequent chapters, but it is useful here

30

to identify the distinctive features of mid-Victorian prostitution that would be affected by the transformation.

Women turned to prostitution as a temporary "refuge from uneasy circumstances." It was often an alternative to proletarianization, one that released them from an oppressive work regime and afforded them readier access to money and social independence. As a temporary occupation, streetwalking did, however, have severe drawbacks: it did not free women from a life of poverty and insecurity, and further subjected them to physical danger, alcoholism, venereal disease, and police harassment.

Similar ironies informed prostitutes' relations with men. Superficially, prostitution seemed to operate as an arena of male supremacy, where women were bartered and sold as commodities. In reality, women often controlled the trade and tended to live together as part of a distinct female subgroup. Prostitutes were still not free of male domination, but neither were they simply passive victims of male sexual abuse. They could act in their own defense, both individually and collectively. They negotiated their own prices, and they were as likely to exploit their clients as to suffer humiliation at male hands.

Although prostitutes were able to manipulate their situation somewhat, they were still operating within the narrow constraints imposed on them by a class-stratified and patriarchal society. Their lives were a piece with the large body of laboring women who had to eke out a precarious living in the urban job market, for whom sexual coercion was but one form of exploitation to which they were subjected. Their story is not one of opportunity and entrepreneurship, but rather of survival. Prostitutes enjoyed certain advantages over other poor working-class women–like the overworked "slaveys" who had to sleep in the kitchen–but these advantages were only relative. There is perhaps no more telling comentary on the exploitative character of Victorian society than the fact that some working women regarded prostitution as the best of a series of unattractive alternatives.

31

2 Social science and the Great Social Evil

An object of fascination and disgust, the prostitute was ingrained in public consciousness as a highly visible symbol of the social dislocation attendant upon the new industrial era. By the 1850s prostitution had become "the Great Social Evil," not simply an affront to morality, but a vital aspect of the social economy as well. Commentaries on prostitution took a variety of forms: novels, manifestos, letters to the editor, and police reports. Embedded in bluebooks on overcrowding, workhouse children, factory conditions, and women's employment were obligatory references to the immorality consequent upon deleterious social conditions.[1] In addition to this public outpouring of concern, recently published diaries of such men as A. J. Munby and W. E. Gladstone reveal the degree to which prostitution constituted a private obsession for some respectable Victorians, or as Gladstone put it, "the chief burden of my soul."[2]

The early-Victorian period also witnessed the elaboration of a new style of social research into prostitution and the formulation of activist programs for its amelioration. The intensity of concern, the style of analysis, the special emphasis on empirical and statistical research are all reflections of this particular moment in British political and cultural history. These early investigations deserve special attention for two reasons. They represent perhaps the most systematic efforts in the 1840s to examine the problem – formally proceeding from an examination of causes to results, extent, and remedies for prostitution. They also set the tone for later "scientific" research into prostitution in the nineteenth century. Later Victorians might debate the absolute necessity of prostitution and try to modify programs for the reform and rescue of "fallen" women, but they entertained very few new questions on the social economy as well as the personal history of prostitutes. As a consequence, the innovative analyses of the 1840s would later crystallize into the conventional wisdom of subsequent decades.

Mid-Victorian defenders of regulation reproduced the style and in-

32

terpretive framework of these early works. However, they reformulated the "problem" of prostitution in ways that reflected the changed social and political climate of the 1850s and 1860s. Early social investigators had identified prostitution as an intolerable evil that threatened the sanctity of the family as well as the social order. For later investigators like Acton, prostitution remained a "social evil," but one that could be contained by a system of police and medical supervision.

Early responses

In the 1840s, the study of prostitution first attracted men of the religious world or doctors and laymen influenced by evangelical doctrine. Prominent among the writers on prostitution were Congregational ministers like the Revs. William Bevan, Ralph Wardlaw, and Robert Vaughn, temperance and moral reformers like William Logan and J. B. Talbot, and evangelical physicians like Michael Ryan and William Tait.[3] These authors presented themselves as brave explorers into the social abyss, but they were clearly uneasy about the "unspeakable" evils they were about to unfold. As a consequence, they adopted a series of protective devices to distance themselves from the subject under scrutiny. Like the rescue of fallen women during this period, their study of prostitution represented more than a philanthropic duty to expose a moral evil and suggest its cure: it was a personal exposure to a sexual temptation, a test of their own moral fiber.

These evangelical writers first condemned male sexual license as a threat to the family and to conjugal love. They upheld the traditional puritan ideal of a patriarchal "marriage of affections" consecrated in the home, a zone of intimacy and refuge from the competitive world of work and politics.[4] Their demand for a single standard of sexual conduct and for the purity of sexual relations was uncompromising.[5] Like the radical sexual reformers of the time, they condemned the arranged marriages of convenience common among the upper class. For Michael Ryan, all marriage was to be a "perpetual compact between man and woman to live together in mutual love and friendship."[6] Adultery and resort to prostitutes desecrated this "holy and inviolable union."[7] Adultery was a "grievous injury to either party," whereas commercialized sex sullied what was supposed to be a spiritual act.

Evangelical writers also concerned themselves with strengthening the patriarchal family because they sought to reimpose the moral and social authority of the father over extrafamilial relations, at a time when the social and material bases of paternalism had been eroded. The patriarch whom they idealized was a nostalgic image, more ap-

33

propriate for the father—head of household of the early modern period—whose authority initially sprang from his crucial role in organizing household production and reproduction among his many dependents, both workers and kin—than for the professional men and industrial employers of "hands" in Victorian Manchester and Liverpool.
However, by reasserting their responsibility for the moral welfare of
"sons" and "daughters," evangelical reformers endeavored to invoke
this earlier authority relationship between the father and his dependents, and thus revive the patterns of deference that had traditionally
bound men and women to their "natural superiors."[8]

As defenders of the patriarchal family, they regarded prostitutes as a
source of pollution and a constant temptation to middle-class sons. A
young man, "cannot pass along the street in the evening without meeting with, and being accosted by, women of the town at every step."[9]
"His path is beset on the right hand and on the left, so that he is at every
step exposed to temptation from boyhood to mature age, his life is one
continued struggle against it."[10] More threatening still to respectable
society were the clandestine prostitutes who as servants were able to
infiltrate the sanctity of middle-class homes. Thus situated, a "sly"
prostitute, or "dollymop," "corrupts and seduces innocence and . . .
[by] assuming appearances the most honorable paralyzes authority . . .
and spreads with impunity the most frightful contagion and immorality
the most flagrant."[11]

Writers on prostitution acknowledged that members of their own
class were often responsible for these women's initial downfall. According to their accounts, ladies' maids and other upper servants fell
victim to middle-class seduction and betrayal, whereas the demand for
prostitution came largely from men of the propertied classes.[12] It was
a great source of public shame that prostitution was "supported and
upheld by men whose positions in society should afford a guarantee
against a morality so lax."[13] Public officials and merchants were also
implicated in this deadly traffic. The poor-law guardians who refused
outdoor relief to widows and unmarried mothers, the merchants who
grossly underpaid their needlewomen, and the shopkeepers who hired
men instead of women all helped to force women onto the streets.[14]
Thus for evangelical reformers the concern over the sexual exploitation of working-class girls by their social superiors was in part a
sincere crisis of conscience, in part an attempt to ameliorate a social
problem that had aroused intense class antagonisms.

Evangelical writers dominated public discourse on the subject, but
theirs were not the only voices raised in protest against prostitution. In
good part, their critique was shaped in response to popular indignation

at the sexual exploitation of working-class women by men of a superior class. On public platforms and in their journals, working-class critics used the discussion of prostitution as a rhetorical opening to hammer away at the "corruption" of the old immoral order and the exploitative character of class relations under industrial capitalism. The attack on upper-class seducers figured prominently in the campaign against the bastardy clauses of the New Poor Law.[15] Socialists and Chartists claimed that these clauses were introduced to relieve upper-class rakes of responsibility to support their illegitimate offspring: "And why was [the bastardy] clause introduced?" asked a Socialist speaker. "Why but to screen a vile aristocracy, who seduce and ruin more young girls than all the other male population put together."[16]

An 1841 article, "British Female Penitent Refuge," published in the *New Moral World,* the organ of Owenite socialism, readily illustrates the way the discussion of prostitution was integrated into a Socialist critique of middle-class paternalism. The article sardonically observed an apparent identity between the "very grave and virtuous seeming gentlemen who fostered vice and solicit prostitutes" and the "grave and reverend gentlemen who step forward now and then to make a formal declaration against it, and a formal demonstration of reclaiming the female practisers of it." Acknowledging that the "vice of prostitution" was a "monstrous evil," the *New Moral World* dismissed the "Refuge" as "of much the same value as was a certain old lady's bucket in emptying the seas." The refuge dealt with symptoms only and was furthermore a hypocritical palliative: "If repentant old gentlemen snatch from the vortex of prostitution one sorrowing victim, their sons are ready on the other side, to thrust in fresh ones." When women leave the refuge, the article continued, "What refuge have they then?" Nowhere was an "unprotected and needy woman safe from the immoral and pernicious approaches of the 'superior' sex." "Socialism" was the only refuge: "It is in Socialism alone that the conditions are to be found for the annihilation of this atrocious – this master vice of civilised life . . . "[17]

Like radical working-class critics, evangelicals manipulated the theme of prostitution for political ends, but in the opposite way. Writers like Wardlaw and Ryan interpreted "female fornication" as symptomatic of the anomic and undisciplined nature of working-class life.[18] Prostitution was seen as another form of disruptive sexual behavior, no different from common-law marriage, concubinage, and other "illicit intercourse of the sexes."[19] London city missionaries blamed the pernicious influence of Socialist ideology for this high level of "prostitution" as well as for increasing rates of illegitimacy and wife desertion.[20] Ralph Wardlaw, who regularly debated Owenite Socialists on the marriage question, described prostitution as the "socialism of the beasts,"[21] and other evangelical missionaries attacked Socialist communities as "brothels," where "all are to yield themselves up to be governed by the unrestrained instincts of nature, in imitation of dogs and goats."[22]

These surveys were political responses to a highly charged political atmosphere. Filled with images of pollution and violation, they convey a sense of horror at the disruption of the natural and social order by public women and working-class radicals alike. At the same time, evangelical writers relied on the method and language of social science to lend authority to their arguments; for, according to Tait, "a searching inquiry and detailed statements are essential, in order to give the public anything like an accurate impression of the desolating effects of this ungodliness."[23]

The social basis of prostitution

A. J. B. Parent-Duchâtelet's study of Parisian prostitutes, *De la prostitution dans la ville de Paris* (1836), served as the model for the British social investigations of prostitution in the 1840s.[24] Dubbed the "Newton of Harlotry,"[25] Parent prepared a demographic study of 12,000 prostitutes who had been inscribed over a fifteen-year period (1816–31). He outlined their former occupation, place of birth, age, social origins, and marital status. He also tried to trace their subsequent history after their names were removed from the police register. To describe these women's social lives, he supplemented police and hospital records with interviews with the women and personal observations of their style of life.

In Parent's study, prostitution emerges as a specialized but transitional occupation for young women of the laboring class.[26] The women generally reflected the social and economic composition of the working poor in Paris. In this instance, there was no rigid demarcation between the "criminal" classes and the "poor." Statistically little marks these women as exceptional or "deviant."[27] The evidence strongly suggests that for these young women prostitution was a stage in their life that they would pass through. Both the age concentration of registered prostitutes in their early twenties and Parent's account of their "sort définitif" substantiate their eventual reintegration into lower-class life.[28]

The publication of *De la prostitution* seems to have sparked a flurry of local surveys in Britain during the early 1840s. Over the next four decades, British publicists referred to Parent's work, and tried to reproduce his catalogue of the social hierarchy, customs, and habitat of the Victorian underworld. They were unable to duplicate his meticulous research because they lacked his precision and did not have access to the kinds of official records that provided him with most of his statistical information. Sometimes their reliance on Parent's typology was more implicit: frequently it is difficult to discern whether generalizations about the social lives and appearances of British prostitutes derived from actual observation or from an unthinking transposition to the British scene of Parent's study of Parisian public women. British writers also made selective use of Parent's findings; they ignored his observations on the fluid social identity of prostitutes, but emphasized the prostitute's sterility, frigidity, dissolute habits, and physical deterioration.

British writers on prostitution also saw their study as part of the larger examination of the "moral statistics" of the population, a subject popular among investigators of the early-Victorian provincial and London-based statistical societies.[29] Such empirical surveys were intended as preliminaries to action; data on a particular social evil were to be accumulated in order to recommend an ameliorative policy. Social science, thus, became "applied Christianity."[30] Yet this social science was a particularly antitheoretical and fragmented sort. Researchers in "moral statistics" viewed society as an atomized collection of individuals; they tended to see social problems as rooted in individual weakness, although they were willing to recognize that certain social situations could tempt and exacerbate this underlying moral frailty.

As a consequence, investigators assumed an uneasy and contradictory stance toward their working-class subjects and even toward their empirical method. Shocked at the abuses of industrialism and urbanization, they saw prostitutes as social casualties of cataclysmic developments, although they felt entirely removed and alien from the class of subjects under examination. This personal ambivalence was manifested in their writings by a tension between moralistic and environmentalist analyses.[31]

William Tait, for example, contributed a number of insights into the economic bases for prostitution. Like Ryan and others, he stressed poverty and unemployment as primary causes of prostitution. "The most distressing causes of prostitution are those which arise from poverty – want of employment – and insufficient remuneration for needle and other kinds of work in which females are employed."[32] In Edinburgh, there was not enough employment for more than two-thirds of the available female work force, and those jobs that did exist were limited to domestic work or the sewing trades, the dangerous "sedentary" trades noted by Parent. Milliners, dressmakers, stay-makers, and bonnetmakers were an absolute glut on the market and could at best eke out a living for only six weeks a year. The local social season and university terms also affected the periodic demand for prostitutes: "In summer . . . there are a third part fewer than in winter, and in autumn the number is still further diminished."[33]

Because he understood the vagaries of the casual labor market, Tait was one of the few male writers on prostitution who looked favorably upon factory work for women.

> It has been remarked, that the morals of the people in large towns, where many factories exist, are more polluted than those of towns of a different description. Yet it is somewhat remarkable, that all the large manufacturing towns contribute a smaller portion of pros-titution to Edinburgh, in proportion to the population, than any other in Scotland.[34]

Yet even an acute observer like Tait submerged his economic analysis in a vast inventory of "natural" or "accidental" causes that led women into prostitution: the "natural" including individual moral failings, such as licentiousness, irritability of temper, pride, love of dress, dishonesty, love of property, and indolence; the "accidental" including the "environmental" hazards of lower-class life, such as se-duction, ill-assorted marriages, low wages, want of employment, in-temperance, poverty, ill-training, obscene publications, and over-crowded housing.[35] Foundering in such a welter of explanations, Tait and others constantly shifted ground in their analyses, frequently em-bracing a single-cause explanation that contradicted the force of the accumulated data. "Invariably," as Philip Abrams notes about all Vic-torian social research, "the writer or speaker cuts his way out of the Gordian knot of social process by seizing on a solution or a main cause which is drawn not from his analysis of society but from his ulterior moral and political principle."[36]

Investigators of prostitution were unable to construct a cultural model that would make a poor woman's move into prostitution com-prehensible within the terms of her social and cultural world. For these middle class writers, working-class culture represented a total negation of culture.[37] From their point of view only a degenerate social milieu that spawned an alienated, antisocial personality pro-vided the setting for women's move into prostitution. For as the studies depicted the types of employment, the social gatherings, and the living conditions that could lead to a woman's downfall, they

38

effectively encompassed the whole of working-class life. As in the case of Tait's study of Edinburgh prostitutes, even tea parties could lead to seduction and procurement, not to mention theaters, penny gaffs, gin palaces, dancing schools, and soirees.[38]

In their analyses, the investigators treated prostitutes as irrevocably "fallen" women whose style of life permanently impaired their intellectual and moral faculties. "Once a woman has descended from the pedestal of innocence," declared Talbot, "she is prepared to perpetuate every crime."[39] Even the gregariousness of prostitutes hastened their dissipation and decline: "in this friendly intercourse which is kept up amongst them, they in some measure acquire the manners of each other; and in this way bad habits and customs are formed which may be said to be common to the whole community of abandoned women." Outcasts from society, ultimately reduced to "the most abject poverty, and wretchedness," subjected to the "most loathing and painful diseases," their fate could only be "premature Old Age and early Death."[40]

Any sympathy for prostitutes arose because of their history, not their present condition. Although these writers' efforts to protect young women from the circumstances leading them into prostitution were enlightened for their class, the treatment for those who had already "fallen" was repression. Writers like Tait demanded that prostitutes be banished from public gatherings and that brothel owners and producers be prosecuted. Prostitutes were labeled public enemies, criminals, and outcasts who had "abandoned the prerogatives of civil liberty."[41]

The Associate Institute

By looking at the social basis of prostitution, investigators had tried to "humanize" the prostitute and to respond seriously to popular criticism of the sexual exploitation of working-class women. But these analyses led to a public agitation that stressed negative and punitive measures against common prostitutes. The attack on the Poor Law and on the inadequate wages paid to women, articulated by Tait and others, inevitably took a backseat to the call for preventive and restrictive legislation to cut off the source of the "supply." Soon after the publication of *Magdalenism,* Tait was appointed secretary to the Edinburgh Society for the Protection of Young Girls, one of a number of provincial societies founded in the early 1840s on the model of the London Society for the Protection of Young Girls and the Suppression of Juvenile Prostitution.[42] The programs of these societies embodied many of the same contradictions found in contemporary writings on prostitution.

39

Dissatisfied with the narrow efforts of the older penitentiaries, these new societies adopted a more activist and preventive approach. They tried locally to repress juvenile prostitution and to prosecute brothel keepers and procurers. Their goal was to ensure a free-trade market for prostitution; for prostitution was "the greatest evil that could befall a woman and a corresponding care [must be] taken that in every case it shall be a deliberate and voluntary act."[43]

The London society and its provincial auxiliaries soon found it impossible to prosecute procurers or brothel keepers under existing statutes. Instead, a new organization, the Associate Institute for Improving and Enforcing the Laws for the Protection of Women, was formed to lobby for legal reforms that would repress the "traffic" in women, punish seducers of minors, and strengthen the police's hand in summary arrests. "A Bill for the Effectual Suppression of Brothels and Trading in Seduction and Prostitution" was introduced into the House of Lords in 1844 by Bishop Philpotts. The bill clearly represented a compromise between parliamentary sponsors of the bill and the members of the institute. It contained no clause against seduction because according to Philpotts, to permit a "fallen" woman legal recourse against her seducer would interfere with her training in penitence. The bill failed in its third reading when members of the government withdrew their support.[44]

When its lobbying efforts collapsed, the institute proceeded to concentrate its efforts on the rescue of adolescent girls and on educating public opinion regarding the fate of "fallen" women. The institute directed much of its attention to a female audience: it established a short-lived women's journal, the *Female's Friend,* and tried to enlist ladies' support for female auxiliaries "as in America." Ladies should be encouraged to "exert themselves in their own province." The institute proposed a sexual division of labor: if ladies "encourage virtue," then "others [men] will be found to put down [vice] with impunity as far as it can be accomplished."[45]

In these efforts the institute reflected the contemporary concern over the welfare of women and children, as manifested in protective labor legislation and the formation of a multitude of associations seeking to aid homeless and distressed women.[46] As conservative reformers, members of the institute were concerned with redressing obvious inequities in order to legitimize male bourgeois supremacy. Furthermore, as one examines the double-edged strategy of evangelical reform – the rescue of some individual fallen souls while consigning the rest to social and spiritual damnation – it becomes readily apparent that solicitude for prostitutes or even their actual redemption were secondary considerations. The agents of moral reform were the principle beneficiaries of the program: activity in a righteous cause tested their virtue while repressive laws and institutions of confinement protected them and their sons from unrestrained moral contagion.[47]

The later moralism: Greg and Acton

Later evangelical writers of the 1850s such as Viscount Ingestre and James Miller exhibited a narrowed and increasingly moralistic perspective on prostitution. Although their writings relied heavily on the language and format of earlier surveys, they were even harsher in their condemnations of lower-class life and prostitution. They lacked the measure of sympathy and practical understanding of the life of the poor that distinguished Tait's work. They skirted the discussion of the economic causes of prostitution, concentrating instead on unsanitary housing and on inferior moral education. Miller was particularly concerned with the demoralizing social environment: "There is literally no room for decency." Living in one small room, never more than two, "the inmates herd together like mere animals."[48]

The intellectual impoverishment observable in the literature on prostitution was a general feature of mid-century social research. The discussion of prostitution was denatured of the political content it had possessed in earlier decades, but this is true of mid-Victorian social investigations in general. With the decline of chartism, bourgeois social commentators were no longer engaged in a debate with their working-class critics. The mid-Victorian atmosphere of consensus and prosperity dulled the cutting edge of social inquiry and discouraged any sense of urgency for social reform. It also inhibited the exploration of radical social theories or even the examination of empirical details that would jar conventional wisdom.[49]

Ironically, the discussion of prostitution assumed a more significant place in public debates as it became more stale and clichéd. For mid-Victorians, prostitution constituted a distressing street disorder that threatened to infect "healthy" neighborhoods, but it no longer represented a social inequity that could spark a revolution. The social order no longer appeared actively threatened by the culture of the dangerous classes, as earlier epitomized by the "illicit intercourse of the sexes."

In the 1850s and 1860s, discussions of prostitution, like temperance, often constituted a diversion from the central issues of class politics. This is well documented in the way growing public concern over prostitution stimulated the repression of open prostitution. It was during the religious revival of the 1850s that prostitution was en-

41

shrined as the "great social evil." The outreach program of evangelicals, begun in the 1840s, gained widespread popularity and momentum at this time, enlisting the aid of women as well as men.[50] Hand in hand with the tremendous expansion of evangelical rescue homes in the metropolis came police crackdowns on the night haunts of prostitutes and their open solicitation in the West End. Police action was clearly stimulated by the agitation of the Society for the Suppression of Vice among the local London vestries. The legal intervention resulted in the geographic reshifting of the supply, rather than in its actual diminution. Successful repression of the fashionable night resorts of prostitutes, such as the closing of the Argyll Rooms (a night house in Piccadilly), created new problems for the police: a spilling out of activity onto the streets and into other areas of the city. This in turn generated vociferous complaints about the intrusion of a "multitudinous amazonian army of the devil" into respectable quarters.[51]

Police were clearly reluctant agents of moral reform who justified their laissez-faire policy by minimizing the social threat posed by prostitutes. When, however, their policy of inaction and toleration came under increased attack in the 1850s, police officials and others sought an alternative to the vicious cycle of repression and geographic dispersion of prostitutes. They increasingly looked to the "continental" system of regulation to facilitate the concentration of prostitutes in a narrowly circumscribed area under close police surveillance.[52]

The writings of W. R. Greg and William Acton were instrumental in generating an intellectual climate sympathetic to regulation. They based much of their argument for regulation on the need to stem the tide of venereal disease threatening to engulf the general population. This sanitary argument will be considered later, but it was linked to an analysis of prostitution very much in keeping with the tradition of social research outlined above.[53]

Greg and Acton presented themselves as moderates on the question of male sexuality and prostitution, arguing for some compromise between strict moral principles and the realities of social life. Their task was to make a regulation system palatable to a society whose official attitudes were increasingly informed by evangelical piety.[54]

For Greg, male access to promiscuous females could no longer be condoned as a time-honored male and class prerogative. It now had to be justified for environmental reasons. Given the "state of society" that required delayed marriages, "illicit intercourse will and must prevail to a considerable extent."[55] Moreover, although prostitution was not an inevitable social fact, it has "invariably been found wherever the population has been congregated in large masses."[56]

42

Although environmental conditions determined the relative levels of the supply and demand for prostitution, the male sex drive remained an "innate" constant. Here Greg's discussion of sexuality incorporated the basic assumptions of the double standard. Although perilous, extramarital sexual indulgence for men could be justified as natural. Greg viewed female promiscuity, however, in an entirely different light. According to Greg, women's sexual passion was dormant prior to sexual initiation. They did not enjoy licentious behavior; therefore their move into prostitution was largely involuntary, in part the work of procuresses and the traffic in adolescents and female children.[57]

In his analysis of human sexuality Greg depicted a world of scarcity that threatened human progress and defied human reason. Women were a perpetual temptation to men. Given the fallen state of humanity, pleasure could never be legitimated and would always exact a heavy penalty. Early marriages foreboded economic disaster; uncontrolled commercial sex fostered the spread of venereal disease. The regulation of prostitution was the only solution to this dilemma. The "rectification of social anomalies," such as the improvement of women's wages and the living conditions of the poor, might inhibit the "supply" but never the "demand" for prostitutes. Greg did not even mention birth control within this discussion. It would become increasingly clear from ensuing debates in the sixties and seventies that it was more respectable to uphold the necessity of prostitution than to advocate the "French" method of family limitation.[58]

Greg introduced the discussion of regulation in the pose of a charitable realist hoping to retrieve prostitutes from their outcast status. Left to themselves, the women were doomed: "The career of these women is a brief one, their downward path a marked and inevitable one; and they know this well. They are almost never rescued, escape themselves they cannot."[59] Greg used Parent's evidence on the subsequent fate of registered prostitutes to argue for the salutary effect of a regulation system. The social reclamation of registered prostitutes was mainly attributed to their custodial treatment by authorities who made "them feel they are no longer outlaws from all law" and thus preserved them from "desperation and utter self-abandonment."[60]

Regulation only entailed the formal recognition of an evil that was already tacitly sanctioned. Greg dismissed the objection that the sanitary supervision of prostitutes, involving the periodic inspection and confinement of prostitutes in lock hospitals, constituted an infringement on their personal liberty. Like Tait and Wardlaw earlier, he declared that "No law" recognized unbounded liberty: "the same rule of natural law which justifies the officer in shooting a plague-stricken

43

sufferer who breaks through a cordon sanitaire justifies him in arresting and confining the syphilitic prostitute who, if not arrested, would spread infection all around her."[61]

Hence, by the time William Acton wrote *Prostitution Considered in Its Moral, Social and Sanitary Aspects in London and Other Large Cities; with Proposals for the Mitigation and Prevention of Its Attendant Evils* (1857; revised in 1870), the topography of the social underground had been extensively delineated. Like Greg, Acton's social observations were largely derivative; the categories of social analysis as well as the actual social details owed much to earlier writers like Parent. Acton himself had a sharp eye for the "specialized character of Babylon" and took his readers on a tour of pleasure gardens, high-class brothels, accommodation houses, music halls, and low lodging houses. His narrative reflects the depoliticized character of mid-century social research. His description of low life entailed no interaction with working-class subjects, nor did his intellectual formulations emerge from an ongoing dialogue with working-class critics. Instead, *Prostitution* was an effort to accommodate and regulate a disturbing social reality that threatened the equipoise of mid-Victorian society, but did not carry any threat of political insurrection.

A specialist in venereal disease and "disorders of the reproductive organs," Acton had studied with the eminent venereologist Philippe Ricord in Paris in the late 1830s. The son of provincial clergyman, he personally bridged the secular and religious worlds.[62] In his writings on sexuality and prostitution, he elaborated a modified evangelical position. Like Greg, he argued for the recognition of a social evil already tacitly sanctioned by English society. His analysis was also shaped by a sense of the perils of male sexual license as well as its inevitability. He looked to regulation to establish some boundaries for this dangerous natural impulse. The need to legitimize a regulation system informed his social portrait of prostitutes as well.

Acton's first plea was for a visual and conceptual reckoning with the prostitute as part of the general urban scene.

> Who are those fair creatures, neither chaperons nor chaperoned: those "somebodies whom nobody knows," who elbow our wives and daughters in the parks and promenades and rendez-vous of fashion? Who are those painted, dressy women flaunting along the streets and boldly accosting the passerby? Who those miserable creatures, ill-fed, ill-clothed, uncared for, from whose misery the eye recoils, cowering under dark arches and among bye-lanes?[63]

Recognition entailed a social identification of the prostitute. Acton tried to place her within her environment and to catalogue the causes of her move into prostitution. Following Greg, he traced the source of prostitution to evil training, seduction, poverty, and overcrowding, with no special emphasis on any primary cause. He dismissed vicious inclination as playing a minor role, for he believed women were generally devoid of sexual appetite. In fact, Acton was quite concerned that young men received the wrong ideas about female sexuality from prostitutes, who simulated sexual excitement to please their customers.

Like Greg, Acton tried to strike a compromise on the question of male sexuality. He admitted that men were subject to sexual impulses that could be partially curbed and regulated but never completely repressed. Premature sexual experience as well as onanism were roundly condemned as dangerous to mental and physical health. Extramarital sexual indulgence was also deplored, but it could not be eradicated, given the present state of society. Within marriage, Acton also argued for moderate sexual indulgence: taking the "hardly worked, intellectual man as a type," he recommended that "marital intercourse" "ought not to take place more frequently than once in seven or ten days."[64] This was a revision of evangelical injunctions against marital intercourse for pleasure rather than for reproduction. This sense of economic balance would inform his views on regulation as well.

In order to justify controlled heterosexual outlets for men, Acton had to answer humanitarian and religious arguments against the sacrifice of female victims to male lust. His reinterpretation of the career of prostitutes was meant to serve this propagandist aim. Whereas Greg had celebrated the reclaiming efforts of the continental system, Acton noted the natural reintegration of prostitutes into working-class life after their brief stay on the streets. He sought to dispel the notion "that the career of the woman who once quits the pinnacle of virtue involves the very swift decline and ultimate total loss of health, modesty, and temporal prosperity." He outlined "three vulgar errors":

1. That once a harlot, always a harlot.
2. That there is no possible advance, moral or physical, in the condition of the actual prostitute.
3. That the harlot's progress is short and rapid.[65]

Women did not suffer this rapid decline, but instead often grew "grey" in prostitution. They had hardier constitutions and were more likely to enjoy good health than their respectable counterparts slaving away in dressmaking establishments or bearing innumerable children. Acton further indicated that there was no rigid demarcation between respectable society and the depraved social underground. Acton tended to downplay the institutions and associations of the underworld – like pimps and brothels – that would mark these women as

45

separate and distinct. The vast numbers of women engaged in occasional and part-time prostitution were able to merge inconspicuously with the respectable poor. English prostitutes did not generally live in explicit brothels, but in lodging houses or "externally respectable establishments," where the inmates had achieved a "quiet truce" with the police.[66]

Prostitution might constitute a stage in a woman's life or a part-time or seasonal activity to supplement her meager salary, as shop-girl, needlewoman, or domestic servant. When Acton called for state regulation of prostitution, he justified his program as a means of enabling the prostitute "to pass through this stage of her existence with as little permanent injury to herself and as little mischief to society as possible."[67]

Conclusion

To what extent, then, did *Prostitution* depart from the conventional Victorian treatment of prostitution? At first glance, Acton appears to have made an imaginative break with past models by stressing the noninstitutionalized, voluntary, and transitional character of English prostitution. In fact, though, these observations did not represent a breakthrough in consciousness nor did they emerge from a more direct and empirical investigation of prostitutes. Parent had discussed the subsequent fate of registered prostitutes; his British followers had simply chosen to ignore it. Acton's British predecessors viewed prostitution as an intolerable social evil that brought moral and physical disaster to all concerned. For them, the "wages" of sin had to be death. Acton, like Greg, accepted the need for male heterosexual outlets. By stressing the free-trade market in prostitution, women's short stay on the streets, their superior health and living standards, and their subsequent reintegration into general working-class life, he more easily rationalized their sexual exploitation.

Rather than a new intellectual venture, *Prostitution* represented the ultimate elaboration of a style, a "literary genre," whose basic assumptions inhibited any further development. The early inquiries into the "causes, extent, and amelioration" of prostitution had gone as far as they could. Parent, Tait, and Acton had successfully documented the inadequate earnings of respectable working women, the seasonal character and the social background of prostitution, and the prostitutes' expectations for the future. The structure and organization of their profession had been outlined, and something of their domestic life had been disclosed. Yet the effort to relate prostitution to existing

46

social structures was undermined by a compulsive need to build defenses against the social reality under investigation. Furthermore, the next field of inquiry–into the prostitutes' own relationship with their community–required a whole new set of postulates. To investigate seriously these questions, the researcher would have had to view these women outside the realm of pathology, as neither pollutants nor the polluted, but as poor women who were integrated into a complex sexual economy.

The stereotyped vision of Acton or Tait would dominate the debates over the C.D. acts in the 1870s and 1880s. Repealers and regulationists both were limited by the confusions and imaginative blind spots endemic to this style of research. Both sides relied almost exclusively on evidence drawn from earlier studies, carefully manipulating social details to bolster their argument for or against regulation. Although they certainly disagreed over the inevitability of prostitution and male license, and the right of the state to intervene in such questions, these differences did not result in distinct or innovative social analyses. Both sides constantly shifted between moralist and environmental explanations. Both combined an apparent solicitude for prostitutes with a distrust for public women. Tied as they were to old formulations, both sides failed to learn from actual social encounters with registered prostitutes and to integrate this experience into a new conceptual framework.

3 *Venereal disease*

By the mid-Victorian period, many doctors and public officials came to assess syphilis as a serious health hazard for the British population. Newly available medical statistics on the incidence of venereal disease in the civilian and military populations had alerted public authorities to the problem and convinced them of the need for preventive measures – in particular, for the sanitary supervision of common prostitutes. The medical rationale for a regulation system was predicated on three assumptions: that syphilis was spread through promiscuous sexual contact with diseased prostitutes; that existing voluntary facilities for treating female venereal patients were ineffective as preventive and therapeutic institutions; that available diagnostic and therapeutic methods were adequate to carry out the medical provisions of a regulation system. A later generation of venereologists would dismiss mid-Victorian confidence in existing therapeutics as naive and misguided. At the time, however, doctors were only dimly aware of their limited ability to cure venereal disease. Nor could they foresee that syphilis would decline "spontaneously" over the course of the nineteenth century, irrespective of medical intervention or the operation of programs for the sanitary control of prostitutes.

Although conforming to accepted medical and clinical standards, the treatment of venereal disease was also governed by the dominant sexual and social ideology. This chapter will explore the various levels of meaning attached to the treatment of venereal disease. It will try to examine how class prejudice and the double standard of sexuality influenced medical treatment, and how these ideological influences shaped institutional facilities for the care of venereal-disease sufferers.

Medical statistics and the incidence of venereal disease

Medical statistics on the incidence of venereal disease structured the dimensions of the problem for Victorian observers.[1] Military medical

returns certainly gave good cause for alarm. Since 1823, military returns had reported a steady increase in venereal disease. By 1864, one
out of three sick cases in the army were venereal in origin, whereas
admissions into hospitals for gonorrhea and syphilis reached 290.7 per
1,000 of total troop strength. Venereal-disease rates were lower for
the navy, but still a source of concern; in 1862, one out of eleven
hospital patients was suffering from venereal disease, and venereal
patients constituted 125 admissions per 1,000 troops.[2]

The only general statistics on venereal disease for the civilian population were death rates due to syphilis, which did not include mortality
rates for parasyphilitic diseases. In 1846, Acton commented on the
mortality rates published by the Registrar General. He noted the very
low mortality rate for syphilis among adults and also observed "a novel
fact of the greatest importance – namely that syphilis is particularly
fatal during the first year of age."[3] Infants under one year old accounted
for thirty of fifty-three reported deaths due to syphilis in London during
the first six months of 1846. During the decades to follow, the devastating effects of hereditary syphilis continued to be a persistent theme of
regulationist propaganda: "The innocent victims of syphilis are infi-
nitely more numerous than the guilty; for it is a disease which follows
vice down to the (third and fourth) generation . . ."[4]

Fragmentary hospital reports, newly available in the mid-Victorian
era, also suggested the general extent of venereal disease among civilians. Inpatient hospital facilities for venereal cases were so limited that
they provided no indication of the actual extent of gonorrhea, chancroid, or syphilis. Outpatient statistics proved more useful. In 1846,
Acton surveyed the outpatients at St. Bartholomew's Hospital, London, and found that nearly half the surgical outpatients were suffering
from venereal complaints.[5] In the 1860s, the Royal Free Hospital
reported an even higher percentage of venereal outpatients. Furthermore, complications due to venereal disease accounted for one-eighth
to one-fifth of the outpatient cases at the eye and ear hospital, and
one-fifth the surgical patients at the children's hospital had hereditary
syphilis. Reports from provincial hospitals in Newcastle, Birmingham,
and Manchester gave roughly the same proportions.[6]

These statistics did not go unchallenged. Contemporary observers
argued that such numbers gave an inflated impression of the actual
number of sick poor suffering from venereal disease. Even Acton acknowledged that syphilis was a "complaint of long duration . . . and
the patient is constantly coming [back] to the outpatient department."[7] Other commentators complained that these statistics only related to surgical outpatients, whereas medical cases constituted the

49

bulk of outpatients. Sir John Simon estimated that only 7 percent of the sick poor in London attending poor-law facilities, hospitals, and dispensaries were suffering from venereal complaints – still a sizable proportion, as many regulationists noted at the time.[8]

In fact, 7 percent would appear to be a conservative estimate of the extent of syphilis among the civilian proportion, judging from data collected on the sick poor in institutions and attending various hospitals and clinics in the early twentieth century. Later statistics would suggest that syphilis was endemic to the civilian population in Great Britain in the Victorian and Edwardian periods and that it was most prevalent among men of the upper and middle ranks and among the casual laboring poor.[9]

Mid-Victorian statistics convinced medical and military authorities that an epidemic of venereal disease was sweeping the nation. Although alarmed, doctors were confident that this epidemic could be stemmed through the sanitary supervision of prostitutes and that existing therapeutic and diagnostic methods were adequate to carry out the medical provisions of such a regulation system.

Syphilis

In the Victorian era, the precise classification of syphilis largely derived from the empirical research of Philippe Ricord, whose *Traité pratique sur les maladies vénériennes* was published in 1838. Ricord's findings were based on research conducted at the Hôpital du Midi, where he had performed 2,500 inoculations on hospital patients. From his human experiments, Ricord was able to distinguish gonorrhea from syphilis and to trace syphilis through its three stages.[10]

Following Ricord, mid-Victorian medical authorities were generally able to agree on certain essential features of syphilis.[11] It was known to be an infectious disease, usually introduced into the system by "impure" sexual intercourse. "General opinion assigns it to the presence of a minute wound or lesion of the part through which the poison is admitted."[12] Within twenty-four days of exposure to infection, an indurated sore would appear at the "site of inoculation."[13] This was followed six to eight weeks later by a febrile disturbance of secondary syphilis, accompanied by a "feeling of lassitude, and depression, a chilling in the joints and limbs, and generalized eruption, usually beginning as pale pink before turning a copper color."[14] Tertiary manifestations might and did appear decades after the original infection. Although sloughing sores and bone disorders associated with tertiary syphilis rarely proved fatal, in its "third form" syphilis was thought to attack the liver, lungs, brain, and muscles.[15] It was also thought to have a generally debilitating effect, like tuberculosis: "Syphilis, *per se*, is rarely fatal in adults; but by altering the structure of the organs of vital importance, it renders the patient unable to resist the inroad of inflammatory action set up accidentally."[16]

Despite the general agreement of medical texts on the outlines of syphilis, some confusion and disagreement remained. Although syphilis was understood to be as "specific a disease as smallpox,"[17] it differed from other specific diseases "in its poison being strictly non-infectious; in its course being chronic and liable to frequent relapses."[18] The longevity of the virus and the "extraordinary manner in which it may lurk for years, absolutely concealed . . . "[19] confused and troubled Victorians. In its manifestations, syphilis seemed to combine the qualities of a specific "virus" and a general degenerative condition.

Mid-Victorian syphilologists also disputed whether chancroid, a local ulceration of the genitals, and syphilis were distinct diseases, whether one attack of syphilis "gave future immunity" to the sufferer, and whether syphilis remained infectious after the initial stage. Most doctors realized that the threat of infection to sex partners and to an embryo diminished over time, but they could not agree upon the duration of treatment or the stated interval after which marriage could be safely recommended to syphilitic patients. Some doctors went so far as to say that they could never guarantee a certain cure to patients, despite the fact that in most cases, "if left to itself syphilis gradually wears out" – that it cured itself "spontaneously" without the pain and trouble of medical treatment.[20]

It is difficult to determine how much these disputes undermined medical confidence in prevailing treatment. Few mid-Victorian doctors would publicly agree with their critics that "*our power* over disease is in no wise proportionate to our knowledge of it . . . "[21] However, the increasing medical emphasis on preventive rather than curative methods to combat syphilis may well have reflected an underlying distrust of available therapeutics.

Preventive methods generally conformed to the view of syphilis as a specific poison that entered the system through a breach in the skin. Parent reported that prostitutes regularly applied oil to the vaginal walls to prevent abrasions that would render them susceptible to venereal infections.[22] Alcoholic and astringent solutions, such as vinegar and water, washed away the "poison," and caustics were used to "destroy" it.[23] These methods were deemed "advantageous as long as absorption [in the blood] has not taken place," for "these various substances are evidently useless when a chancre exists."[24]

Once the syphilitic "poison" had been absorbed into the blood, mercury treatment in the form of pills, vapor baths, or inunction with ointment was generally prescribed. Mercury was a traditional specific for syphilis; however, its popularity had waned and waxed during the seventeenth, eighteenth, and early nineteenth centuries because of the dire effects of the heroic dosages customarily administered to syphilitics.[25]

By the middle of the nineteenth century, mercury regained some of its popularity and continued to be the primary but not exclusive treatment for syphilis until the advent of Salvarsan before World War I. Historians have linked its use to the continued belief in humoral pathology in the nineteenth century. According to humoral medical theory, drastic remedies were necessary to neutralize a dangerous poison; painful side effects were evidence that the drug was exerting the required "alternative" effect to reestablish a healthy balance in the body.[26] Following this theory, mercury was supposed to act by stimulating the flow of pituita, or phlegm, which helped to discharge the vicious humors. "The venereal poison, having entered the body, was compelled to the exterior through salivation and perspiration."[27]

Doctors were reluctant to dispense with a traditionally sanctioned treatment when they could not offer patients a better alternative. Faced with heavy competition from homeopathic doctors and quacks who advertised "nonmercurial" and dietary cures for syphilis, regular doctors struck a compromise: they continued the old remedy in more sparing dosages, avoiding salivation and following a treatment of smaller doses over a prolonged period.[28] They also experimented with alternative drugs, sometimes alternating between mercury and herbal concoctions like sarsparilla, astringents like nitric acid or ammonia, and iodide of potassium.[29]

Mercury also satisfied certain empirical criteria of treatment. As Victorian doctors acknowledged, syphilis was known only by its effects—"Of its physical character and essential nature we know nothing."[30] Mercury seemed to counteract these symptoms: since primary and secondary lesions of syphilis tend to clear up spontaneously, a prolonged treatment with mercury was credited with effecting a cure.[31] Still, doctors recognized that mercury was not a "specific in the ordinary acceptance of the term, and does not appear to exercise any direct influence on the poison of syphilis, but on the effects of the disease only."[32]

This skepticism was well deserved. Despite its persistent use as a specific for syphilis, the therapeutic efficacy of mercury is doubtful. At best mercury relieved some of the symptoms of syphilis and left the infection "simmering . . . so that the disease was constantly progressing towards the stage of tertiary manifestations."[33] At worst mercury treatment greatly aggravated the destructive effects of syphilis. In fact, it is not clear "which of the [past] symptoms of treated patients were due to syphilis and which to mercury intoxication."[34] Moreover, the "curative" dose was perilously close to the "lethal" dose: according to early-twentieth-century actuarial tables (U.S.), untreated syphilitics had mortality rates lower than syphilitics "cured through [mercury] treatment."[35] Not surprisingly, modern medical authorities regarded the small-dose mercury treatment (as opposed to heroic dosages) as the most beneficial innovation in the treatment of syphilis prior to the invention of Salvarsan.[36]

Gonorrhea

> Do you wish to contract clap? This is the way. Take a pale, lymphatic woman, blond rather than brunette, and as leucorrhoeic as possible, dine with her; begin with oysters and continue with asparagus, drink of a good many dry white wines and champagne, coffee, liqueur. All this is well. Dance after your dinner and make your partner dance. Warm yourself up, and drink a good deal during the evening. When night comes, conduct yourself bravely; two or three acts of intercourse are not too much, more are still better. On waking do not fail to take a long warm bath and to make an injection. If you do not get the clap, it is because God protects you.[37]

This advice to young men by Ricord incorporated most of the medical and social assumptions governing the treatment of gonorrhea in Britain and France during the early and mid-nineteenth century.[38] Described by Oliver Wendell Holmes as the "Voltaire of pelvic literature," "a sceptic as to the morality of the race in general,"[39] Ricord firmly believed that sexual incontinence was universal among men. Inasmuch as he also believed that the body could become acclimatized to gonorrheal inflammation, he recommended deliberate exposure to the "clap" to young men starting off on a career of dissipation.

Ricord identified gonorrhea as a purulent inflammation of the mucous membranes, whose primary seat in men was the urethra and in women, the vagina. In his view, gonorrhea was a mild disease for men, and of practically no importance to women. His diagnosis was based on the clinical observation that men acquired gonorrhea from women who appeared to be almost entirely healthy.[40] Although not suffering from gonorrhea themselves, women exuded secretions, including vaginal discharges as well as menstrual fluid, that could excite inflammation of the urethra in men: hence, Ricord's prescription of a "lymphatic blond," as "leucorrheoic [suffering from purulent vaginal discharge] as possible." In addition, alcohol and a rich diet, including asparagus and oysters, could stimulate a local irritation. Disease could further result from excessive sexual intercourse or excessive sexual excitement.

This nonspecific pathology incorporated a series of medical fallacies that seriously affected the diagnosis and treatment of gonorrhea in females. It incorrectly identified the vagina as the site of gonorrheal infection, rather than the cervix, uterus, and fallopian tubes. As a consequence, a number of vaginal infections were undoubtedly confused with gonorrhea. In addition, as most women were asymptomatic in the early acute stage, doctors, relying solely on clinical diagnosis, greatly underestimated the extent and seriousness of gonorrhea in women. This initial diagnostic error resulted in subsequent misdiagnoses: doctors remained unaware that chronic untreated gonorrhea constituted a serious threat to women's health, and that it was frequently the hidden cause of sterility and severe pelvic inflammations among women.[41]

British venereologists tended to accept the nonspecific etiology of gonorrhea, although Victorian texts occasionally listed "contagion" as an additional cause of the disease.[42] Like Ricord, most Victorian specialists viewed gonorrhea as a simple local disorder; the 1864 Committee to Inquire into the Pathology and Treatment of Venereal Disease did not even deem "it necessary to enter upon the subject of gonorrhea."[43] Gonorrhea was presumed to be a "much less common affection in women than in men; and when it does occur the disease is ordinarily much less severe and hence more rarely comes under treatment."[44] The recommended treatment for acute female cases was rest and improved personal hygiene: "A warm bath, rest in bed, and a little lotion causes a complaint which looked very formidable . . . to become a relatively mild affection."[45] This hygienic regime undoubtedly had a salutary effect on those patients who were actually suffering from nongonorrheal vaginal infections, relieving their overt symptoms.[46] Less benign were the irrigations, injections, and cauterizations that were routinely administered to male and female patients. At best, these measures were painful and futile. In the case of women, they probably served to spread the gonorrheal infection further up into the internal reproductive organs, thereby stimulating pelvic inflammations.[47]

54

Social and sexual ideology

However flawed and pernicious, the treatment of gonorrhea and syphilis conformed to accepted medical and clinical standards. Therapeutics for venereal disease were also consistent with moral and sexual attitudes prevailing among the dominant classes of Victorian society. Repressive moralist views still influenced the treatment of syphilis and gonorrhea, despite the new humanitarian spirit in medical practice. Because mercury application was very painful, it remained an appropriately punitive method of treating syphilitics: "Continuation of the unpleasant treatment long after the subsidence of the outward manifestations may well have been motivated by a Calvinistic sadism to discourage the miscreant from further immoral activities."[48] Likewise, the cauterization of male and female patients for gonorrhea served a similar punitive and deterrent function.

Class and sex prejudice also insinuated themselves into medical theory and practice. Cruel medical experiments were performed on poor hospital patients of either sex, who were inoculated with syphilitic and gonorrheal pus, so that doctors could observe the progress of the two diseases.[49] Deep-seated hostilities toward women are also evident in certain diagnostic and therapeutic procedures. Sex prejudice was more overt in the treatment of gonorrhea than syphilis, perhaps because the stages of syphilis were well known and male and female syphilitics manifested the same symptoms. In contrast, the diagnosis of gonorrhea in women was less precise and more amenable to ideological manipulation.

The nonspecific pathology of gonorrhea conveniently suited Victorian sexual ideology. Because they were ignorant of the seriousness of gonorrheal infection for women, doctors readily adopted a cavalier attitude toward treating male patients who continued to cohabit with their wives, though suffering from gonorrhea. According to William Sinclair, British doctors frequently acted as willing accomplices for errant husbands, helping them to camouflage their gonorrheal discharge. In so doing, they were following the lead of French specialists of the day. Diday, a French venereologist whose work was highly regarded in Britain, reported one instance of a young man soon to be married who had contracted gonorrhea and came to him as a patient. There was no time for a cure before the wedding day:

> In these embarrassing circumstances one sovereign remedy remains, only one – injections of nitrate of silver . . . Suppose one employs a medium dose of the solution, in an hour and a half or two hours after the infection there appears a discharge, the simple effect of

traumatism, accompanied by a little smarting in micturition. This slight inflammation lasts five or six hours. But then, precious result, the canal becomes dry; all morbid secretion is arrested, and this condition persists for eighteen or twenty-four hours – quite sufficient time for the bridegroom to seek his nuptial couch in a healthy or, at least, non-contagious state. In exact figures, if the newly-wedded pair ought to retire to their room on Friday morning at one o'clock, the preservative injection ought to be made about nine o'clock on Thursday afternoon.[50]

This pathology also conformed to medical and social theories that looked upon disease as a result of "sin" as well as bodily imbalance and excess. It was assumed that mind and body were generally interrelated, so that morbid spiritual states could exert a harmful physiological effect. Following this theory, gonorrhea was a consequence of unnatural vice and sexual excess. Doctors like Acton regarded gonorrhea as a natural by-product of the "mode of life" of most prostitutes: "It arises, as I believe, in the great majority of cases, simply from the continual irritation and excitement of the generative organs consequent upon their mode of life, though it may be caused, no doubt, occasionally from the urethral discharge of the male."[51]

However, immoral women were not the only ones to stimulate gonorrheal inflammation in men. The vaginal discharge of virtuous women could also generate "disease" in men, thereby contradicting the ideological association of disease and sinful habits (see Chapter 11). This virtuous source of infection also challenged the sexual-moral code that rigidly segregated "pure" women from the "impure." By designating all women as potential pollutants of men and reservoirs of infection, it evoked instead a more general hostility and dread of females and female "nature."[52]

Class and sex prejudice also informed the controversy surrounding the use of the speculum to diagnose gonorrhea and syphilis. In the 1830s the vaginal speculum had gained popularity among Parisian specialists as a means of examining inscribed prostitutes for venereal disease and of applying caustic lotions to local lesions.[53] When, in the 1840s and 1850s, British disciples of Ricord like Acton tried to introduce the speculum into general gynecological practice, they were severely rebuked by their colleagues, who reminded them of the speculum's sordid origin: "The speculum emanated from the syphilitic wards of the hospitals at Paris, and it would have been better for the women of England had its use been confined to those prostitutes institutionalized."[54] Speculum examination might be appropriate to "unsexed women" already "dead to shame," but it constituted a shocking "im-

56

morality" when imposed on virtuous women: "the female who has been subjected to such treatment is not the same person in delicacy and purity that she was before." The uterus, the seat of female reproductive mysteries, had been violated. Medical journals reported cases of women whose minds had been "poisoned" by the experience; it was alleged that these women became addicted to speculum examination, and had degenerated into "uterine hypochondriacs."[55]

These comments suggest the sexual overtones of the examination procedures for female venereal patients. The speculum examination was perceived by patients and by many doctors (at least in the 1850s) as a voyeuristic and degrading act, one that inflicted mental and physical pain on the female sufferer. Seen in this context, the later feminist outcry against the "instrumental rape" of the internal examination was not as extreme as modern historians have alleged. Rather, it reflected the general cultural understanding of the patient-doctor relationship, when it manifested itself through this intrusive mode of diagnosis.

Lock hospitals

Like the therapeutic and diagnostic procedures described above, hospital facilities for the treatment of venereal patients fulfilled a variety of nonmedical functions, and were as much the product of sexual and social ideology as the state of medical knowledge. Frequently, the social and educational services of the venereal disease hospital were at cross-purposes with its proported medical mission; even by Victorian standards, these facilities failed as sanitary and therapeutic institutions.

Although possessing certain distinct characteristics, public facilities for the treatment of venereal patients followed general institutional developments in Victorian health care. With some important modifications, these facilities were organized according to a two-tiered system: voluntary hospitals were the preferred facilities, servicing a nonindigent population, whereas workhouse infirmaries handled the overflow as well as the less desirable patients. Voluntary hospital accommodations for venereal patients may further be subdivided between inpatient and outpatient facilities and between those beds reserved for venereal cases in general hospitals and the inpatient care provided by special venereal disease, or "lock," hospitals. The social makeup of the patients varied according to the admissions policy of each facility, and to a lesser extent, according to the self-selection, or "consumer demand," of the patients themselves.[56]

Victorian medical observers agreed that inpatient facilities for female venereal cases were shockingly inadequate. An 1882 survey esti-

57

mated that there were only 402 beds for female patients in all the voluntary lock hospitals in Great Britain and that, of this number, only 232 were "funded for use." An additional 102 beds were reserved for female venereal patients in the general hospitals of London and six provincial cities.[57] In most locales, female venereal patients had to resort to the "foul" wards of the workhouse infirmaries, whether or not they were paupers. Furthermore, female sufferers from venereal disease faced a widespread pattern of discrimination both in terms of admissions to hospitals and in their institutional treatment, when admitted as patients.

Many general hospitals had rules against admitting venereal patients, although sometimes male patients were surreptitiously admitted to general wards.[58] Other general hospitals and infirmaries reserved two to four beds for venereal patients, and admitted them on a selective basis; they often required letters of recommendation, evidence of "respectability," and extraordinary contributions on the part of venereal patients to their own support.[59] The offensiveness of the "phagedaenic" skin disorders associated with syphilis and the identification of gonorrhea and syphilis as infectious diseases at a time when most diseases were not understood to be infectious undoubtedly contributed to the general reluctance to admit venereal patients.[60] However, restricted admissions were usually based on moral objections, as evidenced in the different policy toward male and female venereal patients. Hospitals were more concerned about isolating female venereal patients, most of whom were presumed to be prostitutes, than their male counterparts. As one hospital survey noted in 1864, "If prostitutes are to be admitted in any large number, it is necessary to keep them under separate custody and even the reception of single patients of bad character into a female ward is sometimes a ground of complaint."[61] On the other hand, the admission of male patients into general wards did not pose the same moral threat: "To isolate cases of male syphilis appears to be entirely superfluous."[62]

When they admitted venereal patients, hospitals found it difficult to apply the same social and moral criteria to them that generally distinguished hospital patients from workhouse paupers. By virtue of their infirmity, venereal patients were deemed unrespectable. Still, certain voluntary hospitals tried to exclude patients from the lowest social class from their lock wards.[63] In other locales, the hierarchical distinction between workhouse and hospital lock patients was blurred. In London, certain workhouse infirmaries refused to admit venereal cases, whereas others maintained an arrangement with the London Lock Hospital whereby they could transfer their lock cases there.[64]

These exclusionist policies generally dated from the eighteenth century. Earlier, in the sixteenth century, both St. Bartholomew's and St. Thomas's, the two royal hospitals in London, maintained a "salvation ward" for the treatment of "pox" by mercury.[65] In the eighteenth century, general hospitals began to exclude various disorders and types of patients from their wards—including infectious diseases, "fever," children, maternity cases, mental disorders, as well as venereal disease. This was done to protect the health and moral welfare of the remaining patients, leaving poor-law authorities with responsibility for most of these rejected cases. In addition, specialized hospitals developed to care for the respectable poor suffering from these disorders.[66]

The founding of the London Lock Hospital in 1746 followed these general institutional developments. Its opening reflected the heightened philanthropic concern over problems of illegitimacy and prostitution at mid-century, as well as the need to provide medical care for a class of patients rejected by other hospitals. Its presence also represents the continuity in Western society of what Michel Foucault terms the "structure" of confinement. By structure he means both a physical and psychological reality, an institution that embodied the principle of exclusion of "social deviants" from society.[67] According to Acton, the lock hospital at Southwark was founded on the site of a medieval house of lepers, who were "formerly kept in restraint." Hence the derivation of the term "lock," "from the French word *loques* signifying rags, bandages, lints."[68] In this case, the lazar house, ancient in origin, had been shaped to meet the needs of the new age. Prostitutes had become the social lepers of the eighteenth century, as syphilis replaced leprosy as the symbol of one kind of dreaded social contagion.[69]

The London and Westmoreland (Dublin) lock hospitals were the only venereal-disease hospitals built in the eighteenth century to continue operation into the nineteenth century. Additional lock hospitals were opened in the nineteenth century: Glasgow (1805), Newcastle (1813), Manchester (1819), Liverpool (1834), Leeds (1842), Bristol (1870), and Birmingham (1881).[70] Most of these facilities first admitted female patients (with prostitutes the target population), and only subsequently opened male lock wards and outpatient clinics that overwhelmingly catered to male venereal patients.[71]

However distinct their medical clientele, the financial structure and social rationale of lock hospitals were organized along the lines of conventional medical charities of the age. Like other voluntary hospitals, lock hospitals were expected to fulfill a variety of social functions beyond the simple medical relief of the poor. As subscribers' charities, they demonstrated the charitable generosity of upper-class patrons through the distribution of tickets of admission to the dependent poor. As educational institutions, they provided clinical training for medical students. They were also intended to serve as a form of self-advertisement and source of professional prestige for the medical consultants attached to the institutions. Finally, they functioned as disciplinary institutions of confinement, subjecting their working-class female inmates to lessons in deference, respectability, and personal cleanliness.

In carrying out these extramedical duties, lock facilities labored under special disabilities. The lock hospital remained a stepchild of the voluntary hospital system – an unpopular charity that was always in financial difficulty. Depending as it did on annual subscriptions, donations, and legacies, it found it difficult to attract the necessary public support. It lacked the "status" of the infirmary and lunatic asylum.[72] Even with its illustrious aristocratic patrons, and despite the success of its chapel, whose Sunday mass was popular among the social elite, the London Lock Hospital suffered financial problems.[73]

In a society where venereal disease was frequently looked upon as divine punishment for "vice," the medical services of lock hospitals appeared morally suspect both to the public at large and often to the governors of the charity themselves. The annual reports of the London Lock Hospital were painfully apologetic: "We may indeed consider the due distemper itself, as a declaration, however greatly a holy God abhors licentiousness; yet hath he mercifully provided medicines which seldom fail, when judiciously used to eradicate it completely."[74] The reports even excused the lack of public support for the charity, while morally condemning their own patients.[75]

The financial difficulties of lock hospitals were compounded by their inability to advertise and engage in certain forms of fund raising. Open advertisements, gala benefits, concerts, and bazaars were considered inappropriate for lock facilities.[76] Lock hospitals were further hampered by the low status attached to venereology as a medical specialty.[77] This was a serious liability, as the prosperity of hospitals was as much dependent on the initiative of doctors as lay benefactors.[78]

Nor did they fare any better in putting themselves forward as educational institutions. Although the London Lock Hospital advertised itself as a "School of Medicine and a House of Mercy,"[79] venereal cases were generally looked upon as routine and "uninteresting" by members of the medical profession. A survey of provincial hospitals found that the "less interesting nature of cases" coupled with the "remote position" of lock wards rendered medical "visits to this part of the

60

[general] hospital less frequent."[80] The report also noted the general physical neglect and poor ventilation of the "foul" wards. The lock wards of the Edinburgh Royal Infirmary were temporarily closed in 1831 because of the high cost of treating lock patients and also because these wards did not contribute to the instruction of students, who were rigidly excluded from them.[81]

On the other hand, the use of the lock wards for the clinical training of students could lead to serious abuses. Acton criticized the practice of open clinical examination of female venereal patients as offensive to any patient's self-respect. In 1870 he regretfully observed that "the indecent system of exposing females before the whole class of students is still pursued ... " at his *alma mater*, St. Bartholomew's.[82] The *Lancet* described the scene graphically:

> It is natural enough (for after all the prostitute is sister to those by our firesides) that one of the great objections of these women to seeking admissions into hospitals is a dread of that clinical mode of teaching which includes the throwing back of all coverings from the poor creature shrinking in her shame and calmly demonstrating the characters of her malady to a promiscuous class of students.[83]

Hence, the social and educational functions of the lock hospital were often at cross-purposes with its medical mission. In all areas, the mid-Victorian lock hospital seemed to operate ineffectively: it failed to attract the kind of professional and financial support necessary for a secure future, and it even failed to attract the necessary number of female patients to fill its beds. Moreover, most lock hospitals felt obliged to compensate for the checkered reputation of their female patients by stressing efforts at their moral reclamation. As a result, lock hospitals subjected female inmates to a repressive moral regime, further discouraging their main source of female patients—prostitutes—from applying for admission.[84]

Inside the hospital, lock patients were subjected to an intense religious atmosphere and coercive discipline. Although strict, the house rules of lock hospitals were not dissimilar to the discipline imposed on the indigent sick in general hospitals. In both kinds of hospitals, interference in the daily lives and habits of the patients was accepted as a legitimate prerogative of the management.[85]

By the 1850s, lock hospitals began to give more publicity to their moral reform efforts than to their medical functions. The annual reports of the London Lock Hospital, for instance, provided no medical statistics on inmates, but they did contain detailed accounts of the "moral statistics" of the patients—their age, family background, place of origin, occupation, religious background, and level of literacy. The

61

social profile of the inmates was meant to elicit sympathy for the sufferers of "complaints" that "arise out of the form of evil which has been called 'the great sin of great cities.' "[86]

Consistent with the moral mission, particular importance was attached to the activities of the lock asylum, a penitentiary, attached to the hospital, for a select group of cured patients. A lock asylum had been connected to the London Lock Hospital since 1787. A similar auxiliary institution was established by the Ladies Committee of the Manchester and Salford Lock Hospital in 1822. Like other "penitents," inmates of the lock asylum were subjected to a rigorous probationary period of three months. They were subsequently trained as servants, laundrywomen, and needlewomen because training in "habits of industry and forethought" were the first steps to "recovery of self-respect and social position."[87] Their education was restricted by moral and financial considerations. Acton reported that women were "instructed in reading in classes, but I was told that writing is forbidden as leading to correspondence with the outdoor world."[88]

Vocational training also took a back seat to the financial interests of the institution, for inmates were regarded as a reservoir of free unskilled labor. The management and staff of the lock asylum were reluctant to go to any added expense to train women in a skilled trade: "the matrons objected to sewing machines, having so many human machines to do their work." Instead, laundry work was the "stable business of the asylum." Moreover, laundry work helped to defray the cost of the inmates' stay; besides the hospital laundry, inmates washed clothes "collected from private families in London."[89]

Doctors familiar with the social habits of prostitutes were critical of this work discipline, and cautioned such rescue institutions to bear in mind the former life-style of their "fallen" women, "in which work of any kind is scrupulously avoided."[90] To Acton, these reclamatory efforts were not only unrealistic but constituted an unfortunate diversion from the primary medical and sanitary purposes of the lock hospital. He looked upon the lock asylum as an exercise in futility that attracted only those women who would soon have left the ranks of prostitution of their own accord.[91]

Even more significant, in the view of Acton and other concerned medical authorities, was the failure of lock hospitals as preventive institutions. As James R. Lane, senior surgeon to the London Lock Hospital, observed: "Voluntary lock hospitals may afford charitable relief to the individual sufferers but from a sanitary point of view, I believe them to be absolutely useless."[92] As admission to the lock hospital was voluntary, Lane went on to explain, young prostitutes only entered the hospital after they had been infectious for some time. Lane continued:

> From long experience of these women, I know them to be, with rare exceptions, far too reckless of consequences to apply for admission and to seclude themselves for treatment until their disease has reached a stage which renders it impossible for them to pursue their calling any longer, and until they have done all their mischief of which they are capable.[93]

On two counts, then, lock hospitals failed to carry through a preventive program against syphilis: they could not detain prostitutes while they were infectious; they did not educate young prostitutes in ablution and prophylactic techniques early enough in their career.

The patients

Statistics available on the female inpatients of lock hospitals bear out Lane's generalizations about these women's age and relative inexperience.[94] Statistics for female inpatients for five lock hospitals and lock wards show them to be young and single. In Glasgow, Liverpool, London, Edinburgh, and Manchester, they were heavily concentrated in the eighteen to twenty-one age bracket. The most frequently given ages were eighteen and nineteen, which seems to correlate closely with the women's first entrance into prostitution. In his survey of women admitted into the Glasgow Lock Hospital between 1870 and 1880, Dr. Alexander Patterson noted that most patients had been on the streets for less than one year. Another authority, M. Berkeley Hill, commented upon the age-specific nature of venereal complaints among prostitutes: "younger girls suffer repeated returns of their disease" and were most likely to be in and out of the lock wards, whereas "older women were more cautious; probably their genital organs are less easily excited into a morbid condition by excessive intercourse."[95]

The social profile of women interned in lock hospitals conforms to the general portrait of working-class prostitutes in other ways as well. In London, two-thirds (64.9 percent) of the inmates were half or fully orphans. They seemed to have followed the usual migration patterns. Approximately 40 percent of the London Lock Hospital inmates had been born in London; of the 60 percent born elsewhere "a large proportion have been furnished by the county of Kent."[96] In the 1850s, over 50 percent of the female inmates at the London Lock Hospital were identified as prostitutes, although annual reports frequently noted that "the vast majority have had respectable livelihoods."[97] At some time or other, most of these women had been servants. At other hospitals,

63

however, occupational background seemed to vary with the forms of female employment available in the region.[98]

The medical profile of the female patients, as reported in medical journals, also tends to support Lane's observation that women only entered the lock hospital in an aggravated state of disease. In the 1870s the majority of female lock patients entered the Liverpool and London lock hospitals as syphilitics. Unfortunately, mid-Victorian returns often did not distinguish between primary syphilis and chancroid; hence, it is difficult to evaluate from statistical tables the stage and character of the disease. Judging from doctors' accounts, however, prostitutes seemed to have entered the lock hospital only when they were too uncomfortable to ply their trade on the streets. It is most likely, then, that primary cases were in fact chancroid, which causes a more painful ulceration than primary syphilis, or else the primary chancre occurred in a particularly painful spot.[99]

Although admitted as syphilitics, female patients actually suffered from multiple venereal complaints, which were aggravated by generally unsanitary habits. In Edinburgh, gonorrhea in "an acute or chronic form was present in almost every patient that applied for admission."[100] Berkeley Hill of the London Lock Hospital remarked that among London prostitutes a "purulent discharge of the uterus" was an "almost universal condition."[101] Only 20 percent of the female inmates of the London Lock Hospital were actually admitted because of gonorrhea, inasmuch as acute gonorrhea in women, when not altogether asymptomatic, was usually too minor an ailment to concern most experienced prostitutes.[102] In general, gonorrheal patients were admitted not because of the complaint itself, but for overall health reasons, "in consequence of ill-health, from long continued habits of dissipation."[103]

The unsanitary and neglected condition of female patients convinced doctors like Lowndes and Lane that diseased prostitutes needed to be interned on a compulsory, rather than voluntary, basis, and that these women had to be educated in sanitary habits. At the London and Liverpool lock hospitals, a substantial part (and by far the most beneficial part) of the medical and nursing care was devoted simply to cleaning the women up and training them in methods of ablution and personal hygiene. This sanitary program would serve both a therapeutic and preventive purpose. It could relieve women's symptoms and in some cases actually cure them of venereal complaints; for instance, antiseptic lotions and mild saline solutions could cure the small early lesions of chancroid, whereas bodily cleanliness helped to minimize the secondary infections of the skin associated with syphilis.[104] More

64

important, doctors believed that the sanitary education of prostitutes was essential to prevent the spread of venereal disease: at the hospital, patients should be taught "not only the comforts and the methods of ablutions but also the immunity from disease that frequent ablution would confer."[105]

From this medical profile, it is also evident that lock hospitals concentrated almost exclusively on treating chancroid and syphilis in women. Gonorrhea was rarely the chief venereal complaint, and hospital authorities seem to have been inexperienced in diagnosing and treating acute cases of gonorrhea in women.[106] Not surprisingly, the medical rationale for a regulation system focused almost exclusively on the need to cure and prevent the spread of syphilis. Based on their experience with lock-hospital and workhouse patients, doctors could not have foreseen that most diseased prostitutes interned under the acts would be suffering from gonorrhea, not syphilis. As the diagnosis of gonorrhea was even more vague and disputed than syphilis, this medical development would certainly complicate the medical and legal defense of the acts.

Conclusion

In conclusion, lock hospitals imposed a social discipline and therapeutic regime on female venereal patients that incorporated the class and sex prejudices of the dominant Victorian culture. Advocates of regulation frequently criticized the repressive moral regime of voluntary lock hospitals, although they did not challenge the medical treatment women received there. Ironically, lock hospitals established under the acts would reproduce this same repressive atmosphere with disastrous results. Doctors working under the acts would also run into difficulties when they tried to rely on the vague diagnoses of syphilis and gonorrhea that had served them adequately in private practice or in the wards of voluntary hospitals. As a result of repeal agitation these diagnoses would be subjected to a new scrutiny in the courts and in the press, since they carried legal sanctions against prostitutes suffering from venereal complaints.

65

PART II

The Contagious Diseases Acts, regulationists, and repealers

4 *The Contagious Diseases Acts and their advocates*

> I trust then before many years have passed away England too will
> have a "Bureau des Moeurs" with a Minister of Health, at its head, a
> large and efficient staff of medical officers in every town and
> throughout the length and breadth of the land as well as sanitary
> police, entrusted with the working of the C.D. Acts, the Vaccination
> Act, the Factory Act, and the suppression of public nuisances, ob-
> scene literature . . . and demoralizing exhibitions of every kind – for
> gentlemen, the end of Government is the Good of Mankind.
> —Dr. C.W. Shirley Deakin, *The Contagious Diseases Acts, 1864,*
> *'66, '68, (Ireland), '69 from a Sanitary and Economic Point of*
> *View*

Historical interest in the Contagious Diseases Acts has principally focused on their cultural importance as explicit manifestations of mid-
Victorian social and sexual ideology. This cultural interpretation, although important, has generally been presented in isolation from the
political background surrounding passage of the acts and the administrative machinery and medical technology that facilitated their operation. The separation of the ideological and the practical origins of the
acts has distorted the historical picture by making the acts appear to
express a more programmatic and coherent social policy than was
actually the case.

This chapter will offer a corrective to this oversimplified approach
by investigating the interaction between ideology and its implementation under the acts. It will also examine the changing public rationale
for the acts, from limited sanitary measures to far-reaching pieces of
social legislation. This transformation was the result both of changing
national policies and of the efforts of local authorities responsible for
the daily administration of the acts in the subjected districts. On the
national level, the political initiative for this change came from civilian
doctors and authorities who organized a campaign to extend the acts
to the north in 1867. Their political agenda was distinctly different
from that of the military authorities and state bureaucrats responsible
for the passage of the first act in 1864. In particular, these civilians
were more explicit ideologues than the early regulationists. For many

extensionists, the acts were part of a grand plan, the first stage in the creation of a moral and sanitary utopia.

Ideology and sexual anxiety

The Contagious Diseases Acts were consistent with a set of attitudes and "habits of mind" (toward women, sexuality,) and class that permeated official Victorian culture. Euphemisms like "Contagious diseases" or "great social evil" reflect both a discomfort and an obsession with sexual questions. The deliberate vagueness of such terms probably focused more attention on "unmentionable" evils than would have any direct reference to venereal disease or prostitution. Characteristically, this linguistic confusion led to awkward attempts at clarification; in the case of the acts, clumsy parenthetical expressions were appended to their titles, such as "Contagious Diseases (Women) Act" and "Contagious Diseases (Not Concerned with Animals) Acts."[1]

This discomfort with sexuality itself contrasts markedly with the clear-cut legal distinctions between genders and classes established under the acts. According to Keith Thomas, the acts represented a "high water mark" of an officially sanctioned double standard of sexual morality, one that upheld different standards of chastity for men and women and carefully tried to demarcate pure women from the impure. "By their bland assumption that prostitution was a permanent and necessary evil and by their direct application of the double standard in that all regulation and medical examination applied to the woman alone they [the acts] yield an interesting commentary on an often forgotten aspect of Victorian England."[2]

An unthinking acceptance of male sexual license set the tone for parliamentary discussions of prostitution, regulation, and the age of consent during most of the Victorian period.[3] However, the very persistence of these traditional libertine views makes it difficult to explain the timing of the acts in the 1860s. It is not at all clear that the official sanction of male "vice" was stronger at that time than, for example, during the 1840s, when Carlyle fulminated against the vicious proclivities of parliamentary members: "I hear it. I hear whoredom in the House of Commons. Disraeli betrays whoredom and the whole House of Commons universal incontinence in every word they say."[4] On the contrary, by the 1860s, the double standard was challenged by a social and moral conscience awakened to the plight of prostitutes by the mid-century religious revival.[5]

The crucial conflict seems to have been between the older male libertine ethos and mid-Victorian social and medical modifications of

70

that ideology. Whereas the right of male access to promiscuous females continued to receive a tacit sanction, influential writers like
Greg and Acton increasingly stressed the dangerous medical and social
consequences of male promiscuity. For public officials in the mid-Victorian period, then, anxiety over male and female sexuality was at
least as important an ideological consideration as traditional libertine
attitudes. Thus the Royal Commission of 1871 couched its defense of
the double standard in the pseudoscientific language of the "spermatic
economy,"[6] transforming a time-honored male privilege into a physiological imperative:

> we may at once dispose of any recommendation founded on the
> principle of putting both parties to the sin of fornication on the
> same footing by the obvious but not less conclusive reply that there
> is no comparison to be made between prostitutes and the men who
> consort with them. With the one sex the offence is committed as a
> matter of gain; with the other it is an irregular indulgence of a
> natural impulse.[7]

Although specifically directed to women, the acts also reflected a
new enthusiasm for state intervention into the lives of the poor on
medical and sanitary grounds. The mid-century sanitary movement
had created a close identification of public order and public health.
The "controlment" of prostitutes as sources of moral and physical
pollution was the logical extension of trends in Victorian public-health
policy.[8] In the late 1860s, regulationists could draw upon a wide
variety of legal precedents – such as the medical clauses of the Poor
Law, Common Lodging House Act, vagrancy statutes, and the new
Vaccination Acts – to justify the sanitary supervision of prostitutes.[9]

The early rationale for the acts

Yet in the early 1860s government officials did not concern themselves
with providing elaborate defenses of the acts because there was no
significant challenge to their legitimacy. At the time of the passage of
the first two C.D. acts (1864 and 1866), their wider social significance
and application remained implicit and undefined. Only when public
opposition mounted in the late 1860s were regulationists obliged to
rationalize the class and sex discrimination underlying the acts. In the
heat of battle they even emphasized the moral and social benefits
attendant upon the acts – post hoc arguments entirely irrelevant to the
original purpose of the first act when it was introduced in 1864.

The acts were initially defended and implemented on narrow sanitary grounds, as exceptional legislation designed to control the spread

71

of venereal disease among enlisted men. As a consequence, they applied to specific military depots in southern England and Ireland and they were overseen by the War Office and the Admiralty. The agitators for regulation were in the first instance military authorities and government bureaucrats. Acton, the *Lancet,* and other influential medical sources may have previously established a climate of medical concern over the incidence of syphilis in the general population, but it was the loss of man-hours and the mounting statistics on venereal disease among the troops that finally spurred legislation on the subject. It was only during the second stage of the agitation, beginning in 1867, when doctors and civilian authorities tried to extend the acts to northern cities, that reform activity in favor of regulation was systematically organized outside the walls of Whitehall and Parliament.

Although applied on a limited basis, the acts involved a more positive extension of governmental responsibility than most mid-Victorian reforms, which were essentially prohibitory in nature. Instead of trying to repress an intolerable evil – like child labor or disorderly houses – they created new medical institutions and a new relationship between private voluntary hospitals and the state. This unprecedented subsidy of civilian lock wards by the state was noted at the time.[10]

The acts reflected a new interventionist approach to social problems that had gained increasing acceptance after 1850.[11] But this interventionist style was dominated by the same antinomies – partially laissez-faire, partially collective – that had characterized early-Victorian social legislation. Social reforms were intended to serve a moral purpose: they were expected to ameliorate certain deleterious social conditions that undermined moral character, thereby, "setting the individual free or equipping him to be thrifty, self-reliant, orderly, clean and in a word moral."[12]

Given this fundamental contradiction, official attitudes toward the larger social and sexual questions raised by the acts were characteristically muddled and inconsistent. Despite the passage of the acts, many officials continued to believe that sexual promiscuity among civilians rightly constituted a private medical risk for the parties concerned. They continued to view venereal disease as a preordained form of Russian roulette for transgressors of the respectable sexual-moral code. Only the exceptional conditions of military life, requiring the effective "celibacy" of enlisted men, justified state protection of sexual promiscuity. In the case of the "civil fornicant," who was freer to make social choices (that is to marry) in keeping with moral responsibility, the effective state subsidy of "male vice" would violate the enshrined laws of economic, political, and moral individualism.[13]

72

The C.D. acts and their advocates

Thus, the initial rationale for the acts hinged on their exceptional status as national defense legislation. It is important to examine the military origins of the acts in order to appreciate their early limited operation as well as the changing social and political focus of the extensionist movement.

The acts before the repeal campaign

> Let those who have never seen a ship of war, picture to themselves a very large and very low room with 500 men and probably 300 or 400 women of the vilest description shut up in it, and giving way to every excess of debauchery that the grossest passions of human nature can lead them to, and they see the deck of a gun ship upon the night of her arrival in port.
> —Admiral Edward Hawker, A *Statement of Certain Immoral Practices Prevailing in H.M. Navy*

The acts were the outgrowth of administrative reforms in the military departments of government. In the 1850s and 1860s, attention was drawn to the inefficient and chaotic administration of the armed forces and to the demoralization of enlisted men. The armed services were plagued by a series of evils, including severe problems of manning and recruitment, desertion, alcoholism, homosexuality, and the prevalence of venereal disease. A concerted effort was made at this time to raise the morale of enlisted men and also to attract a better class of recruits, through reforms in the terms and length of service, better pay, pensions, improved sanitary and medical conditions, and educational and temperance reforms. These reforms reflected a new humanitarian and environmentalist approach to the problems of military life. The environmentalist perspective began to undermine an entrenched belief in the innate depravity of enlisted men and substituted instead a conviction that humane conditions would make for a morally responsible and more efficient soldier or sailor. At the same time, this involved more control over the lives of enlisted men, in particular, a closer supervision of their leisure activities. The division of sailors into three classes, with preferential leave policy for first-class men, and the surveillance activities of a naval police patrol (established in 1860) helped to impose a new social discipline on sailors. In a somewhat less coercive way, naval savings banks, sailors' and soldiers' homes, and temperance campaigns tried to break the hold maintained by the drink trade, crimps, and prostitutes over enlisted men, by offering alternative services and accommodations.[14] These efforts to improve the moral tone of the army and navy were tempered by official distrust of

73

recruits as potentially disloyal. The army continued to prohibit enlisted men from marrying, in order that a "professional bachelor army without family ties" could be "assembled in large depots and moved regularly around the country."[15]

One catalytic agent in changing public consciousness about the state of the military proved to be the medical debacle of the Crimean War (1854–6), where the British army suffered more casualties in hospital than on the battlefield. The bestial living conditions of soldiers and their dependents were brought home by photos and reports in the press. In Parliament, Radical M.P.s like J. A. Roebuck attacked the military departments as bastions of aristocratic inefficiency and corruption, and they obtained a committee of inquiry while the war was still in progress.[16]

The result was the report of the Royal Commission on the Health of the Army in 1857. This report specifically noted the high level of venereal disease among certain troops, acknowledging that "there is doubtless a greater amount of [sexual] dissipation . . . among young men of the same class than in civilian life."[17] However, the introduction of a regulation system was not included in the recommendation of the commission report. In fact, the report specifically called for the discontinuance of the periodic genital examination of soldiers, on the grounds that it destroyed the men's self-respect and was medically inefficacious. Instead, the report focused on rectifying the general environmental conditions that would lead men into temptation: their general ennui and routinized existence and the abominable sanitary conditions of barracks.[18]

Nonetheless, the new stress on humanitarian reforms and on greater efficiency indirectly led to demands for a regulation system. At the recommendation of the Royal Commission, an army statistical department was created that produced annual reports on the health of the army. The navy had published such reports since 1840, but the value and reliability of these statistics greatly improved after the Crimean War. According to Christopher Lloyd, navy medical statistical reports finally assumed a reliable and professional character when Dr. Bryson, "a born statistician, took over the editorship just before the Crimean War."[19] Bryson represented the new style of professional civil servant bent on transforming the navy from an aristocratic enclave to an efficient organ of government.[20]

It was men like Bryson who actively organized opinion on the problem of venereal disease among the military and who advocated a regulation system. The medical statistical reports of the army and navy provided the initial ammunition. They stressed the extraordinarily high incidence of venereal disease in the armed services and the financial and manpower cost of this medical disability. In the early 1860s these V.D. statistics were particularly alarming, owing to the return of troops stationed in India.[21] As mentioned in Chapter 3, in the army one out of three sick cases were venereal in origin in 1864, representing 290.7 per 1,000 of troop strength. The naval statistics were only somewhat less sensational; in 1862 one out of eleven sick cases was venereal, which represented 125 admissions per 1,000 strength.[22]

The statistical reports also included editorial comment on the unusual prevalence of venereal disease in certain garrison towns and home ports.[23] Plymouth and Portsmouth were identified as the worst plague spots: "Whenever the crew of a sea-going ship is permitted to land on liberty at either of these ports, the indulgence is sure to be followed by a sudden rise in the sick list."[24]

These continuing reports had a national and local aspect. They "arrested the attention of heads of departments and attracted the earnest consideration of the highest authorities."[25] They also stimulated the appointment in 1862 of a committee to inquire into venereal disease among the military. But although investigative machinery was set in motion that would lead eventually to the legislative enactment of the C.D. acts, informal arrangements were already underway with local hospitals to provide inpatient care for diseased prostitutes on a voluntary basis.[26]

Opponents of regulation, like Florence Nightingale, had been directly responsible for the creation of the 1862 venereal-disease committee. Nightingale heavily influenced the selection of members and drew up the questions for the committee. Her hope was to air the question publicly and to present effective arguments against regulation. "She considered the continental system morally disgusting, unworkable, and unsuccessful in results."[27] Not surprisingly, then, the report of the committee advised against the introduction of a "continental" system in Britain and attacked the regulation and compulsory examination of prostitutes on sanitary and moral grounds.[28] Instead the committee recommended the establishment of lock hospitals on a voluntary basis; improved sanitary conditions in barracks and greater facilities for private ablution for soldiers; and a policy of penalizing soldiers for concealing but not contracting venereal disease. It took a strongly environmental view of sexual promiscuity, advocating as a deterrent "healthy, innocent and manly occupations and amusements which can relieve the tedium of life in barracks and on board ship." The committee also admonished public authorities in garrison towns and ports for tolerating the immoral conditions of the streets and for permitting public houses to function as brothels.[29]

An important dissent from the report came from Sir John Liddell, director general of the naval medical department, who stressed the need for a regulation system to "arrest disease at its source." He noted that the continental system had the "support of commanding and medical officers." Furthermore, he dismissed the view that such a system would offend public feelings on the subject. On the contrary, he argued, public sentiment was ripe for regulation, owing to recent precedents for state intervention on sanitary matters and to the heightened attention paid to the "social evil."[30]

Liddell's position clearly won out. The environmentalist arguments of Nightingale and the 1862 committee failed to convince politicians like William Gladstone that a standing army could be a "moral institution."[31] In July 1864, Parliament passed the first Contagious Diseases Act, to continue in force for three years.[32] The act applied to eleven garrison and dock towns in England and Ireland; although not legalizing prostitution, it provided that a women identified as a diseased prostitute by a plainclothes member of the metropolitan police undergo examination. If found diseased, she could be detained in a hospital for up to three months. The accused could elect to submit voluntarily to the examination or be brought up by a magistrate (with all the publicity attendant to that event) and then be bound by his orders.

To carry out the acts an administrative apparatus was patched together from a hodgepodge of national and local, civilian and military bureaucracies in operation at the time. The Admiralty and War Office oversaw the operation of the act; naval and army surgeons acted as examining doctors; dockyard metropolitan police (under the Home Office) stationed in subjected districts were responsible for identifying common prostitutes and ensuring their attendance at examination; local "nonstipendiary" magistrates adjudicated legal appeals and infractions; and local general hospitals provided medical services under the act.[33] Crucial parts of this administrative apparatus – particularly the national police network – had been in existence only a short time, a fact that undoubtedly contributed to the timing of the acts as much as mid-Victorian social and sexual ideology.[34]

As later military commentators noted, the "Act of 1864 was allowed to pass as a partial measure of sanitary police, for the benefit of soldiers and sailors of the army and navy."[35] Even at this point, though, broader social and legal questions had been raised in committee and in public debate. The celibate state of the army, the social and living conditions of enlisted men, the structure and organization of

76

prostitution in military districts had all been given some attention. A spate of letters to the *Times* in 1863 on the "social evil," which Florence Nightingale believed to have been deliberately planted by regulationists to aid the passage of the first act, wholeheartedly endorsed the social and sanitary policy underlying regulation.[36] The letters endorsed regulation as a means of controlling "one of those foul streams running through humanity in the mass which proves its tendency to moral decay,"[37] and only regretted the failure to implement a full-scale continental system.[38]

Public response to the proposed legislation was not uniformly favorable. In 1863, Harriet Martineau published a series of four letters against regulation in the *Daily News*.[39] The *British Medical Journal,* later to become a staunch supporter of regulation and extension when Ernest Hart assumed the editorship, opposed the 1864 act as a "most bungling attempt at legislation on a most painful and difficult subject."[40] It criticized the alarmist character of the medical statistics put forth by proponents of regulation: "To believe all that has been seriously said and written we shall be forced to conclude that in the course of another generation, English men will have undergone a thorough process of physical degeneration."[41] It also opposed police surveillance and compulsory internal examination as an unjustified interference with the "civil rights"[42] of subjected prostitutes, here anticipating the later arguments of feminists and civil libertarians.

Military doctors and officials themselves expressed moral and legal qualms about the acts. Even before organized repeal opposition had begun, they were troubled over the direction and legal implications of the acts: whether they were sanitary or police measures; whether they officially licensed prostitutes; whether they violated constitutional or moral principles. They perceived that the regulation of prostitutes was a "delicate" matter and stressed the need to introduce the acts into subjected districts tentatively, in installments, and on a limited basis. Whatever their trepidation, officials and politicians never anticipated an active and organized resistance on the part of a combination of subjected prostitutes and middle-class reformers.[43]

If anything, the early positive reception of the 1864 act encouraged authorities to try to extend their legal and territorial jurisdiction. "So little public opposition had been made to the Act of 1864 that it was thought a more useful measure [periodical examination of all prostitutes] would be passed without difficulty . . . "[44] The press for extension also resulted from certain practical and medical difficulties experienced by officials in the initial operation of the act. Failure to achieve anticipated medical results—in particular the persistence of wide fluctuations in venereal disease among troops—was partly blamed on the migratory habits of prostitutes and their ability to slip out of districts when threatened with hospital internment. One proposed solution was to expand the territorial limits of subjected districts and to add additional military stations to the schedule. Furthermore, doctors criticized the procedure by which police relied on the reports of men in hospitals to identify diseased prostitutes. They argued that this led to an arbitrary application of the act that was bitterly resented by local prostitutes. Finally, doctors and officials complained that the act provided insufficient provisions for dealing with refractory prostitutes and that legal and administrative loopholes actually encouraged insubordinate behavior among the women. In Portsmouth, for example, women defied the control of the house surgeon and "sometimes as many as four would quit the hospital without leave in one day."[45]

Through trial and error, administrators and supporters of the act came to envision a new purpose and function for a regulation system. Their enthusiasm for a wider field of activity and control grew with every partial success, as did their impatience with the narrow limits of the first act.[46] Encouraged by the apparent public acceptance of a regulation system, officials and lobbyists seized upon a favorable climate of opinion to extend their legal powers.

The new clauses of the 1866 act were meant to rectify the initial flaws of the 1864 act and to build on its early success.[47] Chatham and Windsor were added to the schedule of subjected districts. In addition, the act incorporated the chief recommendations of the Skey committee established in 1864 to "inquire into the pathology and treatment of venereal disease," that a "system of periodic fortnightly inspection or examination of all known prostitutes be made compulsory, under a well organized system of medical police."[48] The term "medical police" suggests the new direction of the 1866 act as a more overt system of police control. Relying on the continental model as well as a colonial precedent already operating in Malta,[49] the proposed regulation system entailed close police surveillance of registered women, whose residence and traffic were to be restricted to narrowly circumscribed areas.

Increasingly, the acts became openly linked to a tradition of repressive social legislation that tried to enforce a social discipline on the unrespectable poor.[50] From exceptional medical measures for the military, they had been transformed into an important piece of domestic legislation. Paralleling this development was new official propaganda that stressed the social and moral benefits of the acts. Contagious Diseases Acts authorities collected statistics on the decline in juvenile prostitution and in the number of brothels and prostitutes in the sub-jected districts.[51] Before parliamentary committees, they testified to the improved demeanor and cleanliness of registered women, to the deterrent effects of the acts on the promiscuous activity of "amateurs" and sailors' wives, and to the improved order of the streets in garrison towns and naval depots.[52] Widely publicized, these reports and testi-monies were the only source of information on the workings of the acts prior to the repeal campaign.

The effort to extend the acts

Armed with this evidence, medical men and civil authorities mounted a vigorous campaign to extend the acts to the north in 1867. They relied heavily on evidence of the moral and social improvements under the acts to counter religious arguments against state support of vice. They recognized that the extension of the acts to the civilian popula-tion required a new political and moral rationale, as civilians did not suffer the same social disabilities as enlisted men. It was therefore necessary for proponents of extension to argue forcefully that such a system diminished public vice and public disorder at the same time that it organized and sanitized the practice of prostitution.

The organized public campaign to extend the acts has its origins in the 1867 report of the Harveian Medical Society of London. The report had been prepared at the request of the International Medical Congress that participants survey the incidence of venereal disease and existing facilities for the treatment of venereal disease in their respec-tive countries. It found the apparent incidence of venereal disease so high among the military and civilian populations of Great Britain, and existing facilities for the treatment of civilian cases so inadequate, that it called for effective state action to alleviate the problem. It noted the financial difficulties of lock hospitals and looked to the C.D. acts as an important precedent for the state subsidy of the treatment of venereal disease cases.[53]

The Harveian report led to the formation of the Association for Promoting the Extension of the Contagious Diseases Act of 1866 to the Civilian Population. The association was organized on classical pressure-group lines: its purpose was to educate the public on the evils of venereal disease and the necessity of remediable efforts. To further its ends, it formed branch associations in thirty-two provincial towns and enrolled over four hundred members.[54] It disseminated pamphlets and regularly petitioned Parliament and the Home Office for the ex-tension of the acts. Although it occasionally held special meetings, it

79

depended heavily on the medical press (in particular the *Lancet*) and on regional medical organizations to promote its cause.[55]

The extensionist association was an umbrella group for diverse and sometimes conflicting interests. It contained a much more illustrious list of patrons and politicians than the repeal movement. Tories, aristocrats, and military men lent support to the extensionist cause because they felt it furthered the military interests of the nation, and they tended to share a worldly perspective on the necessity of prostitution and male promiscuity. Anglican clergy were early recruited into the extensionist movement and also identified themselves as part of the established, corporate interests that supported regulation. Unlike evangelicals and nonconformists, Anglican clergy tended to be more concerned with public order and the control of vice than with its total eradication.[56]

Civilian authorities also greeted the extensionist cause with enthusiasm. They supported the extension of a regulation system to northern cities as a means of containing the street disorders of prostitutes and alleviating the local cost of treating diseased prostitutes and their children in the workhouse.[57] Police, in particular, preferred regulation to the suppression of open prostitution. They tended to see prostitution as an inevitable fact of social life; only when public opinion forced them to act vigilantly did they crack down on public solicitation.[58]

Some police officials, however, exhibited a genuine enthusiasm for the new discretionary powers afforded them by a regulation system. William Harris, assistant commissioner of metropolitan police, for example, discussed his plans for the extension of the C.D. acts to London before an investigative committee established in 1868 by the House of Lords to consider the question. He called for extensive powers for the police, who would be entrusted with the surveillance of bawdy houses, the repression of pornography, streetwalkers, clandestine prostitutes, and the apprehension of women who procured abortions. Asked to define a clandestine prostitute, Harris replied, "Speaking of London, I should propose that any woman who goes to places of public resort, and is known to go with different men, although not a common streetwalker, should be served with a notice to register."[59] Harris's views even shocked William Acton, the principal propagandist for regulation, who questioned the vague definition of prostitution offered by Harris:

> It is difficult to know what offences the assistant commissioner requires that a women should be guilty of to justify her registration as a prostitute and it is to be regretted that his evidence is not more explicit on this point, as the question what conduct is to expose a woman to police surveillance is one of no small difficulty.[60]

80

Class prejudice and suspicions of female sexuality were even more
explicit in an 1882 pamphlet on *The Social Evil with Suggestions for
Its Suppression and Revelations of the Working of the Contagious
Diseases Acts,* by an "Ex-Constable of the Devonport Division." The
"Ex-Constable," perhaps a pseudonym for Inspector Anniss of Devonport, argued that the female instinct for promiscuous intercourse
was "inherent." Women entered prostitution for pleasure and vanity,
not out of economic necessity. The author of the pamphlet asserted
as well that attractive women of the lower classes were almost exclusively of low character and likely to engage in some form of clandestine prostitution. "In every large town without exception, where a
woman has a chance of this course and runs no danger of serious
loss or inconvenience, and possesses the means of deluding her
friends, she will embrace it."[61] Only the fear of detection and, in the
case of subjected districts, fear of compulsory examination, kept
these women from "resorting to the streets when the day's work is
done."[62]

Not all extensionists shared these misogynist views. Active feminists
and supporters of birth control were also represented in the extensionist
camp, although they were a distinct minority.[63] They included prominent Malthusians like the Drysdale brothers, Charles and George. In
Physical Sexual and Natural Religion (1855), George Drysdale had
recommended the state regulation of prostitution. He argued that registered prostitutes performed a valuable and virtuous service; they were
martyrs to a "sexual passion" that could not find a legitimate outlet in
conjugal love because of the unnatural marriage customs of the period.
While celebrating prostitutes as "unhappy victims of our natural sexual
difficulties," whose services were at present necessary to social and
physical health, he called for social and sexual reforms that would
remove women's social disabilities and facilitate early marriage and
small families.[64]

Charles Drysdale, who coauthored the Harveian report with J. B.
Curgenven, publicly endorsed his brother's sentiments in the 1860s.
He also tried to balance a defense of regulation with an interest in the
autonomy and welfare of women. Only when repealers convinced him
that a police regulation system threatened the civil rights of working-
class women did he withdraw his support in 1870 and move actively
into the repeal camp.[65]

The views of most extensionist leaders fell somewhere between the
feminism of Drysdale and the fierce misogyny of Harris and the "Ex-
Constable." Spokesmen for extension exhibited a custodial and morally condescending attitude toward both men and women and the

81

working class. The civilian leadership of the movement was generally composed of reforming and often politically liberal doctors committed to public health and sanitary reforms. As such, they were a different constituency from the London medical elite, who endorsed extension but did not actively participate in the public controversies. Spokesmen for extension tended to be specialists in venereology, a specialty that could be well-paying but did not carry much status within the medical profession.[66] A number of these venereologists, like Charles Drysdale, Berkeley Hill, and William Acton, had studied in Paris under Philippe Ricord and were much impressed with the regulation system there. From their stay in Paris, they also seemed to have gained a greater sympathy for centralized state medicine than most of their British contemporaries.[67]

What additionally marked these civilian doctors was their direct experience with the medical problems of the poor. Some of the principal propagandists for extension had worked under the C.D. acts, whereas others had been engaged in hospital work among the poor, as consultants to voluntary hospitals or as medical officers of health attached to workhouse infirmaries.[68] They prided themselves on their practical knowledge of the distress caused by venereal disease among the poor at a time when the plight of venereal patients was ignored by most respectable members of society. They would certainly have concurred with the *Lancet's* self-congratulatory statement: "If the working classes have any true friends, they are to be found in medical practitioners who probably know more of the genesis of poverty and the needs of a working man than any other class in the community."[69]

In keeping with these views, extensionist leaders actively participated in mid-century reformist and social-science organizations, such as the National Association for the Promotion of Social Science, the Dialectical Society, or the Royal Statistical Society. As members of these organizations, they actively concerned themselves with two sets of related social and sanitary problems: sewage, water supply, housing, and epidemiology; and baby farming, illegitimacy, and infanticide. The latter concerns would bring many of them into open conflict with feminists and civil libertarians, who challenged the male medical supervision of women's health and maternal functions.[70]

These divisions would crystallize in the 1870s. Throughout the 1860s, however, feminist repealers like Harriet Martineau, Elizabeth Wolstenholme, and F. W. Newman coexisted with prominent regulationists within the Social Science Association. In part, this coexistence reflected the consensus atmosphere of the 1850s and 1860s that encouraged a dialogue between divergent social and political views.[71] But it also may suggest a political and social affinity between members of opposing camps. Despite their position on regulation, subgroups on both sides undoubtedly shared a similar rhetoric of reform and similar perspectives on class, the social order, and respectable social behavior.

This shared ideology had a social basis. The social background of some repealers and extensionists was strikingly similar. For instance, F. W. Newman, a prominent repealer (and John Henry's brother) and M. Berkeley Hill, the secretary of the extensionist association, both came from families with Paineite and nonconformist or Calvinist traditions.[72] Hill had been raised in a prominent Unitarian family, but as the family prospered, most of its members had joined the Church of England. Newman was originally confirmed as an Anglican; as a young man, however, he suffered a crisis of faith and subsequently rejected orthodox Christianity, stressing instead the importance of personal ethics and moral institutions. Both Hill and Newman were influenced by a tradition of philanthropic and public service, although members of the Hill family were notably committed to "regulator" roles and to coercive programs for the control and rehabilitation of the socially "unfit,"[73] whereas Newman adhered to an antistatist and personal-rights position.

Although both were professionally connected with University College, London – Hill as professor of surgery and pathology at the medical school and Newman as professor of classics – they moved in different political and social circles. Despite his nonconformist background, Hill was integrated into the military and medical establishments that were anathema to Newman, whose pamphlets regularly condemned the materialist and libertine doctrines of "aristocratic" doctors and the military.[74] Hill was a member of the London medical elite, married to the daughter of Sir Thomas Howell of the War Office; he had been educated at the Hill family's experimental school at Bruce Castle, but he sent his son to Eton.[75]

On the question of women's rights, however, the differences between the two remain unclear. Hill did not take a public position on the subject, but his family was actively involved in the suffrage movement from the start. The Women's Suffrage Society of Bristol held its first meeting in 1868 at the home of Berkeley Hill's father, Matthew Davenport Hill, the great penologist. Charter members included Hill's sister, Florence Davenport Hill, and a number of women who soon became active in the repeal struggle. The first honorary secretary of the Bristol society was F. W. Newman.[76]

In their personal responses to prostitutes, ironically it was Hill, the

83

regulationist, who manifested more sympathy for the "fallen." True to his Unitarian origins, he had moral scruples about the acts, never acknowledging that they actually licensed prostitution. He was sufficiently concerned with their humane and legitimate operation that he toured various subjected districts and interviewed registered prostitutes, investigating their social origins and their treatment by police under the acts.[77] Here he demonstrated a greater intellectual curiosity and personal concern for the women's welfare than other regulationists, who were content to accept the glowing reports of the C.D. acts authorities without troubling themselves to verify them. In fact, Hill showed a more active interest in the women than Newman, who, despite his feminist pretensions, was frankly appalled by streetwalkers. On at least one public occasion, Newman expressed his personal repugnance for prostitutes: "When he had been accosted by those women [prostitutes] he had not known what to do, as it were; he had recoiled with a shudder from them, feeling it was out of his power to help them."[78]

In certain respects Hill was an "atypical" extensionist leader. He was more socially prominent and professionally successful than most spokesmen for extension. His academic position and contact with nonconformist circles was also unusual. If we compare him to John Brendon Curgenven, the other secretary of the extensionist association, we may gain a somewhat fuller impression of the kinds of men active in the extensionist cause.

Like Hill, Curgenven was in his mid-thirties at the time of the first organization of the extensionist association – a young man on his way up.[79] Unlike Hill, he was an outsider to London circles – a provincial from Cornwall. His choice of profession followed family tradition; in 1847 "he became a pupil of his uncle, Peter Brendon . . . at Highgate." Curgenven lacked Hill's university education, although he did study at one of the major London hospitals, St. Bartholemew's. Hill had also studied abroad with renowned medical specialists – in Vienna with Virchow and in Paris with Ricord – whereas Curgenven gained his foreign medical experience in the military, by accompanying Lord Ward to the Crimea as "medical attendant and private secretary."[80]

Curgenven was engaged in a "large general practice" and never received the same hospital appointments and honors that were awarded to Hill throughout his career. Instead, Curgenven seems to have sought status and recognition through participation in the large number of voluntary organizations and medical reform activities that illustrate the growing social and political influence of "reforming" doctors. Many of these activities – particularly those related to the

84

medical supervision of childbirth and infancy–drew strong criticism from feminists. A partial list of his voluntary efforts: As a member of the Parliamentary Bills Committee of the British Medical Association, he assisted in the drafting of the first Habitual Drunkards bill and a bill on Infant Mortality; he also helped to draft the bill for the Examination and Registration of Midwives (1869). He promoted the formation of the Paddington Committee of the Charity Organization Society (1869) and served on various local sanitary and relief fund committees in the late 1860s.

As these examples suggest, both male repealers and male extensionists laid claim to the role of humanitarian reformers. On both sides, enlightened social views coexisted with class prejudice and, in some cases, a fear of and hostility toward female sexuality. The result was a repressive humanitarianism that was a marked feature of extensionist arguments and programs. As philanthropists, extensionists argued that the medical aid provided under the acts contrasted favorably with the comfortless penitentiaries and empty preaching of evangelicals. Penitentiaries did not help the prostitute "in the days of her prostitution."[81] Moreover, they imposed an unrealistically harsh and tedious work discipline on women unaccustomed to menial labor. Extensionists also held up to scorn traditional religious views on venereal disease as divine punishment for "vice," arguing instead that "to give these unfortunate women health was the likeliest means of reclaiming them."[82]

In taking a hard line against religious "fanatics," extensionists re-echoed a long-standing medical contempt for the "narrow" principles of moral reformers "who distribute freely moral principles but [withhold] bread and soup."[83] Ironically, extensionists systematically avoided discussing the real "bread and butter" issues relating to prostitution–the economic and social discrimination that forced women into prostitution in the first place. They concentrated instead on the medical impediments to female penitence, assuming indeed that it was *females* who needed to be penitent and ignoring all other material factors that might keep women in prostitution.

Like so many other mid-century reformers, extensionists only partially broke with a moralist perspective on prostitution. In fact, they argued that the acts aided the moral reform of prostitutes: medical supervision exposed prostitutes to the civilizing influence of the surgeon who is "generally regarded among our lower classes much as the mysterious medicine man of yet wilder tribes."[84] As William Acton noted, "The mere fact of seeing periodically a man aloof from the life they lead must have a good effect upon them."[85]

85

Regulationists and repealers

The repealers' challenge

In 1868 and 1869, the confidence of extensionists was shattered by formidable opposition on two fronts. First, in his 1868 Report of the Medical Officer of the Privy Council, Dr. John Simon advised against the extension of the acts to the north and challenged extensionist arguments on all grounds. He dismissed their sanitary arguments, claiming that their statistics on the incidence of venereal disease among the sick poor were greatly exaggerated and that, in any case, syphilis was the only venereal disease "important to society," and only a small proportion of those who suffered from true syphilis actually experienced permanent damage. He claimed that the cost of extending the acts to the civilian population would be prohibitive and that the sanitary benefits of regulation did not outweigh the violation of moral principles involved in such a state action. He dismissed the evidence of moral and social improvements under the acts as incidental to their operation. He also argued that the sanitary requirements of the acts were essentially unenforceable in a metropolis like London, as the large body of clandestine prostitutes would inevitably escape supervision. For all these reasons, he advised against any change in the "neutral" position of the state toward prostitution.[86]

Simon's report ended any immediate prospects for the extension of the acts to civilian areas in Britain. The House of Lords committee still proposed such an extension in 1868, and an extensionist bill was introduced in the Lords that year, with its proponents noting that a number of northern cities had already applied to have the act extended. However, the bill was later withdrawn.[87] Significantly, the 1869 Select Committee of the House of Commons made no recommendation for the extension of the acts; instead, "the Committee confined their inquiries to those districts in which the Act had been applied, and to the alterations thought necessary to secure more satisfactory results."[88] The committee's recommendations were incorporated into the 1869 act, which extended the C.D. acts to five additional districts; stiffened the discipline imposed on the women by setting nine months as the maximum period of detention in hospital; provided for the moral and religious instruction of the women so confined; required the detention of women "unfit" for examination; extended the jurisdiction of the acts to within a ten-mile radius of the subjected districts; and made the acts effective for an indefinite period.[89]

By 1869, extensionists were on the defensive. Although they continued their public agitation, the cause had clearly lost some momentum. Having established regulation in military depots, the government

seemed reluctant to extend the acts to the north, especially in the face
of mounting public opposition (see Chapter 5). With the emergence of
public repeal agitation in 1869, the tone of the extensionists decidedly
changed. Extensionists had defended their cause vigorously against
Simon's criticism, but they were stunned and annoyed by the challenge
now mounted by "ladies" and "provincial members" of the medical
profession. They responded with openly misogynist attacks on prostitutes and their female supporters.

A change of tone is apparent in Acton's presentation before the
Medical Officers of Health in 1869. With his prized sanitary legislation under attack by feminists and personal-rights advocates, his position on prostitutes hardened—or at least the overlay of humanitarian
concern began to wear thin. "The public should be made fully aware
of the fact we are not legislating for 'soiled doves' but for a class of
women that we may almost call unsexed . . . "[90] Whereas he had
previously pleaded the cause of prostitutes who would only remain on
the streets for a brief period, prostitutes now became a class of women
separate and apart from the rest of humanity. Common prostitutes
were such an obvious class that they needed no formal statutory definition. Acton denied that the absence of this definition under the acts
posed any "practical threat to modest women":

> it is a remote possibility that any woman should be charged with
> being a common prostitute, unless her conduct was notoriously and
> openly bad, and it is obvious that any distinct statement of the Acts
> that shall render a woman liable to be included in the class supplies
> by the definition the means of evasion.[91]

This is a remarkable statement in light of Acton's own writings on the
fluid social identity of prostitutes, as well as the importance attached to
classification and identification of the unrespectable poor by enthusi-
asts for state intervention. But in a sense, the failure to provide a statutory definition of the common prostitute is consistent with the traditional legal treatment in Britain of women and outcast groups—as the
"Other," an entirely negative and collective presence before the law.[92]

However hostile Acton appeared toward prostitutes, he vented most
of his spleen against the "ladies" who cried out against the "instrumental rape" of workingwomen through the internal examination.
These ladies not only challenged the male medical role, but they
openly discussed subjects inappropriate for "pure" women and tried
to politicize other respectable females on these issues. The extensionists countered repeal exposés of the "medical lust of dominating and
handling of women"[93] with a vituperative attack on the "immoral"
literature distributed by the "shrieking sisterhood."[94]

87

> The subject is a very unsavory one for public discussion, and it is not they [the extensionists] who have dragged such ghastly matters to light, and paraded them before the eyes of the young and pure. . . . if the promoters [of extension] are obliged to defend these laws against the grossest misrepresentation and exaggeration, against hysterical shrieking and bigoted fanaticism, the blame is not theirs, but their opponents – who have scrupled at nothing.[95]

From the start, the struggle between extensionists and repealers was a heated and emotional one, a struggle that involved deep-seated sexual hostilities on both sides. As we shall see in subsequent chapters, middle-class women embraced the repeal cause out of loyalty to their "fallen" sisters and also out of hostility to male power and influence. On their side, extensionists responded to the feminist repeal campaign with an anger that also seemed to be fed by a hostility toward assertive women and fear of female autonomy. To many antisuffragists, the public participation of women in such a campaign came to signify the dangers of women's involvement in the political arena. As one M.P. declared, "He looked upon their conduct respecting that movement as a foretaste of what the country might expect if women were engaged largely in politics."[96]

More generally, the feminist repeal campaign raised the threat of a female rebellion against male domination on all levels – a struggle that would be fought on the domestic front as well. In his 1875 edition of *Functions and Disorders of the Reproductive Organs*, Acton warned against the threat posed by advocates of women's rights to the sexual supremacy of men in marriage. He specifically noted the case of a "lady who maintains women's rights to such an extent that she denied the husband any voice in the matter, whether or not cohabitation should take place. She maintained most strenuously that as the woman bears all the consequences . . . a married woman has a perfect right to refuse to cohabit with her husband." It appears that this "strong-minded female" would lend no ear to his arguments that such "conduct on her part might be . . . highly detrimental to the health of the husband."[97]

Conclusion

In summary, by 1869, the Contagious Diseases Acts had been extended well beyond their initially defined limits as exceptional legislation for the military. They broke new ground as domestic social measures, creating new medical institutions and new precedents for police and medical supervision of the lives of the poor. By 1869, when organized opposition to the acts first emerged, the ideological disputes surrounding the operation of the acts assumed a new intensity and cultural importance. The ensuing conflict over the C.D. acts would spotlight the clusters of social forces vying for political hegemony in the 1870s and 1880s. The political legacy of that conflict would cast its shadow over medico-legal policy as well as the feminist struggle through World War I.

5 The repeal campaign

In 1869 the men and women who first organized public opposition to the Contagious Diseases Acts were dismissed as a small sectarian group of "eccentric cranks" and religious zealots. For most of the 1870s the repeal movement continued to be regarded as a "forlorn hope" even by its staunchest supporters. By 1880, however, the social and political climate had changed. The image of the repeal movement as a collection of cranks still persisted, especially in certain official circles, but the political power and popular appeal of the repealers could not be ignored. By this time, these "eccentrics" had been able to impose their views on a significant part of the general public and also to dictate Liberal party policy on the subject of regulation. Their political influence could be felt at national and local levels. In 1883, for example, Joseph Rowntree recounted a conversation he had had recently with a political acquaintance in York. The gentleman had asked him, "have you any fads in York?" "I said, 'Yes, any Liberal candidate must be against the C. D. Acts.'"[1]

How did repealers move from the periphery of social and political power to center stage? They certainly benefited from the reorganization and domination of the Liberal Party by Radicals in the early eighties.[2] But structural change in the Liberal Party apparatus tells only part of the story. The repeal of the acts also reflected a new public consensus on prostitution and the double standard. Over the sixteen-year period from 1870 to 1886, repealers had mounted an impressive public campaign aimed at transforming social attitudes and influencing opinion among the political elite. This chapter will briefly outline the political highlights of the repeal campaign and analyze its tactics and propaganda.

Most repeal groups were organized as conventional pressure groups. To influence opinion about the acts, repealers, or abolitionists, as they were also called, organized branch associations, mass public meetings, petition campaigns, and electoral leagues. They also distributed mountains of propaganda and put forth medical and statistical evidence against the acts to counter pro-acts propaganda. These conventional pressure-group efforts sometimes masked more radical impulses and activities, as well as ideological differences, among repealers. An important division on strategies and ultimate goals existed between libertarian and religious interests, between men and women, and between working-class and middle-class participants. We shall identify the points of agreement here, and discuss more fully the internal conflicts among repealers in following chapters.

The chronological and political history of the repeal campaign

It was not until the late 1860s that organized public agitation against the acts mounted, in response to efforts to extend the acts to the north.[3] This public opposition reflected the newly charged political climate. The Reform Act of 1867 had stimulated a wave of political activism among middle-class nonconformists and working-class radicals. The extension of the franchise to "labor aristocrats" also gave impetus to the early beginnings of political feminism in Britain; the first women's suffrage societies were formed in 1866 and 1867. All these groups could be depended upon to lend a sympathetic ear to a critique of the medical and military establishments and to be hostile to a centralized state.[4]

In 1867, Berkeley Hill approached Daniel Cooper, of the Rescue Society of London, to solicit his support for "the alleged medical and ameliorative effects" of the acts and for their proposed extension to northern cities.[5] Alarmed at this prospect, Cooper organized a meeting of the managers of the London female rescue homes, and initiated propaganda to "bring this infamous legislation under public notice." In 1868 and 1869, Cooper and his associates published a series of pamphlets that exposed the "false statistics" of the moral benefits of the acts. The results were disappointing: "We spent more than £100 in the circulation of our papers, and with what results? I am ashamed to say that very little effect was produced. The utmost apathy prevailed; people would not believe our words and would not stir. The infamous Act of 1869 was passed in spite of all our efforts."[6] Still, as Cooper's associate, R. B. Williams, noted in 1886, "we were doing the necessary sub-soil work, were scattering information, and preparing the ground for other more influential agitators to follow."[7] A Nottingham doctor, Charles Bell Taylor, corresponded with Cooper, and agreed to help organize public opposition to extension. Aided by a fellow Not-

91

tingham physician, Charles Worth, Taylor chose the 1869 meeting of the Social Science Congress in Bristol to launch the public agitation.[8]

At the health section of the congress, two papers were presented in support of the acts: one by Berkeley Hill, arguing for extension, and the other by Paul Swain of the Royal Albert Hospital, Devonport, detailing the beneficial working of the acts in the Devonport district. Numerous opponents of the acts were present in the audience, which was chiefly composed of doctors and clergymen, as ladies had been excluded from the meeting. Medical authorities from the subjected districts were also present in considerable numbers. According to the local Bristol newspaper, the health section was turned into a "bear garden" during the discussion of the papers, when opponents of the acts vigorously contested the morality and constitutionality of the acts. At the end of the discussion a "hot debate" ensued over a proposed resolution in favor of extension. The resolution was defeated; instead, the "meeting resolved by an overwhelming majority that the National Association for the Promotion of Social Science should protest against the Acts and take steps to resist their extension."[9]

Encouraged by their first public success, opponents of the acts held a meeting the next day and formed "The National Anti-Contagious Diseases Act Extension Association." This cumbersome title was soon altered to "The National Association for the Repeal of the Contagious Diseases Acts," also reflecting the revised goal of the society to include total abolition of the acts.[10] Hundreds of branch associations of the National Association were soon formed at public meetings in the Midlands and the north. By the mid-eighties, it had an annual income of £3,000 and a membership that fluctuated between 334 and 750. As these numbers might suggest, even in good years most branches rarely had more than a handful of subscribers. Although initially based in the north, the National Association moved its headquarters and its organ, the *Shield,* to London in August 1870. Both the association and its journal were dominated by the cosmopolitan, republican, and constitutional wing of the repeal movement. As a London-based society, the National Association was expected to be the parliamentary and legal arm of the repeal movement, generally responsible for lobbying efforts and electoral activities. Initially, it was also expected to build a popular base of support in London and to oversee public agitation throughout the country. However, the small clique of freethinkers and Unitarians who dominated the executive board appear to have been totally unsuited to these latter two tasks, and their regional responsibilities were soon restricted to supervising repeal activity in the south of England and in the subjected districts.[11]

92

The repeal campaign

The National Association had excluded women from its first meeting, although it soon opened its membership to them. This exclusion resulted in the formation of a parallel but separatist female organization, the Ladies' National Association for the Repeal of the Contagious Diseases Acts (LNA). In December 1869, Elizabeth Wolstenholme, who had attended the congress, immediately contacted Josephine Butler, a feminist active in the higher education of women and also in rescue work, and asked her to organize a women's campaign against the acts. Butler soon emerged as the moral and charismatic leader of the crusade. Although her hold over the day-to-day political affairs of the repeal movement gradually lessened, she always retained a magnetic sway over popular audiences and a devoted following among repeal workers.

Butler later recalled discussing early plans for repeal agitation with two Quaker friends, Mary Priestman and Margaret Tanner. "What shall we do?" she asked them. "Well, we must rouse the country," was the response. "So gentle, so Quakerly, yet convinced that we three poor women must rouse the country."[12]

By the end of December 1869, a general committee of the LNA had been formed and a Ladies' Protest published in the *Daily News,* with 124 signatures of prominent feminists and female members of the Society of Friends. The protest outlined the essential arguments of the LNA: the acts violated the "legal safeguards hitherto enjoyed by women in common with men"; they allowed police absolute power over women; they "punish the sex who are the victims of vice and leave unpunished the sex who are the main causes both of the vice and its dreaded consequences"; they made vice safe and smoothed the "path of evil" for "our sons"; and they failed as moral and sanitary legislation.[13]

The Ladies' Protest and the formation of the Ladies' National Association gave notoriety and vitality to the fledgling repeal movement. By 1871, fifty-seven branches had been formed, with 811 subscribing members. As Daniel Cooper remarked, "But for the Ladies' National Association we should have had no discussion and the Acts would by this day [1871] have probably been extended throughout the country."[14] Female participation in repeal efforts astonished and perplexed the press and public officials and greatly annoyed regulationists. In 1870, the British public was unused to women speaking publicly before mixed audiences on such matters as prostitution, venereal disease, and internal gynecological examinations. The *Spectator* was impressed with the women's courage and tenacity: the Ladies' Protest "gives us a new ideal of women's intellectual courage and capacity of political life."[15] Other press reaction was less generous. The *Saturday Review* inveighed against the "shrieking sisterhood,"[16] and John Morley, the Radical editor of the *Fortnightly Review,* warned the female signatories that their manifesto "encouraged the presumptuous notion, current among men of the world, that resort to declamatory *a priori* methods is the incurable vice of women when they come to political subjects."[17]

Hence, from the beginning, the most important division between participants within the repeal camp was on the basis of sex. Men and women formed separate organizations and began to define distinctive concerns and methods of agitation for their own membership (see Chapter 7). Class divisions also became readily apparent. As the first annual report of the LNA explained, the repeal movement had two popular constituencies: "first the more educated artisans, clerks, warehousemen and tradesmen who study politics, and are honest devotees of justice to all classes and races"; "second, those with whom religion takes the lead, and with whom virtue and the laws of God are the paramount interest." The report further explained that although each "class includes persons of the upper ranks, . . . it appears that it is only in the middle and humbler ranks that a great majority is zealous for justice or virtue or both."[18] Whatever their political differences, working-class and middle-class repealers were united in their hatred of "profligate aristocrats," who they believed dominated the government, the military, and also the medical profession.

Over the next sixteen years (from 1870 to 1886), repeal groups continued to proliferate, reflecting the special interests of groups within the repeal camp and the changing political focus of the campaign as a whole. Regional electoral leagues, principally the Northern Counties League and the Midlands Electoral League, were first organized in 1872 and 1873 to promote the repeal cause during parliamentary and municipal elections in the provinces. By the mid-seventies Quakers, Wesleyans, and Congregationalists had also organized their own repeal groups. In 1875, a separate workingmen's association, the Working Men's National League, was formed in Liverpool, under the sponsorship of the LNA and the Friends' Association. In the late seventies more specialized professional and political societies followed.[19]

Jurisdictional disputes among constituent groups were bound to occur as these societies frequently worked the same geographic area and tried to tap the same financial sources. On the other hand, national and regional groups would often sponsor meetings together, share voluntary and paid agents, and jointly embark on various local and national projects. Moreover, most repeal leaders held membership in more than one repeal organization.[20]

In their early public agitations, repealers and their agents aroused strong popular feeling against the acts in the north and even in some subjected districts. They were able to mount impressive challenges to Liberal Party candidates at three important by-elections in 1870 and 1872. This popular success forced the government to take note. In response to a repeal bill introduced by William Fowler in 1870, the government proposed to set up a committee of inquiry, the Royal Commission of 1871, to study the administration and operation of the acts.[21]

For six months, the commission listened to the testimony of military personnel and police and medical authorities responsible for the local administration of the acts, in addition to a few repeal spokesmen. Many commissioners found it an onerous chore; A. J. Mundella recalled the "six weary months on the commission such as I hope never to pass again," whereas "Professor Huxley and other eminent gentlemen shrunk from it in disgust."[22] Some commissioners, like F. D. Maurice and Robert Applegarth, who had initially favored the acts, changed their minds as a result of hearing the testimony. Nevertheless, the commission's final report supported the continuation of the acts, with one important revision. In deference to strong public sentiment on the subject, the report called for the abolition of the compulsory periodic examination. The majority report also supported additional reforms that would raise the age of consent, send prostitutes under sixteen to homes or industrial schools, and punish more stringently publicans or lodging-house keepers who housed prostitutes.[23]

The government failed to act on these recommendations. Instead, H. A. Bruce, the Home Secretary, proposed a compromise bill in 1872. The bill would have repealed the C.D. acts, prohibited solicitation, and required that any woman prisoner submit to internal examination. If found diseased, she was to be detained in the prison infirmary for up to nine months. Another part of the bill raised the age of consent from twelve to fourteen, introduced heavy penalties for harboring girls under fifteen for purposes of prostitution, and provided for the summary conviction of keepers of bawdy houses.[24] This combination of punitive measures against prostitutes and clauses to protect the morality of young girls would become the paradigm for numerous pieces of moral legislation proposed throughout the seventies and eighties.

Bruce publicly defended the bill as a more efficient substitute for the C.D. acts, one that would eliminate the danger of entrapping innocent girls into a police registration system but would nonetheless extend the medical provisions to a greater number of female miscreants. "If we have made the meshes larger, we have given the net a wider sweep."[25] Repealers were divided over the bill. The parliamentary leadership and spokesmen of the National Association accepted it as a useful compromise, a first step toward the eventual abolition of the acts. The LNA stood fast against Bruce's bill, objecting to it on constitutional and moral grounds, as a dangerous extension of state power and sanction of the double standard.[26] The bill was never passed, as it satisfied neither opponents nor supporters of regulation.

With the defeat of Bruce's bill, repeal leaders turned their attention to preparations for the next general election. They began to take stock of themselves and to note their organizational chaos. Initially, repealers had not anticipated a lengthy struggle and had not mapped out a long-range political strategy. As a result, repeal groups had been organized spontaneously and little had been done to coordinate efforts. By 1872, however, repeal leaders began to appreciate the political forces arrayed against them and to realize that the repeal campaign was just in its "infancy."[27] Writing to Henry J. Wilson of Sheffield in that year, Butler supported plans for a northern electoral union (later called the Northern Counties League) that would offset the inactivity of the London-based National Association and would also stir up support for the repeal cause in the forthcoming general election.[28]

Still, between 1872 and 1874, the repeal campaign limped along and was unable to capture the attention of Parliament and the general public. The national press had lost interest and refused to cover the campaign; instead repealers had to rely on their own journals and on the provincial newspapers.[29] Repeal bills were introduced into the House of Commons almost every year throughout the 1870s, but they rarely secured more than 100 votes.[30] Electoral intervention declined in the mid-seventies, as repeal leaders feared that their candidates would suffer embarrassing political defeats.

A crisis came in 1874 with the general election. The Liberal government fell, destroying any immediate prospect for the repeal of the acts, as repealers could not hope to exert any political leverage on the Conservatives. In this "season of discouragement and general apathy," Butler undertook a mission to the Continent to spark abolitionist efforts there.[31] These international efforts gave a psychological boost to the flagging morale of repeal workers at home, although some repeal supporters feared, with some justification, "that the foreign work would divert attention from home work."[32]

The fall of the Gladstone government in 1874 also facilitated James Stansfeld's endorsement of the repeal cause. Stansfeld had been one of the three leading Radicals serving in Gladstone's Cabinet. A Unitarian brewer, he was part of a cosmopolitan, feminist, and republican circle in London. Although he had many friends and relatives prominent in the repeal campaign, he had previously felt constrained from openly opposing government policy on the acts. After the dissolution of the government, however, he freely declared himself for repeal and quickly assumed the national leadership of the movement. His 1874 Bristol speech in favor of repeal was widely covered by the press, thus ending the "conspiracy of silence" on the acts. In general, the national press was troubled by his support of such an unseemly cause. The *Times,* for example, sincerely regretted "to find a statesman of Mr. Stansfeld's eminence identifying himself with the hysterical crusade against the Contagious Diseases Acts."[33] Stansfeld withstood these public assaults bravely and with good humor; writing to Butler on his public advocacy of repeal, he announced that he "hopes to be the best abused man in England within twelve months."[34]

Upon assuming the political leadership, Stansfeld set about shaping the repeal movement into a more effective political pressure group and propagandist effort. Additional electoral leagues were added to the list of repeal organizations; renewed efforts were made to interest work-ingmen and residents of the subjected districts in the repeal cause.[35]

Building and sustaining popular support constituted only one of Stansfeld's political strategies. He was also concerned to place the repeal argument on a scientific basis, to "beat the supporters (of the Acts) on their own ground."[36] Although he agreed with most repealers that important moral and constitutional issues were at stake, he also stressed the need to counter regulationist arguments with scientific and empirical "facts" that supported repeal. To this end, Stansfeld encour-aged the formation of the National Medical Association in 1875, thereby enlisting medical opinion in support of repeal. He also advised repealers living outside subjected areas to undertake rescue work or to support local lock hospitals in order to demonstrate their sincere phil-anthropic interest in the welfare of prostitutes.[37]

Repealers' careful lobbying had made sufficient inroads in official political circles that another committee of inquiry was appointed by the Conservative government in 1879. This committee continued to meet and hear testimony on and off until 1882. A number of repeal supporters were initially asked to serve on the committee, although most of its members were still drawn from the military services and the medical profession. In 1880, the Liberals returned to power and new members of the committee were appointed, including Stansfeld, to replace M.P.s who had lost their seats or had moved into the ministry. Until 1881, the witnesses before the committee consisted of medical experts testifying for or against the medical benefits of the acts; a later group of witnesses were subsequently examined on the moral effects of the acts.[38]

By 1882, repealers and regulationists on the committee seemed to have reached a stalemate, with each side refusing to concede any points to the other and instead throwing up a "barrier of statistics" to confound opponents.[39] Despite extensive testimony against the acts, the majority report uncritically praised the regulationist system, wholeheartedly endorsing official accounts of their beneficial operation. Members supporting the majority report were particularly impressed with the success of the acts in Devonport and with the strong local support for their continuation.[40] In contrast, the minority report, written by Stansfeld and signed by six other members of the committee, repudiated official statistics and attacked the acts on moral, constitutional, and sanitary grounds.

The majority report notwithstanding, the repeal argument was clearly gaining wider credence among Liberal M.P.s and the general public. In 1880, "new men" had been elected to Parliament, strong Radicals committed to a platform of repeal and other moral issues. They had been able to penetrate the power structure of the Liberal Party by organizing the National Liberal Federation.[41] Formed in 1877, the federation was an important component of a developing extraparliamentary party organization, whose annual conference tried to frame a party program and impose discipline on M.P.s. Organizers of the federation also hoped that, by "providing one body that could speak on any question that might arise with 'all the authority of the voice of the nation,'" the federation could harness the energies of various pressure groups, like the repeal movement, that had proliferated outside the Liberal Party.[42]

In 1882 Stansfeld returned to the Cabinet, signaling Gladstone's tacit support for repeal and the removal of the "disability prohibiting a Cabinet member from advocating a moral cause."[43] A wave of popular support for repeal among radical workingmen's clubs in the East End in the early eighties, coinciding with a surge of repeal activity among middle-class women in the West End, undoubtedly gave additional weight to the lobbying efforts in Westminster.[44] Another boost to the repeal effort came from the formation of a political committee of Liberal politicians agitating for repeal within party circles. Henry J. Wilson and his coworkers in the provincial leagues were largely responsible for the creation of the political committee, having wearied of the National Association's uninspired lobbying efforts.[45]

These organizing efforts began to reap positive results by 1883. On April 12, 1883, the National Liberal Federation supported the repeal of the acts. The stage was then set for Stansfeld's motion before the House on April 20 that "the House disapproves of the compulsory examination of women under the Contagious Diseases Acts."[46] The resolution was carried 182 to 110. With the suspension of the compulsory examination clauses of the acts, their entire abolition seemed inevitable.

Repealers still had some political hurdles to jump. One was the general indifference of the Liberal Party leadership, who, although nominally committed to repeal, were preoccupied with Irish affairs and unwilling to introduce a repeal bill until the Home Rule bill had passed.[47] Moreover, strong opposition to repeal persisted among Conservatives and members of the military and medical establishments. Three important Cabinet members, Lord Hartington, Vernon Harcourt, and Lord Northbrook – the "lovely trio," as Butler called them – steadfastly opposed the repeal of the acts.[48] On the other hand, even the *Lancet* acknowledged that without the compulsory clauses the acts were ineffective; better to abolish them altogether than to try to implement useless half measures.[49] A further impetus to repeal may have been the popular indignation over alleged official corruption and aristocratic libertinage stirred up by Stead's exposés of white slavery in the *Pall Mall Gazette*.[50] To head off total abolition, regulationists tried to propose alternative measures that at least ensured the detention of diseased prostitutes in hospitals. By and large, though, the opposition to repeal had been battered down, apparently exhausted by the petitions and "disgusting literature" that regularly appeared at their offices and on their breakfast tables.[51]

The acts were repealed in 1886. After repeal, most repeal groups were dissolved, although the Ladies' National Association continued to exist until 1915 and to agitate against regulation in the colonies. Other regional groups were absorbed into the National Vigilance Association, a more prurient moral reform group that eschewed the feminist and constitutional goals of the repeal movement.[52]

The repealers

On the whole, middle-class repeal leaders were drawn from the same social constituency that supported other mid-Victorian reform groups, like the United Kingdom Alliance, the Liberation Society, the National Education League, and the antivaccination movement.[53] Male leaders were generally wealthy industrialists and merchants residing in northern cities, although a core of important repeal supporters lived in Bristol and London. Politically important in their own locales, they nonetheless saw themselves as provincial "outsiders" from the London social and political establishment that upheld the C.D. acts. Most were

99

staunch supporters of the Liberal Party and many belonged to its Radical wing. They were overwhelmingly nonconformists, with a heavy concentration of Quakers in leadership roles.

No one more exemplified the northern middle-class Radical repealer than Henry J. Wilson of Sheffield.[54] Wilson was an industrialist and self-made man, from a family with a long tradition of religious dissent. His radicalism was mainly informed by a hostility to privilege, as embodied in aristocratic enclaves like the Established Church and the military. He believed in a meritocracy, but did not support any further extension of democratic principles to social or political relations.

Self-righteous, punctilious, and determined, Wilson bullied agents and middle-class supporters of repeal into effective political action. His aggressive manner frequently annoyed other repeal workers. A. J. Mundella, for instance, described him as "a capital fellow in *harness* . . . who . . . is only dangerous when he has nothing to do. . ."[55] Still, Wilson's local influence within the Liberal Party, as well as his connections with a series of Radical pressure groups, enabled him to organize the Northern Counties League in 1872. Although he had contact with local working-class leaders, he supported the Liberal Party's policy of discouraging autonomous working-class associations and personally resented any expression of political independence on the part of workingmen. Consequently, he strongly objected to the formation of the National Working Men's League in 1875 and repeatedly chastised working-class agents who dared to speak authoritatively on repeal in public, rather than remain in the background of the agitation.[56]

In the 1880s Wilson began to assume a major role in planning the political strategy of the repeal campaign at the national level. As mentioned previously, he was instrumental in organizing a national political committee within the Liberal Party to agitate for repeal. Elected to Parliament in 1885, he vigorously supported repeal in the House of Commons; after 1886 he continued to oppose regulation in the colonies. One historian has characterized him as the prototype of the Radical M.P. of the 1880s, who never achieved prominence, "but the Radicals in parliament consisted of row on row of men like him."[57] Outside of Parliament, Wilson was attracted to the newly emerging social-purity movement, and soon became a popular speaker on male chastity and the dangers of "self-abuse."

In his correspondence, Wilson frequently railed against the "inefficient manner" in which the National Association was conducted.[58] Like Josephine Butler, he regarded the leadership of the National Association as ineffective "do-nothings," with no conception of how to

100

carry on a public agitation. His characterization, although harsh, was not inaccurate. As already noted, the small clique who controlled the executive board of the National Association failed to develop any popular constituency in London or elsewhere. They even failed to capitalize on the support of prominent trade unionists like George Howell and Henry Broadhurst by declining their offers to work for the cause.[59]

William Shaen (1821–87) typifies the London group.[60] Between 1870 and 1886 Shaen served as chairman of the National Association executive board. Educated at University College, London (like most of the men in his circle), he initially worked in the firm of William Henry Ashurst, a prominent Radical solicitor of London. Through Ashurst, he made the acquaintance of Emilie Ashurst Venturi and James Stansfeld, who was married to another Ashurst daughter, Caroline. Through these associations, he was introduced to the larger Radical circles in London. Over the years, Shaen embraced dozens of humanitarian and republican causes that defended individual rights and sought to further political democracy at home and abroad. He was an antislavery proponent, a staunch ally of Giuseppe Mazzini and republican nationalism, and an early supporter of suffrage and higher education for women. He was also active in rescue work and social purity as legal advisor to the Rescue Society of London, founder of the Social Purity Association and Moral Reform Union, and active spokesman in the campaign against white slavery in the 1880s.

Shaen also had direct associations with working-class radicals: in the early forties, he had been a moral-force Chartist; later he taught in the Working Men's College and publicly supported both the secularist movement and the Land and Labour League. Yet Shaen was never able to exploit his contacts with secularists and radical workingmen's groups for the repeal cause. Although not lacking in good intentions, Shaen's cold and aloof manner evidently did little to inspire loyalty and enthusiasm among either working-class or middle-class groups. One repealer described him as a "clear thinker but as a worker [he] needs to be lifted by a whirlwind of enthusiasm. He is too slow and cool."[61]

Leaders of the LNA shared the republican and feminist sentiments of the National Association executive. However, they combined these political principles with a religious fervor that aroused intense emotional loyalty among their own general membership and facilitated outreach work among workingmen and women. The LNA's political following also owed a great deal to the charismatic appeal of Josephine Butler, whose speeches against the "instrumental rape" of work-

101

ing women under the acts electrified popular audiences across the country. Unlike her male provincial counterparts, Butler had a genuine respect and sympathy for working people that was entirely reciprocated. And from the start, she envisioned the repeal movement as a popular crusade against male vice and social injustice, whose principal standard bearers would be middle-class women and workingmen.[62]

Not surprisingly, religious conflicts periodically arose among middle-class repealers and were linked to regional antagonisms. Northern evangelicals were deeply suspicious of the secular and constitutional priorities of the freethinking deists and Unitarians who dominated the National Association in London. These suspicions were frequently misplaced, inasmuch as most Victorian freethinkers like Shaen adhered to as stern a code of morality as any evangelical zealot. Agnostics and atheists in the repeal movement were opposed to sensual gratification and were generally attracted to other "anti" causes founded on self-control and sensual renunciation. In their repeal literature, they regularly inveighed against the materialist and libertine doctrines of medical men and the military.[63]

Religious differences also existed among working-class repealers that would influence the extent and character of interclass alliances in different regions. In the north, nonconformity provided an important organizational and cultural link between middle-class reformers and workingmen. As a consequence, chapel-going trade unionists and radicals in the north readily endorsed repeal and collaborated with middle-class repeal leaders on other projects as well. In London, where working-class radicalism had developed along more insular and autonomous lines, the absence of a religious tie made it difficult for middle-class repealers (even for secularists like Shaen) to bridge the social gulf separating them from workingmen.[64] Sometimes, religious differences even exacerbated class distinctions and were the source of mutual hostility and distrust. In 1881, for example, George Dyer, the middle-class editor of the *National League Journal,* lamented to a chapel-going audience in Shoreditch that "He was a bit of a parson in his way, so he supposed the Radical Clubs in the borough would not hear him, or he would like to go among them, and speak on the question."[65] The 1880s, however, witnessed a great spurt of radical activity in London and the expansion of secularist and radical clubs in the East End. Spokesmen for repeal made the rounds of these clubs, where their attack on "vicious aristocrats" responsible for the acts enjoyed an enthusiastic reception. They were, however, not "parsons" like George Dyer, but secularists and local officials of workingmen's clubs, like F. A. Ford, president of the Finsbury Radical Clubs association.[66]

Whether secularist or evangelical, workingmen tended to stress constitutional arguments against the acts over moral objections to the state support of vice.[67] However, the repeal campaign also presented labor aristocrats with an opportunity to demonstrate their own social and sexual respectability and to dissociate themselves publicly from the "bestial" immorality of the "residuum." Not surprisingly, their defense of inscribed prostitutes was sometimes ambivalent and contradictory. This ambivalence is well illustrated by Robert Applegarth's reaction to evidence presented before the Royal Commission of 1871. A prominent trade unionist, Applegarth was the only member of the commission to suggest that registered prostitutes be interviewed; he himself visited the Devonport district, interviewed women in the Royal Albert Hospital, and concluded that workingwomen were bullied and abused under the acts.[68] In his questions, he also evinced great concern over the impact of the acts on general working-class life. Most specifically, he questioned a number of witnesses about the movement of prostitutes out of "disorderly houses" into respectable lodgings as a means of avoiding registration. He feared that this social underground would spread its moral pollution to the respectable working class. His responses here suggest the manner in which most "self-respecting" trade-union leaders viewed the casual laboring poor in a custodial manner, as members of a different class and culture.[69]

Paid agents also constituted an important working-class presence within the repeal camp. The men and women employed as paid agents for repeal groups were frequently veterans of earlier radical causes, like moral-force chartism. Some, like William Burgess and W. T. Swan, were skilled organizers who had worked for the teetotal United Kingdom Alliance and could command annual salaries of £250 to £300. Others were quite humble men, like "Peters" who did odd jobs for the LNA but left to become a porter. John Marshall of Plymouth had been a dock laborer and was only paid £50 a year by the National Association. Yet he seems to have made a professional career out of his repeal experience, and ultimately became a preacher after repeal. The female paid agents were paid distinctly less than the men and, with the exception of Jessie Craigen, who split her time among the suffrage, antivaccination, and repeal movements, never attained national stature as a first-rank agent.[70]

However necessary paid agents were to the prestige and vitality of the repeal campaign, they were also a source of conflict and controversy. Many prominent repealers, notably Stansfeld and Butler, were concerned that paid agents not substitute for the voluntary efforts of

103

middle-class supporters. Others, like Henry Wilson, resented any attempt at autonomous political activity on the part of agents or other working-class participants.

Repeal tactics

In their public agitation, repealers sought to educate public opinion on repeal as well as to influence elite political circles in Parliament. Popular agitation and private political lobbying were intended to complement and supplement each other; in reality, these activities moved repeal groups in different political directions and frequently strained political consensus within the repeal campaign.

To demonstrate popular support for the repeal cause, repealers organized large public meetings in religious assemblies, mechanics' institutes, radical workingmen's clubs, and in great halls like the Corn Exchange in Leeds or the Free Trade Hall at Manchester. These meeting places were centers of nonconformist middle-class culture or trade-union and radical working-class life. Collectively they constituted a network of social and political institutions across Britain that served as the institutional backbone for the Liberal Party and for Victorian reform movements against privilege and established institutions.[71] Later, in the 1880s, repeal meetings would also be held in mission halls, Salvation Army halls, and in open-air assemblies – thereby capitalizing on the new wave of religious revivalism at the time. Most public meetings were attended by both men and women, although smaller mothers' meetings for working women and drawing-room meetings for "ladies" were also held to introduce women to the repeal cause.[72]

In preparation for the meetings, voluntary and paid agents would canvass the district, distributing handbills, hanging posters, and placing advertisements in local newspapers.[73] The meetings often turned out to be great political events and sources of popular entertainment. Local political dignitaries usually presided over the meetings, and arguments against the acts were put forward by prominent national repeal figures like Butler or Stansfeld. In her *Reminiscences,* Butler recalled one packed meeting she addressed at a tiny place, Alnwick, Northumberland. "I did not expect opposition at Alnwick. I thought the only difficulty might be to keep my audience awake! When I arrived I found the Town Hall already packed to excess. I dare say the meeting was an exciting event in the dull old town."[74] After rousing the audience, a local repeal supporter would usually conclude the meeting with a public resolution against the acts and a proposal to form a local repeal committee.[75]

104

petition

Following the excitement of the meeting, branch members and paid agents would get down to the difficult task of maintaining local interest in the repeal cause. Local committees expended most of their efforts collecting signatures for the numerous petitions sent to Parliament in favor of repeal. The petition not only demonstrated popular support for the repeal cause, but also served as a useful organizing technique. In 1877, for instance, the Manchester committee of the National Association organized a systematic house-to-house canvass, "carried with the aid of well-trained women missionaries."[76] These female missionaries would make frequent visits to the houses.

> By the second time the mission woman's appearance had probably aroused attention, neighbours had spoken one to another of her work, and greater readiness to admit her would be manifested. If she succeeded in awakening any interest on the part of the woman of the house, she might be asked to call again in the evening, when the husband would be at home . . .[77]

Although some "thousands of signatures to petition were obtained by this means," the primary object of the canvassing was the "diffusion of information on the existence of the Acts and the immoral principle involved in them."[78]

Fetes or special occasions were only sparingly organized by repealers, given the moral delicacy of their cause. In 1879, however, a Fancy Fair was launched on behalf of Benjamin Lucraft's candidacy for a parliamentary seat in Tower Hamlets.[79] Featured at the Fancy Fair was an exhibition of "belongings of the Arctic explorer," an antique coin collection, and "some splendidly carved oak work representing the celebrated pictures of Sir Edwin Lancaster."[80] Busts of Mrs. Butler were offered for sale, as well as the handicrafts of "ladies of high social position."[81] Workingmen and women also contributed their share. The "proud member" of the Working Men's National League, "whose brawny frame, and labour-stained hands, bespeak a genuine son of toil, is exercising his skill in making some article connected with his trade," announced the *National League Journal*. Meanwhile his wife, "whose heart bursts with indignation as she thinks of the 'great' politicians of both parties who concur in consigning her fellow women to the slavery of men's lust, is knitting away at some useful piece of work."[82]

Local committees also tried to induce "clubs, literary societies and discussion classes" to debate the C.D. acts. They queried political candidates for local and national office about their position on the acts and sent deputations to the Home Office to appeal for their abolition.[83] They tried to impress upon politicians of both parties their

105

Most successful tactic—challenge of Liberal Party candidates in by-elects.

intention that "Questions of party or place will be held subservient to the one great question of National Morality and National Justice."[84]

The repealers' most successful tactic for demonstrating popular support was their challenge of Liberal Party candidates at by-elections.[85] On three occasions they successfully used by-elections to publicize their cause and to embarrass a Liberal candidate closely associated with the workings of the acts. At Newark in spring 1870, repealers opposed Henry Storks, who had implemented a regulation system as governor of Malta. Storks was a staunch supporter of the C.D. acts and closely associated with the military interests in government.[86]

Repealers pursued Storks in his next effort to gain a parliamentary seat, during the by-election at Colchester in Autumn 1870 (see Figure 1). Their intervention was deeply resented by local Liberal Party members, including the Liberal Working Men's Committee and many local subscribers to the National Association.[87] Nonetheless, male and female repeal leaders descended upon Colchester and placarded the town with Storks's declaration defending the necessity of prostitution and endorsing a plan to subject soldiers' wives to the acts. Sandwichmen perambulated Colchester with this infamous proposition. The women were furious with Storks, "who seemed the incarnation of the medico-military sentiment."[88] Storks's supporters were composed of all respectable Liberals, members of the military establishments, as well as brothel keepers and publicans "who knew their craft was in danger"[89] should repealers succeed. This latter group formed themselves into a crowd of roughs and physically abused and threatened repealers.[90]

At Colchester, repealers put up their own candidate, Baxter Langley, a well-known Radical, in order to split the Liberal vote and effectively to ensure the election for the Conservative candidate. Although Langley ran on a repeal platform, his campaign literature also identified him as a supporter of public education, direct representation of labor, the ten hours' bill, tax reform, a national citizen army, and arbitration as the means of settling international disputes.[91] A few days before polling, Langley withdrew his candidacy. The Conservative candidate, Learmouth, won over Storks, as a result of massive abstentions on the part of Liberal voters. Repealers were elated and claimed a major victory. At her home in Liverpool, Butler received a telegram with two words: [the Bird] "shot dead."[92]

Butler's activities during the Colchester by-election substantially contributed to this impressive show of support for the repeal cause. Chased by a crowd of brothel keepers and their flunkies in Colchester, Butler and a Mrs. Hampson sought refuge in the cellar of a "Methodist" grocer, who installed them "amongst his bacon, soap and

106

THE
ELECTORS OF COLCHESTER
TO
SIR HENRY STORKS.

So you're coming to Colchester, Stork, King Stork!
And you think to succeed with your talk, tall talk;
    But you very well know
    You won't dare to show
Your face on the hustings, King Stork, King Stork.

You succeeded at Malta, King Stork, King Stork,
In expelling disease with a fork, with a fork:
    Yet the evil recurs,
    For Nature demurs
To be crushed by enactments, O Stork, King Stork!

You came down to Newark, O Stork, King Stork;
And appeared on the platform, King Stork, King Stork:
    But at the first sight
    Of the Blue Book took flight,
Not liking to stand by your colours, King Stork.

And the women of Colchester, Stork, King Stork!
Will rival their sisters of Newark, King Stork,
    When they know who's come down
    To give laws to the town,
Where Boadicea once fought, King Stork.

Contagious Diseases are bad, King Stork;
But Tyranny's worse than disease, King Stork:
    So off to your bogs,
    And your own native frogs,
For *we* won't be swallowed by you, King Stork!

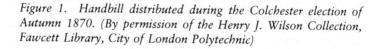

Figure 1. Handbill distributed during the Colchester election of Autumn 1870. (By permission of the Henry J. Wilson Collection, Fawcett Library, City of London Polytechnic)

candles."[93] They later encountered the same kind of opposition in Pontefract. During the by-election of 1872, a women's meeting was held in a hayloft. Hired bullies then set bundles of straw afire while the metropolitan police casually looked on. Butler and Charlotte Wilson were able to make their escape by jumping down the hatch of a trapdoor: "It was not so much personal violence that we feared as what would have been to any of us *worse than death;* for the indecencies of the men, their gestures, and threats, were what I would prefer not to describe."[94] In both Colchester and Pontefract, local public opinion was outraged by these attacks and expressed itself forcibly against the Liberal regulationist candidate in the polls.[95]

Repeal arguments

Over the course of the campaign, repealers bombarded politicians and the general public with highly colored propaganda against the acts. Repealers attacked regulationists as a mid-Victorian embodiment of "Old Corruption" – as licentious aristocrats who conspired to control women through state sanction and monopoly. Regulationists of all stripes were made to fit this aristocratic stereotype, whatever their actual social position; Butler, for instance, repeatedly condemned those "terrible aristocratic doctors," when in fact medical spokesmen for regulation were ambitious members of her own social class.[96]

Repealers also identified their own struggle against a centralized state and police with the traditional defense of the rights of the free-born Englishman. In her speeches before popular audiences, Butler raised the specter of a popular revolution against the ("speculum") and the vicious aristocrats who supported the acts.[97] She frequently referred to Wat Tyler's revenge on the rape of a poor girl by a government official during the peasant revolt of 1381. Tyler's head had emblazoned the banners of Chartist marches, and Butler hoped to reinvigorate the flames of radical political protest for the repeal cause.[98]

A vivid elaboration of this iconography is contained in J. J. Garth Wilkinson's pamphlet, *The Forcible Introspection of the Women for the Army and Navy by the Oligarchy Considered Physically* (1870). Wilkinson cited two factors that made for the enactment of the C.D. acts: first, "the medical love of power possible through royal chartering" previously embodied in the "Compulsory Vaccination Law"; and second, the "medical lust of handling and dominating women," complemented and supplemented by the "police lust of hunting and persecuting women."[99]

108

The repeal campaign

Repealers also emphasized the urgent need for reform by detailing instances of police brutality and the entrapment of virtuous women under the registration system. Butler's letters to the *Shield* on the "Garrison Towns of Kent" exposed the brutal and corrupt operation of the acts.[100] In her reports Butler attacked the hypocrisy of the double standard, by identifying officials responsible for punishing prostitutes as the same men who also bought their sexual services. She told the story of one poor "unfortunate" "committed to prison by the Bench at – – –," who said, "It did seem hard ma'am, that the Magistrate on the bench who gave the casting vote for my imprisonment had paid me several shillings a day or two before, in the street, to go with him."[101]

Accounts of official malfeasance and the resistance of registered women also appeared regularly in repeal periodicals and pamphlets. During the early years of the campaign, the *Shield* usually devoted a column of its front page to "intelligence from the subjected districts," reprinting local newspaper accounts of petty session trials of registered women who defied the regulations of the acts and who rioted in governmental lock wards. As the level of resistance was directly related to local repeal agitation and to promises of legal assistance, not surprisingly these accounts dwindled when public agitation in subjected districts declined after 1871.

Lurid tales of the "instrumental rape" of registered women were further evidence of the urgent need for reform. Repeal propaganda specifically warned workingmen and women that the extension of the acts to the north would impose the "disgusting examination under the Contagious Diseases Acts" on virtuous wives and daughters of workingmen falsely accused of being prostitutes.[102] At public meetings, repeal spokesmen would display the vaginal speculum and explain its use to a horrified audience.[103] Vivid and detailed accounts of the instrumental torture figured prominently in repeal propaganda.

> It is awful work; the attitude they push us into first is so disgusting and so painful, and then these monstrous instruments – often they use several. They seem to tear the passage open first with their hands, and examine us, and then they thrust in instruments, and they pull them out and push them in, and they turn and twist them about; and if you cry out they stifle you. . . .[104]

Indignant letters by workingmen, published in a 1871 pamphlet entitled *Vox Populi*, demonstrate the appeal of this propaganda.[105] The correspondents were stern, self-respecting, nonconformists from Scotland and the north of England, who frequently identified themselves as trade unionists, members of benefit societies, masonic groups,

109

class

and radical political societies. These men attacked the acts first as "class legislation," as "un-English" "unprincipled pieces of legislation" that had been smuggled through Parliament. Most of all, they resented the proposed extension of the acts as threats to virtuous poor women, specifically to female members of their own families. As Thomas Gibson, a workingman from Kendal, wrote: "I have done what I can, and will still do all in my power, to help you get the Acts repealed, so that our mothers, wives and daughters may still feel that they are in a noble and honorable land. . ."[106] William Gilliver, secretary to the Trades Council in Birmingham, voiced the same sentiment: "I heard more than one man (especially fathers) say: 'If any policeman were to touch my child or sister for such a cause, I would beat him down with the first weapon I could lay hold of.' "[107]

Repealers also used the widely publicized suicide of Mrs. Percy, a music-hall entertainer from Aldershot, to illustrate the evils of regulation. Because she refused to submit to examination, Percy had been blacklisted from all the music halls in town. She then wrote a letter of protest to the *Daily Telegraph*, complaining of police abuse and intimidation. After a short stay in Windsor, Percy returned to Aldershot, for an engagement at "The Queen's Tap"; once again, the police forced the proprietor to dismiss her. She ultimately committed suicide in order to vindicate the reputation of herself and her daughter. The suicide made national news in 1875 and brought new life to the fading energies of the repeal movement. Butler, for one, could not hide her delight.

instru. rape
false entrapment

> This suicide at Aldershot has created a great sensation. It is in every newspaper; and already three London newspapers (of course not *The Times*) have leading articles strongly condemning the Acts. Every good cause requires martyrs, and this poor woman's death will, I believe, be a means in the hands of Providence, of shaking the system more than anything we could do.[108]

Stories of instrumental rape, false entrapment, and pitiful suicides had the virtue of appealing to all supporters of repeal – to working-class radicals and middle-class nonconformists alike. These accounts tended to depict registered women as innocent victims of male lust and medical and police tyranny; as such, the women remained appropriate objects of solicitude, even for middle-class moralists who chiefly condemned the acts for making "vice" safe.[109]

Although sensational tales had enormous propagandist value, they inhibited a sober examination of working-class prostitution in the subjected districts. Because they found it politically expedient to depict "fallen women" as passive victims of evil machinations, repealers were understandably not moved to scrutinize the actual motives, social origins, and current life-styles of registered prostitutes. Instead, they relied on Acton's study or fell back on the already familiar stereotypes outlined above.

Occasionally feminists and personal-rights advocates did acknowledge that registered women were experienced prostitutes whose move to the streets was voluntary and gradual. They further denied that prostitutes were a class apart; instead, they stressed the casual nature of prostitution as a temporary occupation for women down on their luck. It was the regulation system, they argued, that doomed these women to a life of sin, by publicly stigmatizing them and preventing them from finding alternative respectable employment.[110] On the whole, however, the discussion of voluntary prostitution received far less publicity than exposés of innocent girls forced into the ranks of prostitution by the "spy police."

Elsewhere, repealers tried to buttress their a priori objections to the acts by documenting their failure as police and sanitary measures. One early effort along these lines was *An Exposure of the False Statistics of the Contagious Diseases Acts (Women),* published in 1873 by the managers of the metropolitan reformatories and rescue homes. This report disputed regulationist claims that the acts had resulted in a real decline in juvenile prostitution and in the number of brothels and prostitutes in the Devonport area.[111]

Repealers also challenged the published medical statistics on venereal disease among the military stationed in subjected districts. Dr. Birkbeck Nevins served as the principal medical statistician for the repeal cause, regularly issuing cost analyses and statistical reports that attacked the acts as sanitary failures. According to Nevins, the acts did not lower the incidence of venereal disease among either registered prostitutes or the troops stationed in subjected districts. In particular, he tried to demonstrate that the acts failed to control the spread of syphilis, the only serious "constitutional" form of veneral disease.[112]

Repealers relied on Nevins's arguments to present their case against the acts at statistical societies and debating clubs. They also badgered members of Parliament with this "scientific" evidence, both through the mail and in testimonies before parliamentary committees. In the late seventies, the resources and time of repeal supporters were increasingly devoted to preparing such testimony. Whether intentionally or not, governmental investigations had effectively channeled repeal efforts away from popular agitation to scientific exposition and specialized lobbying efforts. This undoubtedly pleased certain members of the National Association, who found political activism personally dis-

111

tasteful. But it was a source of concern to LNA leaders like Josephine Butler, who looked upon the select committee "as a great farce and waste of time."[113] In 1882, Butler sent out a general circular to the LNA executive committee, expressing "immense relief" at having "got rid of the incubus of the long drawn out Parliamentary Enquiry." It was difficult to "maintain any vigorous agitation while in this state of suspense."[114]

In the later years of the campaign, Butler and other activist leaders warned against the dangers of "substituting office work for the vitality of missionary zeal" and placing "organization" above "individual initiative and independent personal effort."[115] How may we evaluate these complaints? Do they represent the normal disillusionment of aging leaders? Or do they accurately identify a real change in political focus and direction of the repeal campaign? On balance, these complaints do seem to reflect certain trends in repeal efforts. As the repeal movement gained political respectability, it moved away from the popular and feminist focus of its earlier phase. Feminists in particular regretted the single-issue focus of the later repeal movement as a retreat from an earlier social and political radicalism. They also looked upon the specialized political lobbying efforts of the repeal movement as a threat to their own political influence within the repeal camp. It is to the "revolt of women" and the social and political divisions within the repeal movement that we next turn.

6 The leadership of the Ladies' National Association

> We know how to manage any other opposition in the House or in the country, but this is very awkward for us—this revolt of the women. It is quite a new thing; what are we to do with such an opposition as this?
> —An M.P. to Josephine Butler, quoted in *Josephine E. Butler: An Autobiographical Memoir*, eds. George W. Johnson and Lucy Johnson (London, 1909), p. 90.

As an association of women only, the Ladies' National Association claimed itself to be "unique in the political history of the country."[1] The LNA would demonstrate the capacity of women to get along with each other and to organize for a political objective. Mary Priestman, a member of the executive board, wrote in 1907, "It has been often said that women are not loyal to women and that they do not work well together—the experience of the LNA is contrary to this . . ."[2]

The LNA gave political expression to a supportive female subculture in the mid-Victorian period. Its feminist leaders were composed of a small group of nationally prominent women who were fiercely loyal to each other and to their organization. A biographical profile of the thirty-three members of the LNA executive board helps to identify the formative political and social experiences that prepared these women for national leadership. From this profile, they emerge as an older generation of feminists, linked together by long-standing bonds of friendship and family as well as by shared political experiences.[3]

In assessing the general characteristics of the LNA leadership, two questions immediately present themselves: How much did LNA leaders differ from male repealers? What was the role of Josephine Butler in the LNA? At first glance, LNA leaders closely resembled their male middle-class counterparts in the Midlands Electoral League and Northern Counties League. LNA executive-board members were predominantly provincials from the north (with the important exception of the Bristol group), nonconformists, and the wives and daughters of wealthy industrialists and merchants. Most were Radicals, combining political individualism with a strong social conscience. Although members of wealthy and influential families, they nevertheless saw themselves as "outsiders" and political insurgents against the Liberal Whig establishment.

Nonetheless, the political experience and collective consciousness of LNA leaders set them apart from most men in the campaign. As female national leaders, they had had to overcome practical obstacles not faced by male leaders. They were in the political vanguard of their sex, and enjoyed certain advantages not generally shared by women of their own social station. Finally, LNA leaders were fully aware of their exceptional status and of the significance of their collective endeavor.

Although most LNA leaders were strong-minded and formidable individuals, one woman, Josephine Butler, stands out among them. By sheer force of personality, Butler was able to dominate the LNA and guide its policy. Beautiful and histrionic, she was adored by men and women alike. A charismatic leader and gifted speaker, she was able to capture the popular imagination and inspire a personal loyalty among her coworkers that bordered on idolatry. Mary Priestman's first encounter with Butler was typical. She and her friend, Mary Estlin, had gone to hear Butler speak at a meeting in Bristol in 1870 to "find for ourselves whether she was really one whom we could follow in the dark path we had entered on." The hall was filled with ladies "waiting amid silence for the speaker." A few minutes later, the door opened and Butler entered, "slight and graceful— almost young & very beautiful [she was forty-three at the time]." "As she moved to the table she raised her eyes with such a look of inexpressible sadness, as if the weight of the world's sin & sorrows rested on her innocent head. A woman Christ to save us from our despair was the involuntary thought that came into my head & has never left it."[4] Butler's periodic illnesses and breakdowns invariably sent waves of insecurity throughout repeal ranks. In 1875, during Butler's most severe illness, Margaret Tanner remarked that the "mere thought of her being ill paralyzes some of our workers, who almost exist by her inspiration."[5]

Men also responded to her magnetic appeal, even those who disagreed with her. After hearing her testimony before the Royal Commission of 1871, one member of the commission was moved to remark: "I am not accustomed to religious phraseology, but I cannot give you any idea of the effect produced except by saying that the spirit of God was there."[6] She was also sexually attractive to men. Meticulously coifed, dressed in the height of fashion, she held popular audiences spellbound with tales of "instrumental" rape, police brutality, and aristocratic corruption. The voyeuristic character of these spectacles was undoubtedly enhanced by the physical charms of the "lady" speaker.[7]

Butler's life illustrates not only her own extraordinary qualities but encapsulates many political and social experiences common to the LNA leadership.[8] She was born in 1828, the seventh child of John and Hannah Grey of Dilston, Northumberland. She was the only LNA leader with family ties to the ruling Whig aristocracy: Lord Grey, the Whig prime minister during the struggle over the Reform Act of 1832, was her father's cousin. Despite her aristocratic connections, she always identified herself as a member of the provincial middle classes and remained unconditionally hostile to the London social and political elite. "Democratic in all her instincts,"[9] she preferred the company of honest workingmen to members of the "refined 'better' classes": ". . . my sympathies are wholly with the non-privileged, even when they drop every 'h.' "[10]

From her father, a great agricultural reformer and antislavery advocate, Butler gained a love of justice and a "horror of slavery and all arbitrary power." John Grey encouraged Josephine to acquaint herself with the political and social questions of the day. In early adolescence, she was aware of "what had come to be known as the 'Condition of England Question.' " With her father, she read the government "Blue Books" and exposés on the abominable treatment of paupers in the workhouses of the New Poor Law.[11]

From her mother, a Moravian, Butler was imbued with a deep attachment to "vital" evangelical Christianity. In her late adolescence, Josephine experienced a religious crisis and conversion that left her with a mystical sense of "calling." Her later public oratory, which recalled the Methodist preaching of the north, also bore the imprint of her evangelical upbringing.[12]

Two other women were important influences in her life. Her aunt, Margaretta Grey, was a strong-minded feminist in the Enlightenment tradition. She "was so disgusted at finding she was not allowed to attend Parliament when her cousin was leader of the Whigs – there was no Ladies' Gallery in either House at the time – that she made it a custom to obtain admission by dressing as a boy."[13] Josephine also formed strong attachments with all her sisters, but particularly with her sister Hattie, who later married a Swiss banker and settled in Naples. Through her father, sister, and future husband, Butler subsequently gained entrée into republican circles throughout Western Europe.[14]

Josephine was married in 1851 to George Butler, an educator and Anglican clergyman. The Butlers were eminently suited to each other in temperament and social outlook. Theirs was a "marriage between equals";[15] George always encouraged Josephine in her public work and suffered setbacks in his own career on account of her notoriety.

The Butlers first lived in Oxford, where George was appointed Examiner to the University. Josephine resented the narrow and misogynist atmosphere of the all-male society at Oxford, and was deeply offended by the open acceptance of the double standard by the "gentlemen" of the university. Their stay in Oxford was cut short by Josephine's respiratory illness; a lesion on her lung had been diagnosed when she was eighteen, and the Butlers were now warned that the climate of Oxford might be fatal to her health.[16] Josephine would suffer physical and nervous breakdowns of this sort throughout her long life (she lived until 1906).

To escape the Oxford damp, George accepted the post of vice-principal at Cheltenham College in 1856. Their four children—a girl and three boys—were born in Cheltenham. When the American Civil War broke out in 1861, the Butlers, who supported the Union cause, found themselves socially ostracized. This was Josephine's first experience with political agitation in support of an unpopular cause: "The feeling of isolation . . . was often painful . . . but the discipline was useful."[17]

The accidental death of her daughter Eva, in 1864, was a "turning point" in Josephine's life and precipitated her move into rescue work. When the Butlers moved to Liverpool in 1864, Josephine "became possessed with an irresistible urge to go forth and find some pain keener than my own, to meet with people more unhappy than myself."[18]

"It was not difficult to find misery in Liverpool," she wrote of her early social work there. In 1866, she began to work among the women of the Liverpool workhouse in the "oakum shed," a women's vagrant ward and Bridewell. From the workhouse, jails, and streets of Liverpool she brought poor young women, some "unfortunates," some simply friendless, all physically worn out from their hard lives, to be nursed by her in her own home. Her widowed sister helped her in this "work without a name which came upon us." In 1866 she opened her own "House of Rest." She had the help of Mrs. Cropper, a Quaker and a pioneer "in the advocacy and practice of the modern methods of kindness in rescue work," who had recently established a family "home" in Liverpool. A few months later, with financial support from a number of Liverpool merchants, she established a small envelope factory as an industrial home for friendless girls. Besides these two "modest" institutions, she always had a few dying prostitutes residing in her home.[19]

Butler's rescue work not only met a personal need, but conformed to her broader feminist interests. As we shall see, she always placed prostitution within this larger context, not merely as a question of morality, but of political economy as well.

During the late sixties Butler became increasingly involved in feminist agitation. From 1867 to 1873, she served as president of the North of England Council for Promoting the Higher Education of Women. In 1868, she petitioned Cambridge to provide special examinations for women. She published her first pamphlet, *The Education and Employment of Women,* in 1868, where she pleaded for the higher education of women and the removal of legal and customary restrictions on their employment. In 1869 she edited a collection of essays, entitled *Women's Work and Women's Culture.* In her introduction, she acknowledged that women's sphere was the home, but called for the diffusion of the "home influence" in the general society. She celebrated the feminine form of philanthropy, "the independent, individual ministering, the home influence" against the masculine form, "the large comprehensive measure, the organization, the system planned by men and sanctioned by Parliament."[20]

Like many other American and British feminists, Butler only partially challenged the basic Victorian assumptions related to sex roles and women's separate "sphere." She defended the right of women to maintain legal, political, and economic identities outside the family, but she also sought to exploit the notion of women's moral preeminence. As pure wives and mothers, as members of religious congregations, "ladies" could defend their public actions in the name of morality and religion. It was thus the peculiar mission of women to defend the home, the family, and the single standard of chastity in the political arena.

Just as Butler's feminism combined two distinct tendencies—advocating sex equality while celebrating the virtues of a distinctive women's culture—so too her defense of prostitutes moved in two directions. Butler undertook rescue work, according to W. T. Stead, "to save DAUGHTERS. Motherhood was to her the sacredest thing in the world."[21] Butler's defense of motherhood was a political device, aimed at subverting and superseding patriarchal authority: it gave mothers, not fathers, the right to control sexual access to the daughters. In this way, Butler sanctioned an authority relationship between older middle-class women and young workingwomen that, although caring and protective, was also hierarchical and custodial.[22] At other times, however, she approached prostitutes on a more egalitarian basis, as sisters, albeit "fallen" ones, whose individual rights deserved to be respected, and who, when they sold their bodies on the streets, had the right to do so unmolested by the police.

117

In sum, by 1869, when she was asked to spearhead the campaign against the acts, and to serve as honorary secretary of the LNA, Butler was a mature woman who had already attained national prominence as a feminist and moral reformer. Deeply religious, she was also intimately connected with political radicals in England and abroad. Yet she had rarely spoken in public and, by her own confession, had no "head for organization." She knew, instead, that her gift was to "breathe a little fire and courage into *individual* workers and so gradually to influence a good many."[23]

The LNA leadership

Fortunately, Butler collaborated with a devoted and hard-working band of women who shared her political views and commitments. Over the sixteen-year campaign, the LNA executive board was dominated by a small group of women. Between 1870 and 1886, thirty-three women served on the LNA executive board. Of the fourteen original members, ten were still serving on the board in 1886, and executive board members each averaged almost ten years on the board. Once appointed, only seven left before repeal had been achieved; these departures were occasioned by illness, death, or the counterattraction of a related feminist cause.[24]

Between 1870 and 1886, the average age of a board member during her first year of service on the executive was forty-seven years (based on twenty-two out of the thirty-three members whose date of birth is known). This mature age reflects two important characteristics of the national leadership. First, most members had reached a stage in their life cycle when they were relatively unencumbered by family responsibilities. Second, LNA national leaders constituted a generation of feminists whose formative political experience had occurred decades before their involvement in the repeal cause.

As mature, affluent women, LNA leaders enjoyed an unusual freedom to engage in public activities and to move about the country. By forty-seven a woman would have passed the childbearing age and most of her children would have reached adolescence. Moreover, a substantial proportion of executive-board members were unmarried, widowed, and/or childless: twelve out of thirty-three (36 percent) were single; another six were widowed; and a total of twenty (61 percent) are known to have been childless.

To be sure, family obligations other than childbearing and childrearing could also have impeded a woman's public activity.[25] Wifely obligations often restricted women's full involvement in political work.

118

Conversely, widowhood seems to have impelled a number of these women into public life. The death of her husband encouraged Margaret Tanner to find a new kind of social responsibility: "After her husband's death in 1869, the way opened for her to greater activity, and in the following year she roused herself from ill health and sorrow to begin a work for public morality under Josephine Butler."[26] Margaret Bright Lucas's public career followed a similar pattern: after her husband's death in 1865 she began "a period of probation for a 'more public life.'"[27]

Because of their family wealth, executive-board members could delegate household tasks to female servants. Although agitating for more industrial employment for women, feminist repealers rarely displayed personal qualms over the fact that they owed their leisure and domestic freedom to the drudgery of workingwomen. They basically accepted this relationship as a natural feature of existing class relations. They did, however, acknowledge a special obligation to represent and defend the interests of workingwomen. At the 1876 annual meeting in Hull, Mrs. Steward of Ongar explained: "When I think, said she, what we women who are in easy circumstances owe to working women—that our clothes are made by them, washed by them; our food cooked by them, our children nursed by them etc. I cannot understand how we can bear not to pay back, to the best of our power, the debt we owe to them. The wages we pay them are but a poor part of the debt we owe! and where is our justice, our gratitude, if we can stand by and see a terrible wrong done ... to them who cannot speak for themselves if we do not rise up and speak for them."[28]

Hence, by virtue of their maturity and social situation most LNA leaders were able to overcome the practical impediments that generally prevented women from engaging in reform activity at the national level. Moreover, middle age also conferred the necessary respectable status on women to speak openly on such delicate matters as prostitution, the internal examination, and venereal disease. Similarly, married status also enhanced a woman's eligibility to speak for fallen women.

It is therefore striking that more than one-third of the LNA executive was single, twice the proportion of single women found among the general members of the LNA in 1870. In part this reflects the high concentration of Quakers on the board, as the Society of Friends seems to have encouraged single women to devote themselves to public causes. It also testifies to the independent feminist character of the leadership cadre, who ignored popular prejudice on this question. Finally, it suggests that, on a national level, the practical advantages enjoyed by single women outweighed the conventional prejudices against their participation. The personal independence of single women helped them gain national prominence in the first place; it also enabled them to travel more easily and to commit their time to national repeal work. As we shall see, these advantages did not operate as decisively on the local branch level.

Although mature single women of prominence were invited to join the LNA executive, social constraints dictated that the principal female spokeswoman for repeal have the status of mother and wife. According to W. T. Stead, Josephine Butler was approached by Elizabeth Wolstenholme Elmy for this reason, rather than other prominent female philanthropists like Harriet Martineau and Florence Nightingale, who were too old and infirm, but also unmarried: "it was thought . . . that the woman who first had to plead for the inviolable sanctity of woman's right to her person should herself be a matron with the experience and standing of a wife and mother."[29] Like Butler, other LNA leaders did not completely break with traditional family roles nor did they fully reject the domestic ideology associated with those roles.

In addition, these women constituted an older generation of female political activists. Of the twenty-two members whose date of birth is known, five were born before 1820 and thirteen, like Butler, between 1820 and 1830. Most of these women came from families that were deeply involved in the political agitations of the 1830s and 1840s. As girls and women, LNA leaders developed a political consciousness and were exposed to a style of political agitation that was populist, extraparliamentary, and far less decorous than mid-Victorian bourgeois reform efforts.

From their home environment, these women gained a familiarity with the important issues of the day. Most had received only a rudimentary formal education but were permitted free access to their fathers' libraries. They were also exposed to lively political and social discussions within the family circle. As a young woman, Emilie Venturi "had plunged in an informal way into legal studies," using the resources of her father's law offices.[30] Despite their conservative Quaker upbringing, Margaret Tanner and Mary Priestman were introduced to national political life through their elder sister's marriage to John Bright, the leading Quaker politician of his day.[31]

This support and encouragement from male relatives later extended to repeal work. Nine women had husbands active in the campaign; others had brothers, brothers-in-law, and other close relatives who were repealers. Many of these men, such as Duncan McLaren, James

120

Stansfeld, J. P. Thomasson, and Jacob Bright, were outstanding feminists and collaborated with their female kin and friends in other feminist projects. Two husbands, J. P. Thomasson and Edward Backhouse, were the principal backers of the repeal movement in general, and of the LNA in particular. Other male relatives, like Stansfeld (Venturi's brother-in-law), sacrificed their own careers to work in the repeal cause. As mentioned earlier, George Butler was repeatedly denied preferment in the Anglican church because of his wife's repeal activity. Nonetheless, he unfailingly defended her position and was a great source of personal emotional support:

> As her domestic mainstay, George was tireless, waiting to meet her [Josephine Butler] from her interminable journeys, at Liverpool railway stations, at all hours, and in all weathers, careful for her health and strength, anxious lest she over tax herself, and offering her continual assurance that should she ever need him, he would immediately come to her.[32]

Although the leader of the "revolt of women," Butler gave special credit to the support of her husband and sons: "It seems strange that I should have been engaged in taking up the cudgel against men when my father, brothers, husband and sons have all been so good."[33] One notable exception to this general pattern of support was John Bright, who systematically opposed both women's suffrage and the public repeal campaign. Nonetheless, his close female relatives formed the feminist core of the LNA leadership. Ironically, many of them had learned the tactics of political agitation decades earlier, while aiding him in the Anti-Corn Law struggle. For example, Margaret Bright Lucas, Bright's sister, recalled her first political work in connection with the Anti-Corn Law League, "when so many ladies both worked for the great bazaars, and raised money by canvassing from house to house, and I well remember how the doors were sometimes slammed in my face when they learnt my errand."[34]

The leadership of the LNA received emotional support from the other women on the board. Most had been recruited to the executive board on the basis of preexisting friendship and kinship relations. A female network of friends and relatives is readily evident: Mrs. Kenway and Mrs. Richardson were sisters; two of Josephine Butler's sisters served with her on the board at various times; and as mentioned above, six female relatives of John Bright also served on the board. In addition, strong friendships between members emerged over the years. In her *Reminiscences,* Butler described the "Bristol group," made up of the "sisters Priestman," Margaret Tanner, and Mary Estlin, as her "body guard, a *corps d'elite* on whose prompt aid, singleness of purpose, prudence and unwearying industry I could . . . rely upon at all times."[35]

Religious affiliations also united members of the LNA executive and served to legitimize their political role in the repeal movement. Nonconformist representation was particularly strong: of twenty-two women whose religious background is known, twelve were Quakers, four belonged to other nonconformist sects, four were agnostics or atheists, whereas only two were Anglicans. Many LNA members shared Josephine Butler's faith in a "vital" Christianity – a social gospel that viewed conversion not only as a "fitness of the individual for a future life, but some attempt to make the world a more suitable place to which Christ should return."[36]

Religion also aided these women's transition from private to public roles. This is most evident in the case of the female members of the Society of Friends. The preponderance of Quaker women on the LNA executive, as well as among the original signatories of the Ladies' Protest in 1870, may be traced to a number of factors, two of which were the prior public experience of these women and the supportive character of the Quaker community itself. Josephine Butler once remarked to an Irish Quaker how she wished she had been a "Friend"; "*they* would have understood her mission." "She would have gone out on her mission backed *by the whole strength of the Society* and the world would have recognized the *right* of a Quaker woman to speak in public."[37]

Although enjoying a certain amount of spiritual equality among their coreligionists, nonconformist women still had to fight for their rights within their own sects. The *Shield*'s obituary of Mrs. Wells recalled her "fearlessness" when "the Congregational Union of England and Wales decided to discuss a resolution against the Contagious Diseases Acts without the presence of women; she and her sister would only withdraw from the hall when requested to do so and withdrew under protest."[38] When a young male Friend refused to admit Josephine Butler into the Friends' annual meeting (on the grounds that she was not a Quaker), Eliza Wigham, with her "plain Quaker bonnet," "seemed to be suddenly transformed from a lamb into a lion and fought her way past these young men dragging me [Butler] with her."[39]

In her memoirs, Butler steadfastly asserted that "We *never* asked of our adherents what their religious views or non-views were." Nonetheless, nonbelievers and agnostics were always kept at a distance by other members of the LNA executive. Moreover, at certain times open disputes over religious orthodoxy erupted. When Margaret Tanner

122

and Mary Priestman objected to the exclusion of Ursula Bright and Emilie Venturi from a "joint conference of Christian bodies," Josephine Butler defended the decision on the grounds that Venturi and Bright were not Christians. Bright was an agnostic, and Venturi "talks of the 'Carpenter's son,' meaning Christ, with some respect, but she considers our faith in Him an old and injurious superstition." Butler proceeded to defend herself against charges of narrow-mindedness, reminding them that "I imbibed from childhood the widest ideas of Christianity; only it *was* Christianity."[40]

Whether nonbelievers or devout Christians, most LNA leaders subscribed to strict principles of personal conduct. There were two exceptions: Emilie Ashurst Venturi and Elizabeth Wolstenholme Elmy, who both embraced a personal code distinctly at variance with mid-Victorian standards of respectability. Although notable exceptions, these women's very existence contradicts the common assumption of a universal prudery and sexual repression among mid-Victorian feminists. Elizabeth Wolstenholme Elmy, for instance, modeled her life on the "example and teaching of Mary Wollstonecraft" and

> in view of the legal disabilities then attached to married women, she united herself to Ben Elmy [in 1875] without any legal ceremony. When it was obvious that she was pregnant, there was much fluttering in the suffrage dovecots, and eventually Mrs. Jacob Bright induced the two to marry on the plea that their continued refusal would be harmful to the suffrage cause.[41]

Hardly less conventional was Emilie Ashurst Venturi, a cosmopolitan, cigar-smoking divorcée, who was Mazzini's literary executor. Venturi's father, William Ashurst, had been a great feminist and friend of Robert Owen's; hence as a young girl Venturi was exposed to radical feminist theories and proceeded to order her adult life in disregard of most established institutions and social norms. One of her sisters had actually run away to France in order to emulate the life of Georges Sand. Venturi herself evinced great disdain for the moralistic pieties of the provincial "goody goodies" who dominated the repeal campaign.[42]

More typically, LNA leaders moved toward feminism through their involvement in moral crusades like abolitionism and temperance. The rhetoric and political imagery of the antislavery cause would carry over to the "New Abolitionist movement," a term frequently used to describe repeal efforts. Eliza Wigham, for instance, was described in her obituary as a "life-long supporter of the Abolitionist cause; the transition was natural to her from fighting against Negro slavery in the West Indies and in South America,

123

to fighting against the attempted enslavement of women to a life of vice."[43]

The antislavery movement also provided older women like Elizabeth Pease Nichol with dramatic evidence of male prejudice against women's public activity. Nichol had been among the female British delegates to the World Antislavery Convention of 1840 who were "roused to white heat" over the exclusion of women at the conference.[44] Their continued contact with American delegates, like Elizabeth Cady Stanton, who went on to organize the women's suffrage movement in America, undoubtedly influenced their early support for suffrage in Great Britain.[45]

In addition to abolitionism and the Anti-Corn Law League, LNA leaders gained entrée into a national reformist network from participation in the annual meetings of the Social Science Congress. In the 1860s, the Social Science Association was the parent group for a series of feminist activities organized for the educational, professional, and legal advancement of women.[46] Held in a different city each year, the public discussions of the Social Science Congress brought together reformers from all parts of the country. These discussions were open to women and often exposed them for the first time to feminist issues. When the Social Science Congress met in her city (Belfast) in 1867, Isabella Tod "was ready to be drawn into active connection with the questions of education for women and married women's property laws, which were prominent subjects of discussion that year."[47] Six members of the LNA executive were active in the Social Science Congress prior to 1869, and four other members attended the 1872 meeting of the congress in Plymouth, where "notice" was given of "public meetings in connection with the C.D. Acts and Permissive Bill (Temperance)."[48]

By participating in the Social Science Congress, LNA leaders were also introduced to a style of analysis that would inform their repeal propaganda. Early in the campaign, feminist repealers found that they had to buttress their a priori objections to regulation by scientific documentation of the failure of the acts as sanitary and social legislation. The empirical investigations and surveys of the Social Science Congress would serve as their model for repeal fact-finding efforts.

Participation in the abolitionist struggle, the Anti-Corn Law League, and the Social Science Congress placed LNA leaders in the political vanguard of their generation. These earlier political experiences prepared them to assume national leadership roles by providing them with agitational skills, a practical education in feminist issues, and entrée into a national reform network.

124

A look at these women's subsequent voluntary activities in the 1860s and 1870s reveals a coherent set of political and social values that helped to shape LNA national policy. Feminism, medical reform, and moral reform were the three principal voluntary activities of the executive-board members. Their feminist commitment preceded their repeal work and probably stimulated their initial objection to the acts, whereas their involvement with medical reform and rescue work largely grew out of their abolitionist experience.

Feminism

By the late 1860s, leaders of the LNA who had earlier participated in the antislavery campaign and the Anti-Corn Law League had transferred their energies to the struggle for women's rights. Seventeen prominent suffragists served on the LNA executive. Many of them had helped to found local suffrage societies in Belfast, Dublin, Edinburgh, Bristol, and Manchester in the three or four years immediately preceding the formation of the LNA.[49] Although sharing personnel, the LNA and provincial suffrage groups promoted their causes separately; in London, prominent members of the London society like Millicent Fawcett had dissociated themselves from the repeal campaign, deeming it disreputable. A total of twenty-two LNA leaders (66.6 percent) were involved in some form of feminist activity. Besides suffrage, these activities included higher education for women, legal reforms, and medical education of women (see Table 1). At this early stage suffrage was an important feminist goal, but not the overriding concern it would become for subsequent generations of feminists.

Mid-Victorian feminists defended female autonomy against the prevailing social view of women as "relative creatures," who were defined by their familial relationships with men. They also upheld the ideal of a companionate marriage, one that would involve social as well as spiritual equality between husband and wife. Although fully acknowledging the social value of wifehood and motherhood, they argued nonetheless that these roles did not entirely establish nor exhaust the limits of female identity.[50]

This feminist commitment strongly influenced the LNA leadership's perspective on the repeal campaign, which they viewed as part of a larger program for women's emancipation. They treated prostitution as the end result of the artificial constraints placed on women's social and economic activity: inadequate wages and restrictions on their industrial employment forced women on to the streets, where they took up the "best paid industry" – prostitution.[51] Prostitution also served as a para-

125

Table 1. *Voluntary activities of the LNA leadership*

LNA leader	Anti-slavery	Anti-Corn Law	Abolition of tests	Social Science Association	Higher Education for women	Suffrage	Married Women's Property Act	Vigilance Association	Medical reform[a]	Social purity[b]	Rescue work	Temperance	Peace	Republicanism	Liberal political affiliation
K. Backhouse									x		x				x
L. Becker				x		x	x	x	x						
A. Bewicke								x		x					
Blackburn						x		x							
U. Bright				x		x	x	x							x
J. Butler	x			x	x	x	x	x	x	x	x	x			x
M. Estlin	x					x		x	x					x	x
M. Garston														x	x
Haslem					x	x	x	x	x				x		
Hindley[c]													x		
H. Kenway	x														
M. Lucas	x	x		x		x				x		x	x		x
P. McLaren	x	x			x	x			x				x		x
H. Martineau	x	x		x	x	x			x		x				x
L. March Phillips								x		x	x				
M. Merryweather									x						
E. Pease Nichol	x	x	x	x	x	x			x			x	x		x

M. Priestman	x		x			x		x			x			x
J. Reid[c]														
M. Richardson			x		x	x		x	x	x	x	x		
F. Smyttan									x					
M. Steward									x					
M. Tanner	x		x				x		x		x	x	x	x
K. Thomas					x	x		x	x		x	x		x
K. Thomasson					x	x		x	x		x	x		
I. Tod			x	x	x	x		x		x				x
E. Venturi	x			x	x	x	x	x	x	x	x		x	
L. Walker					x		x	x		x				
Wells[c]														
C.M. Whitehead									x	x				
E. Wigham	x			x	x			x	x	x	x	x	x	
L. Wilson					x	x		x	x					
E. Wolstenholme-Elmy			x	x		x		x	x					
Total	10	5	1	10	8	8	17	14	16	12	8	7	7	5	13

[a] Medical reforms include antivivisection, antivaccination, rational dress, RSPCA, mesmerism, hydropathy, alternative medical institutions (such as the Old Park Lock Hospital in Bristol and medical education for women).

[b] Social purity includes Social Purity Association, National Vigilance Association, participation at the Hyde Park Demonstration.

[c] No information available.

digm for the female condition; it established the archetypal relationship between men and women, repeated in perhaps a more veiled and subtle manner within the confines of genteel society. Mary Hume-Rothery, a prominent LNA speaker, explicitly associated bourgeois mercenary marriages with prostitution: in an "open letter" to William Gladstone, Rothery looked forward to the day "when women shall dare poverty, loneliness, contempt, starvation itself rather than sell themselves, whether to wealthy husbands, or less eligible purchasers."[52]

At a time when women were trying to establish some public standing as moral and rational beings, the double standard, which justified male sexual access to "impure" women, harkened back to the pre-Victorian view of women as "the Sex," as sexual objects to be bought and sold by men.[53] Feminists realized that the popular sentimentalization of "female influence" and motherhood only thinly masked this older distrust and contempt for women. State regulation of prostitution further institutionalized these social prejudices, by treating registered women as denatured social outcasts and by allowing male clients, doctors, magistrates, and police access to and control of the female body.

Middle-class feminists were by no means alone in regarding the C.D. acts as a vast male conspiracy to degrade women. Their indignation was shared by female popular audiences across the country, and also by registered prostitutes, who keenly sensed the misogynist character of the regulation system. One woman bitterly complained to Josephine Butler:

> It is *men*, only *men*, from the first to the last, that we have to do with! To please a man I did wrong at first, then I was flung about from man to man. Men police lay hand on us. By men we are examined, handled, doctored, and messed on with. In the hospital it is a man again who makes prayers and reads the Bible for us. We are up before magistrates who are men, and we never get out of the hands of men.[54]

Through the repeal campaign, LNA leaders hoped to educate their constituency on feminist questions, but they still found themselves constrained by the single-issue strategy of the repeal movement. Although Joseph Butler believed that the repeal cause gave "additional impulse" to the suffrage movement, she also expressed fear that repeal work diverted feminists away from the more urgent struggle for women's suffrage.

> My own cogitations have led me to feel and fear that we shall, shortly, be utterly swamped if we don't get it [the parliamentary

franchise], and that it is a more urgent matter than I thought. . . But we *cannot* drop the repeal work – I try now to join the two as much as possible tho' it *does* annoy some people.[55]

The vote, she explained to Mrs. Wilson of Sheffield, was "*a means of self-preservation* – we cannot *always* depend on the self-sacrificing efforts of noble men, like your husband, to right our wrongs . . . " With the enfranchisement of agricultural laborers in 1884, women remained the "one unrepresented section under a government which will become more and more extended, more popular, more democratic, and yet wholly masculine. Woe is me! That people cannot see!"[56]

The leadership of the LNA partially resolved the conflict between repeal work and their broader feminist interests by forming auxiliary societies to "work against all those disabilities and injustices which affect the interests of women." The "vitality of our Crusade," reported Butler, "appeared . . . to cause it to break through the boundaries of its own particular channel, and to create and fructify many movements and reforms of a collateral character."[57] The most important feminist offshoot was the Vigilance Association (formed 1871), to which fourteen members of the LNA executive board belonged. Organized by leaders of the LNA and National Association (both male and female), the Vigilance Association shared premises and agents with the LNA and the National Association. It also held joint or paired meetings with the LNA around the country and regularly exposed the nefarious activities of the LNA's archenemies – the military, police, and medical profession – in the pages of its journal.[58]

Medical reform

The leaders of the LNA were also attracted to various kinds of medical and health reforms, including the antivivisection and antivaccination movements, water cures, and dress reform. Feminists supported popular health movements as an alternative to the "materialist" and libertine doctrines of the regular medical profession. They protested against the encroachments of those "terrible aristocratic doctors" who condoned male promiscuity as a physiological necessity, who as "male midwives" had usurped a traditional female occupation, and who received state sanction to torture and corrupt the innocent bodies of women, children, and animals.[59]

The feminist attack on the periodical examination was central to the antimedical thrust of the repeal campaign. In highly colored language, LNA literature denounced the examination as a surgical outrage, an "espionage of enslaved wombs."[60] The examination was depicted as an unnatural, voyeuristic intrusion into the womb that degraded any female, whether she be a private patient or a public prostitute. "For myself," wrote Butler, "I had much rather die than endure it, and I believe that at this moment there is a very general feeling of penitence on the part of women for ever having submitted to this, for now it is made a plea by such men as– – –for wholesale outrage of our poorer sisters."[61]

By focusing on the speculum examination, feminists sought to bridge the social and moral gulf between "pure" and "impure" women. In her letter to Prime Minister Gladstone, Hume-Rothery decried the "horrors of the lazar jail," and defended the "sacred shame left in all but the basest."[62] This feminist identification with outcast women angered regulationists, who denied that the examination could offend "the most depraved classes of prostitutes." Feminists countered that it was the examination itself that ultimately destroyed these women's self-respect and rendered their rehabilitation virtually impossible.[63]

Feminist repealers also challenged the medical rationale underlying the acts, namely that prostitutes "polluted" men.[64] Whereas the acts penalized women for spreading disease, it was actually vicious men, they argued, who infected each other. "Among men," Butler wrote in a private communication, "the disease is almost universal at one time or another." Thus, "to try to stem disease by curing women who are immediately infected by men" was a hopeless task.[65] Even when a prostitute was beyond the infectious stage of syphilis, the disease could still be communicated from one man to another having connection with her, through "mediate contagion."[66] Male and female repealers occasionally carried this argument a step further and charged Admiralty officials with using prostitutes as scapegoats to cover up homosexual practices in the Royal Navy. Butler conjured up a "familiar scene": a ship docked and

> 70 men were found affected by recent venereal sores of a bad kind, not one of them having seen the face of a woman for more than a year. To such dissolute soldiers the cowardly official says, "Inform, inform us of the *woman* who has infected you." The men ashamed to confess that they had infected each other point to any woman who comes first.[67]

Feminist repealers also tried to offer alternative voluntary medical services to prostitutes suffering from venereal disease. Local repeal supporters had founded the Old Park Lock Hospital in Bristol in 1870; in 1877, the Bristol branch of the LNA officially took over the management of the financially beleaguered institution.[68] In the same year the Belfast LNA also lent support to the local lock hospital attached to the rescue house of the Midnight Mission,[69] and in 1884 Josephine Butler opened a small lock hospital in Winchester "for the reception of the poor outcasts."[70] These efforts were expressly intended to provide a "practical answer to those who affirm that the Ladies of our Association are ignorant of or indifferent to the frightful diseases which result from vice, and to the victims of those diseases."[71] Furthermore, these hospitals would dispense medical treatment consistent with the laws of morality. Under her care, Butler reported that venereal patients were cured without undergoing the internal examination: "When my poor girls have dreaded such an ordeal, when the doctor said it would be needful, I have asked them to pray and we all prayed, and then got well without any examination."[72]

Moral reform

Feminist leaders undertook rescue work, like medical reform, as an extension of their repeal efforts and specifically as a means of furthering the political goals of the organization. Some of them, like Butler and Katherine Backhouse, had been active in rescue work prior to 1870. By engaging in rescue work, the leadership was carrying on the tradition of "women's mission to women" begun by evangelical moral reformers in the 1850s, when the Great Social Evil was increasingly gaining public interest and attention.[73]

In the mid-Victorian period, female moral reformers used rescue work to carve out a special place for themselves in public life. While extending their social influence outside the home, these women justified their new political preeminence as a continuation of their traditional role as moral guardians of the family and the community. Rescue work also reinforced women's self-conscious participation in a distinct female subculture: female reformers rallied to the defense of members of their own sex while militantly opposing the sexual prerogatives of men.

Female identification of this kind, however, did not necessarily entail a commitment to feminism, nor did it represent a sustained challenge to the restrictions and social inequalities imposed on women. A significant discrepancy existed between the rhetoric of female solidarity and the actions of most female moral reformers. Female reformers might identify with women's special interests, but more often than not their actual relationship with working-class women was hierarchical, controlling, and punitive. Even on an ideological basis, only a small

131

ried to give new political meaning to traditional moral re-
rts.[74]

he particular achievement of Josephine Butler and the LNA
that they publicly linked moral reform to the wider goals of female
emancipation. They identified poverty, not "sin," as the principal
cause of prostitution. "Economics," Butler claimed, "lay at the heart
of practical morality."[75] Most LNA leaders followed her lead. Still,
the feminist repeal effort was not entirely free of the ironies and contradictions outlined above. Even feminist repealers had an unstable
emotional relationship with their "fallen" sisters: they became morally
indignant when confronted with a registered woman who did not
desire to be rescued and reformed.

Early in the campaign, LNA leaders urged the rank and file to
undertake rescue work in their local areas as part of their repeal
efforts. Through rescue work, female repealers tried to demonstrate
their practical knowledge of the conditions and temptations faced by
poor women. This in turn legitimated their right to represent those
poor and "fallen" women in the ensuing political struggle.

The LNA received encouragement in this endeavor from James
Stansfeld, in an 1876 letter publicly addressed to LNA members.
While in Plymouth Stansfeld had been struck by the work of John
Marshall, the paid agent for the National Association stationed there.
Marshall's combination of repeal and rescue work was held up as a
model to all committees. In his letter, Stansfeld stressed the political
importance of this combined effort, both as a way of breathing new
life into moribund repeal organizations and also of answering some of
the pointed criticisms of their opponents.

Petitions and propagandist work were not enough to keep members
occupied. In contrast, rescue work would draw women into the LNA
and give them something satisfying to do. Stansfeld did not expect
such efforts to degenerate into "mere charity," but rather hoped that
women would gain a personal understanding of larger social problems
through this experience, and that they would be able to arm themselves with facts to combat the exaggerated expertise of official and
medical advocates of the acts. Most important, this personal missionary effort would dispel criticism that repealers were "wanting in
Christian charity toward the women and made no provision for bodily
cure." It was incumbent upon repealers to devise a program encom-
passing rescue work and also physical care so that "those not dream-
ing of escape should be ministered unto."[76]

Stansfeld's message had a dramatic impact on the national movement. As mentioned above, Bristol and Belfast LNA members immedi-

132

ately responded to his appeal and began to cooperate with voluntary lock hospitals. His suggestion for a rescue mission to the fallen evoked an even more widespread response. Bristol, Edinburgh, York, Leeds, Birmingham, Dover, and Plymouth all reported new efforts to establish rescue homes, night homes for the friendless, registry offices for servants, and watches at railways stations "on the days of servants' terms, to meet young girls from the country, and, if possible, to render them assistance in finding their way, procuring lodgings, etc., lest they should fall into evil snares."[77]

The leaders of the LNA could correctly argue, as did the local secretary of the Glasgow branch, that they had laid the groundwork for the later social-purity efforts of Ellice Hopkins: "The effect of our long-continued efforts to enlighten public opinion was evident in the preparation thus made for the favorable reception accorded to Ellice Hopkins' lectures on social purity. Without *our* previous work, *hers* would have had little effect."[78]

The LNA leadership at first encouraged Stansfeld's plans, as consistent with its basic philosophy, and many members of the LNA executive like Mary Priestman and Lucy Walker guided the moral reform efforts of their local branches. Yet as early as 1878, the LNA leadership had grown wary of the rescue impulse, which by then had captured the imagination of its membership. There were a "hundred women" who would engage in rescue work for the "one" who would bravely enter the political arena to combat the acts.[79] The LNA correctly feared its membership would be seduced away from the hard work of repeal toward the more personally gratifying and socially acceptable work of reclamation. Moreover, leaders like Butler took a dim view of female penitentiaries because they contended it was men who needed to do penance, not women.[80]

The LNA rank and file

The LNA attracted hundreds of middle-class women to the political arena for the first time. Was the LNA a successful training ground for aggressive feminism? To answer this question, one must look beyond national policy to the activities and composition of local branches. More work on grass-roots associations needs to be done. At this point, we can only offer a brief and tentative assessment of the LNA rank and file, although a closer study of the Plymouth and Southampton branches will be presented in Chapter 8.

By 1884, there were 104 local branches of the LNA scattered throughout Great Britain, with a total of 981 subscribers.[81] Between

1870 and 1884, seventy-eight branches were active for over ten years. A small, stable leadership core controlled these branches, similar to the tight female network operating at the national level. Of these seventy-eight branches, sixty-three (80.8 percent) had one or more secretaries who served for more than ten years, whereas the average term of office for branch secretaries was nine years.

The numerical and financial strength of the LNA was centered in areas where national leaders were also located: York, Liverpool, Bristol, Leeds, Newcastle, and London (in the 1880s).[82] In fact, twelve executive-board members also served as secretaries of their local branches and therefore helped to bring local membership in line with national policy. On the other hand, the wives of outspoken opponents of the feminist and libertarian policies of the LNA also served as local secretaries for their districts. Not surprisingly, LNA branches under their leadership tended to eschew the populist and unconventional political style of many national feminist leaders.

With the suffrage movement in its infancy in Great Britain, for most local members the repeal campaign represented a first exposure to political activity. One typical recruit to repeal was the mother of W. T. Stead, whose early participation in the local LNA was recalled by her son: "... in 1870 my mother and the mother of my future wife canvassed the women of our village for signatures to a petition for repeal. It was the first time I had ever seen my mother promote a petition for Parliament."[83]

If few local members had previously engaged in political agitation, still fewer had ever spoken up in public. Charlotte Wilson, in her memoirs, recounted the shock of her first public announcement: "I well remember, having to make some business announcement at the close of a women's meeting, how appalled I was at the sound of my own voice – the first time I had heard it at a public hall!"[84]

For these women, the religious connection was even more crucial than it had been for national leaders. In an article on "Ladies' Branch Associations," Mary Priestman stressed the importance of the religious setting as a familiar and reassuring social ambience to recruit middle-class women into the LNA:

> It has been found very useful to hold meetings among the attendees of our places of worship when the minister's wife, or some ladies of the congregation, will call them together for explanation of the subject, and for prayer and guidance for such an important matter. The influence of religious fellowship and acquaintance is of great value, in overcoming the natural shrinking from a painful subject which cannot but be felt by everyone.[85]

134

The religious association dominated the outlook of the LNA general membership and tended to obscure the feminist and libertarian objectives of the national leadership. As a consequence, the fears of national leaders that its members could be easily sidetracked into rescue work and led astray by social-purity forces were well founded. However committed the leadership may have been to the welfare of the prostitute, the attitude of the rank and file was decidedly more confused and ambivalent. Local members vigorously protested against the medical outrage of inscribed prostitutes as an insult to all "womanhood," but they frequently failed to distinguish between opposing the state sanction of vice and supporting moves to repress open prostitution.

In addition, many local branches seem to have actively discouraged single women from joining. A significantly smaller proportion of branch secretaries were single as compared to national executive-board members. Additionally, only 15 percent of the subscribers were single in 1871; their proportion increased to 24 percent in 1884. Two factors account for the more limited role of single women at the branch level, particularly during the early stages of the campaign. First, married women could more easily combine domestic responsibilities with repeal activity at the local level. More importantly, local prejudice tended to discourage the participation of single women. In 1870, Gertrude Wilson had to keep in the background at a Leeds LNA meeting, as she was only one of two "unmarried ladies" there. Furthermore, some married members objected to a single woman like herself distributing repeal leaflets to factory girls.[86]

Another issue that exposed the conservatism of local branches was their preference for segregated meetings—a policy that, if followed in a thoroughgoing fashion, severely restricted women's public role in the repeal campaign. Branches of the LNA often avoided holding mixed meetings with men in deference to local public opinion. Charlotte Wilson explained the position of the Sheffield branch on this question: "Though our first public meeting was so successful, there were many persons who fancied that the subject could not be suitably discussed in mixed meetings. Therefore while not abandoning public mixed meetings, we got ladies from time to time to address Mothers' meetings . . ."[87] Wilson did not specify whether the objections to mixed meetings came from women or from their male allies. Certainly her husband, Henry, evinced little sympathy for the "conjoint action" of women and men. In the Butler correspondence there were frequent complaints against other male repealers who discouraged women's active participation in various locales.[88]

Not all local branches were so timid and dependent on male approval. The Bristol chapter, with its large feminist constituency, presents a contrasting picture of local branch life. Two notable features of Bristol members are readily apparent from the subscription lists. First, the Bristol branch had the highest persistence rate of members of any large local chapter, with 48.6 percent of subscribers in 1870 continuing their membership through 1875, and almost a third of the original subscribers belonging to the LNA in 1884.[89] Moreover, a very high proportion of the Bristol members were single, increasing from 42 percent in 1870 to 49 percent in 1884. This undoubtedly reflected the high concentration of Quakers and Unitarians in the branch. As noted earlier, it was also an indicator of the independent and feminist character of the branch. The Bristol group further distinguished itself by its activism and political initiative. Bristol members undertook personal missions to the subjected districts, where they agitated among the subjected prostitutes. As, as mentioned, in 1877 they also assumed the management of the local lock hospital in Bristol, thereby giving institutional expression to this professed solidarity with their "fallen" sisters.

7 *Class and gender conflict within the repeal movement*

The aggressive feminism of LNA leaders inevitably brought them into conflict with some male repealers. Although a number of men in the campaign shared the feminist and libertarian sentiments of the LNA leadership, they tended to be concentrated in the politically ineffective National Association. As Josephine Butler frequently complained in her letters, the London-based National Association focused too narrowly on parliamentary lobbying and left popular agitation to others. Instead, the LNA had to look to northern industrialists like Henry J. Wilson and Edward Backhouse for money and support. Although tireless in their efforts, provincial leaders like Wilson had little sympathy for the personal-rights libertarian concerns of the LNA. The LNA leadership, then, found itself bound to two unsatisfactory middle-class allies: the "do nothings" of the National Association, who were nonetheless ideologically correct on most feminist issues, and the "goody goodies" of the provincial electoral leagues, who, while often antifeminist, could be counted on to assume active political roles in support of repeal.

As a consequence, feminist repealers felt obliged to wage a woman's battle on two fronts. In public, LNA leaders fought for the right of women to control their own persons against the arbitrary control of police and doctors. In private, they fought for their own political rights and authority within the repeal movement. Political differences with middle-class leaders forced them to enter into an interclass alliance with workingmen and more generally to identify a special mission for themselves within the repeal camp.

The attack on conventional tactics and programs

On a number of occasions the women of the LNA showed themselves remarkably innovative and obstinately unwilling to play according to accepted political rules. Many of their actions expressed their dissatisfaction with male political institutions and centers of power. Early in

137

the campaign, for example, the LNA asserted its political independence by refusing to cooperate with the Royal Commission of 1871, which was charged with investigating the operation of the acts. Whereas the National Association could "without inconsistency" work with and criticize the Royal Commission, the LNA stood aloof on moral and constitutional grounds. It did not desire to perfect the working of the acts; it wished them abolished. The leadership of the LNA went so far as to accuse the all-male commission of voyeurism. The annual report of 1871 asserted: "The Royal Commission gives a number of gentlemen the opportunity of being acquainted in the indecent details of an odious system."[1]

In a positive way the LNA leadership often distinguished itself by its flexibility and comparative activism. The personal political style of LNA leaders was distinctive; they participated more actively in public agitation than their male counterparts in the National Association, who tended to leave organizing efforts to their agents. To capture popular support, LNA leaders resorted to sensational propaganda and daring acts of heroism. During the Colchester and Pontefract by-elections, for instance, Butler and her associates were chased and threatened by a crowd of brothel keepers and their flunkies.[2] Nor were these the only occasions when Butler and her colleagues were subjected to physical danger and abuse. In Cardiff, "crowds of men" threatened Butler and assured her that "they must and would have women."[3] In Glasgow she was attacked by medical students; in Manchester a gang of roughs attacked her while she was speaking in a theater, covering her with flour and excrement, tearing her clothes, and bruising her badly.[4] There was a certain dramatic flair and glorification of danger in these enterprises. Not only did feminists identify with outcast women, they tried to act out their roles as well – to give some reality to their spiritual identification with the fallen sisterhood.

Feminist leaders also descended upon the Plymouth and Southampton districts, where they encouraged registered prostitutes to fight an organized battle against the police, local doctors, and magistrates who embodied the C.D. acts. They sought out subjected women in the hospitals, low streets, and workhouses. They knew they were dealing with women of unsavory character and also with lodging-house keepers who profited from letting rooms to prostitutes. Yet they worked with these women largely on their terms – providing legal advice and defense along with moral uplift. They taught them how to fight the arbitrary actions of the police, and in some cases how to elude the law. They treaded a thin line between providing legal and tactical advice and encouraging the women to commit civil disobedi-

138

ence and resist legal authority. In one instance, a Mrs. King physically resisted the police herself. These were brave personal acts that reflect militancy and deep commitment.[5]

Role of women in the campaign

The LNA leadership also defended female autonomy within the repeal camp. It took a consistently strong stance on organizational autonomy and the important public role that women should play in repeal. Although defending the legitimacy of a separate women's group, LNA leaders still aspired to public leadership of the campaign as a whole. It was therefore important that women speak and participate at mixed public meetings. Many men, however, clearly begrudged women a public role in repeal, and mixed meetings emerged periodically as a sensitive issue. Those men who opposed mixed meetings were the same ones who generally undervalued women's participation and leadership in the movement.[6]

The power struggle for control of the repeal movement boiled over in 1877, when Josephine Butler was increasingly concerned over external and internal threats to the political mission of the LNA. From the outside she saw the movement for women's emancipation threatened by the proposed enfranchisement of agricultural workers and protective industrial legislation for women in the factories. Furthermore, the "strong diversion of forces" into rescue work, following James Stansfeld's directive, as well as into Ellice Hopkins's social-purity efforts, threatened the integrity of the organization and its feminist political position.[7] Internally, although Butler repeatedly asserted that she had "no head for organization," and although she herself had brought him into the movement, Stansfeld's undisputed preeminence in the national movement must have caused some concern as well – if only as a symbol of the shift in the balance of power from female to male leadership.[8]

But Butler sensed more specific efforts to undermine the authority of the LNA. In 1877 she sent out a circular to the LNA executive on "the necessity of the united work of men and women together." But she also pointed out the "ease" with which men combine together "for any cause," "quite naturally excluding women . . . and on the other hand women from long habit have naturally quite stood aside and allowed men to work alone, whilst they themselves try very faithfully to exercise that unseen or domestic influence alone which has hitherto been permitted them."[9] In another message to the executive, she expressed concern over the

139

tendency which I see among men to allow women to drop out of the foremost ranks in this crusade, the general tendency both at home and abroad to consider that our question having now attained the rank of a scientific and international question advocated by distinguished and learned men, it is less necessary that women should be the inspiring, and even the guiding power.[10]

Women must not give way to the experts: "We must claim a place in the foremost ranks even of the scientific and political advocacy of our claims."[11]

Butler sensed all along that Henry Wilson, although one of her important allies against the inaction of the National Association, harbored these prejudices against women. In 1899 she summed up her general estimation of him: "I grieve to find Mr. Wilson's tendency to exalt the man's work a little at the expense of the woman's. He is of a strong, aggressive nature."[12] Wilson deeply resented the presumption that repeal was especially a women's question. And he had a very difficult time dealing with strong-minded women.[13]

Repression of prostitution

The LNA had as much reason to distrust Wilson's "soundness" on the issue of prostitution as it did his disdainful attitude toward women in the campaign. In 1870, Wilson wrote his sister Gertrude, who had just joined the newly formed Leeds LNA, of his impressions of the C.D. acts and their critics. He discounted her fears that modest women like herself could be falsely accused by the police. Furthermore, he did not object to the arbitrary power given police over women's lives; rather he opposed the acts because they sanctioned rather than suppressed vice. Let "the police act as public prosecutors in cleaning the streets of prostitutes, putting down brothels, aiding in prosecutions for indecent assaults," and he would have no quarrel with them.[14]

In contrast, libertarians in the LNA and National Association steadfastly defended prostitutes as victims of social injustice rather than as criminal miscreants. They opposed police repression of solicitation on two grounds: it would constitute a dangerous extension of state power, and it was directed solely at women rather than at male profligates. Male and female feminists did, however, support certain legal measures that would restrict the "trade in vice," such as raising the age of consent and punishing seducers and third parties. But even while allowing for limited state intervention, Butler and others warned that the repression of brothels might render prostitutes homeless and further accentuate their outcast status.[15]

140

Class and gender conflict

By 1875, however, Wilson and his associates in the Northern Counties League had moved well beyond the LNA's qualified approval of restrictions on the "trade in vice" to a proposed attack on the "vice" itself. Dissatisfied with the "negative" program of repealers (that is, the simple repeal of the C.D. acts), Wilson and Joseph Edmondson hit upon a plan for "constructive legislation" that would outlaw fornication. To feminists, this further evidenced their limited imagination and total lack of regard for personal rights.[16]

The leaders of the LNA also suspected that men's enthusiasm for cleaning the streets of prostitutes masked a prurient interest. When male coworkers objected to the presence of ladies in the visitors' gallery of the House of Commons during the debate on the C.D. acts in 1883, Butler disdainfully remarked upon their evident pleasure at being present themselves.[17] She also complained of a Dr. Hoopell's total want of decency: "at meetings he has held in the North, he is in the habit of displaying . . . the instruments used at the examination and describing minutely their use. I protest against this as needlessly and grossly indecent. He says it rouses men against the Acts more than anything."[18]

Workingmen's Associations and paid agents

Thus LNA leaders suspected that within the ranks of male repealers there existed the same hatred, contempt, and lust for women that drove "those terrible aristocratic doctors" and members of the "decadent upper classes" to entrap women in the C.D. acts. Feminists' alliance with working-class men in the repeal campaign reflected, in part, their distrust of men of their own social class. Similarly their support for an independent working-class repeal organization mirrored their own concern for female autonomy within the repeal camp.

The LNA's alliance with workingmen and its encouragement of an autonomous Working Men's League was consistent with the long-standing republican sentiments of leaders like Josephine Butler. Leaders of the LNA repeatedly expressed a desire for the widest participation of persons of all classes within the repeal movement. A broad-based support not only reflected the genuine populist convictions of the leadership but also furthered certain of its long-term political goals. Through repeal, feminists sought to educate public opinion on the subject of prostitution and the double standard. They hoped that repeal would reflect a "revolution" from below, both a real transformation in social attitudes and habits and a populist attack on established centers of political power. Moreover, they realized that to the extent that the repeal cause concentrated narrowly on political lobby-

141

ing (where money and access to elite political circles were paramount), the role and status of women and workingmen within the movement would be diminished.

The LNA always regarded the newly enfranchised labor aristocrats of the industrial north as its natural allies: "The people" were "more just, more manly than those who rule them" proclaimed the LNA annual report for 1871.[19] Nonetheless, the feminist message to workingmen was mixed and somewhat contradictory: it attacked the double standard of sexual morality as well as male political prerogatives, but it also encouraged workingmen to assume custodial roles toward their own women. Thus, the LNA reminded men of their patriarchal responsibilities as defenders of the family. One LNA poster, prominently displayed during the Colchester by-election, warned "Working Men!" to "Look to the protection of your wives and daughters. They are at the mercy of the police where these Acts are in force."[20]

Ironically, the LNA frequently patronized its working-class male allies in a similar fashion. The LNA annual report for 1876 welcomed the formation of the Working Men's National League, with the confidence that "no more fruitful results" could be obtained by any combination of workers than the "co-operation of cultivated ladies with working men."

> All that is most generous and noble in our working men is drawn out in this combination; they are not unwilling to follow the gentle guidance of a grave and educated lady in a crusade which concerns so deeply the interests of women and the homes of the poor, and they are found to be willing to devote their brief hours of leisure and the whole influence of their votes and character to the cause, when the right chord in their hearts and consciences is touched by a delicate hand.[21]

Local branches of the LNA responded enthusiastically to the new alliance with workingmen. In the LNA annual report for 1876, a number of local correspondents announced the formation of workingmen's organizations under the aegis of the LNA, and a new public assault on the acts by local workingmen and ladies. "During the latter part of the last year," the Leeds correspondent reported, "the Leeds ladies' committee determined thoroughly to arouse the working men, and obtain a public expression of their own opinion."[22] The special bond between LNA members and workingmen was also stressed by the Edinburgh correspondent of 1884: "We have . . . held a few meetings with working men . . . to enlist their help in procuring repeal of laws which affect them and their families, and ourselves as women, in a closer manner than they can do to other classes of the community."[23]

The LNA's support of autonomous workingmen's associations infuriated many male repealers, who viewed this alliance as a threat to their own leadership and a breach of class solidarity. Upon hearing of plans for the new league, Henry Wilson wrote to Butler and begged her "to promise not to form this association." In vain she protested that she had learned of the league after it was an accomplished fact and that it was a spontaneous popular response to the Percy case. Although not responsible for it, she was "only too thankful to see the working men thus moving without being pushed by people above them. . ."

> I believe they will feel much more interest in the movement and much more committed to it if allowed to call *their own* meetings, collect their own money and organize themselves. I do not think that feeling of responsibility could live and grow and be extended among that class unless they were to act more as a class in that matter.[24]

Although more supportive of working-class initiative, LNA leaders still had significant political differences with their new allies. At the same time that Butler and her friends were trying to build bridges with the organized working class, they actively opposed Mundella's factory legislation bill that would restrict female employment.[25] They argued instead that shorter hours should be won through the organized and collective effort of women themselves.[26] They knew they were treading on dangerous ground here. In 1876, Butler hesitated from pressing the point at the annual meeting of the TUC: "I think it might be wise for us not to raise the question of the restrictions on female labour in the Trades Congress, this year. . . . It is such a serious question for the future, that we must try to avoid that awful thing—a real breach between women and working men."[27]

Workingwomen and the LNA

Although focusing its attention on workingmen, the LNA did not entirely ignore its female constituency in the working class. Early in the campaign the LNA held large public meetings for workingwomen, such as the 1870 meeting at Leeds attended by 800 or 900 "mill hands" and organized by local workingmen. Circulars advertising the meeting and also explaining the operation of the acts had been distributed to women at the factory gates. Over the years, LNA annual reports noted the strong feeling "amongst the poorer women . . . against the inequity of this class legislation," and the attendance of women of the "humbler" class at general public meetings and mothers' meetings.[28] In Liverpool, Bristol, and elsewhere, periodic attempts were made to organize separate workingwomen's organizations whose dues were set at sixpence rather than the usual two shillings and sixpence. However, announcements of these organizations were rarely followed up by news of their continued activity.[29]

The leadership of the LNA publicly regretted their failure to galvanize working-class women into active participation in repeal groups. In a 1870 letter to the LNA, Butler stressed the importance of recruiting workingwomen into the repeal cause. She noted with dismay "a great falling off in the numbers of women attending the various meetings held on behalf of Repeal." The collective presence of workingwomen at meetings was necessary to maintain the public vitality of the LNA. The ladies of the LNA would act as their spokeswomen: "Now the only way in which great numbers of women can . . . openly assert their view is by their *presence* at our meetings: for it is only the few who can speak or write."[30]

At by-elections workingwomen substantially contributed to the popular show of support for repeal. Much of the LNA activity at Colchester and Pontefract was aimed at generating popular female indignation against regulationist candidates. In Colchester, circulars addressed to the "Women of Britain" detailed the horrors of the internal examination inflicted on registered prostitutes.[31] Public meetings of workingwomen were held at the time, where Butler and other LNA agitators were greeted with enthusiasm. When Butler and Mrs. Hampson were forced to seek refuge in a grocer's cellar from a male mob, they overheard "women going past in groups who had been at the meeting, and their conversation was mostly of the following description: 'Ah she's right, depend upon it she's right. Well, what a thing! Well, to be sure! I'm sure I'll vote for her whenever I have a vote.' "[32]

Even without a vote, workingwomen could still influence their newly enfranchised husbands. In her *Reminiscences,* Butler recounted "an amusing incident" of the election to demonstrate the effective working of "female influence":

> I was walking down a bye-street one evening when I met an immense workman, a stalwart man, trudging along to his home after work hours. By his side trotted his wife – a fragile women, but with a fierce determination on her small face. At that moment she was shaking her little fist in her husband's face, and I heard her say, "Now you know all about it; if you vote for that man Storks, Tom, *I'll kill ye.*" Tom seemed to think that there was some danger of her threat being put in execution.[33]

The fact remains, nonetheless, that workingwomen could only exert indirect political influence. For effective political support, the LNA had to look to husbands like "Tom." Workingmen were already

144

experienced in political organization and public agitation. With some financial assistance, they could more easily organize themselves. They were accustomed to the same political language as the "ladies" of the LNA and they were more readily their political equals. As a consequence, LNA leaders were probably more comfortable in their presence. It was not until late in the campaign, in 1877, that the LNA discharged its male paid agent and replaced him with a workingwoman.

Yet the failure to draw workingwomen into repeal groups cannot be blamed simply on the elitism and indifferent organizing efforts of the LNA. It may have reflected deeper problems of organizing workingwomen at that historical moment. At face value, the repeal cause should have been extremely attractive to working-class women. Its combination of class and moral questions had traditionally activated women to public action in the past. In the 1830s women of the artisanal class had been active in both Chartist and anti-Poor Law campaigns. In their political role, women acted as defenders of the family and as the voice of justice and morality in the community. Female indignation was particularly strong against the bastardy clauses of the Poor Law, which were viewed as "prostitute-making" laws.[34]

Why, then, did workingwomen in the 1870s fail to use the repeal campaign to carve out a moral territory for themselves in public life, similar to their middle-class female counterparts? Dorothy Thompson has suggested that structural changes in working-class life may have impeded female political participation by the late 1840s. In the early Chartist period, female chartists were frequently employed outside the home and were integrated into the social and political activities of the working-class community. After the 1840s, important changes in the social relations between the sexes seem to have occurred, particularly among the skilled sectors of the working class. The separation of workshop and home, the decline of female employment outside the home, and the privatization of social life resulted in the growing isolation of workingwomen from public life. This trend was undoubtedly reinforced by the enfranchisement of male labor aristocrats in 1867. The low profile of workingwomen in the repeal campaign, then, may have been symptomatic of the general social and political demoralization of working-class women in the mid-Victorian period.[35]

Although workingwomen were underrepresented in repeal organizations, they readily gave informal support to repeal. The conversation between "Tom" and his wife is one example; the large attendance of workingwomen at repeal meetings is another. Moreover, poor workingwomen in subjected districts articulated the neighborhood senti-

145

ment against the acts. As we shall see, the attitude of female neighbors toward registered prostitutes was decidedly mixed. It may well be that prostitutes posed a social and sexual threat to respectable working-women in the northern cities as well as in subjected districts. Middle-class "ladies" could take up the cause of prostitutes with impunity, whereas working-class women clung to a social respectability based on shakier material foundations. As a consequence, they may have felt decidedly more ambivalent toward prostitutes, perhaps more ambivalent than their husbands.

Conclusion

How then do we evaluate the achievements of the LNA? Its ties to organized labor contrast sharply with its failure to organize working-women against the acts. Nor was it entirely successful as a training ground for militant bourgeois feminism. Although hundreds of middle-class women were drawn into the political arena, the leadership's efforts to indoctrinate its rank and file on constitutional and feminist issues had mixed results. The sixteen-year repeal campaign had success-fully aroused and focused deep female anger at male sexual license; unfortunately, this sense of grievance was not always translated into effective political action nor accompanied by an active concern for the welfare of prostitutes. In most districts, the rank and file focused on moral and religious objections to the acts and were readily susceptible to the counterattractions of the more repressive purity crusades of the 1880s.

Nevertheless the positive efforts of the LNA should not be over-looked. On numerous occasions, the LNA leadership showed itself to be keenly sensitive to radical historical possibilities. The feminist alli-ance with workingmen demonstrated an ability to overcome some class limitations and a willingness to defy the conventions of reform politics. This alliance highlighted the struggle against middle-class men, who held power as a class and gender prerogative. In marked contrast to most interclass reform movements, the feminist repeal ef-fort tended to accentuate rather than obscure class differences.

The LNA's defense of prostitutes was also impressive. Its leaders rejected the prevailing social view of prostitutes as pollutants of men, and instead depicted them as the *victims* of male pollution, as women who had been invaded by men's bodies, men's laws, and by that "steel penis," the speculum.[36] The prostitute as hapless victim was, nonethe-less, a restrictive and moralistic image, one that inhibited a more searching inquiry into the motives and self-perception of the women themselves. At times, however, feminist repealers exhibited a social understanding of prostitution that transcended this kind of abstract moral coding. As we shall see in later chapters, ladies and their agents defended the right of women to live monogamously outside of marriage and even recognized that "promiscuous" behavior among poor women did not consign them to an outcast category by the standards of their own community. They acknowledged the multiple social identities of poor women: of prostitutes who were not irrevocably "fallen" and of brothel keepers who were in reality female lodging-house keepers struggling to support their families. In this way, feminist repealers resembled the registered prostitutes of Plymouth and Southampton who repeatedly contested the acts in the courts and on the streets. Both groups of women exhibited a courage and independence that went far beyond what might have been anticipated, given the limits of class, sex, and previous political experience.

147

PART III

Two case studies: Plymouth and Southampton under the Contagious Diseases Acts

8 Plymouth and Southampton under the Contagious Diseases Acts

The Contagious Diseases Acts . . . have both directly and indirectly promoted the objects of sanitary and municipal police. They have purged the towns and encampments to which they have been applied of miserable creatures who were mere masses of rottenness and vehicles of disease, providing them with asylums where their suffering could be temporarily relieved even if their malady was beyond cure, and where their better nature was probably for the first time touched by human sympathy. . .
—"Report from the Royal Commission on the Administration and Operation of the Contagious Diseases Acts 1866–69 (1871)," P.P., 1871, XIX, p. 11.

In 1882, repealers glumly reviewed the select committee's favorable report on the working of the C.D. acts. The ordeal of the long-drawn-out inquiry had ended badly for the repeal side. Most committee members had simply accepted official accounts of the beneficial operation of the acts while dismissing repeal arguments and evidence of police abuse as unsubstantiated and malicious propaganda. The majority report included some additional thrusts at the repeal movement. It observed that "the majority of the more intelligent and respectable classes in these districts would be strongly opposed to the repeal of the Acts," and pointedly noted that "the strength of the opposition [to the acts] in each locality is [proportional] to its distance from the places where they are in operation."[1]

However strong their support in the north, the failure of abolitionists to sway public opinion in subjected areas remained a serious flaw in their overall political strategy. It would not prove to be an insurmountable barrier to repeal, as the acts were eventually abolished over the vehement objections of local authorities in subjected districts. Still, the pro-acts sentiment among the "respectable" inhabitants of garrison towns and ports brought under the acts undoubtedly strengthened the regulationists' position. It enabled them to defend the acts as consistent with the principle of "local option" and as promoting the interest of public order and morality as well as public health.[2]

The repeal leadership was aware of the strategic importance of win-

151

ning over the subjected districts and periodically sent down deputations and paid agents to stir up public feeling against the acts. Repealers were most active in subjected districts in 1870, during the early popular phase of the campaign, and later in 1876, when under Stansfeld's leadership they tried to revive public interest in repeal. In the early 1870s, repeal agitation was most successful in two southern ports, Plymouth and Southampton, that were placed under the supervision of the Admiralty. In both districts numerous public meetings in support of repeal were held, local branches of the LNA and National Association were formed, and hundreds of registered prostitutes were incited to resist the legal requirements of the acts.

These cities provide a comparative local study of the repeal campaign and the operation of the acts in two subjected districts. The local campaigns in Plymouth and Southampton were in many ways a microcosm of the national movement. Because of their smaller dimensions, it is possible to scrutinize the motives and interests of supporters and opponents of the acts that were also played out on the national level.

Plymouth and Southampton also contained some special features that make these two districts particularly worthy of investigation. With its vast military installations, Greater Plymouth was readily subject to governmental pressure. It soon emerged as the "pattern station" of the C.D. acts, where the government lavished more resources and energy toward their effective operation. As the *Shield* commented in 1870, it was the statistics from Plymouth "they always parade[d]" to demonstrate the diminution of V.D. among the military and the moral reclamation of registered women.[3] For their part, repealers regarded Plymouth as the "Citadel" of the acts, where the practical accomplishments of the regulation system could best be challenged. Southampton, conversely, was a commercial port, and more independent of state policy. The repeal campaign enjoyed larger indigenous middle-class support there; this in turn encouraged Southampton prostitutes to mount the greatest legal resistance to the acts.

Unlike other subjected areas like Aldershot and Portsmouth, neither Plymouth nor Southampton was completely controlled by the military. Both districts had substantial civilian communities and a similar band of Liberal nonconformists who readily committed themselves to repeal. Even local regulationists were a more diverse group than one would find in most of the garrison towns brought under the acts. As a Plymouth repealer noted, they included in their ranks "enlightened" sanitary and moral reformers as well as the "purely inhuman military despotism that wanted the Acts as a policy of

152

convenience."[4] Consequently the local debate between repealer regulationists was a more exacting test of the "Liberal conscience" and more focused on issues of social reform and social control than in other subjected districts.

Of course, a local study of two subjected districts reveals more than the attitudes and identity of regulationists and repealers. The discussion that follows deepens the study of the C.D. acts in four important ways: it demonstrates the impact of local political and social conditions on the practical outcome of the acts; it studies the institutions established under the acts; it investigates the experience of prostitutes brought under the acts; and it examines the actual encounters among repealers, regulationists, and the subject working-class population. Indeed, it is only in the subjected districts that all three groups came together and personally confronted each other. The local study, then, makes it possible to investigate how the various participants shaped each other's response to the acts.

The setting

In Greater Plymouth (population 132,792 in 1871) and Southampton (population 53,741) the local response to the Contagious Diseases Acts was largely conditioned by the political and social economy of these two southern dock towns. Although cut off from the industrial development of the north, both districts experienced considerable population and commercial growth in the mid-Victorian period as a result of railway and dockyard expansion. Southampton emerged as a major mail and emigration depot whose economy was dominated by a few large firms. Commercial efforts in Greater Plymouth (made up of Devonport, East Stonehouse, and Plymouth, and known as the Three Towns) were overshadowed by government installations. In 1871, one out of every three men over twenty there was either in military service or a civilian employee of the Admiralty.[5]

Between 1851 and 1871, the population of the Three Towns grew by more than 20 percent. Southampton's growth was even more remarkable; its pace of expansion was double that of the Three Towns and comparable to that of northern industrial cities. Their new urban population was drawn from the surrounding countryside, impelled by rural poverty and, in the case of Plymouth, the financial collapse of the mining industry in Devon and Cornwall. Emigrants were likely to be young and uneducated, with little or no industrial training. Males could find employment in the large casual labor force on the docks of Southampton or the Three Towns. Employment in large-scale commercial or governmental establishments, in towns with little economic diversity, left its mark on lower-class life there and contributed to the politically disorganized and quiescent character of the laboring poor in these communities.[6]

Women fared much worse than men in these districts. Many had come to Plymouth or Southampton after their fathers, brothers, or husbands had migrated overseas. Both cities had uneven sex ratios: in civilian sections of Plymouth, at least three out of five adult residents were women in 1871. Plymouth also contained the most extreme cases of female destitution, as well as the largest proportion of casual prostitutes. In the 1860s relief rolls there doubled, providing one indicator of the extensive destitution of women and children left to shift for themselves.[7]

But young single women were not permitted outdoor relief. The symbiotic relationship between women's sweated labor and the seasonal dockyard work open to men in London's East End existed in neither Southampton or Greater Plymouth–thus further restricting employment for women. The jobs open to women were in service industries that generaly catered to the seafaring population and to resident county societies of Southampton and Plymouth. Much of this employment was underpaid and highly irregular. If they lived outside their families and the homes of employers, these women were in dire straits. One obvious recourse was prostitution: in the spring of 1871, 40 percent of single women, aged fifteen to twenty-nine, who resided alone in lodgings in Plymouth were registered prostitutes.[8]

The urban centers these immigrants encountered were neither attractive nor hospitable. Greater Plymouth and Southampton experienced all the urban ills attendant upon a rapid influx of population—overcrowding, insufficient public services, and an inadequate police force. The subsequent extension of municipal government in the Three Towns and Southampton was largely a response to the need for efficient sanitary and law-enforcement agencies.[9] Bylaws to facilitate police control over the streets and "disorderly houses," as well as those that would regulate common lodging houses, were passed in the 1840s and 1850s.[10]

In both districts, then, local authorities had identified the casual laboring poor, and particularly "fallen women," as a threat to public health and decency before the C.D. acts were enacted. In the 1860s, local police were granted new powers to control drunken and disorderly streetwalkers. However, no serious effort was made to repress the trade and police continued to maintain a working relationship with prostitutes, who assisted them with inquiries "about wanted men and goods smuggled off foreign ships."[11] In exchange, prostitutes were left to ply their trade as long as they remained within demarcated areas.

In the Three Towns, some alteration in the character of prostitution did take place as a result of mid-century reforms. Most dramatically, the enforcement of the new licensing laws in the 1860s contributed to the decline of Castle Street as the center of prostitution and the drink trade. Castle Street, alias "Castle Rag" or "Damnation Alley,"[12] was the most notorious sailor district in Plymouth during the first half of the nineteenth century. Situated right along the Plymouth quay, it was filled from top to bottom with taverns and pubs with such nautical-sounding names as the "Blue Anchor" and the "Lord Nelson."[13] Here the sailor lodged while on shore, bought his provisions and clothing from the slop merchants and tailors, and spent or lost his pay on drink and the prostitutes who also resided in the pubs. His relationship with these women was decidedly ambivalent. Sailors' shanties graphically detailed the mutual exploitation between Jack and the prostitutes of Sailortown. A drunken night on the town frequently ended with "Jack all alone" left "stark naked on the bed" while "me watch an' clothes an' eighty pounds with me fancie one they fled."[14] The "flash packets" he met strolling down "Damnation Alley" often turned out to be "fireships" (V.D. carriers) in disguise, who later drugged, robbed, and shanghaied him, leaving him with "three pair of sox" and a "dose of the pox."[15]

Unseemly behavior was by no means restricted to the pub interior. Open brawls between prostitutes and sailors, and particularly between sailors and soldiers competing for the same woman were nightly occurrences. Shop windows were broken, stabbings were not infrequent, and respectable citizens, poor or rich, were afraid to venture out after dark.[16]

Such disorders continued until the late sixties, when police used their new powers under the licensing acts to clear out the Castle Street dives and almost every other pub and beer shop operating as a brothel throughout the Three Towns. By 1871, not one beerhouse or tavern remained on "Damnation Alley."[17] This was as much due to the declining economy of the area as to police vigilance: the number of troops stationed at the Citadel, only 200 yards from Castle Rag, significantly declined, whereas the completion of the Millbay docks to the west changed the destination of mercantile shipping.[18]

Prostitutes followed their customers west and resettled in the Octagon area of Plymouth. This relocation entailed more than a geographic reshifting of the supply. In the Octagon area, prostitutes no longer resided in pubs but took private lodgings in back alleys nearby. Street brawls, as well as other predatory behavior between prostitutes and their customers, continued, but in a notably subdued form.[19] Similar developments seem to have occurred in Southampton. By 1871, Southampton prostitutes also resided in private lodgings in the Simnel Street area, where they lived among the casual poor in streets notorious for their unsanitary condition and for the "low" character of the inhabitants.[20]

In both districts, the connection between prostitution and the drink trade persisted beyond the 1860s, as prostitutes continued to resort to pubs to find customers. As late as 1896, Plymouth pubs were fitted up with "snugs," small private compartments that facilitated sexual intimacy. Snugs could be entered through the back alley, and drinks were served through a slit in the partition.[21] Police surveillance of the drink trade was constrained by local political realities, for licensed victuallers wielded considerable influence at elections and generally had friends on the watch committee.[22] Prostitutes could also prove to be fierce adversaries. When attempts were made in the late 1860s to remove the licenses of publicans and beerhouse dealers who entertained or harbored prostitutes, the women marched in a body to the Plymouth workhouse: "they went there four deep, beating tin kettles and blowing tin whistles." Mr. Cox, the receiving officer, explained "that he couldn't take all of them although he added that he had plenty of oakum for them to pick." On Monday, "they found new quarters in Devonport."[23]

Prostitutes would have been loath to accept Mr. Cox's offer, as the repressive regime of the workhouse made it thoroughly unpalatable to any person with the resources to keep out. Only the most vulnerable members of the working class—the old, the sick, unwed mothers, widows, and children—entered the workhouse in any numbers. In both districts, women brought up on vagrancy charges frequently preferred prison to a workhouse ticket.[24]

Prostitutes only resorted to the workhouse at the time of their confinement or when they were physically incapacitated from carrying on their trade. Once in the "house," "females of dissolute and disorderly habits" were separated from "those of a better character."[25] They were sometimes forced to wear a stigmatizing costume and were deprived of visitation rights when ill and of any outside communication. Venereal-disease patients were left to "rot" in the foul wards, under the worst sanitary conditions, with only a pauper nurse in attendance.[26]

This public network of control and confinement was supplemented by local voluntary efforts to cut off the female supply or divert the male demand with more wholesome amusements and surroundings. Agnes Weston established the first Sailor's Rest in Devonport in 1868, as an alternative to "grog shops" and sailors' women who traditionally lodged and entertained "Jack" in port.[27] In the Three Towns the condition of fallen or homeless females also excited a great deal of local charitable attention. With the exception of hospitals and dispensaries, the most numerous and important voluntary charities were the female penitentiaries, rescue homes, and orphanages that took in destitute and improvident girls and trained them to be domestic servants.[28] Rescue homes in Southampton were less abundant, although preventive institutions like the Southampton Female Orphan Asylum were dominated by the same mercantile and patriarchal ethos as their Three Towns counterparts, housing female orphans and training them, as the Southampton town directory inadvertently put it, for "domestic servitude."[29]

As a result of these municipal and voluntary efforts, repealers could argue that the social habits of the poor and the conditions of the streets had markedly improved prior to the enactment of the C.D. acts. In 1878, W. T. Swan, a paid agent for the national repeal groups, responded critically to assertions that a "great improvement" in public order had taken place in the dock towns since the operation of the acts:

> That a great improvement has taken place ... since twelve years ago, no one need deny. "The roaring profligacy of the streets after nightfall," is no longer so general, nor so frequent, but this is equally true of Liverpool and other seaports where the Acts are not in operation. The early closing of public houses: better police regulations; the attention now given to the moral and intellectual improvement of seamen, and the greater care taken when vessels are paid off to encourage the investment of savings through Sailors' Homes, etc. etc., have all helped to bring about an improved state of things.[30]

The introduction of the acts in Plymouth: 1864–9

Local authorities in Greater Plymouth welcomed the C.D. acts as a supplement to their own efforts to control street disorders and also as a means to defray the cost of poor-law medical relief. Officials of local medical institutions were less favorably inclined toward the acts. In 1858 the authorities of "the Civil Hospital at Plymouth [South Devon and East Cornwall Hospital] and of the Devonport and Stonehouse dispensary declined to entertain any proposals for the treatment of infected prostitutes," undoubtedly for traditional moralist reasons.[31]

In spite of this initial rebuff to Admiralty officials, communication continued between the Admiralty and the local Devonport dispensary, as Devonport needed a hospital and the Admiralty wanted lock wards for public women. A marriage of convenience was eventually arranged. In 1861 Thomas Woollcombe, "a gentleman of considerable local influence, of great business ability, deeply convinced of the advantages of preventive legislation against syphilis, was made Chairman of the Dispensary Committee, and set himself seriously about carrying out the wishes of the Admiralty."[32] He was responsible for the amalgamation of the existing charity with a "new undertaking, to be styled 'the Royal Albert Hospital.'" Construction was finished in 1863, and for eighteen months prior to the enactment of the C.D. acts the medical treatment of diseased prostitutes was conducted on a "voluntary basis."[33]

The Admiralty hoped that cooperation with the local hospital charity would favorably influence public opinion in the district and gain influential local advocates for the acts. Certainly no one more vigorously defended the acts than Thomas Woollcombe, who viewed the regulation system as inseparably tied to the interest of the Royal Albert—his "creation." A local newspaper characterized him as the "father" of the Royal Albert who "from the day of its birth has watched over it and trained it with true parental love . . . " In "short, his soul—one would almost say—is thrown into the Hospital."[34] Woollcombe used his local influence to defend the acts and the Royal Albert both behind closed doors at town council meetings and openly in public meetings; on one occasion "when the supporters of Repeal monopolized the speaking until ten o'clock, he resumed the argument and continued it for two hours."[35]

Other public officials in the Three Towns shared Woollcombe's enthusiasm. William Luscombe, a Plymouth magistrate testifying before the Royal Commission of 1871, praised the acts for improving the demeanor of "public women." When asked about the state of the streets before the enactment of the acts, Luscombe described the audacious and offensive habits "of a great number of the lowest class of women to go far away from their homes into the better streets and the best part of town without hat or bonnet."[36] He claimed that the metropolitan police curtailed these excursions, and would also meet and send back the "mining girls from Cornwall who knocked about in the neighborhood of the mines and think there must be more freedom in a large town."[37] Poor-law guardians also regarded the acts as an opportunity to reduce the poor rates and to remove prostitutes and their diseased children from the workhouse.

Hence local advocates of the acts believed that the regulation system served the interest of public order as well as public health. Officials of the Royal Albert also felt obliged to justify their support for regulation on moral grounds, well before central authorities felt any similar compunction. Since its opening, the Royal Albert provided for the moral and religious instruction of interned prostitutes (such instruction became a mandatory policy for all districts only under the 1869 act). The social conscience of regulationists was further salved by Inspector Anniss's statistics on the moral improvement of the Devonport district since the introduction of the acts. In his reports, Anniss charted a precipitous decline in the number of brothels, pimps, prostitutes, and promiscuous juveniles in the Three Towns district as a result of the acts.[38] Although local police officials objected to the exaggerated claims of the metropolitan police, judicial and municipal officials from Plymouth were prepared to give the "water police" the lion's share of the credit.

The moral and social preoccupations of local authorities frequently resulted in a more coercive policy than the procedures officially sanctioned by the Home Office and Admiralty. Some of the more repressive measures associated with the C.D. acts in Plymouth – such as restrictions against the receipt of correspondence in the hospital and the detention of refractory lock patients in confinement cells – were the work of civil authorities acting at their own discretion. This informal assumption of power was paralleled and reinforced by the new power delegated local officials by Parliament under the 1866 and 1869 acts.[39]

The new clauses of the 1866 bill requiring periodic examination vastly increased the discretionary powers of the police, whose control now extended over a much larger group of lower-class women, not simply diseased prostitutes, but also women suspected of promiscuous behavior. There had to be a corresponding change in the system of police surveillance. Previously, police had relied on reports from the men admitted to the military hospitals. Now they were expected to go out into the community and maintain a tight surveillance of places where public women might congregate, principally working-class leisure sites and residential areas – pubs, beer shops, music halls, fairs, private lodgings, and common lodging houses. Moreover, police supervision resulted in the segregation and identification of a certain class of prostitutes. In the case of Plymouth, for example, soldiers' and sailors' prostitutes were required by the police to reside in the Octagon area.[40]

159

1868 - compulsory exam

Two case studies: Plymouth and Southampton

Even before the repeal campaign, the local operation of the acts encountered some opposition from registered prostitutes. After the compulsory examination was put into full effect in 1868, many women simply left the district. In 1868 and 1869 a total of 473 inscribed prostitutes left the Three Towns, most of them returning home or migrating to nearby villages. The women who remained on the register were older, more indigenous to the district, and more tied to a life of prostitution.[41]

A pattern of low-level conflict and insubordination is also observable among the lock patients in the Royal Albert, who clearly resented the harsh and moralistic regime of the hospital. In the early years, whenever a ship docked in Plymouth harbor, patients would simply pick themselves up and leave the ward. Officials complained that such actions encouraged a general attitude of defiance and resistance among the women of the town. They argued that the efficient working of the acts could only be ensured if the women's lives were regimented within and without the hospital—if they felt they had no place to go after they had escaped.[42]

In 1869 a very serious conflict over authority within the hospital emerged. On the one side were Admiralty officials, the visiting surgeon, and the chairman of the managing committee of the hospital; on the other side were the local medical officers of the Royal Albert in charge of the lock wards. The conflict operated on two levels: it was both a question of internal hospital politics and a struggle between local and central authorities responsible for administering the acts, a struggle that spawned middle-class opposition to the acts among local authorities. Most of the insurgent civil doctors and members of the board of governors were also local magistrates who felt their judicial prerogatives had been undermined by the punitive measures taken by the hospital against refractory patients. The conflict thus provides some perspective on the power structure of Devonport and on the muddled state of knowledge relating to venereal disease.

Difficulties between medical officers and the Admiralty and police officials first surfaced in 1868, when local civilian doctors objected to the discretionary powers of the police in identifying diseased prostitutes.[43] At the same time a number of Admiralty officials were displeased with the performance of the local doctors. Testifying before the Select Committee of 1869, Dr. Sloggett, then visiting surgeon at Plymouth and later inspector of hospitals under the acts, and Mr. Romaine, Permanent Under-Secretary of the Admiralty, both remarked on the incompetence of the civilian medical staff of the Royal Albert. Romaine complained that the local doctors, who vol-

160

untarily gave their services, kept the women in the hospital longer than necessary.[44]

This provoked an angry response from the four senior surgeons of the Royal Albert. In September 1869 Sloggett informed the Admiralty that the medical officers had circulated papers to the local press, claiming that they stood as a check against the visiting surgeon and the police.[45] This publicity was the cause of much insubordination and resistance among the subjected women. The local medical officers and the visiting surgeon differed over "the classes of disease considered contagious," with the former arguing that the visiting surgeon was sending in women who were not suffering from disease or at too advanced a stage to be contagious. According to Sloggett, these medical disputes impeded the effective working of the act and explained "why there has not been as great a diminution of disease as expected."[46]

Vernon Lushington, the Under-Secretary of the Admiralty, saw the problem as practical, not ideological. He commented that he could discern "no motive" "so far as I can see on either side; it was either a difference of professional opinion or some feeling of mutual jealousy."[47] No subversion of the acts or principled opposition to their general character was intended. Woollcombe would, however, argue that the intentions of the doctors were indeed malicious, that "while holding their office . . . they [the four surgeons] are quite ready to write letters in the public [press] well calculated to raise the opposition to the workings of the Act."[48]

The Admiralty and Woollcombe won all these early battles, as they sought to draw the net closer around the women and head off any possible middle-class opposition. They discharged the house surgeon, Sedley Wolferstan,[49] and took steps to hire a resident medical officer to free them from relying on the four senior surgeons. On November 22, 1869, Woollcombe and the four surgeons confronted each other at a special meeting of the hospital board of governors. The meeting had been called by eleven members of the board of governors to investigate the dispute over control of the lock wards. A proposed investigation was quashed, but the identity of the eleven signers of the petition is worthy of note. Five were magistrates for Devonport, as were three out of four of the insurgent medical officers. All told, ten Devonport magistrates were directly involved in the dispute.[50]

Not surprisingly, then, the insurgents took their battle out of the hospital and into the magistrate's court. In late November the Devonport magistrates passed a resolution, criticizing the treatment of refractory patients within the Royal Albert.[51] Woollcombe considered it a most "mischievous resolution," engineered by the "secretary of the Managing Committee and others who voted in the minority" against him earlier that month.[52] This political disagreement would affect judicial decisions in later C.D. acts cases. In December 1869, for example, Woollcombe noted the difference between Devonport and Plymouth magistrates: in Devonport magistrates seemed to have a "real sympathy" with the women, a problem that could be solved by appointing a stipendiary magistrate.[53] The "real sympathy" of the Devonport magistrates who opposed the acts was more realistically a response to an infringement on their local prerogatives, whether as doctors at the Royal Albert or as sitting magistrates.[54] The same eight magistrates who sent a resolution to the Home Secretary critical of the Royal Albert's by-laws also signed an 1870 petition in favor of the acts.[55] Their opposition arose from local resentment at external intervention in what was perceived as local affairs, a fact that was misinterpreted by repealers.[56]

Plymouth regulationists

The acts enjoyed the overwhelming support of public officials throughout the Three Towns.[57] Pro-acts sentiment cut across party and religious lines: Conservatives, military men, and Anglican clergymen could be counted upon to lend their support to the regulationist cause, whereas a large number of civic-minded Liberals and nonconformists also defended the acts, on the grounds that they served the interest of public health and morality. The acts received the public endorsement of the editors and publishers of the two Plymouth daily newspapers, the *Western Daily Mercury* and the *Western Morning News*.[58]

As elsewhere, the principal spokesmen for the acts were local doctors. Medical proponents of regulation generally came from professional families and many had Liberal, nonconformist connections. Besides wielding considerable political influence, they were active in philanthropic endeavors relating to public health and rescue work. Christopher Bulteel, for example, was treasurer of the Plymouth Female Home and a member of the Plymouth Artisans Improved Dwelling Society. Although supporting state intervention in matters regarding public health, medical advocates of the acts could also be found embracing nonconformist and liberal causes like temperance, the National Educational League, and even women's suffrage. As we shall see in Chapter 9, these men moved freely between the rhetoric of social control and public order and the ideals of sanitary and moral reform.[59]

Throughout the seventies and eighties, the acts continued to enjoy the tacit or active support of most respectable middle-class residents in the Three Towns. Despite all their efforts, repealers were unable to alter the favorable climate of opinion about the acts or to undermine the alliance of doctors, military men, public officials, and newspaper editors who supported their local operation. On the other hand, regulationists found (and actually sought) few adherents among the working class, with the exception of some of those directly involved in the drink and prostitution trade – the brothel keepers, publicans, and their hangers-on – who stood to benefit materially from cooperation with the metropolitan police. If they were willing to act as spies, they could gain additional control over the women residing in their houses or frequenting their pubs.

The most vociferous working-class supporters of regulation were the metropolitan police employed under the acts. As servants of power, held in mild contempt by their masters and generally despised by the poor, the "water police" (as they were called by the poor) occupied a difficult position. They were expected to divorce themselves from their class identities and attachments. Some, like Inspector Silas Anniss, played their official part brilliantly. Anniss was a perfect symbol of an emerging state bureaucracy, cold, self-righteous, authoritarian, and efficient in his duties. As a member of the dockyard police, he had distinguished himself in the apprehension of naval deserters, receiving a reward for each man brought in.[60] His talent for espionage and surveillance work seems to have helped him in his new responsibilities. In his official capacity, Anniss was notably disdainful of women and working people. Yet he was never accused of bribery or official corruption, but of brutal and callous mistreatment. A target of repeal propaganda over a period of sixteen years, he was a clever propagandist himself: for example, he tried to steal repealers' thunder by distributing religious tracts to prostitutes in the examination room.[61]

An ambitious man, Anniss used the acts to advance his own career. He found a loyal and powerful ally in Thomas Woollcombe, who regularly put him forward as a tireless and disinterested civil servant.[62] In the end, Anniss proved to be an embarrassment for the many Liberal doctors who preferred to look upon the acts as a sanitary rather than a police measure. And he was bitterly resented by local police officials and even some Devonport borough magistrates who regarded him as an arrogant and power-hungry competitor.

Few metropolitan police carried out their duties with the professional aplomb and detachment of Anniss. Many water police "lorded it" over

163

the women and bullied them into compliance. Some established a friendly, even flirtatious, relationship with registered women.[63] Other police, however, lacked the stomach for their duties.[64] As one officer from Woolwich remarked, "I was six years an Inspector under the Contagious Diseases Acts. I was thoroughly disgusted with the duties and was glad to get out of them."[65]

Plymouth repealers

Plymouth repealers were recruited from a different constituency than local regulationists, although both sides included civic-minded reformers who frequently served together on the boards of local charities. Repealers, however, were almost exclusively nonconformists and less politically influential than regulationists. The repeal cause also tended to attract individuals vehemently opposed to the military and to a centralized state. Most significant, Plymouth repealers included in their ranks two groups that had little or no representation among regulationists: middle-class women and workingmen.

In 1907, Alfred Balkwill, a Plymouth Quaker, gave an account of the origins of repeal organization in the Three Towns. According to Balkwill, Josephine Butler had first approached his two cousins, the Misses Bragg, who welcomed her as the "daughter of their father's friend." They then introduced Butler to his mother who, "from the first, tho' in the decline of life, threw her whole sympathies into the movement." Balkwill himself was thoroughly captivated by Butler:

> My first impression of Mrs. Butler as a speaker was that of her splendid courage. I did not need to be cousined: I was on her side by nature and by circumstance and by the charm of the cause being so unpopular. From the first she carried every meeting she addressed at Plymouth and formed a small band that stood by her to the end.[66]

This small band of Quakers formed the core of Plymouth repealers throughout the repeal campaign. Their early engagement is consistent with the national pattern, as Quakers were the first sect to give their wholehearted financial and personal support to the repeal campaign. They perceived it as another abolitionist struggle and closed ranks in support of the effort. The Quakers provided a network of small communities located in various sections of Britain, whom Butler and other repealers could call upon as the first contacts in the area. Plymouth Friends were certainly the single most socially committed, cosmopolitan, and geographically mobile members of the local middle-class community. They were not as wealthy as some of their counterparts in

164

the north. Rather, they were generally prosperous shopkeepers: Mr. Sellick was a bookseller; Alfred Balkwill, a chemist; and Richard Bishop, a draper who lived above his shop. But they were united by friendship and marriage to the Quakers of Bristol and the north, who formed the backbone of the national repeal campaign. And, as Balkwill's letter suggested, they were generally related to each other.

It is significant that Josephine Butler first contacted Quaker women, even though her connection with them had been through her father's antislavery activities. Although most of the Plymouth citizens who stood on the platform beside her at public meetings were men, their wives and sisters were the early agitators within the Quaker community. With the exception of A. M. Richardson (who lectured on the acts throughout the southwest), the sister of Alfred Balkwill, they never achieved national status as spokeswomen for the LNA. They generally spoke only before women's meetings in the Three Towns. Along with Caroline Nicholson, an elderly schoolteacher and Congregationalist, the core of Quaker women took responsibility for most of the repeal activities run by local women in the Three Towns.[67]

Members of the ladies' committee were middle-aged, either unmarried, childless, or with grown children. Unlike LNA national leaders, most Plymouth women did not come from wealthy backgrounds and could not have delegated all the housework involved in superintending a growing family to a large number of servants. They were overwhelmingly nonconformists; besides the Quaker core, half a dozen ministers' wives attached themselves to the repeal cause in the late seventies and eighties. They frequently shared a philanthropic interest in temperance and mission work, but had not previously engaged in any feminist or political agitation.

The Plymouth ladies' committee was a strategically important and active chapter. Branch members assisted national representatives in agitating among the prostitutes and brothel keepers of the Three Towns and participated in an underground railroad that spirited subjected women out of the district. Thus, from the very beginning, repeal and rescue work were intimately connected in Plymouth. A few women had previously engaged in rescue work, like Caroline Nicholson, who had earlier visited prostitutes in the Devonport workhouse but then found herself excluded from the Royal Albert and supplanted by a male chaplain.[68] Others became active in rescue work as an outgrowth of their participation in the repeal movement.

The Plymouth chapter also contributed some colorful propaganda tracts used by the national campaign. Miss Nicholson composed a series of fly sheets known as the "Devonport Series" on the horrors of life in Devonport district under the C.D. acts. They included such titles as "What I Saw at the Royal Albert Hospital," "A Plea for Soldiers," and "Abolition of Slavery on the Gold Coast: Is It Consistent with the Establishment of Slavery at Home?" The tracts criticized the patriarchal regime of the hospital, the regulations forbidding soldiers to marry, and the secrecy by which the "slavery" of the "outcast daughters of poverty" was conducted so that "special care" was taken "that the middle-class religious people of the land shall be kept in the dark as to what is going on."[69]

Although notable for their courage and comparative activism, female repealers in Plymouth lacked the political finesse and feminist commitment of the LNA national leadership. The Plymouth group generally ran separate meetings for women, and they relied on men to run public mixed meetings and to carry on the debates in the letters-to-the-editor columns of the local newspapers. After 1874, when the resistance campaign among prostitutes had substantially diminished, branch life settled down to the conventional pattern of drawing-room meetings, petitioning, and the questioning of political candidates. Without a feminist or libertarian perspective, many local members were readily susceptible to the appeal of social-purity forces in the late seventies and eighties.

Like the ladies' committee, the gentlemen's committee in Plymouth revolved around a few key persons. Whereas the Plymouth LNA was never larger than twenty or twenty-five members, the gentlemen's committee had a larger and more fluctuating membership (as many as forty to fifty). The men were middle class, nonconformists, and Liberal Party members, with only slight political influence. The original male supporters of repeal were Quakers, but the committee later recruited members of other denominations that had nationally committed themselves to repeal.[70]

Alfred Balkwill, the chairman of the gentlemen's committee, was known in Plymouth for his championship of unpopular causes. In his obituary, the *Western Morning News* remarked on his affection for the poor, the downtrodden, and "the moral underdog." "It was often said that to get Mr. Balkwill's assiduous love and affection one must qualify to be very bad."[71] Another who could always be called upon to support the repeal campaign was William Littleton. Littleton was registrar of marriages and a navy clothier in Devonport who "suffered seriously in his business by his persistent and prominent support of repeal."[72] The local repeal agent, John Marshall, also played a vital role in the Plymouth operation. Formerly a dock laborer at the Millbay docks, he was hired as the resident agent of the National Association in 1870. He and his wife ran the rescue home and local offices of the National Association on Union Street, in the midst of the pub and entertainment center of Plymouth. With roots in the working-class community, Marshall was able to establish an effective intelligence network among the poor. In his "rescue and defense" mission, he was expected to inform women of their legal rights under the acts and to help them to escape the clutches of the "spy police."

Repealers were able to attract working-class support during the first six months of their agitation in Greater Plymouth. As part of a general "stirring up" of the working class in the Three Towns, a working-men's committee was formed in August 1870. Members included prominent local working-class spokesmen, like S. P. Cook and J. Pike, who were also active in the temperance and nine-hour movements. In 1876, the Plymouth police chief, Frederick Wreford, actually chaired a meeting of the workingmen's committee, probably out of spite at Anniss for disparaging local police efforts.[73] Despite this illustrious recruit, the local workingmen's committee was never a viable, autonomous group; like the workingwomen's committee, news of its formation or revival was not subsequently followed by accounts of its active operation. Sustaining local working-class organizations was a national problem for repeal forces, but this difficulty was undoubtedly aggravated by the generally disorganized and quiescent state of the working class in the Three Towns.

Southampton — commercial port

An entirely civil population, Southampton was subjected to the acts only in 1870, largely because of the complaints of the authorities in Portsmouth (seventeen miles away) that diseased women from Southampton were coming into their town. The serious opposition that greeted the acts here came from within the community: from prominent Southampton religious and community leaders, but also from a number of borough magistrates. The Admiralty was unable to provide hospital accommodations in Southampton for the women who had been found to be diseased because the Royal Hants Infirmary, whose managing committee was dominated by stalwart repealers, adamantly refused to cooperate in the construction of lock wards.[74] The women had to be sent instead to the Portsea Hospital in Portsmouth, a notoriously inefficient and run-down establishment.

Reverend Edmund Kell, a Unitarian minister, and his wife were the focal points of repeal activity in Southampton. Until his death in 1874, Reverend Kell spoke at every public meeting on repeal, contributed

167

numerous letters to the local newspaper and to the *Shield,* and was present with his wife at every court trial involving a C.D. acts offense. He had been among the first residents of a subjected district to alert Josephine Butler to the moral and constitutional dangers posed by the acts. Like Plymouth repealers, his personal connection with Butler stemmed from his earlier involvement in the antislavery movement. Kell was a classic reformer in the Liberal, nonconformist tradition. From his vigorous support of the Reform Act of 1832 to his charter membership in the Southampton Women's Suffrage Society in 1867, he embraced virtually every major liberal political and social cause of the day.[75]

Southampton supporters of repeal were a more influential group than Plymouth abolitionists. Aside from the thirty-seven clergymen and ministers who signed repeal petitions during 1870, twenty-three other middle-class men spoke at repeal meetings. Of these twenty-three, five were doctors, seven magistrates or prominent political officials, and five were merchants. Even a few local public health officials gave their support to repeal. More predictably, critics of state medicine readily lined up against the acts, such as Dr. Edwin Hearne, a local magistrate and noted foe of compulsory vaccination.[76]

Members of the Southampton ladies' committee tended to be the wives of male repealers – middle-aged women married to merchants and ministers. In contrast to the Plymouth LNA, Southampton ladies did not initiate the local campaign and were far more reluctant to engage in repeal agitation or in rescue work. Only Mrs. Kell undertook personal missionary work among registered prostitutes.[77]

As elsewhere, middle-class repealers used constitutional rather than moral arguments to appeal to local workingmen. The "Southampton Working Men's Branch of the Anti-Contagious Diseases Acts Association" was formed in January 1871, and was chiefly composed of labor aristocrats and small shopkeepers. Most of the speakers were also radicals and members of the Land and Labour League, who were attracted to the repeal cause because of its antiaristocratic and antimilitary ethos.[78]

The workingmen's association, however, seems to have remained active only through 1871. Later attempts to revive it coincided, as in Plymouth, with efforts by the national associations at general agitation in the subjected districts. Yet neither of the workingmen's groups in Southampton and the Three Towns ever joined the Working Men's National League, founded in 1875, or contributed a list of their membership to the national rolls, published in the *National League Journal.*

Southampton regulationists also resembled local advocates of the

168

acts in the Three Towns. They tended to be doctors, military men, and local officials who praised the acts as enlightened sanitary and police measures. Some regulationists were principally attracted by the pecuniary advantages of the acts for local ratepayers. Local poor-law guardians demonstrated their enthusiasm for the acts by offering to send all the female patients in the lock wards of the workhouse to the Portsea Hospital to be interned. Their thinking was clear: any poor woman with venereal disease was unrespectable and hence a prostitute.[79]

Not all regulationists were so biased and mercenary in their treatment of the poor. John Aldridge, the local extensionist secretary for Southampton and examining surgeon under the acts, identified himself politically with the interests of the workingman. In 1874, he ran unsuccessfully in a municipal election as a Liberal and "laboring man's candidate." His platform endorsed sanitary reform (sewage), public service, and working-class education.[80] He seems to have treated registered women with discretion and courtesy; in 1875 he even complained to the Admiralty of the "rough use of the speculum" by the other examining surgeon in Southampton.[81] The Radical politics of a few regulationists notwithstanding, pro-acts forces were still unable to generate popular support for their cause. The only public meeting organized in support of the acts in 1870 was taken over by repealers, who defeated all resolutions in favor of the acts.[82]

Conclusion

In Plymouth and Southampton, then, the local conflict between regulationists and repealers reproduced national political alignments over the C.D. acts. In both districts, regulationists were mainly recruited from those groups who stood to benefit substantially from the local operation of the acts – from municipal officials, doctors, military men, and, in the case of Devonport, hospital authorities. Even these special-interest groups could, on occasion, express dissatisfaction with the regulation system. Disparaging remarks by central authorities often offended local pride and stimulated angry resolutions by the local town council. Territorial conflicts between local and national authorities also flared up over the years. But these conflicts represented only temporary irritations and not principled opposition to the acts.

The material advantage of the acts to local residents made it difficult to wage a repeal campaign in these districts. For a number of reasons, Southampton repealers did not suffer the same handicaps as those in Plymouth: Southampton was not a military town; the acts had only recently been introduced; no local charity like Devonport's

Royal Albert benefited from their operation; and from all indications, Southampton was not so disorderly a town or so overrun by "fallen women."[83] Initially, Reverend Kell could more easily persuade community leaders that the acts did not serve the best interest of their city and that they were only introduced in Southampton to benefit Portsmouth.

In both districts, the backbone of local repeal support came from nonconformists, moral reformers, and foes of the military and the centralized state. For many men, repeal activity was only one of a series of "anti" causes that they espoused. It was nonetheless a cause that had special relevance because it involved an "intolerable evil" so near to home.[84]

In contrast, middle-class women and workingmen who supported repeal tended to regard the acts as a more direct threat to their status and well-being. Workingmen condemned the acts as a "class" bill that applied only to their women.[85] Female repealers like Mrs. Kell also viewed regulation as a personal affront, "an insult to the whole womanhood of England" in its "ruthless sacrifice of female liberties to the supposed interest of profligate men."[86] The state sanction of the double standard, the usurpation of the female missionary role by male chaplains, and the medical "outrage" of the speculum examination degraded some women and undermined the proper moral role of others.

In the long run, local public opinion and political power would rest with the regulationists. Nonetheless, for a short period in the early 1870s repealers in Southampton and Plymouth were able to wage a full-blown struggle in the press and in the streets. It is to that early popular phase of the local agitation that we next turn.

9 The repeal campaign in Plymouth and Southampton, 1870–4

On a midsummer day in 1870, Eliza Binney, a prostitute living in Plymouth, emerged from an examination house where a doctor had just certified that she was suffering from venereal disease. Binney was ordered to go to the lock hospital in Devonport, escorted by a plain-clothes metropolitan police officer. As they were about to set out, the pair encountered two middle-class repeal agents, Mrs. Elizabeth King and Mr. Daniel Cooper. Mrs. King, parasol in hand, pressed Binney not to go unless she had signed the voluntary submission provided by law. A scuffle ensued as Binney resisted the officer and King "pushed the constable aside and took hold of Binney by the waist, upon which Inspector Anniss, who had come out of the station, took Mrs. King by the arm and pushed her aside."[1]

Meanwhile, a crowd of about a hundred and fifty people had collected to watch the incident. King and Cooper were charged with interfering with the police and were later forced to stand trial. Eliza Binney, for her part, was dragged off screaming to the hospital. Examination there revealed that she was not diseased after all. Hospital officials released her the next day, but she was still subject to police surveillance and fortnightly internal examination.

The trial of Cooper and King on July 28 represented the dramatic high point of the "Siege of Devonport," a period of intense local political activity against the Contagious Diseases Acts. Middle-class repealers and their working-class agents had descended upon the Devonport district in the spring and summer of 1870. They organized public meetings and also agitated among the brothel keepers and prostitutes, counseling them to resist the requirements of the acts. Mrs. King had established her headquarters in Bath Street, in the center of the brothel area, using the front room of Mrs. Harris, a well-known brothel keeper. From her headquarters, she distributed petitions against the acts to local residents as well as leaflets that informed prostitutes of their legal rights under the acts.[2]

171

Two case studies: Plymouth and Southampton

The persons assembled at the King–Cooper trial represent the various political and social forces struggling over the Contagious Diseases Acts on both local and national levels. Many of the contradictions and ironies that surround the public debate over the Contagious Diseases Acts also emerged during the trial. The trial was intensely political; all the sitting magistrates were outspoken supporters of the acts, which they largely saw as police measures to control public prostitution and street solicitation. For local authorities, the trial was intended to deliver a punitive lesson to repealers, whereas repealers themselves regarded the trial as an opportunity to air their views publicly and to demonstrate popular support.

Let us begin with the dramatis personae. First, Eliza Binney, a "common prostitute" subjected to the Contagious Diseases Acts. At the trial, Binney was described as "very respectably dressed and . . . gave her account in a becoming way," although one witness remarked that she was "rigged differently" at the time of her arrest.[3] Her history was known since 1869, when an inquest was made into the death of a naval surgeon who was visiting her in a brothel on Summerland Place; Binney seems to have stuck by him while he was ill and, as the local newspaper noted, she refrained from taking advantage of his vulnerable state to empty his pockets or steal his watch.[4] At the time, the presence of a gentleman in Summerland Place excited some attention in the local press inasmuch as that street was in a notorious "brothel" area where prostitutes mainly plied their trade among enlisted men. At the King–Cooper trial in 1870, Binney argued that she had moved out of the brothel, to Wolsden Street, and was then living with a gentleman – therefore no longer a "common prostitute."[5] She also maintained she had never signed a second voluntary submission after her first visit to the hospital and did not know she had a right to apply to the magistrates if she wanted her name removed from the registration list. In sum, Binney was an experienced young prostitute, not an innocent "soiled dove" mistakenly brought under the acts, who nonetheless had no idea of her rights before the law. And ironically, she had been sexually involved with a naval surgeon, and in fact naval surgeons were the medical officials at the examination house.

At her trial, E. M. King was described as a forty-year-old "naval officer's widow" from Australia who had recently returned to England so that her children could be educated there.[6] Upon learning of the Contagious Diseases Acts, she offered her services to the Ladies' National Association as a voluntary agent to go down to Plymouth and to agitate against the acts. This activity proved to be the start of King's career as a feminist and activist, much of which was later devoted to

172

antimedical and antimilitary crusades and to reforms related to working-class women – that is, to issues that attacked male centers of power and sought to bridge class differences among women.[7] Like Josephine Butler, King stressed the economic basis of prostitution as early as 1870. In a letter to the *Shield* she said, "If the Government had but spent the money they have on the Royal Albert Hospital [where the lock wards were located] and the police, on setting up a factory where the poor girls would get work and a morsel of bread they would have done some good, and taken hundreds off the street."[8]

Her stay in Plymouth, although a noble effort, proved to be something of a disaster – she seems to have irritated authorities and alienated the respectable members of the town while unrealistically raising the expectations of prostitutes concerning the political and legal assistance that would be forthcoming from repealers. Wiser from her struggle in Plymouth, she went on to agitate in Woolwich and Colchester, other garrison towns under the acts, linking the repeal cause with a general critique of the military.[9]

Daniel Cooper represented the evangelical side of the repeal movement. He strongly influenced both the style and organization of rescue work in the 1850s and 1860s, the period of its great institutional expansion, and was also one of the first agitators against the acts when he learned in 1868 that there were plans to extend them to northern cities.[10] His objections to the acts were mainly moral, not libertarian: the acts legislated vice and they degraded the women registered under them, making them less amenable to reformation. His attitude toward prostitutes was essentially patriarchal and puritanical. Although he admitted that economic necessity could drive women into prostitution, he tended to stress evil training, broken homes, and the habits of the poor as the causes for women's lapse from virtue.[11]

Despite their differences, King and Cooper could work together on the streets of Plymouth. Their activity represented a dramatic departure from the traditional pressure-group tactics of petitioning, parliamentary lobbying, and educating public opinion through pamphlets and public meetings that characterized repeal efforts in the north. As a consequence, their methods in Plymouth must have shocked the staid members of the repeal camp, who took a dim view of civil disobedience as well as of political alliances with brothel keepers and prostitutes.

It certainly shocked Inspector Silas Anniss, the principal local antagonist of repealers in Plymouth. For repealers and the local poor, he came to represent the "evil genius" behind the local operation of the acts in Plymouth. As late as 1900, fourteen years after repeal, antiregulationists were still talking about his "sinister" presence: "It was

173

there [Plymouth] that there reigned a petty tyrant, the chief of the spy police, Mr. Anniss, whose name may still convey a thrill of horror to those few now living who remember his cruel methods, his mendacity and the credence given to him by the Government and officials at the time."[12]

However melodramatic their characterization of Anniss, repealers were nonetheless accurate in assessing his strategic importance. It was Anniss's statistics concerning registered women that advocates of regulation "always parad[ed]" as evidence of the social and moral benefits of the acts.[13] Because of his efficient supervision and because of the kind of cooperation he received from local authorities, Plymouth became the "model station" of the Contagious Diseases Acts.

Many of the poor residents who had witnessed the struggle between King and Anniss crowded into the Plymouth courtroom on the day of the trial. Samuel Dennaford, a beershop owner, had been among the crowd of a hundred and fifty in Flora Lane; at the trial, he testified for the defense. During cross-examination, Dennaford indicated that he actively supported repeal efforts and regularly distributed the *Shield* on the streets.[14] He proved to be something of an embarrassing supporter for the repeal cause; police officers claimed he regularly catered to prostitutes in his beershop, whereas he maintained that they had to resort to drink before facing the ordeal of the internal examination.[15]

The conduct of the King–Cooper trial reveals the individual prejudices of the Plymouth magistrates. Although generally more hostile than Devonport magistrates, some were more open to general discussion and criticism of the acts than others. Whereas one magistrate, Mr. Norrington, thanked the defense counsel for new information on the acts, the mayor, Mr. Luscombe, lashed out at King for encouraging the women. The prosecution also manifested a particular hostility toward King, referring to her as a "paid agent," and calling for her imprisonment (while requesting a lighter sentence for Cooper, who was also charged with obstructing the police). In the end, the bench decided against both Cooper and King, and fined them each £5.[16]

The decision of the bench "was greeted with hisses which were immediately suppressed." Furthermore, a "very large crowd of persons assembled around the door of the Guildhall at the conclusion of the enquiry and loudly sympathised with Mrs. King and Mr. Cooper."[17]

To the *Devonport Independent,* the only local paper in the Three Towns mildly sympathetic to repeal efforts, the King–Cooper trial signified that repealers had successfully galvanized subjected women to "resist . . . as much as they can." Furthermore, repealers had convinced the general public that the acts were class legislation, that they were

174

administered in a sinister and arbitrary manner, and that they posed a threat to modest workingwomen: "Whether it be right or wrong – or to whatever cause it may be attributed – it is nevertheless a fact that there exists a fear [among] the respectable females to walk in the street after dark, lest they might be interfered with by the 'spy police.'"[18]

How had repealers aroused such intense public feeling in the Three Towns? In the three months preceding the trial they had worked hard at building a popular base of support, by holding public meetings, circulating handbills, and forming local branches of the LNA and National Association. For a brief time, they also succeeded in thoroughly disrupting the local operation of the acts. To local officials, however, the most shocking feature of the "Siege of Devonport" was the active role of women in the agitation.

According to Admiralty accounts, the early agitation in the Devonport district was the work of a "ladies association" and its "agents."[19] Official chroniclers of the repeal campaign essentially agreed with this interpretation, and acknowledged the impetus given the Plymouth campaign by the Bristol branch of the LNA. In the spring of 1870 the Bristol LNA had sent a Miss Duffett to Plymouth as its agent "to spread information concerning the working of the Acts and the movement for repeal."[20] Miss Duffett had formerly lived and worked in Plymouth as a seamstress, but

> left after her mother's death because she had seen that there was NO SAFETY FOR A WORKING WOMAN living alone in a town where a malicious whisper, or the *mere suspicion* of a policeman, paid in proportion to his success in bringing up unhappy women, was sufficient legal evidence to condemn to intolerable punishment, with consequent loss of character and employment.[21]

The Bristol LNA supported an office in Plymouth between 1870 and 1872, when that financial obligation was taken up by the National Association. A number of its members, including Mary Priestman, Mary Estlin, and Margaret Tanner, visited Plymouth in 1870 and worked among the prostitutes there. Two other female agents had prolonged stays in Plymouth during the spring and summer months: the celebrated Mrs. King, and Mrs. Lewis, a professional rescue worker from Birmingham, who had been asked by a "ladies association" "to undertake a mission to Plymouth just to investigate the matter to satisfy the public and the committee on this question [of exploitation of poor women by the acts]."[22] Finally, these paid and unpaid agents were aided in their efforts by local members of the Ladies Committee, by local men like John Marshall, Alfred Balkwill,

175

and William Littleton, by Josephine Butler, and also by Daniel Cooper and R. B. Williams, of the Rescue Society of London.

Repealers soon found that they were unable to make much headway with the respectable middle-class citizens of the district, and turned their attention instead to "stirring up" working-class sentiment. Advocates of the acts complained, "In calling public meetings they issue inflammatory circulars to the working classes, appealing as they also do in their addresses, to the passions more than the judgment of the people and ensuring anything but a dispassionate consideration of the subject in hand."[23]

The meetings of workingmen and women in early June stimulated great popular excitement.[24] The *Shield* commented on the June 10, 1870, meeting of men at Mechanics' Hall, Plymouth: "the exertions of Mr. Daniel Cooper and Mr. Williams had roused the alarm of the opponents of repeal, and the addresses of Mrs. Butler had raised the enthusiasm of the working classes. The excitement in the Three Towns in consequence was almost without parallel."[25] In August, prominent working-class agents of the national repeal groups came down to the Three Towns to speak at a meeting of workingmen and women. The *Shield* described the meeting as "attended by working men, convened by working men, and addressed by working men." A number of "middle-aged women," "wives" of the men, were also present. One outcome of the meeting was the formation of a workingman's committee.[26] The *Devonport Independent* commented on the "new phase" the campaign seemed "to be entering in becoming a class matter." "It is repeatedly pointed out to the working classes that the Acts are degradation to them specially; and that they endanger the liberty and virtue of their wives and daughters whilst those of the men of the upper classes are safe."[27]

Workingwomen also lent their voice to the public protest against the acts. At women's meetings throughout the spring and summer, working "women" mixed with "ladies" to hear condemnations of the acts as class and sex legislation. Speaking before a public meeting of women in Plymouth, Butler expressed her pleasure at the large assemblage of well-dressed ladies there; but she was "the more glad to see a great number of my humble sisters present because it is to them that I desire principally to speak." It was the peculiar mission of the LNA to bring women together. "In a large town, or even in an assembly like this, there may be persons of many different shades of moral character but let us for this evening put away distinctions; let us for once bridge over the gulf which separates class and class; the virtuous from the fallen . . ."[28] As we shall see in the next chapter,

176

workingwomen also played a central role in aiding prostitutes' resistance to the acts.

Local repeal agitation gained added momentum from the wide-ranging and occasionally heated debates between C.D. acts advocates and repealers in the letters-to-the-editor columns of the daily newspapers during the spring and summer months of 1870. Most of the letters in favor of the acts were written by local doctors and dealt with the deterrent effect of the acts and the responsibility prostitutes had for "causing" venereal disease. They generally reflected a continuity with the long-standing fears of women and of the dangerous classes that traditionally informed legal statutes and confinement institutions for prostitutes.

"Medicamentarius" opened the debate with a letter defending the acts as deterrents to clandestine prostitution among "married women whose husbands were at sea."[29] "Fair Play," on the other hand, criticized the one-sided character of the acts, in that only women were examined. This seemed especially ludicrous as "syphilis only breaks out it seems after an east wind blows ships into Plymouth harbor."[30] Whereas "Fair Play" maintained that contagion affected males and females alike, and to examine and confine one sex alone would be analogous to vaccinating only one sex, "Medicamentarius" insisted that only women "generated contagion," "plied a trade," and "could hide the disease" so well. Responding to the vaccination analogy, he argued that if only male children could thus engender "small pox," then females should go unvaccinated.[31]

A number of the letters also tried to probe the causes and origins of prostitution. Dr. A. R. R. Preston wrote a series of letters on the subject that were a hodgepodge of social analysis—a "bestiary" of natural and accidental causes for prostitution that often contradicted one another.[32] In most of his letters he held the view that women "fell" by virtue of their personal shortcomings and the fundamental degradation of working-class life. In his last letter, however, he focused on poverty as a principal cause of prostitution, and he suggested that the large fund amassed for the repeal of the C.D. acts be used instead to aid indigent, honest workingwomen. Poverty led to prostitution, as the women in Plymouth could not "honestly earn enough to live on."[33]

Christopher Bulteel's letters exhibited these same internal contradictions and fluctuations in tone and emphasis. Bulteel's series of thirteen letters to the *Western Daily Mercury* were collected into a pamphlet for the Extensionist Society and advertised as treating the C.D. acts in their "moral, social, and sanitary aspects." This characterization sug-

177

gests the scope of Bulteel's remarks and their resemblance to past inquiries into prostitution. Bulteel was reworking a genre epitomized by William Acton: his letters contain the familiar union of concern over the fate of prostitutes with a presumption of their degraded status. In addition, they represent a growing frustration and anger at repeal efforts in the Three Towns and annoyance at the failure of repealers to acknowledge the beneficial effects of the acts.

In his early letters, Bulteel presented himself as the secretary of the Plymouth Female Home and as one of the four senior surgeons who had circulated pamphlets critical of the acts in 1869. He began by retracting his opinion of a year ago that Inspector Anniss had grossly exaggerated the amount of prostitution in the Three Towns previous to the acts and underestimated the amount of secret prostitution that subsequently existed. Prostitution had significantly decreased (from 1,770 "prostitutes" in 1864 to 600 in 1870), and the women were now cleaner and better behaved on the streets. While in the hospital, the women had the benefit of a chaplain, and the Admiralty allotted £150 a year for reclamatory work. Most important, the acts deterred women from clandestine prostitution and were an important check on the sexual promiscuity of the "lower-class of domestic servants."[34]

R. B. Williams and Daniel Cooper responded to Bulteel's pro-acts letters with an attack on the veracity of Anniss's statistics.[35] They further tried to expose the injustice done to innocent young women by a corrupt system. They collected cases of mistaken identity and of police abuse and regularly reported them to the *Shield* and local newspapers.[36] These wronged innocent women tended to be friendless girls – orphans or newly arrived immigrants from the country – who strongly resembled the inmates of the Rescue Society homes in London. They satisfied the image of "victim" demanded by the readers of the *Shield,* and they may indeed have been the kind of women most receptive to the solicitations of Cooper and Williams. In reality, the court cases exposed repeal involvement in a more ambiguous kind of social underground.

Besides the workings of the acts, public debate centered on the tactics of the repeal movement. The distrust and contempt for women reflected in the letters on prostitution extended to the "ladies" engaged in repeal activities.[37] Both prostitutes and feminists had mischievously entered the public sphere, a fact sometimes even regretted by local supporters of repeal.[38]

On June 5, the editors of the two Plymouth papers advised "ladies at Plymouth and Devonport" not to attend the meetings scheduled for that day and the next. "For decency's sake, we hope none but married

178

ladies will go." The question had been forced into "pure family circles" enough already: "To be obliged to discuss the questions in public newspapers is bad enough; to have it expounded by ladies and brought up at the breakfast table afterwards, is . . . terrible . . . the next thing, we suppose, will be to bring home for family reading certain portions of Mr. Mayhew's work in *London Labour and the London Poor*."[39]

Editorials in the newspapers manifested a positive fixation on the defiling of the "breakfast table" by the "filthy" circulars that arrived at that hour.[40] That time of day probably represented a special moment when all members of the middle-class family came together, sat before the patriarchal head, and engaged in some communication with each other. Feminist literature on the horrors of the internal examination that came in the post threatened to pollute innocent minds; it also raised the specter of sexual insurrection against familial and political authority.

Although national figures like Josephine Butler spoke before men, audiences in the Three Towns were generally segregated according to sex. Nonetheless, the newspapers complained of the "strange, indecent commingling of the sexes" at public repeal meetings and noted with disapproval the "motley crowds" that attended the women's meetings during the spring and summer in 1870. Calling the "movement of women" unnatural, "A Friend of Women" was shocked to see the presence of dissolute women among "poor ignorant young girls in their teens" and respectable married women.[41] Charges of indelicacy were also leveled at female speakers like Butler for candidly discussing prostitution and venereal disease in public. A. R. R. Preston further criticized middle-class women for turning a cold shoulder to fallen women and thereby hastening their ultimate downfall.[42]

Feminists did not let these charges go unanswered. Mary Hume-Rothery, a prominent antivaccinationist and speaker for the national LNA, was in town to speak before a meeting of women in Devonport. She correctly perceived the misogynist ideology behind these allegations.

> Not all the gibes or revilings or sneers or lies of Saturday Reviewers or Pall Mall Gazetters or of the smaller fry who scribble anonymous letters to newspapers all over the kingdom, will avail to turn us one hair's breadth from our course, or be felt as anything but a compliment considering the quarters from which they emanate.[43]

In a letter to the editor of the *Western Daily Mercury*, Butler herself refuted Preston's charges of the "coldness of virtuous women": "Sir, I should not feel that I had a right to speak as I have ventured to do in

179

public on the subject of the great social evil if I had not previously engaged in practical efforts to diminish it."[44]

Thus, by the summer of 1870 the repeal campaign had become an omnipresent fact of life in Plymouth. The stage was now set for the second phase of the agitation: the legal resistance of registered women. Female repealers played an even more crucial role here than they had in the general agitation. It was the "ladies" and their female agents who visited the "low" streets, made contact with the brothel keepers, distributed handbills, and visited prostitutes in the workhouses and hospitals. Through their agitation, female repealers had established a political arena that made possible the resistance of prostitutes and their community.

To a certain extent, repealers encouraged others in illegal activities and acts of civil disobedience, and they broke the law themselves. However, most of their ("obstructive" efforts entailed advising poor women of their rights under the acts and providing them with legal counsel at their trials. In 1870, an aid and defense fund was formed for this purpose and local solicitors were retained. The National Association principally subsidized this endeavor. The repealers' defense efforts not only disarmed the authorities but encouraged the women. The police and Admiralty had not expected to have to deal with women who were informed of their rights. As Inspector Sloggett remarked, who would "have foreseen that an association could exist of ladies who would employ men known for their skill in legal casuistry to explain to prostitutes all possible methods by which they could evade the provisions of the Acts."[45]

E. M. King's leaflet, "Women of Plymouth and Devonport Suffering Under the Contagious Diseases Acts!" gives us some idea of the feminist appeal made to prostitutes. Decrying the internal examination as the "lowest and grossest insult," an affront to all women, King promised help for those who wished to escape this degradation. "Many ladies have taken great trouble, have been put to great expense to come and speak to you. . . . Are you glad they are come? Are you grateful to them?" Then, "Reform and Resist." "Don't go *willingly* to the examination or to Hospital, but let them *make* you go."[46] The moral and social condescension is readily apparent. However, juxtaposed with obvious class prejudice was a sense of female solidarity with the "fallen" sisterhood of Plymouth and Southampton. This profession of female solidarity was based on a shared experience of oppression, as symbolized by the male medical "outrage" of women by the speculum examination.

Mary Hume-Rothery reported that when she offered a pamphlet of

180

this sort to women leaving the examining room at Devonport, they thankfully accepted it and promised to read the contents. Standing outside the walls of the Royal Albert Hospital, she "was touched to see a group of four . . . go away slowly and seemingly consult together," until "one made a spring and flung one of our papers over the wall into the hospital yard or garden, in the kind . . . hope that it might reach some of the illegally detained inmates."[47]

By mid-July, organizing efforts among registered women began to show results. The acts' first test case came when Harriet Hicks petitioned the Devonport magistrates to be released from the Royal Albert Hospital. The trial proceedings, which were reprinted in the *Devonport Independent,* under the heading "Illegal Detention of a Woman at the Royal Albert Hospital, Devonport," were widely distributed as a handbill by the repealers.[48] The Hicks case reveals much about the character of the C.D. acts resistance movement in the Three Towns and the experience of women caught up by the acts.

On July 13, 1870, at the Devonport Petty Sessions, Mr. Adams, a local counsel for the repeal association, made an application on behalf of Hicks, declaring she was wrongfully detained at the Royal Albert Hospital. Adams maintained she had never knowingly signed a voluntary submission form, and she was neither a prostitute nor suffering from venereal disease. Ebenezer Simmons, a butcher, testified first. He had been living with Harriet Hicks, a former prostitute, for six or seven years, and he had one child by her that had "died of miscarriage." In 1868 they had moved to Devonport from Falmouth, Cornwall, and taken a furnished room in a lodging house in Cornwall Street, one of the poor and, as police would later point out, "disreputable" streets in the borough. Shortly after her arrival Hicks was placed on the police register and, in 1869, was detained in the lock hospital for three months. The couple had subsequently moved to Plymouth, and for the past five or six months had been living in a furnished room in a poor working-class district there. Ebenezer Simmons testified that seven weeks previous to this application, two of the "water police" (metropolitan dockyard police), Inspector Anniss and Constable Angear, "came into their room" and "demanded Hicks," saying "they had come for her and she must go with them as they had information she was diseased." "They did not say what the disease was." Hicks protested, "it was no such thing . . . she had not been with any one, not having occasion to, as he [witness] always brought her his weekly wages."

Mrs. Lewis testified next. She had gone to the Royal Albert Hospital on July 6 to see Hicks and told her "she had heard from her husband

[Simmons] that he sent her a message, and that he was keeping steady, not having been drinking as he had the last time she was here." As a result of their discussion, Lewis contacted the solicitor and laid the application before the court.

Mr. Woollcombe, representing the Royal Albert, objected. There was no evidence that the "woman Hicks" had requested this hearing herself. Court was adjourned until the following day, at which time the principal protagonist of the courtroom drama, Harriet Hicks, was finally brought in. This was the first meeting she had had with her solicitor, Mr. Adams. She was clearly a passive participant who in no way had authorized the proceedings or requested release from the authorities. Only in the most tentative manner did she acknowledge asking Mrs. Lewis for help: "I told the lady who came to see me that I was detained, but I did not ask her to try and get me out. I told her I should like to go out. She did not say she would try and get me out but she would talk to the doctors when I was gone out of the room."

Simmons was then recalled as witness. Although he acknowledged that before Hicks "lived with me, she was a prostitute," he declared his trust in her:

> Q. But for five or six years so far as you know, she has kept herself strictly with you?
> A. You cannot answer for a woman being in all day long but she was home night times, and when I came home I always found my meals, and if I could not come home they were brought to me.
> Q. You had no fault to find with her?
> A. No, and I don't think anybody else has.

She had discharged her conjugal obligations in all other areas; there was no reason to question her fidelity in sexual matters.

The defense counsel tried to rest the case here. Through Simmons' testimony, he argued, he had shown reasonable proof of Hicks's character. As Simmons declared himself undiseased, he had also demonstrated that Hicks herself was free of contagious disease. Woollcombe objected and asked to bring medical evidence before the court that would justify her detention.

Mr. Moore, the resident medical officer, was called. He was asked about the disease Hicks was harboring:

> Q. Is it syphilitic?
> A. She has a disease which comes under the Acts.
> Q. What term do you enter it in your returns?
> A. ... Under the head of syphilis.

Moore then explained that the sore was a vaginal ulcer and not "truly

182

Hicks case

syphilitic." "It might not give syphilis, but it might produce gonorrhea or a like sore." He was asked by the magistrates and Hicks's solicitor to clarify his definition of venereal disease.

A. All genital diseases, in man or woman, arising from excessive or impure sexual intercourse.

Q. How did this sore arise, do you think.

A. I believe it arose from excessive sexual intercourse.

Q. But persons might be faithful to each other, and yet have excessive intercourse, might such a sore arise from it.

A. It might; but I should not think it probable.

The court ordered Harriet Hicks's discharge, and the decision was roundly applauded by the spectators in the courtroom.

The Harriet Hicks case affords a glimpse into the life of the unre-spectable poor – an unmarried couple living together with a single room for a home – conditions familiar to the overwhelming majority of poor Plymouth families regardless of size. The woman was married to another man who had not supported her; she subsequently left him and went into prostitution. Separation was the working-class form of divorce. Simmons, a workman, was willing to acknowledge her previous history in court, although he now declared she lived faithfully with him. It was her status as a kept woman that secured her freedom.[49]

The case also tells us much about the abuses committed under the acts: of illiterate women forced to make their X's on documents they did not understand; of police barging into working-class residences at any time without warrants; of doctors interning women in the hospital on the basis of confused medical diagnosis. At a time when syphilis was well distinguished from gonorrhea, Moore's diagnosis was impre-cise even by Victorian standards. Advocates of the acts had always scoffed at repealers as medieval in their belief that venereal disease was divine punishment for vice, but Moore's diagnosis of disease en-gendered by "excessive sexual intercourse" was founded on a similar notion of moral retribution for sexual impurity.

Local C.D. acts officials were outraged by the decision. In their report to the Admiralty they complained that a number of the Devon-port magistrates showed a "real sympathy" for Hicks and an "unmis-takable animus" toward the police and the operation of the acts. As a consequence, they urged the appointment of a stipendiary magistrate to handle C.D. acts cases. Most of all, they worried that Hicks's successful petitioning might encourage further insubordination among registered women.[50]

Their worst fears were soon realized. The Hicks case provided regis-tered women with an important political lesson and stimulated an ava-

183

lanche of legal resistance. Twenty-nine women were brought before magistrates in the Three Towns for violations of the C.D. acts in the summer months. This represented only a fraction of the women in actual defiance of the acts. At the time the law courts were thoroughly swamped and only a selected number of recalcitrant women were brought up. To deal with this insurrection, the Home Office had to station additional police in the district, while Admiralty officials complained of an increase in V.D. among enlisted men. The "Siege of Devonport" had for a short time brought voluntary submission to an end.[51]

Most of the C.D. acts cases brought before the magistrates in the next two months involved women who had refused to attend examination or sign a voluntary submission (which was posted as a violation of the law in the hospital). All these women acknowledged that they had formerly been prostitutes, but quite a few claimed to be presently living with one man or otherwise desirous of quitting prostitution. They accused the "water police" of preventing them from becoming "respectable again" by hunting them up and exposing them to their neighbors, informing their employers, and threatening their families and lovers. Even women who professed no desire to "reform" resented their treatment under the acts. They expressed extreme aversion to the periodic examination and complained that they were interned in the hospital when there was "nothing the matter with them." They also complained of callous and abusive treatment by the police. When found suffering from venereal disease, police would not permit them to return home to make arrangements for the care of their possessions or children, but dragged them off directly to the hospital. Police would enter their rooms without knocking, uncover them to see who was in bed, and bid them get up and get dressed while still remaining in the room.[52]

At their trials, registered women and their working-class supporters were subjected to further ridicule and humiliation. In November 1870, for instance, John Marshall, the local repeal agent, was brought to trial for interfering with the special C.D. acts police. Unlike King and Cooper, he was not given the option of a fine but was sentenced instead to two months of hard labor. Marshall, however, was not the only working-class person treated shabbily at the trial. Sarah Mach, the woman he had allegedly incited to resist, was asked if she had been bribed to speak in Marshall's defense. She defended her integrity, "I think we are allowed to know our own feelings: we are not beasts of the field."[53]

In defending these women, repealers had to cooperate with the "social underground" of greater Plymouth. They also had to adapt

184

their own notions of respectable sexual behavior to the accepted mores of the casual laboring poor. Indeed, the *Shield* waxed indignant at the "Prostitute-Making" acts by which "women like Harriet Hicks and Mary Ann Bowden, who have lived faithfully for many years with their partners, although not legally married to them, are registered as common prostitutes."[54] Furthermore, Josephine Butler, in defending the "moral reclaimability" of the prostitutes, reminded her audience "that among the poor – the classes dealt with by the Contagious Diseases Acts – the boundary lines between the virtuous and vicious is so gradually and imperceptibly shaded off, that there is no one part at which it would be possible to affix a distinct name or infallibly assign a class."[55] Admiralty authorities took careful note of this argument and treated it as "subversive." Inspector Sloggett reported that it "was . . . clearly explained to the women that immoral or adulterous intercourse if confined to one man at a time was not illegal."[56]

Repealers further struggled against attempts by police and Admiralty authorities to isolate brothel keepers and prostitutes as a "special class" for whom constitutional guarantees no longer applied. Police reports frequently accused repealers of collusion with brothel keepers who did not favor the acts. Repealers were certainly aware that the lodging-house keepers they defended regularly permitted prostitutes to stay with them. In 1876, for instance, their solicitor defended a Mrs. Gunn against charges of harboring a diseased prostitute. In order to apprehend the young woman, Emily Barnett, Inspector Anniss had broken into Mrs. Gunn's house without a warrant. The executive committee of the National Association considered pressing charges against Anniss for trespassing. They were dissuaded, however, by their solicitor on the grounds that the house was indeed a brothel and no jury would convict the police.[57]

Yet how enduring and self-sustaining was this resistance movement? How much time and money were repealers willing to invest to support the local agitation? And how sincere were their sympathies for the prostitutes they aided?

By August 1870, repeal workers began to despair of the immensity of their undertaking in Plymouth. Shortly after her trial, for example, King wrote a rather angry, frustrated letter to the *Shield*. There had been enough "of talking, and speechifying and petitioning" in Plymouth. Now that repealers had brought voluntary submission to an end, "The whole power of the Admiralty staff retained to put the Acts in force, is brought to bear upon the women. They look to us to help them." To keep up resistance they needed "men" and "above all, we

185

want money, our private funds are well exhausted."[58] Mrs. Hampson, a "lady" rescue agent from London, who was working among the poor women in Plymouth in the autumn of 1870, also perceived the futility of her endeavor. "I got on with the poor women myself very well. It is hard work to keep up hope in them – of our willingness to help them they feel sure, but that we can do so they have some little doubts." These women were under the thumb of the civilian as well as metropolitan police. Mrs. Hampson tried to explain to them that they could not escape unless they left their "calling": "I tried to comfort them all I could, but felt it difficult work."[59]

Josephine Butler's letter to the annual meeting of the LNA in 1870 echoed Mrs. King's urgent request for women workers in the subjected districts. "It is suggested that two or three, or more, might visit together for a time one or other of the localities under the Acts, their places being taken by others when other duties possibly necessitated a change. This is a mission worthy of the noblest and the best."[60]

The LNA, much more than the National Association, sent members of its executive board to Plymouth, rather than just its paid agents. Butler frequently suggested missions and the setting up of public meetings in order to stir up feeling for repeal in the Devonport district. Yet there still remains, in the letters and executive-board minutes of both national groups, a general repugnance toward the subjected districts – a certain contempt for the people of the south by northerners, and a sense that in these districts there existed a different kind of working class and a different kind of prostitute than they were generally accustomed to dealing with. Butler, who had worked extensively with poor women in Liverpool, felt personally estranged from the prostitutes of the garrison and dock towns of the south. During her tours of the various subjected districts in 1870, she frequently commented on the hardened character of the "fallen" women she encountered there and on her inability to crack their defensive shell. At the annual LNA meeting held in Plymouth in 1872, she expressed her dismay:

> She had travelled through many towns and she never found one unfortunate woman without [modesty] left in her; but when she came into garrison towns of Plymouth and Devonport, where the Acts were in force, those unfortunate females did not meet her frankly. They looked cold and hard, and they told her callously that they were registered, that they were doing no ill, no harm, because they went regularly to their examination.[61]

In 1870, repealers had defended the constitutional right of prostitutes to petition their government like anyone else. However, in 1872, when advocates of the acts tried to turn the trick around and organized a pro-acts petition signed by prostitutes in the Three Towns, repealers responded with shock and moral outrage. "Which Shall Prevail?" contrasted the high moral principles of repealers to the debased sentiments of "Queen's Women" (as registered prostitutes allegedly called themselves): "For the women who sign this petition are **not reclaimed women** or women seeking to be reclaimed but they are practising as *Prostitutes under Government Sanction;* whereby . . . they procure increased custom, more money, and a recognised social position."[62]

By 1871 public activity in Plymouth had diminished considerably. There were far fewer deputations to Plymouth and fewer public meetings. Women still continued to resist the acts in the courts in significant though diminished numbers (thirty-two in 1871, twenty-one in 1872). Repealers complained that local newspapers no longer printed letters critical of the acts.[63] The only public debate in 1871 occurred over the public reference by Mr. Bruce, the Home Secretary, to Anniss's statistics on the reclamation and decrease of Devonport prostitutes since the acts were in force. Mr. Bruce had given an "exaggerated account" "as to the disgraceful condition of Devonport previous to the passage of the Acts, and the wonderful improvement effected by them." This "called forth a burst of indignation from the Town Council, the Press, and the public generally, which compelled Mr. Bruce to apologize and try to explain away his statement."[64]

Like the earlier controversy over the policy of the Royal Albert in 1869, this debate did not represent a serious questioning of the basic principles underlying the acts. The Devonport Town Council was angered because the Home Secretary had given their town a bad name and impugned the virtue of its women (as a statistic representing one out of nine women between the ages of fifteen and thirty-five as common prostitutes might well do). The dispute caused a temporary political irritation, but not something that could form the basis of a sustained political opposition.[65]

By 1872 the Three Towns had settled down to a general compliance with the acts. Inspector Sloggett reported that "there is no place under the Acts in which so favorable a report can be made, and it is to be attributed entirely to the zeal and assiduous attention of Inspector Anniss in the discharge of his duties."[66] In 1873 he assured the Admiralty that the repeal cause was dead in Plymouth: "a reaction seems to have taken place in the minds of the public in reference to the Acts and the immediate active opposition at Devonport, Southampton, and other places has subsided. The local agencies have either been withdrawn or they continue their hostility in silence."[67]

Two case studies: Plymouth and Southampton

Southampton

Although the acts did not take effect in Southampton until May 1870, the public debate over them began that February. On February 26, the Royal Hants Infirmary met to determine whether it would cooperate with the Admiralty in the construction of lock wards. Trouble was already brewing. In a letter to the editor of the *Weekly Hampshire Independent,* "M.D.", a supporter of the acts, was alarmed over the "likelihood of an opposition to the above Act by that portion of the community in Southampton to whom we are accustomed to look as the personification of every virtue and the guardians of society's morals."[68] At the meeting of governors, Reverend Edmund Kell spoke against the acts, emphasizing their unconstitutionality and ineffectiveness. The meeting voted to oppose selling the Admiralty any land.[69] Soon afterwards, the Admiralty purchased land independently to build its own lock wards. It also toyed with the idea of constructing an "asylum or refuge" for fallen women alongside the planned lock hospital in order to assuage the moral objections of the local repealers. Opposition was so vehement, however, that the Admiralty decided to send the women over to the Portsmouth Hospital instead.[70]

Repealers captured the initiative during the spring and summer of 1870 with large public meetings, petitions, and the organization of ladies' and gentlemen's committees.[71] The Southampton movement received aid and support from the national associations, which paid the fees of Mr. Harfield, the local solicitor, and also the salaries of the local repeal agents. Nonetheless, the national groups were less interested in Southampton than Plymouth, and the level of their financial support reflected this. The success of the repeal movement largely depended on the efforts of local repealers headed by Reverend and Mrs. Kell.

The most successful aspect of the Southampton campaign proved to be the intense legal resistance to the acts, which began in September 1870 and was sustained for seven years. During this period, 420 C.D. acts cases were brought before the magistrates, 133 for "non-submission" and 287 for refusal to attend examination. In contrast, the Three Towns had only 118 such cases, 75 of them during 1870 and 1871.[72] The Southampton women brought to trial closely resembled their counterparts in the Three Towns. Most were acknowledged prostitutes who resented the publicly humiliating procedures of the acts or who expressed a desire to quit prostitution and wanted to be taken off the register. Many complained of entrapment by the plainclothes police, who "ape[d] the manners of profligate gentlemen."[73]

Some Southampton women resisted as many as three, four, and five

188

times. Many factors contributed to the persistence of the Southampton resistance. Women generally received a more sympathetic hearing in Southampton than in Plymouth or Devonport. A minority of cases were dismissed, and many women were ordered to examination for three to six months rather than the maximum of twelve customarily given when they signed the voluntary submission. An 1871 Admiralty report on the general working of the acts in Southampton complained that the women never received a "fair trial" due to the "strong opposition shown by the Anti-C.D. Acts Society." They had an "office on High Street" with a "very influential committee of ministers of religion, ladies, and other persons who have thrown every obstacle in the way of the Acts being enforced.... Even some of our Borough Magistrates have been influenced by the opposition society." Finally, the repeal organization's principal defense attorney, Robert Harfield, was a "highly respected solicitor."[74]

As in the case of Plymouth, Admiralty officials argued that the legal resistance of subjected women was instigated by outsiders like Daniel Cooper and Mary Hume-Rothery, who arrived in Southampton in late August 1870. Cooper clearly tried to foment another "Siege of Devonport" in Southampton, by visiting the women and encouraging their resistance. Local repealers also established a political climate conducive to the women's noncompliance by writing letters to the editor and holding large public meetings. As in the Three Towns, the first successful court case triggered extensive legal resistance on the part of subjected women.

The women were supported in their efforts by the presence of Mrs. Kell and several other members of the Southampton ladies' committee at their trial. The appearance of ladies in court elicited the same "scandalized" reaction from a number of magistrates as did the presence of Elizabeth King and Mary Hume-Rothery in the Plymouth and Devonport courthouses. Repealers kept up a running battle with local magistrates on the question of open courts and the right of "ladies" to remain there. The *Shield* remarked on the continuing trials:

> In constantly requesting all ladies to leave the court while cases of this nature are being heard, the magistrates seem entirely to ignore the feelings of the women who are thus left to bear the terrible shame and humiliation of the trial in the presence of men alone, and totally unsupported by the sympathy of any one of their own sex . . .[75]

At women's meetings, the ladies of Southampton defended their presence at the trials. Without relinquishing their social prerogatives as ladies, they nonetheless expressed a certain identity of interest with

189

fallen women. To charges that it was "unladylike" to state her opinion publicly on the subject of the acts, Mrs. Bradley responded: "She hoped she was a lady and should have been ashamed not to be present that night (applause) . . . for this was a woman's subject and every lady was a woman was she not?" As women and ladies, she called on all present to "stand by the side of their fallen sisters." Hume-Rothery, who was the main speaker of the evening, further remarked that the acts were definitely "a woman's question, for it was the mission of woman to elevate the moral and spiritual character of man."[76]

Magistrates openly disputed the presence of ladies in court and the essential morality of the acts among themselves. In February 1871 it was announced at Southampton petty sessions that Rose Carsons, who was charged with refusing to attend examination, could no longer face "the ordeal" of the examination and broke up her household to move to London. She was now living a dissipated life, whereas she had formerly been "kept" by a gentleman. At that point Dr. Hearne, a sitting magistrate, "volunteered an opinion in the cause of morality, that the Acts worked badly by tending to increase prostitution." He was rebuked by his fellow magistrates, and told not to discuss the acts on the bench.[77] In a letter to the *Weekly Hampshire Independent,* Dr. Hearne explained that he had already incurred the wrath of the chair because of his earlier objections to the improper and unfair insults leveled at "the respectable and self-denying ladies" who attended open court.[78]

The legal aid and defense of Southampton women was an extremely effective tactic in Southampton, but it was not complemented by personal missionary effort among the subjected women. Southampton lacked that small band of stalwart supporters, like Littleton, Marshall, the Balkwills, the Misses Bragg, Mrs. Bishop, and Mrs. Richardson who readily went among the "fallen" or poor women of the Three Towns and counseled them on the acts. It never received the numerous deputations and agents from the London and national LNA. The one exception here was Mrs. Kell. Before the Royal Commission of 1871 she testified that she could find no other member of the ladies' committee to accompany her on her visits to prostitutes in the low lodging houses of Southampton. She also had great difficulty in persuading young girls to go to the London homes of the Rescue Society; she had convinced four to enter the homes and then could find no more interested applicants.[79]

As in Plymouth, prostitutes' resistance was linked to the strength of middle-class support and to the general level of repeal activity in the district. When Mrs. Kell died in the spring of 1872, active resistance to

190

the acts as well as public repeal activity ground to a halt. Admiralty officials confidently reported that "immediate active opposition" to the acts had subsided: "At Southampton the agent [Mr. Knott] has long discontinued his attendance near the examining room, and summonses have been issued against thirteen only."[80] The National Association considered closing its office and discontinuing its agency.[81] However, the ladies' committee began to revive in September 1872. Reverend Kell's donation of £50 to the LNA in 1873 in memoriam to his wife made it possible for the national groups to retain an agent there.[82] Legal resistance to the acts by subjected women picked up accordingly. In 1873, the number of summons issued for "non-submission" and "non-attendance" jumped to seventy-four.[83] Letters in the press on the C.D. acts began to reappear. Public meetings were again held. Sloggett acknowledged in 1873 that Southampton was one of the three towns where resistance was still active, principally because of the efforts of the "ladies' association" and the "agents."[84] With Reverend Kell's death in 1874, Southampton never found another committed leader for the local struggle. This may account for the failure to revive interest and activity there after 1876, at which time national groups tried to organize a Subjected Districts League. By the end of the 70s, an influential pro-acts segment would join Plymouth officials in a protest against the suspension of the acts.

Why did the repeal agitation ultimately subside in Plymouth and Southampton? Repealers had never anticipated how protracted and difficult a battle they would have on their hands, both nationally and locally. They certainly had not estimated the amount of human and financial resources necessary to sustain an agitation among subjected women. Only dimly did they perceive the network of control and confinement that loomed over these women's lives, particularly in a government town like Plymouth. The casual laboring poor that they encountered in both districts were different from the industrial working class of the north and were not easily organized for any social and political purpose. Finally, as Mrs. Hampson dimly perceived, repealers had little more than solace and a stay in a dreary London rescue home to offer the women in return for their cooperation. Ironically, the publicity associated with the repeal agitation may have reinforced these women's outcast status, destroying their relative anonymity and rendering their move out of prostitution more difficult. This would be the dilemma confronting repealers in their subsequent rescue and defense efforts.

191

10 *The making of an outcast group: prostitutes and working women in Plymouth and Southampton*

With middle-class support, many registered prostitutes in Plymouth and Southampton forcibly resisted the requirement of the Contagious Diseases Acts. Their experience under the acts constitutes an important chapter in the social history of an outcast group in Victorian England. Although the acts were ostensibly passed as sanitary measures to control the spread of venereal disease, their local administration extended well beyond the sanitary supervision of common prostitutes. As single women residing outside their families, registered women were perhaps the most vulnerable members of their community; consequently, official intervention into their lives offered police an easy opportunity for general surveillance of the poor neighborhoods in which they resided. These women were used as a leverage on the working-class community, not simply because of their marginal status within that community, but in good part because they shared social characteristics in common with the mass of the urban poor. Their temporary moves into and out of prostitution reflected the fluid social identity among the casual laboring poor who so violated Victorian society's sense of order and place. In the districts where the acts were enforced, prostitution, petty theft, and the seasonal migration of the poor into the countryside to pick hops and strawberries were all means by which the chronically underemployed endured through hard times. The Contagious Diseases Acts were part of institutional and legal efforts to contain this occupational and geographic mobility.[1] At the local level, they were used to clarify the relationship between the unrespectable and respectable poor, and specifically to force prostitutes to accept their status as public women by destroying their private associations with the poor working-class community.

By establishing the general social profile of Southampton and Plymouth prostitutes, we may begin to assess the degree to which the lives of registered women were integrated into the conventional framework of working-class life. In particular, the first section of this

192

chapter outlines the options open to women who moved into prostitution and the way in which prostitution represented a transitional stage
in their adult lives. The second discusses the impact of the Contagious
Diseases Acts on registered women and their community. It examines
the extensive public resistance mounted against the acts by the "unrespectable" poor as well as the degree to which the poor ultimately
acquiesced in the social isolation of prostitutes. In conclusion, we shall
connect the experience of registered women to long-term changes in
working-class prostitution and in the social economy of the laboring
poor in the late Victorian and Edwardian periods.

A *social profile of the prostitute*

No systematic survey of motives and social origins of registered prostitutes comparable to the work of A. J. B. Parent-Duchâtelet in Paris or
William Sanger in New York was undertaken by C.D. acts authorities
in Plymouth or Southampton.[2] It has nevertheless been possible to
construct a general profile of the women registered under the Contagious Diseases Acts from hospital and police records, from local newspaper reports of petty-sessions trials of prostitutes, and from the public testimonies of local authorities and repeal workers. In December
1871 there were 503 registered women in Greater Plymouth and 160
women in Southampton.[3] From these sources the uniform picture that
emerges closely resembles that of Victorian prostitutes in other urban
areas: these were young single women, mostly half orphans, who were
born in the immediate district or in the surrounding countryside.[4]
They resided in private lodgings and catered to a working-class clientele.[5] Their migration patterns appear to be no different from those of
the general population for the two districts or for young single women
in particular.[6] In general, the registered women of both districts appear more indigenous to the two districts than suggested by the official
testimonies of local police and magistrates, eager to blame "social
disorder" on nonresidents. Census and hospital records for Plymouth
nevertheless indicate that a significant number of women were recent
arrivals from the local countryside–about half–although local authorities overstated their proportions.[7] Such women came to Southampton or to Plymouth for many of the same reasons as other rural
migrants, although, as half orphans, they were especially obliged to
shift for themselves at an early age.

Family conflict as well as economic necessity may have also motivated young women to leave their homes to move to the city or to take
another residence in town. The discomfort of poor, overcrowded

193

homes, and the problems of family life, beset by high birth rates, high mortality rates, and the emigration of men overseas, may have rendered domestic service in more prosperous households (initially at least) an attractive alternative. Some women clearly left their families simply to get away, with not much forethought about their future. Police and rescue workers cited substantial numbers of youthful runaways who found themselves in notorious brothels soon after their arrival in the city.[8] Young women, impatient with the subordination and fatalistic acquiescence expected of their class, may have been most likely to make this break. Registered women in these districts were noted for their independent and aggressive behavior. Their present mode of life may have reinforced this defiance and insubordination, but such distinctive behavior also suggests that they were a special group more inclined to self-assertion than most of their working-class contemporaries.

These women's early sexual experience generally conformed to the pattern of sexual activity for young women who entered prostitution, as outlined in Chapter 1.[9] Registered women frequently testified that they has passed through various stages of sexual involvement with workingmen before going on the streets – whether it be serial monogamy or more general promiscuity.[10] Yet few indicated that the need to support a child precipitated their move into prostitution. In these districts, as elsewhere, illegitimacy seems to have been a social problem distinct from prostitution.[11] There were, of course, some exceptions. Laura Clarke, for example, came to Plymouth to be confined and to escape the claustrophobic social pressures of her rural village in Cornwall. She put her child out to nurse, took a position as a domestic servant, and only subsequently moved into prostitution after her child died. In her case, then, pregnancy and illegitimacy did force her to uproot herself, leave the scene of her disgrace, and establish new social relations in a nearby urban area.[12]

On the whole, occupational dislocation seems to have been a more decisive factor in women's moves into prostitution then premarital sexuality and pregnancy. Plymouth and Southampton officials generally agreed that the previous work experience of registered women had been as maids of all work – the bottom rung of the ladder of domestic service – although their moves into prostitution had usually been occasioned by a period of unemployment. As one doctor remarked, "they get out of place and they have nowhere to go and they adopt this as a last resort, as a means of livelihood; some go back to service and again return to the streets."[13] However, the 1871 census listings for women previously identified as common prostitutes in Plymouth indicates a more diverse occupational background. Of thirty-one

194

women between the ages of fifteen and twenty-nine who were traced to residences on three notorious streets in Plymouth, only two were actually listed as prostitutes and four as domestic servants, whereas the rest were listed as dressmakers, tailoresses, seamstreses, bookbinders, or as unemployed.[14] These listings were by no means an accurate reflection of their present occupational status–at their trials none of them claimed to be holding down respectable jobs; rather the listings may have reflected what they might have done in the apst and what they could expect to go back to when they finished their present career. The listings also represent an attempt to blend into the neighborhood–to give occupations appropriate to the working-class community in which they resided. These *were* the employment opportunities for workingwomen in Plymouth and Southampton; as milliners, dressmakers, tailoresses, domestic servants, or laundresses, young women would rarely earn more than six to eight shillings a week, working fourteen hours a day–barely half what a male day laborer would earn. And as "improvers," slopworkers, or general maids of all work they earned considerably less. Much of this employment was highly casual, structured around the demands of the local season and the provisioning trade. If living outside their families, these women were subject to periodic layoffs, and hard pressed to survive on their won without a "friend." Placed in a vulnerable economic and social position, some women who could not rely on family, relatives, or lovers may have found the shorter hours and better pay of prostitution a temporary and relatively attractive solution to their immediate difficulties.[15]

Indeed, the standard of living of prostitutes was perceptibly higher than that of other poor workingwomen. When the ships came in, a prostitute, even a sailor's woman, could easily earn the weekly wages of a respectable workingwoman in a day. Prostitutes had a room of their own; they dressed better; they had spending money and access to the pub, the principal facility in the working-class neighborhood that provided heat, light, cooked food, and convivial sociability.[16] Venereal disease and alcoholism were occupational hazards for these women, but they regarded their general standard of health as better than the dressmakers and laundresses who slaved away fourteen hours a day. Consumption, the disease generally associated with overwork and undernourishment, was the great killer of adult females, not syphilis.[17] But although the proceeds of prostitution raised the prostitutes' living standard to that of unskilled male workers, this by no means represented economic mobility out of the lower strata of the working class. Moreover, theirs was an unstable income, subject to the availability of clients. Finally, economic benefits have to be weighed against the ex-

195

posure and physical danger of the occupation as well as the likelihood of its diminishing profitability as the women aged. For practical and psychological reasons, most women were probably ill equipped to endure the rigors of the "profession" for more than a few years.[18]

Whereas periodic unemployment influenced women's move into prostitution, other seasonal factors were at work as well. Local police from dock and garrison towns reported an enormous increase of streetwalkers and disorderly behavior among prostitutes upon the arrival of ships or new regiments. Clearly the high profitability of prostitution at this time attracted women to the streets and the districts.[19]

For most "public" women prostitution represented only a temporary stage in their life. The age concentration of registered women in their early twenties supports the likelihood that they had had prior work experience outside the home as well as noncommercial sexual activity. In addition, registered women appear to have stayed in prostitution for only a few years, leaving in their mid-twenties at a critical point in their lives—when most working-class women were settling into some domestic situation with a man. The timing here is important, for as long as prostitution represented a temporary stage in a woman's career, and as long as she could leave it at her discretion, she was not irrevocably scarred or limited in her future choices.

Although the age of Plymouth and Southampton prostitutes fell within the normal age range for Victorian prostitutes, by 1871 registered women were concentrated in the older portion of that range. On the whole, registered women were a few years older than most new recruits to prostitution in towns where the acts were not in effect. The registration process had already begun to prolong their careers in prostitution and to deter younger women from going on the streets. Plymouth women, for example, were on the average four years older then the women placed on the register there in 1866.[20] They were also older than Southampton prostitutes in 1871: whereas 38 percent of Southampton women were under twenty-one, only 10 percent of registered women in the Devonport district were in the same age category.[21] The recent enforcement of the acts (1870) in Southampton probably accounts for this age difference: there was insufficient time for the acts to have had a significant impact on the lives of subjected women in the district or to have inhibited the recruitment of young women into prostitution.

Some information is available on the subsequent history of registered women. From all the public testimonies, the likelihood of their returning to respectable employment without leaving the two districts was small. Rather, women escaped registration in two ways. Some left the district entirely—with more than 70 percent of Southampton women (who could migrate to nearby urban areas) and 20 percent of Plymouth women exercising this option over the period in which the Contagious Diseases Acts were enforced.[22] Others, after a few years on the streets, tended to settle into a more permanent relationship with one or more sailors, living with them when they were in port, and drawing their half pay in their absence. They also sometimes supplemented that income with the proceeds of casual prostitution.[23] This pattern seems to have been widespread among sailors' prostitutes elsewhere and suggests prostitution's ambiguous relationship to working-class sexual and social norms.[24] As one observer noted, "concubinage" was "not only the door into prostitution, but also the door out of prostitution very often."[25]

Although prostitution represented a temporary stage in a woman's life, one would like to know whether she was rendered a social outcast during that transitional period. For prostitutes lived among the casual laboring poor, who were accustomed to hard times and who also had to make difficult, temporary accommodations to pressing social necessity. Poor neighbors were nonetheless of different minds about prostitutes. Some saw prostitution as a threatening and illegitimate form of social behavior. Others came to understand and tolerate prostitution as one of a series of strategies adopted by women to survive.

Plymouth and Southampton prostitutes resided in narrowly defined areas that were readily subject to police surveillance. In Plymouth, registered prostitutes inhabited the cramped streets and alleys radiating out of the Octagon, the pub and entertainment center of the Three Towns. The Octagon was centrally located on Union Street, Plymouth's major commercial thoroughfare. Here Plymouth prostitutes walked the streets in full view of respectable society, so much so that the wives of naval officers on their way to the penny bridge at East Stonehouse kept to the south side of Union Street, leaving the north side to public women and their customers.[26] In contrast, Southampton prostitutes were mostly concentrated in the Simnel Street neighborhood, a closed-in area without good access to the new commercial district.

These disreputable "low" streets were repeatedly condemned in the local newspapers as infested with brothels and as sanitary abominations. The connection between the physical condition of the streets and the immoral behavior of the inhabitants was made clear in the town clerk's quip following the conviction of Maria Stevens, Granby Street, Plymouth, for brothel keeping in 1872: "The clerk jocosely remarked that the street was very unhealthy, its level being as low as the sea, and the inhabitants still lower."[27]

197

Two case studies: Plymouth and Southampton

Although these streets were notorious as brothel districts, in reality a more diverse social and economic life was present there.[28] Residence on these streets was largely determined by economic necessity, although the general neighborhood tolerance of certain illegal or unrespectable behavior, as well as the availability of accommodations for transients, may have also attracted the large number of single men and women living outside their families.[29] Although highly visible, these young people formed a distinct minority of the street population. Most people lived in families; even in brothels, prostitutes were outnumbered by members of the brothel keeper's family and by other lodgers living in families. The family operated as the main support system among people who existed just at or below subsistence level, where all adults and most children were required to contribute to the family income.

For most residents of these neighborhoods, the conditions of casual employment not only enforced economic cohesion within the family, but also required men and women to oscillate between casual work in large governmental and commercial establishments and odd forms of self-employment. Hence, fluctuations in income and occupation were experiences that neighbors shared in common with prostitutes. In addition, residents often found themselves on the wrong side of the law as well as physically constrained by institutions like the workhouse, prison, or in the case of prostitutes, the lock hospital, that were used interchangeably for the confinement of the social deviant.[30]

The irregular pattern of these people's lives permitted and sometimes required a certain amount of geographic mobility. The movement of prostitutes and brothel keepers brought before the courts can be traced from one "furnished apartment" to another within a confined area. However, any "common" woman who ventured too far out of her neighborhood was highly suspect to the police, and the social isolation that existed among poor residents in different parts of town is striking. On the other hand, the summer exodus remained an established tradition among the Southampton and Plymouth poor. Although their migration into the towns was more or less permanent, this did not preclude an excursion during the summer to pick strawberries in Hampshire or to follow the fair circuit through Cornwall. Prostitutes also participated in the annual exodus: police noted that they regularly camped out in the summer and returned to town for the winter.[31]

The unstable economy of the area encouraged a high degree of predatory behavior among the local residents. As is the case today, most victims of crime were poor, and police columns of the news-

198

papers frequently carried stories of women stealing blankets, sheets and any other moveable items from their lodgings to be pawned. Seeking legal redress for stolen property, however, could be a tricky business. Poor complainants sometimes found themselves victims of a process they had initiated. This was the experience of Harriet Smith of Southampton, who had brought charges against Elizabeth Baker, a prostitute, for stealing a silk dress from her premises. Mrs. Smith let out rooms to Baker and to two other women in order to support herself and two children. "She made the women fine clothes," but this particular dress was stolen by Baker and pawned for seven shillings. Baker was sent to prison for one month; Mrs. Smith, for her part, was still required by the court to pay the seven shillings to the pawnbroker in return for the dress, as a way of penalizing her for her "life."[32]

Exploitative behavior also existed between prostitutes and their customers. Drunken brawls and petty thefts between women and their clients were frequent occurrences. Yet this mutual exploitation too had its limits, and from time to time a glimpse of class solidarity inadvertently emerges from the police columns. In 1878, for example, Mary Cousins and Mary Hearn, "two women well known to the police," were charged with stealing money from Henry Holl, a general laborer, at a lodging house in Southampton. Holl had accompanied Cousins to her house, had fallen asleep, and was awakened "by hearing the two women disagreeing about money, one of them remarking to the other, you should not have cleaned the poor man out like that, for he is a working man!" A clear implication of the discussion was that if Holl had been a rich swell no such moral qualms would have obtained.[33]

Poor residents also adhered to standards of sexual and social behavior that were in sharp contrast to conventional Victorian mores. In 1882, the local clergyman of St. Peter's parish, Plymouth, asked his lady visitor to report on the moral condition of one of the streets in his parish. The street surveyed contained no lodging-house brothel but was adjacent to the notorious prostitute district. In her report, the lady visitor noted that many female residents who professed to be "respectable" were actually living with men out of wedlock. Most of the women had formerly been married, had been deserted or had exercised the traditional working-class option of self-divorce, and had subsequently established a new relationship with another man. To the shock and consternation of the lady visitor, the women defended the propriety of their action. "I," for example, had "three children by different fathers. Now living with a sailor, and passes for a married woman; says she is not ashamed of her baby – she never professed to be a Christian, and is not so bad as many that do make a profession." "W" was equally unrepentant. She was "married at registry office to a man whose wife is living, and argues that it is all right, as he first wife is remarried, and wrote a letter to give him leave to follow her example."[34]

This flexible view of marriage and sexual respectability partially underlay the neighborhood toleration of prostitutes. The lady visitor also uncovered extensive financial connections between prostitutes and their more respectable neighbors. Some were "dressmakers to the girls," whereas others had relatives directly involved in the trade. "S," for example, "Seems to be living respectably now, but has her mother's likeness framed with the text round it 'Blessed are the dead that die in the Lord.' You remember the case. Mother kept a bad house."[35]

The economy of prostitution on these streets hardly appears to have been highly formalized or rationalized: women were self-employed, paying only rent to lodging-house keepers, who nonetheless made larger profits off prostitutes than other lodgers, charging them anywhere from three shillings and sixpence a week for room only to thirteen shillings for room and board. Still, it would be incorrect to characterize the older women in charge of "disreputable" lodgings as the exploitative professionals generally associated with the term "brothel keepers." They were largely women with families, left to shift for themselves. Taking in lodgers represented one of the few ways that women could support their family. These women did not own the houses; they rented them from male landlords. And at least four Plymouth and Southampton women pleaded in court that they ran brothels to "keep the children off the parish."[36]

Despite many shared experiences, prostitutes remained distinct from the social profile of their neighborhood in a number of ways. First, as mentioned earlier, their standard of living was perceptibly higher than that of other women. Second, their living arrangements also set them apart. Young women residing in lodgings appear strikingly cut off from the family system that was the organizing social and economic principle of these streets. Not only were they residing outside their families, but they were living independent of lovers and children as well. Prostitutes tended to form personal attachments with sailors who were not permanently in residence. As a consequence, sailors could not exercise the same kind of control over their women's lives as men who habitually lived off the wages of sin.[37]

When not residing with their families, their lovers, or their own children, prostitutes did have female companions. Single women

200

tended to live together in clusters of three or four in a few residences on Southampton streets and scattered throughout the notorious Plymouth streets. These groups formed the basis of an important and supportive female subculture. Most prostitutes were recruited into prostitution by other women – a process that is best understood as a system of access and initiation similar to that operating in other occupations.[38] Prostitutes usually walked the streets together in twos and threes, both to protect themselves against physical abuse and to insulate themselves from the harassments of young boys. Repealers who visited their neighborhood made a special note of the "kindness and sympathy of those poor girls towards each other and their anxiety to aid and assist each other when in distress of any kind . . ."[39]

Hence, prostitutes resided in special working-class districts as part of a distinct female subgroup. They lived among a very poor population that stood to benefit substantially from their commerce. It may be that many residents tolerated prostitutes more out of financial need than out of any strong sympathy and understanding of the women's plight. Yet this toleration easily wore thin if official pressure was brought to bear on neighbors and relatives who led very fragile social and economic lives.

The impact of the C.D. acts

In their struggle for survival, the very poor maintained a delicate balance between private interest and public responsibility, between toleration and the segregation of marginal social behavior. This fragile social equilibrium was upset by the enforcement of the Contagious Diseases Acts. On the one hand, the acts generated an extensive public resistance movement among the women and their community. On the other hand, by forcing prostitutes and their neighbors publicly to acknowledge what had been informally tolerated marginal behavior, they may well have forced a stricter redefinition of permissible behavior, thereby heightening the social isolation of prostitutes.

Among the prostitutes themselves one may observe a shift in attitudes and self-perception, forced upon them by the public exposure of the police registration and examination procedures. This is most plainly seen in the women's reaction to the periodical examination. Their vehement hostility to the internal examination may have partially been a reaction to the brutality of the doctors, as feminists alleged. No more than three minutes was spent on each examination; the instruments may have still been hot from immersion in boiling water (if they were sterilized at all).[40] And of course, a tense, resistant woman could find the examination by speculum painful. Annie Clark found the examination "painful" and "disgraceful" and declared, "I would rather spend fourteen years in prison than submit to it."[41] Elizabeth Hounsom, who held the record for multiple jailings – five – for refusing to attend examination, also maintained she preferred imprisonment to the "degradation" of the examination: "She tore the summons up when it was served upon her and did not appear at her fifth trial."[42] Another woman who vowed to go to prison rather than to submit to examination told Josephine Butler, "We ought all to show the officers that we have some respect for our own persons."[43]

Like the middle-class feminists, registered women regarded the periodic examination as a peculiarly unnatural and degrading experience, a form of "instrumental" rape.[44] When a repeal agent asked two women the difference "between exposing themselves to any man who came to have connexion with them and showing themselves to the doctor," they turned upon him "fiercely" and replied:

> I should have thought you'd have known better nor that. Ain't one in the way of natur', and the other ain't natur' at all. Ain't it a different thing what a woman's obliged to do for a living because she has to keep body and soul together, and going up there to be pulled about by a man as if you was cattle and hadn't no feeling, and to have an instrument pushed up you, not to make you well (because you ain't ill) but just that men may come to you and use you to thersils [sic].[45]

Nonetheless it would be misleading to dwell exclusively upon the brutal and sadistic character of the examination; more subtle means for humiliation were built into the whole procedure. In a society so profoundly class-bound as that of England, an examining physician would have had to do or say very little to make a registered woman feel worthless and degraded. The examination was demeaning because of its public character. Streetwalking at night was one thing; being forced to attend examination during the day, often taunted on the way by young boys who loudly questioned whether the woman were going up to the "Bougie Fair" or the "meat market," was another.[46] One woman confided to a female missionary that "it was no use trying to reform now, she was registered as a prostitute and everybody would know what she had been doing, and what she was. Going up for examination, she said, was worse than going with 20 men ..."[47] The domiciliary visitation by the police and the central location of the examination house made it impossible for a subject woman to keep her private and public worlds apart. This is what destroyed her "self respect."

202

The making of an outcast group

In this way the acts forced prostitutes to adjust their self-images. Repealers complained that the acts hardened the women by forcing many "who may not have made up their mind to continue as prostitutes" to acknowledge their outcast status. Although women appealing for legal aid to repealers made no attempt to hide the fact that they had been prostitutes, some certainly evidenced a strong ambivalence about their past and even expressed confusion as to what it meant to be a prostitute. Clearly the categories of acceptable social and sexual behavior were not that well defined. Harriet Hicks is a case in point.

When asked at her trial in 1870 whether she was still a prostitute, Hicks responded, "No, only to the one man." A sympathetic magistrate then intervened and explained to her, "You mean that you are not a prostitute, other than as living with one man without marriage?" to which Hicks meekly replied, "Yes, that's what I mean."[48] Hicks's confused response that she was a prostitute "only to the one man" suggests that she may not have understood the question – that the very word "prostitute" might have been foreign to her general usage. One must question whether a poor woman's testimony before a middle-class audience truly reflected her private self-estimation. It is unlikely that prostitutes fully internalized the notion of being "fallen" when they knew they could "rise" again. Moral reformers and rescue agencies appear to have failed to elicit any inner compulsion to be consistent in their public and private lives. Rather, these women seem to have effected a practical and psychological compartmentalization of their lives, except when subjected to concerted public stigmatization.

In fact, public shaming was one of the principal functions of police registration and surveillance. The "water police" made daily visits to known brothels; there they obtained the name of new arrivals and endeavored to place these women on the register. In many ways, they resembled both an occupying military force billeted on a subject population as well as a general morals police. Inspector Anniss actually lived above the examination house on Flora Street in Plymouth, around the corner from the most notorious Plymouth streets. Over the years, he was frequently called upon to testify at divorce cases, affiliation cases, and petty theft cases where a woman's character had to be ascertained.[49] Likewise, after the acts were suspended in 1883, James Disberry, a former metropolitan police constable, was actually hired as a rescue agent because of his intimate knowledge of the women.[50]

Through their surveillance and harassment the police made it impossible for a woman, once placed on the register, to have her name removed unless she left the district or married. Women complained

203

bitterly of the "policemen a hunting you up . . . coming to your house, threatening you, and letting all the people around know what you are. If you wants to live quietly in your neighborhood, you can't do so. I've shifted more than once, but they were soon after you ordering you up to that beastly place."[51] A Devonport magistrate, generally sympathetic to the acts but concerned about police intimidation, cited the case of Bessie Blewitt, who had abandoned prostitution and had gone to live with a man in a private house. In investigating the basis for her request to be removed from the register, the police went "several times to this house, where, in every probability . . . the persons she was lodging with would refuse to allow her to remain," forcing her back into a brothel.[52] Indeed, according to the magistrate, Mr. Ryder, numerous women testified in court that they were remaining in brothels because they could not get any other place. This locked them into public registration as a prostitute. In the case of Elizabeth Bond, the justices said that "while she was lodging at a brothel the presumption was . . . that she was engaged in prostitution."[53]

Numerous cases were reported to the Royal Commission of 1871 that demonstrated the obstacles women encountered in extricating themselves from prostitution under the acts. These cases also underscored the difficulty faced by any member of the laboring-poor community seeking to help the women in establishing bona fide respectable credentials before the law. Such was the dilemma of Eliza Kemp, who "took the line upwards from prostitution" by settling down with a sailor, but who was nonetheless interfered with by the police. "Her story was that, 12 months ago she was a prostitute but from that time had been living with a man named Martin, who had gone to sea, leaving her an allotment of £2 a month, and that is strong evidence in her favour. That is looked upon as nearly as good as marriage among that class." Police charged her with going with another man and the repealers took up her case. Like Harriet Hicks, the woman appeared helpless before the complexity of the legal entanglements as well as reluctant to implicate her friends. "Now it is curious when we first asked this poor girl whether she had any witnesses, and what her defense was, and it is was only by suggesting and pressing her with questions that we dug out of her where she lived, and who her friends were, and at last we found they were most valuable witnesses." In fact, when observed by the police, Kemp had been in the company of a Mr. and Mrs. Thornton, who themselves were discredited as unrespectable, hence unreliable, witnesses by the prosecution. On cross-examination Mrs. Thornton admitted she "was not married to Thornton, but she had lived with him for six years and had two children by

204

him." Speaking of Mrs. Thornton's position, the repeal spokesman noted, "that whole class is one in which marriage is an exception; but on the other hand, it is extremely important that any remnant of decency remaining should be taken hold of and respected . . ."[54]

The resistance of registered women and their community to the acts must be seen in the light of the economic and legal sanctions applied against those who tried to protect registered women. In the case of the Plymouth area, perhaps the police's greatest weapon was their power to inform against governmental employees and naval pensioners who let out rooms to prostitutes. If a pensioner proved uncooperative, his pension could be stopped, dock laborers and artisans could be dismissed, and pubs and beer shops harboring diseased prostitutes could be placed "out of bounds" for the men in service.[55] The police also established a certain "discipline" among the unrespectable poor; brothel keepers brought to court on the complaints of moral reformers were sometimes exposed as police spies, reporting any new woman who took a room to the police in order to buy protection.[56]

It is thus impressive that 420 cases of violation of the C.D. acts were brought before the Southampton magistrates between 1870 and 1877, whereas the Three Towns, where government influence was far stronger, had 118 such cases, 75 of them occurring between 1870 and 1871.[57] These cases represent only a small portion of the women refusing to attend examination during the periods of intense political resistance. In these early years, the resistance of subjected women was stimulated by repeal agitation and offers of legal assistance, but the women also received substantial support from members of the laboring-poor community.

The collective and individual support accorded prostitutes by their friends and neighbors underscores the role of women in those neighborhoods. Women seem to have been the organizing force behind public demonstrations in the defense of registered women. In their response to the Contagious Diseases Acts, they appear motivated by personal sympathy for the plight of a neighbor as well as by hostility toward the metropolitan police as interlopers in their community. Nonetheless the women of the community were clearly divided in their reaction toward registered women. Some bitterly opposed the presence of prostitutes on the streets. And even respectable women who aided prostitutes appeared ambivalent toward registered women; in some cases a deep resentment against the "water police" may well have overpowered a certain repugnance and distance they felt toward prostitutes.

Many of the women who intervened on behalf of registered women

205

were prostitutes or brothel keepers themselves, but repeal workers also reported complaints by "poor but respectable neighbors" of the "heartless way in which the girls [brought under the acts] were treated."[58] When the police tried to apprehend Mary Ann Ferris of Granby Street, two of her female friends struggled to release her from their custody, while a sympathetic and curious crowd assembled that "became large and followed the policemen and the women through the most public streets to Devonport [where the lock hospital was located]."[59] In addition, popular support for the women and hostility to the police was manifested in the courtroom. For instance, the acquittal of Inspector Anniss in 1876 from the charge of molesting a virtuous young shopgirl was met with "a perfect storm of indignation and the Bench was literally hissed and howled at from all parts of the Court, and particularly from the crowded gallery." The newspaper account specifically noted the behavior of women in the mob: "Men and women – indeed, the *women seemed ten times more fierce than the men* – stamped their feet, shook their fists and fairly grinned at the magistrates, and the Court ultimately broke up in confusion" (emphasis added).[60]

Women brought under the acts were often assisted by individual neighbors: hidden when police came, lent money, or permitted to pay their rent when they had the money. In 1883, at the trial of Mrs. Lang of 11 Central Street, Plymouth, for brothel keeping, Ellen de Courcy was asked how much she paid for her room: "She took a room from Mrs. Lang and paid her what she could."[61] Although this may have perpetuated a system of indebtedness to brothel keepers,[62] it also reflects the tradition of mutual aid among the poor, who understood much better than most middle-class reformers and philanthropists the character of seasonal and irregular employment and the hazards of poverty.

Female neighbors not only protected women from the police; they were also instrumental in aiding young women's escape. Since 1870 there had existed in Plymouth a kind of underground railway that spirited women out of the district to rescue homes in London. The local rescue worker indicated that two-thirds of the young women who applied for help had been found or brought there by poor women.[63] Lodging-house keepers often assisted in prostitutes' escape, although they may have been instrumental in bringing these young women into the trade. R. B. Williams, of the Rescue Society of London, reported one instance where a "lodging house keeper, more merciful than the agents of the law" had hidden two new arrivals in a cupboard and

206

with a transient compunction of conscience or with a desire to compound for other misdoings, which I have not unfrequently seen amongst this class, took the two girls the same night to a benevolent person at Plymouth, who has frequently sent girls to the Rescue Society, remarking, "These poor things are very unhappy-minded about theirselves [sic] and, as they will soon be made as bad as others if they go up to Flora Lane [the examination house], I shall be glad if you will try to get them into a Refuge, or anywhere where they can get respectable again . . ."[64]

Prostitutes also maintained important relations with their families. Many of these young women had left home for financial reasons; hence, on a day-to-day level these women were expected to rely on themselves. Nonetheless the aid they could receive in times of crisis was a testimony to the enduring family support that persisted. Thus although a number of young girls were apparently orphans, they could still depend on a series of female relatives when faced with legal prosecution. At their trials aunts, mothers, and married sisters who resided in town or in the neighboring countryside would appear and testify on their behalf, often at great personal sacrifice. Bessie Bunker's mother was threatened with being prosecuted under the Contagious Diseases Acts if she tried to protect her daughter.[65] In addition to their supportive presence at trials, relatives defended these women in other ways. Some relatives promised to take the women away if they were taken off the police register. Others like Fanny Churchward's mother and Mary Jeffries physically defended their daughters from the police.[66] The parents of Mary Ann Ferris, Jane Jeffries, and Alice Osman were identified as "consenting parents" who encouraged their daughters in prostitution and ran brothels themselves.[67]

Some parents were not sympathetic. The fathers of Mary Ann Holman, Emma Edwards, Jessie Clarke, and Elizabeth Baker would not take them back.[68] Some could not afford to have them return home, as in the case of Mary Hayles's mother, who explained that her husband was an unemployed laborer.[69] The rejection of these marked women was often the consequence of social and economic constraints. In one case, a young woman who had left prostitution and returned to her family was still required by the police to submit to examination. Threatened with the loss of her stepfather's job with the Southampton Corporation if she refused to sign the voluntary submission, she eventually complied although it meant exclusion from her family: "So at last I signed, and was then examined, and as father had said, I shouldn't stay at home as I was brought under the examination."[70]

In the face of glaring publicity, the women's support from neigh-

207

bors, relatives, and friends inevitably crumbled. Many landladies experienced the same ambivalence toward subjected women as the latter's relatives. A basic concern over public respectability recurs in several cases. What bothered respectable neighbors was not the "immorality" of a young woman as much as the notoriety gained by police visits and the economic sanctions that could result.[71]

A significant portion of the local community was hostile to prostitutes from the start, although their antagonism may have been exacerbated by the police and examination system. A petition to the Home Office in 1870 from forty-five inhabitants of the neighborhood surrounding the Southampton examining house complained that "their feelings have been outraged and scandalized, and their interest in many cases injured" by the placement of the examination house in their neighborhood.[72] In general, local "matriarchs" acted as the voice of righteous indignation in the neighborhood, objecting to the presence of "bad" women as well as the scandal of the examination in their vicinity. One woman commented that the "neighbours made it a rule to shut themselves indoors until it [examination hours] was all over."[73] Another woman expressed concern that children had begun imitating examining procedures: "My little girl came to me the other day and asked me what the young women went into the examining house for; she understood they went in there to undress."[74] Mothers were equally distressed over the invidious comparison their impressionable offspring drew from the greater affluence of prostitutes and the lesser income of respectable workingwomen. Children outside the examination house were overheard discussing: "It is more than mother got who went out washing. My mother is out now, one little girl said, and will be tired to death. Wait a bit and I shall go as well, and my mother shall not go out to wash like that . . . and they live better than we do. See how fine they dress, and they get more than we do."[75]

One can only speculate on the feelings of certain groups in these working-class communities who remained silent in the midst of the C.D. acts controversy. Young workingwomen who were not prostitutes articulated very little public response to the acts, although they may have participated in crowd activity on the streets and some may have signed the petitions against the acts that were circulated in these neighborhoods. Like the indignant married women cited above, young single women who chose to eke out a pitiful though respectable living may well have resented the flamboyant dress and easy spending habits of prostitutes. Part of their reticence may also have stemmed from motives of self-preservation, inasmuch as association with prostitutes

208

rendered a woman's character suspect to the police and could lead to her name being placed on the registration list. One milliner who actually left Plymouth because of the system of police intimidation claimed that malicious neighbors contributed to this reign of terror by threatening "you with the Water Police." She also noted that the general neighborhood response to subjected women was condemnatory: "When girls are arrested, all look on them with disdain; some perhaps with pity."[76]

Although police officers acknowledged that registered women subsequently experienced difficulty in obtaining respectable employment, the social exclusion of these women from the general poor community may have more seriously disrupted the normal pattern of their lives. Of special significance was the abandonment of women by their lovers in the military services. To be sure, at the height of legal resistance in Plymouth in the summer of 1870, seven men defended their women in court; they claimed they were living monogamously with the accused, although they frequently acknowledged that these women had checkered pasts. But not all workingmen responded in this way. Esther Levi, Elizabeth Bond, Matilda Brown, and Lavinia Lambert all pleaded in court that their men had either abandoned them or refused to marry them until they were taken off the register.[77] The metropolitan police seemed to have actively harassed some of the men: Maria Barnett's fiancé, a sailor, was upbraided by Inspector Anniss for planning to marry a prostitute.[78] In addition police were known to report an enlisted man's liaison with a prostitute to his commanding officer.[79]

By 1883, when the Contagious Diseases Acts were suspended, the character of prostitution in Plymouth and Southampton appears to have been distinctly altered. The women subjected to the acts were clearly getting older; much larger numbers were in the over-30 category. In the Devonport district, 106 out of 403 (26.3 percent) "known common women" were listed as thirty-one years and older for 1881, although there had been only 54 out of 557 (9.7 percent) in this age group in 1870. Southampton showed a similar trend: 4 out of 154 (2.6 percent) in 1870, as opposed to 20 out of 110 (18.2 percent) in 1881. Similarly, lock-hospital records document the increasing recidivist rate of registered women admitted to the lock wards throughout the 1870s. Hospital authorities acknowledged that their rehabilitation program only worked at all effectively with first-timers – women who had not yet entered upon a professional career of prostitution.[80]

Contemporary reports confirm this trend toward professionalization. Both repealers and C.D. acts authorities noted that women were staying longer in prostitution, but predictably they disagreed on the

209

reasons for this trend. Police officials tended to stress the improved health and increased longevity of prostitutes under the acts; repealers emphasized the stigma attached to being a registered woman. The latter also acknowledged that the women who remained in the districts profited from the system and bragged about being "Queen's women" – sanctioned by the government. What the change does suggest is that prostitution had become more profitable; because of police surveillance the amateur dollymops had been "deterred" and a streamlined, rationalized "work force" resulted. Also, as prostitutes became public figures through the registration process, it became increasingly difficult for them to gain respectable employment, and to move in and out of their other social identities.[81]

The changing character of prostitution

The history of the women of Southampton and Plymouth suggests the process by which working-class prostitutes were transformed into a specially identified professional class. But most of the accumulated evidence on subjected women presents a picture of poor women integrated rather than excluded from the community of the casual laboring poor. The eventual isolation of prostitutes from general lower-class life was largely imposed from above, although it received the passive acquiescence of the poor themselves.

It may well be that the experience of registered women was symptomatic of important and long-term changes in working-class life: a growing inflexibility in social norms and habits, a restriction in occupational identities and personal mobility. The isolation of a separate criminal class may have been a necessary corollary to the increasing social and legal pressures placed upon the poor to adhere to a more rigid standard of public respectability. Thus, it could be argued that the Contagious Diseases Acts, by establishing an unusually effective system of police surveillance and public stigmatization, simply accelerated a process occurring more slowly elsewhere. Criminal statistics for the late nineteenth century lend support to this thesis. The changing composition of registered women anticipates the national trend toward a general narrowing down of "antisocial" behavior among a smaller but more readily identifiable group of women – as indicated by declining arrest rates for women for both summary and indictable crimes, and by increased recidivism among women prisoners, who increasingly were to be found in older age categories.[82]

Some indications of the changing character and dimensions of prostitution may be observed as well. If criminal statistics for the early twenti-

210

eth century and the post-World War I periods are compared, in London, for instance, there was a notable decline in arrest rates for "known prostitutes," a change in the occupational background for those imprisoned, as well as increased recidivism among those imprisoned.

These changes were in part the result of new repressive public sanctions that stigmatized prostitutes and contributed to their social isolation as forcibly as the C.D. acts. The suspension of the acts in 1883 and their full repeal in 1886 extinguished any hope police might have cherished of using the acts to institute a national system of regulation, with formal brothels that would contain prostitution within carefully demarcated areas of cities. For some time the police in cities like Plymouth, Cardiff, and Liverpool tried to contain prostitutes in segregated districts. However, under pressure from social-purity groups in the last decades of the nineteenth century, police were forced to resort to an alternative policy of suppressing street solicitation and closing brothels.[83] These repressive activities were facilitated by two new pieces of legislation – the Industrial Schools Amendment Act of 1880 and the Criminal Law Amendment Act of 1885. The Industrial School Amendment Act enabled police to remove children summarily from brothels and place them in industrial schools. Its intent was blackmail; working-class families were to be prevented from taking in prostitutes to supplement the family income, on pain of losing their children. Additionally, the Criminal Law Amendment Act of 1885 provided for easy summary proceedings against brothel keepers. Like the C.D. acts, these new measures helped to drive a wedge between prostitutes and their community. They were even more effective at destroying the brothel as a family industry, undermining the social and economic autonomy of prostitutes, and increasingly rendering them social outcasts.[84]

Between 1890 and 1914, the systematic repression of lodging-house brothels was carried out in almost every major city in Great Britain. These clean-up campaigns were generally instigated in response to local pressure by social-purity groups.[85] Purity crusades of this sort were conducted in Plymouth in 1904 and 1905, and the prostitute area in Southampton was deliberately cleared to make way for "civic improvements" in the 1890s.[86] In many locales the legal repression dramatically affected the structure and organization of prostitution. Prostitutes were uprooted from their neighborhoods and had to find lodgings in other areas of the city and in the periphery.[87] Their activity became more covert and furtive. Cut off from any other sustaining relationship, they increasingly were forced to rely on pimps for emotional security and for protection against legal authorities. This trend was noted with alarm by police and judicial authorities at the time. In

211

1895 one London magistrate waxed indignant at the self-righteous actions of vigilance committees, who were forcing prostitutes into the hands of pimps. The recent increase in the numbers of bullies, he maintained,

> has to a great extent been caused by those, who, in their excessive zeal, have made it impossible for a prostitute to live in apartments without a man living with her who appears to be her husband. The result of this has been that almost every prostitute is under the control of some bully who causes her to be a thief as well as a prostitute.[88]

Of course, pimps were not always the wicked villains that public officials and purity advocates made them out to be. A husband or lover often drifted into being a "bully . . . much as women . . . drift into prostitution. It is a refuge from uneasy circumstance."[89] In return for their keep, pimps provided some practical and emotional services: "Prostitutes like to have a man with them whose presence enables them to get apartments, to have protection from robbery and violence, and to have companionship in their off-time."[90] Even so, the prevalence of pimps in the early twentieth century meant that prostitution had shifted from a female to a male-dominated trade and that there now existed third parties with a strong interest in prolonging women's stay on the streets.

Thus, by the outbreak of World War I, the organization of prostitution had undergone significant changes, mostly as the result of legal repression. Other long-term social and economic changes also helped to constrict the market for prostitution. Such trends began in the nineteenth century but culminated in the 1920s. The demand for commercial sex seems to have diminished by the postwar period, both because of the competition of "amateurs" and because of a decline in the unmarried transient male population.[91] A similar decline in the "supply" seems to have taken place as well, a result of the economic transformation of the casual laboring-poor community. Historians have argued that decasualization in the late nineteenth century, and especially after World War I, transformed the life-style of the urban lower classes, affording the unskilled steadier incomes and higher real incomes. Despite high unemployment rates in postwar years, chronic casual poverty—which was the basic precondition for the kind of prostitution found in nineteenth-century cities like Plymouth and Southampton—had largely been eliminated by industrialization, a rise in real wages, and a decline in the birthrate and in overcrowding.[92]

Nevertheless, it is unclear what the net effect of this improved living standard was for women. It may well have afforded women greater

212

economic opportunity to support themselves, inasmuch as the real wages for women substantially exceeded prewar levels and increased mechanization expanded their employment opportunities.[93] But it also may have made men more viable as supporters of the family, whether as husbands or fathers. The decline in mortality and birthrates and the easing of overcrowding may have helped strengthen the lower-class family unit, perhaps making it more possible for young women to remain at home longer. These developments may have further contributed to a privatized, home-centered culture and stimulated lower-class antagonism toward women who supported themselves as "public women."

More stringent public sanctions against unrespectable social behavior as well as economic access to the means of maintaining a respectable life-style seem to have had a decided impact on public prostitutes, poor workingwomen, and working-class culture in general. Decasualization may have meant higher real incomes and greater economic security, but also a significant loss of autonomy. As a result, the lower strata of the working class would be permanently enclosed within city walls, within the home, and within the bounds of respectable behavior, whereas the poverty and prostitution that persisted would be more invisible, isolated, and desperately anonymous.[94] The history of Southampton and Plymouth prostitutes suggests the early outlines of this process, for their ultimate isolation from the community of the laboring poor marked an important formative stage in the making of an outcast group.

11 *The hospitals*

On January 1, 1873, Julia Clark, a lock-ward patient at the Royal Portsmouth Hospital, complained "of the quality of the soup and potatoes given [inmates] for their dinner" and began to throw the plates and tableware about. The resident matron admitted that the soup was watery and managed to quiet the room. The next day, further disturbances broke out in the same ward, and three women were locked in dark cells. That night, the rioting erupted anew; when it had ended two days later, the police had arrested seven women and eight others had been locked in confinement cells.

Five days after the commencement of the "soup" riot, Inspector Sloggett arrived at the hospital to investigate. He carefully interviewed each refractory patient "first alone, in her place of confinement, to hear her complaints" and "to take measures for her immediate re-lease." He found Julia Clark sitting on a bed in a small room without light, with an untouched pile of bread and butter next to her. She had been in the room for five days, and Sloggett now described her as "contrite and submissive." She insisted that she had no complaints, except in reference to the soup and potatoes, although she was visibly disappointed at not receiving her discharge.

Sloggett then visited two other women in confinement cells. Laura Lewis, who had protested because a letter she was expecting had been withheld, had been in the "dark" room for three consecutive days. "As soon as the door was opened, I saw lying on the bare floor what seemed a huddled mass of woman's clothing; the woman 'Laura Lewis,' lying with her garments rolled over her head just inside the door; fragments of earthen ware strewed about, and farther back the floor sloppy and dirty: the cell contained no utensil for personal wants." Next he dis-covered Violet Hill, who had complained of harsh treatment by the surgeon, in a room upstairs filled with broken glass. She had no clothes or furniture with her and had also been confined there for three con-secutive days. She was so battered by the experience (reacting with what

Sloggett called such "obstinacy and false shame") that she asked to remain in the "room" rather than return to the ward.[1]

After further questioning, the meaning of the "soup riot" became clear. The resident medical officer had been "too readily disposed to adopt coercive measures in the repression of any acts of insubordination." Because he felt some of the women had been "saucy" with him, the doctor had refused to examine them the next week. Angry and disappointed, the women lashed out at the conditions most immediately intolerable: watery soup, restricted access to their mail, and generally harsh treatment. Fundamental, though, was a simple desire to get out. As Sloggett wrote later, "I have found that many are discontented at what they think is often an unnecessary detention after they are fit to be discharged. I have to believe that most of the riots in the Hospital originate in a wish to go out on the part of some one or other of the ringleaders."[2] It was no coincidence that the day after Sloggett's arrival Laura Lewis was declared cured and discharged.

Sloggett was clearly shaken by his visit and appalled at the way the hospital staff had handled the disturbance. This was not the first time he had had cause to find fault with the hospital management. Riots occurred annually at the Royal Portsmouth, and Admiralty inspectors regularly complained of the insanitary state of the lock wards. Only four months earlier, Sloggett had described Portsmouth as the "worst" lock hospital under his supervision; on that visit he had found the patients untidy, facilities dirty, and the nurses understaffed and inefficient.[3]

Two weeks after the "soup riot," Sloggett made a tour of inspection of the Royal Albert Hospital in Devonport. There, order and cleanliness prevailed. The women had "no complaints" about their treatment and many seemed anxious to abandon their former life. The contrast between the Royal Albert and the chaos at Portsmouth could not be more striking: "It seems difficult to believe that the two establishments can be conducted and maintained by similar governing boards and on the same principle in reference to their position with the Board of Admiralty."[4]

The hospitals as moral and social institutions

The Royal Albert and the Royal Portsmouth (where Southampton and Portsmouth women were interned) hospitals were both civil hospitals that operated lock wards under the supervision of the Admiralty.[5] Both functioned as confinement institutions under the acts; their principal purpose was to isolate women until they were either "cured" of venereal disease or they were past the contagious stage. The same class

215

of patients was interned in their lock wards and placed under the supervision of a professional staff that relied on the same pathology to diagnose and treat their ailments.

Nonetheless, the facilities and custodial policy of the two institutions differed markedly. In 1863, a general survey of provincial and metropolitan hospitals found the Portsmouth Hospital totally deficient: built like a private house in 1849, the wards were "mere chambers, none of them having any through ventilation."[6] The internal discipline of the lock wards also reflected this slipshod character. Despite persistent outbreaks by lock-ward inmates, hospital authorities were slow to tighten their controls on the women and to institute a more consistent and rationalized regime. After the "soup riot" of 1873, a succession of resident medical officers did endeavor to introduce disciplinary procedures. Their efforts invariably ended in disaster. When Portsmouth authorities tried to enact a correspondence rule comparable to the one in effect at the Royal Albert since 1866, another riot broke out. As Inspector Sloggett noted at the time, the rule worked at the Royal Albert because the patients were used to it.[7] Anarchy reigned at Portsea, and the women had grown accustomed to the freedom and latitude that resulted. In 1873, soon after the "soup riot," Dr. O'Connor complained to the Admiralty that he was fighting a systematic attempt by the women to control the hospital. O'Connor had been appointed chief medical officer there on January 1, 1873, "under very difficult and trying conditions." Formerly, patients could roam about at will. The new regulations he tried to institute met with strong organized resistance:

> The worst characters feeling this change very much as a place where they formerly ruled Supreme, have commenced lately to organize a regular series of rows in the wards, such as smashing windows, crockery ware, etc., openly boasting that my predecessor had been removed because they made rows in the wards and I should have to leave for the same reason; and that my successor will allow them to do as they please once more.[8]

According to O'Connor, he received little support from local authorities. The bench gave refractory inmates only seven to fourteen days for the "most outrageous conduct." As a consequence, the offenders "openly make light of such punishment." Finally he complained that the hospital staff was inadequate to deal with this spirit of insurrection; each nurse had patients in three separate sections, so that when she attended those in one section "they commenced to smash things in the one she has left."[9] To deal with the present rebellion, he had used confinement cells and even asked permission to cut off the hair of any

216

refractory patient, as was done in the Vienna hospital—a request that, sensibly, was denied by Admiralty authorities.[10]

Inspector Sloggett, in one of his private reports to the Admiralty, gave another side of the picture. He attributed most of the problems there to the boredom of the women and to inept management. When later that year he visited Portsmouth without prior warning, he found the lock wards quiet and orderly with "some [women] reading or working but the majority with nothing to do."[11]

For the next ten years, disturbances continued to erupt at Portsmouth with greater frequency and intensity than at any other lock facility certified under the acts. Admiralty officials were at a loss to explain these persistent outbreaks, but they tended to blame the indifferent performance of the staff. In his reports on later riots, Inspector Sloggett complained that the hospital staff, particularly the matron, had made no effort to relate personally to the women and to win their respect and confidence. They had failed, in effect, to adopt the strategy of control advocated by "progressive" reformers—the replacement of visible forms of restraint with the bonds of obligation and personal attachment to figures of authority.[12]

The Royal Albert, in contrast, was a model Victorian institution, where discipline was more consistent, rationalized, and hence more effective. The same 1863 hospital survey that found the Portsmouth Hospital deficient warmly praised the plans for the Royal Albert. The building, dedicated in 1863, was a monument to Victorian revivalist taste—a dark, gloomy, gray stone edifice in the Renaissance style, very much resembling the fortresslike urban *palazzi* of Florence. The *Illustrated London Times* admired its view and situation: "From the windows in the western wing will be obtained one of the most beautiful panoramic views probably in the west of England, the harbour, the stupendous bridge at Saltash, with the chains of hills in the distance"[13]—a view the women in the lock wards would be able to enjoy only until 1869, when the glass in their windows was made opaque and barred.[14]

The Royal Albert was to be a modern facility, equipped with all advanced medical and nursing techniques. House surgeons were to be "Doctors or Bachelors of Medicine of one of the Universities of the United Kingdom, or Fellows or Members of the Royal College of Physicians of London practicing exclusively as Physicians."[15] Plans were underway for a training school for nurses "under the Nightingale system." As such, the Royal Albert stood as the symbol of local munificence and advanced scientific thought—a substantial incarnation of Victorian philanthropy. All the military and civic dignitaries of Devon-

217

port served on the board of governors. The charity was a corporation whose investments reflected the commercial and transportational boom of the mid-Victorian period; its major investments were in railroad stock, particularly the South Devon Railway, whose chairman was Thomas Woollcombe.[16]

From its beginning, however, the Royal Albert was caught up in a double identity: as a general hospital "supported by voluntary contributions" – a motto emblazoned on its facade to this day – and as an institution built and subsidized by the Admiralty, inextricably bound up with the fortunes of the Contagious Diseases Acts. The Royal Albert diligently tried to promote its first image. Nonetheless, the insubordination of its medical officers, the public attacks by repealers, the periodic riots of the women interned in the lock wards, and the public knowledge of the massive subsidies received from the Admiralty drew attention to its other official capacity.

As a general hospital, the Royal Albert was expected to tend to the needs of the deserving poor in Devonport, to offer them an alternative to the workhouse infirmary. Its ticket system for admission also provided the social elite of Devonport with an important avenue for dispensing patronage: for an annual fee of one guinea, subscribers were allowed to recommend one inpatient or twelve outpatients every other year. Through "Hospital Sundays," churches regularly contributed to the hospital charity, affording ministers "the personal means of relieving the poor of their own congregation by the use of tickets." In the 1870s, the working class of Devonport was encouraged to make contributions in its own right, through membership in the Provident Dispensary and "Hospital Saturdays," when collections were made at the workplace.[17]

These financial schemes and promotions did not liberate the Royal Albert from its basic dependence on the Admiralty for most of its running expenses and capital expenditures. Throughout the 1860s, Admiralty subsidies to the Royal Albert accounted for more than three-quarters of its annual income. Between 1869 and 1871 the hospital reported large surpluses and the consequent investment of £1,300 in South Devon railway debentures. Unfortunately, this was not a stable income, as it was tied to the number of lock patients attending the hospital. By 1870, the annual number of cases had declined from a high of 1,536 to 1,033, and Admiralty subsidies diminished accordingly. The financial crisis worsened over the decade, as fewer women were placed on the registered rolls.[18]

The Royal Albert simply could not find private means to make up for the loss of Admiralty income. It never captured widespread sup-

218

subscriptions decline K 70 due to public prejudices against CD Acts.

object to Acts

port; only individual large subscriptions and legacies kept it afloat. There had even been a falling off of general subscriptions from past years. The annual report for 1870 expressed concern, although it quickly rationalized the decrease: "The falling off in the subscription lists, not to be wondered at in a changing community, is nevertheless a matter which calls for the serious attention of friends." Although the report for the next year showed an improved financial picture, that was principally due to a single large legacy.[19]

Some members of the board of governors were less reluctant than the annual report to identify political reasons for the decline in public support. At the Royal Albert's annual meeting in November 1870, Reverend Binns, a repeal supporter and member of the board of governors, attributed the falling off of subscriptions "to the feeling that had grown throughout the town in reference to the C.D. Acts." Dr. Frederick Row, one of the insurgent medical officers, took the occasion to blame the repressive regime of the hospital management and the recent altercation with the medical officers for this decline.[20]

In 1875, Thomas Woollcombe complained that unfortunately

> for the charity the prejudice against the C.D. acts operates very much against the Hospital. We find our annual subscriptions and donations gradually but sensibly falling off. And we know of a recent instance in which a Lady diverted upwards of £4,000 from our funds to those of other charities on the ground of her decided objection to the Acts.[21]

According to Woollcombe, the steady reduction in the occupation of the lock beds meant that the hospital found itself £500 in arrears from the lock side.

Inspector Sloggett did not concur with Woollcombe's analysis. According to his own calculations, the hospital had realized a substantial profit from the lock side in the last two years. However, he did acknowledge that public subscriptions had fallen steadily since 1870 on account of public hostility to the acts and also because it was widely assumed that Admiralty support rendered the hospital financially independent. Sloggett suggested a partial compromise, by which the Admiralty would guarantee the financing of a minimum of beds. He strongly recommended continuing the connection with the Royal Albert. The success of the acts, Sloggett argued, was in large part due to the energetic support of the hospital committee and subscribers, "while the opposition has been greatly checked by the influence direct and indirect of those desirous of promoting the interest of the charity."[22]

As indicated earlier, "promoting the interest of the charity" could entail letters to the editor, vigorous defenses of the acts at public

219

meetings, the boycotting of repealers' businesses, and favorable court decisions by magistrates who were also staff members of the hospital or members of its board of governors. Repealers charged that the financial arrangement between the Royal Albert and the Admiralty encouraged doctors to keep women in the hospital who were not diseased or to keep them there for a longer period of time than necessary. Perhaps the most telling comment on the relationship between the network of control set up by the acts and the practical needs of the hospital was that of Thomas Woollcombe in 1869: "By the most extraordinary exertions on the part of Inspector Anniss we have now got all our beds full."[23]

In addition, the Admiralty underwrote various other expenses entailed in the special treatment of lock patients: the cost of building walls around the hospital and reglazing the windows with opaque glass; a subsidy of £150 to £200 for the samaritan fund that paid for the women's stay in rescue homes or transportation back to friends and relatives; and the construction of a chapel out of an unused lock ward. The last two items were all examples of the preferential treatment given the Royal Albert and were the envy of Portsmouth authorities. The samaritan fund also represents the early interest in reclamatory work on the part of the management of the Royal Albert. Soon after its opening, the Royal Albert began a small samaritan fund with private donations.[24]

Thus, from the very beginning, the Royal Albert had committed itself to both the moral and physical rehabilitation of the women under its "care." The lock wards were to become the center of a new moral regime. The treatment was mainly purgative: the C.D. acts were "necessary harsh measures to eradicate evils which are so engrained into the social habits of a large body of our people." Authorities engaged in a colonizing effort; they sought to enforce "discipline based on personal kindness and affection." Women who were previously "untouched by human sympathy" were now personally known to the hospital authorities and the police: they had "thus acquired a sense of individuality before unknown to them" and their behavior was more orderly in consequence. Their confinement in the hospital represented an "opportunity given during a necessary period of seclusion, for the encouragement of religious and moral influence which so seldom reach fallen women, too often treated as the hopeless outcasts of society."[25]

The women could only be transformed if order was put into their lives and a strict regime enforced. Accordingly, the inmates were subjected to work and time discipline: their daily lives were punctuated by work, prayers, mealtimes, lessons in ablution, and reading classes.[26]

220

The hospitals

This disciplined program replicated the regime of other confinement institutions for "fallen women" – a decided irony, as early regulationist propaganda had pointedly criticized the repressive regime of voluntary lock facilities and female penitentiaries.

In both hospitals, women were expected to perform various chores, such as laundry work for both the civil and lock sides and maintenance of their own wards. Laundry work helped to underwrite the cost of the women's confinement, but it also served a more symbolic function. Through laundry work, women could do penance for their past sins and purge themselves of their moral contagion: "Clear starching, it would seem, cleanses all sin, and an expert ironer can cheerfully put her record behind her."[27]

Repealers frequently exaggerated the inhumane character of the patients' work load: letters appeared in the *Shield* "exposing" the oppressive working conditions there. By and large, repealers conceded that the menial work expected of the women was not worse than the general lot of workingwomen. They argued, however, that prostitutes were unwilling and ill equipped to do such work; many women had resorted to prostitution in order to be liberated from precisely that life of drudgery. Furthermore, they complained that the women were not provided with the necessary warm undergarments to wash the hospital floors.[28]

In the hospital the women were also trained in deference and subordination. The social world of the hospital reproduced the patriarchal and class order of Victorian society. The male doctor was to reign supreme as the chief disciplinary and medical officer. The matron, usually a middle-aged spinster or widow, would act as his subordinate and female role model to the inmates.[29] Nurses were to be respectable workingwomen who, like the C.D. acts police, had divorced themselves from their original class identity. All the members of the staff were expected to maintain a professional distance from the inmates, yet still gain their confidence and respect.

As one might expect, this utopia never materialized. Sex and class conflict, which pervaded the operation of the C.D. acts outside the walls of the hospitals, also insinuated themselves inside. Members of the professional staff frequently failed to live up to their idealized role: some entered into collusions with the patients, while others exercised authority in an arbitrary and inconsistent manner.

From the start, Admiralty and medical officials were extremely ambivalent about employing women under the acts. They vehemently denied that the subjected women found an internal examination by a male doctor offensive; on the contrary, they asserted that the women violently objected to the presence of a female nurse at the examina-

221

tion.[30] They also attempted to exclude lady visitors from lock hospitals under the acts. As mentioned above, women like Caroline Nicholson, who had previously visited prostitutes in the workhouse, found themselves closed out of the Royal Albert and supplanted by a male chaplain. Feminists regarded this exclusion of lady visitors and the assumption of their role in moral reform by men as part of the male conspiracy to divide women.[31] Butler waxed indignant:

> When men of all ranks, thus band themselves together . . . and place themselves like a thick impenetrable wall between women and women, and forbid the one class of women entrance into the presence of the other, the weak, the outraged class, it is time that women should arise and demand their most sacred rights in regard to their sisters.[32]

Miss Bull, the matron of the Royal Albert, was not as apocalyptic as Butler, but she too resented the male hierarchy of power in the hospital. In the early 1860s, Bull had been in charge of moral reform efforts in the lock wards; these duties had since been transferred, over her objections, to the chaplain. When asked whether "reformatory work" was as "efficiently discharged by the resident chaplain [as by herself]," she replied, "I think that a woman's influence is greater than a man's, but the chaplain was desired to give his whole time, and I do not think that divided authority is good."[33]

Nurses constituted a more insidious threat to the social hierarchy of the hospital. Despite efforts to recruit respectable women into nursing and to raise the status of nursing to a profession, many nurses at both hospitals were workingwomen who had not yet adopted the same custodial attitude toward the inmates as the doctors or matron. Earning only £20 to £25 a year, they were readily susceptible to bribes and to other "unprofessional" schemes for enhancing their incomes.[34]

Whatever their misgivings, hospital and Admiralty officials still relied on nurses and the matron to inculcate the women in moral and social values. Aside from lessons in ablution and personal hygiene, nurses and needlewomen were expected to train the interned women in "women's work" and domesticity. The presumption was that these women had been, in Acton's words, "unsexed,"[35] and that they had to relearn the feminine role as a first step to their rehabilitation.

At the Royal Albert women were set to work sewing clothes for "small children,"[36] and they were permitted to bring their own babies into the hospital. According to the 1873 financial agreements between the two hospitals and the Admiralty, lock patients could be admitted with "infant children" not exceeding three years of age. Authorities were motivated by both medical and disciplinary considerations. If

222

they refused to admit prostitutes' babies, children with constitutional syphilis would be sent to the workhouse, which meant certain death for them. Admiralty officials agreed that "irrespective of the sanitary advantages . . . their [the infants] admission tends to promote the good behavior of the mother."[37]

It was as domestic servants, rather than as mothers, that public women were to be returned to the private sphere. In 1873 Inspector Sloggett noted the respectable appearance of the women at chapel service at the Royal Albert: " . . . clad alike in dark blue serge dresses, their hair neatly draped and wearing muslin caps, they seem rather like a number of respectable young women in domestic service than registered prostitutes."[38] Masquerading in new clothes and a respectable persona, they resembled the standardized nonentities of the Aldershot Lock Hospital, as celebrated by William Acton: "The demeanor of these women as we passed along was most respectful; there was no noise, no bad language, no sullenness, no levity."[39]

Nonetheless, the lessons in respectability and "self-respect" had only a temporary effect. The recommittal rate for the hospital was high,[40] and hospital authorities readily acknowledged that their rehabilitation program only worked at all effectively with first-timers – women who had not yet entered upon a professional career of prostitution. The annual report of the Royal Albert for 1870–1 announced that "of the women admitted for the first time and placed in a separate ward – 27 (or 25.32 percent) have been sent to Reformatories or returned to their friends . . . . Out of 220 women placed in the other wards during the same period, only 19 (or 8.63 percent) have been so disposed of."[41]

The Royal Albert's system of personal surveillance and punitive measures helped to minimize disturbances within the hospital but could not prevent the periodic outbreaks that occurred after 1868. In the early seventies internal disturbances were often responses to outside political agitation. Hospital authorities bitterly complained that every sensational trial or wave of repeal agitation encouraged insubordination among the lock-ward patients. There is some direct evidence for this: on October 24, 1870, five women applied to be discharged from the Royal Albert on the grounds that they were not diseased. They were defended by a solicitor retained by the repealers. Three "spontaneously withdrew" their application, and a fourth woman was discharged from the hospital just prior to her trial. The last applicant, Susan Edyr, had her request denied on the basis of the testimony by a Mr. Swain, the senior surgeon at the hospital, who examined her. Swain also happened to be sitting on the bench as one of the presiding magistrates. That evening, there was considerable disruption in the

223

wards of the Royal Albert, and five women were placed in segregation wards for "bad language and disorderly conduct." Two of them, Margaret Ward and Susan Edyr, were among the women who had petitioned for release.[42]

Most protests in the hospitals related more directly to internal conditions and restrictions than to outside agitation against the Contagious Diseases Acts. They took two forms: attempts at escape and "breaking out." The breaking of glass was stereotyped protest behavior for women under confinement: "The *disease* consists in smashing the windows of the cell, breaking the furniture, tearing up the blankets and bedding – the [general] remedy for this being confinement in a dark cell, with a bread-and-water diet." Commentators blamed the monotony of institutional life for the frequent breaking out among female inmates. Extreme tedium could also stimulate "insane frenzy," "singing, dancing, *swearing,* or destroying the blankets and rugs given them to sleep in."[43]

Lock-ward patients were undoubtedly bored to tears by the dull routine. When not doing their chores, they sat "about in groups" and "gossiped."[44] This inactivity afforded them the time and means to organize insurrections against hospital authorities. Many women also believed that there was "nothing the matter with them" and that they had been unnecessarily detained in the hospital.[45] They grew resentful when any new restriction was introduced, or when they believed the doctor or nurses had exercised their authority in an arbitrary or vindictive fashion.[46]

The hospital regime was constantly refined and elaborated, as authorities found themselves dealing with refractory patients who refused to be deferential. In 1869 it was argued that the women could only be transformed if they were cut off from their past associations. Hence, we have the frequent discussions in Admiralty records over raising the walls ever higher and limiting patients' correspondence.[47] Some women not only had to be cut off from their past but from each other. Segregation wards were built in 1869 in order to isolate refractory patients yet keep them within the hospital. And in the early 1870s the hospital developed a strict classification system, separating the hardened old-timers from the impressionable young women.[48]

The Admiralty watched nervously as Royal Albert authorities extended their control over the lives of the women interned in the hospital. They became particularly alarmed over the case of Elizabeth Cotzibitch, who began a glass-breaking riot in 1876 after being deprived of a "mourning note." Cotzibitch was sentenced to one month's imprisonment, although the Devonport magistrates questioned the legality of the correspondence rule.[49] Anxious not to overstep its legal boundaries, the Admiralty castigated the resident medical officer for his intemperate and illegal behavior and directed Woollcombe to modify the correspondence rule.[50]

Instead, Woollcombe vigorously defended the procedure. He explained to the Admiralty that the patients were permitted one letter a week, although "any letters of importance would not be withheld." The hospital committee had considered it their "primary duty to effect the reclamation of women – to this effect a correspondence rule was necessary." Otherwise, it would not be possible to get "gentlemen" to work for the charity. The fact that the Royal Albert was the only hospital to operate with such a rule explained its good order and discipline. "Elsewhere [that is, Portsmouth] its absence has led to contrary results." Without a limit on their correspondence, the women "would be in constant communication with their men outside and the result would be the setting up of jealousies between them with violent quarrels, fights and disturbances."[51] Segregation wards were also necessary to maintain internal discipline within the hospital without recourse to external authorities. Sloggett reported strong feeling on the part of the hospital committee that unnecessary publicity be avoided: the chairman of the committee had spoken "temperately" but "firmly"

> as to the strong feeling even now held by many supporters of the Hospital against the Acts and what they consider as the doubtful financial benefits derived from the civil Hospital Committee being engaged in the administration of the Acts. He considers that in case of it becoming necessary to bring patients before the Magistrates for refractory conduct in the wards more frequently than has been done hitherto the circle of objection will be largely extended . . . . [52]

The Admiralty was greatly surprised by the vehement reaction of the hospital authorities and backed down almost completely on its demands.

In both hospitals, the suspension of the acts in 1883 stimulated open hostility between the women and hospital authorities. Part of this was due to a misunderstanding on the part of the women: soon after the suspension of the acts, five women scaled the walls of the Royal Albert, believing they were no longer legally interned there.[53] For the first time in five years, Royal Albert authorities had to apply to the magistrates for assistance in punishing the women. With the suspension of the acts, the metropolitan police had been transferred to other duties, or in the case of Inspector Anniss, quietly pensioned off.[54] The *Western Morning News* lamented, "had not the Metropolitan Police been withdrawn from duty under the Acts the women would not have been at large for any time. Five years ago when two others escaped, and Inspector Anniss was communicated with, they were brought back again in a few hours without any trouble."[55]

Although the women were imprisoned for their actions, they had good reason to suspect they were illegally detained; they had been subject to a series of illegal and arbitrary acts by hospital authorities in the past. This illegal activity continued beyond the suspension of the compulsory clauses of the acts. After 1883, numerous cases were brought to the attention of the Admiralty where doctors and the police tried to force women to be examined and to enter the hospital. In 1884, the chief of constabulary in East Stonehouse ordered prostitutes to be examined by the visiting surgeon, who "declined to do so except with their voluntary submission." In the same year, women were sent to the Portsmouth hospital from Southampton without signing a voluntary release.[56]

These arbitrary measures merely underscored the fact that internal and external controls had broken down. The Admiralty received complaints from both hospitals that women refused to do the washing and laundering assigned to them. Inspector Sloggett reported that because the women had entered the hospital voluntarily they did not feel they had to do the "necessary needlework" for the hospitals and for their own clothes.[57]

The outbreaks of the women, financial pressures, and embarrassing court trials all served to focus adverse public opinion on the closed world of the lock hospitals. But in the long run it was the discomforting statistics on the increase of venereal disease that most severely damaged their credibility as effective sanitary and therapeutic institutions.

The hospitals as sanitary and therapeutic institutions

Medical proponents of regulation had originally assumed that the prostitutes interned under the acts would resemble the female inpatients at voluntary lock facilities. That is, they would be young women, in their late teens, with fresh cases of syphilis, who could be confined for a short period of time while they were visibly contagious.[58] This did not prove to be the case. By 1871, the women confined in the lock wards of the Portsmouth and Royal Albert hospitals were in their early and mid-twenties and suffering from gonorrhea.[59]

A different selection process partially accounts for this discrepancy. Most voluntary hospitals only admitted "serious" cases of venereal

226

disease, chiefly syphilis, whereas prostitutes themselves would not apply for admission unless incapacitated from carrying on their trade: "Their custom is to neglect their malady or treat it with purges or lotions obtained from the chemist until it either disappears or becomes so severe that they are no longer able to move about . . . "[60] Under the acts, however, the general examination of all registered women led to the internment of women with venereal ailments not ordinarily treated in the hospital, like gonorrhea.

The low proportion of syphilitic patients at Portsmouth and the Royal Albert may have also reflected the changing composition of registered women in the districts. When periodical examinations were instituted in 1868, women with syphilis may have simply left town in order to avoid a long hospital confinement. Fewer young women moved into prostitution to take their places. The women who remained on the register eventually passed through the primary and secondary stages of syphilis and entered the later latency stage of the illness that would go undetected clinically.[61]

Hospital finances may have also influenced this distinctive selection of lock-ward patients. In the late sixties, the lock wards at both facilities had been considerably expanded, in anticipation of a large influx of venereal patients detected by means of the periodic examination. By 1871 the supply of diseased women had declined precipitously and the lock wards stood half empty. To fill the beds, examining surgeons may have been more inclined to order a registered woman with the slightest discharge into the hospital.[62]

These developments caught C.D. acts authorities off guard. They had never anticipated that prostitutes interned under the acts would be suffering from gonorrhea, not syphilis. This fact complicated the medical and legal defense of the acts and led to a serious conflict between the patients and doctors.

Women resented their confinement in the hospital for so minor and commonplace an ailment as vaginal discharge. They were also frustrated and angry at the hospital treatment, consisting of rest, improved hygiene, and the application of lotions. Women interpreted this sanitary program as no treatment at all, and grew restless and insubordinate at their confinement.[63]

Like the interned prostitutes, most medical authorities also regarded gonorrhea in men or women as a minor local "affection" and one that did not really justify state intervention. Even the *British Medical Journal,* a staunch supporter of regulation, acknowledged that the acts "would never have become law as a protection against gonorrhea."[64] As one might expect, repealers lost no time denouncing the confinement of gonorrheal patients in the hospital as a waste of money and distortion of the original purpose of the acts.[65]

Repealers also criticized the diagnosis of gonorrhea as too imprecise and arbitrary to justify enforced confinement in the hospital. "No man on earth can say, by any system of periodical examination that can be devised, whether a woman is in a contagious condition or not."[66] Women could conceal their diseased state by "syringing out the vagina before examination" to "get rid of the mucus [discharge]."[67] Even C.D. acts authorities admitted that women could camouflage their disease: Inspector Sloggett reported that occasionally he had to remove "from the vagina, by means of forceps, large pieces of sponge" and "nearly the whole of the foot of a stocking" introduced there for the purpose of "misleading" the surgeon.[68]

Opponents of the acts also challenged positive diagnoses of gonorrhea on the grounds that it was impossible to distinguish gonorrhea from "natural" discharges of virtuous women. "It is perfectly possible for a woman to have a point of ulceration in the vagina; a pure healthy woman; and for that spot to secrete a pus, which will produce in a male distinct gonorrhea."[69] Defenders of the acts waffled on this point. The nonspecific pathology that underlay their diagnosis assumed that a host of vaginal secretions could excite gonorrheal inflammation in men. Dr. Lane of the London Lock Hospital admitted that "virtuous women, or at least quasi-virtuous women, undoubtedly do communicate gonorrheal disease to men."[70] Inspecter Sloggett and Dr. Moore of the Royal Albert disagreed. They vehemently denied that the two categories of women could be medically confused. Instead, they argued that "in a prostitute there is a [purulent] discharge from the uterus which is never or seldom present in a virtuous woman," and that this uterine discharge was usually a result of excessive sexual intercourse.[71]

This muddled diagnosis may have sufficed for doctors in private practice or those working in voluntary lock facilities, but it would not stand up in court. In 1870, Elizabeth Bond and Mary Ann Jeffries successfully petitioned the Devonport magistrates to be released from the Royal Albert on the grounds that they were free of venereal disease. Medical witnesses for the defense testified that the women suffered from discharges that were not "inconsistent with a virtuous life."[72] Later that year, Agnes Snowden, another lock-ward patient, also applied to the court, but was released by Royal Albert authorities just prior to her trial. She had been confined in the hospital as a patient suffering from gonorrhea for two days. Mr. Ryder, one of the Devonport magistrates, remarked dryly that if the woman got well in two

imprecise diagnosis of ~~guar~~ gonorrhea

days, it was obviously not a "serious case." He also asked whether the Royal Albert stood to "gain" by her unnecessary detention.[73]

Imprecise diagnoses of gonorrhea also led to conflicts between medical authorities responsible for the operation of the acts. A difference of medical opinion precipitated the 1869 dispute between the four senior surgeons of the Royal Albert and Admiralty officials. The Devonport doctors had publicly accused Sloggett, who was then the medical officer in charge of periodic examinations, of sending in gonorrheal cases "of a very trivial character . . . in many cases we have been able to discover no trace whatever of contagious disease."[74] They noted that between 1866 and 1869 a total of 609 cases had been dismissed from the Royal Albert within ten days of admission.[75] The conflict was eventually resolved by the appointment of a resident medical officer who deferred to Sloggett's medical opinion.[76] Sloggett later defended his diagnosis before the Royal Commission of 1871 on the grounds that virulent symptoms of gonorrheal discharge could rapidly subside after a few days of hospital treatment.[77]

Similar controversy surrounded the diagnosis and treatment of syphilis. Although the three stages of syphilis and its latency periods were well known at the time, the prevailing medical attitude was to treat the disease symptomatically. Women were confined in the hospital for thirty days until their primary sores went away. It was then assumed that they were "cured" or at least no longer contagious— authorities cared less about their ultimate cure than about curtailing *mercury* their sexual behavior while they were visibly contagious. Mercury, in ointment or spray form, was administered to inhibit the progress of their disease. However, it had serious side effects and could damage the teeth and kidney system. Furthermore, the lethal dose was perilously close to the "curative" dose. Small wonder that women complained of being burned and "tortured" in the hospital.[78]

Repealers contended that the brief internment of syphilitic prostitutes in the hospital afforded no sanitary protection to male clients. They argued that nearly all prostitutes had contracted syphilis at some early point in their career, well before they were detected by the C.D. acts police, and that they remained infectious for a considerable time. "The *secretions* of syphilitic women may communicate constitutional disease, although she herself presents no visible symptoms of disease."[79] Even when a woman was beyond the infectious stage, syphilis could be communicated from one man to another also having connection with her through "mediate contagion."[80]

Throughout the 1870s these arguments against regulation represented a minority medical opinion. Despite some ambivalence, most

229

doctors continued to believe that the sanitary supervision of prostitutes could be effectively administered with existing diagnostic and therapeutic techniques. By the 1880s, however, the climate of medical opinion had changed. Both the military medical returns and recent breakthroughs in the diagnosis of gonorrhea had successfully undermined earlier optimism.

Advocates of the acts had always dismissed repealers as "religious fanatics" and assumed the mantle of enlightened scientific reformers for themselves. Whatever the moral questions involved in the dispute, they would stand by "the logic of figures and results."[81] By the late seventies, however, these "figures and results" began to work against the regulationist position. Military and workhouse statistics showed a general decline in venereal disease since 1860 (before the acts were in force), with the important exception of the period between 1876 and 1882. In this interval both gonorrhea and secondary syphilis increased among enlisted men. To make matters worse, this increase was proportionately greater in subjected districts than in nonsubjected districts.[82]

These statistics also coincided with a reversal of medical attitudes. Venereologists on the Continent had begun to grow skeptical of the sanitary effectiveness of regulation: Fournier's surveys of men in venereal-disease hospitals, for instance, revealed that most had been infected by young clandestine prostitutes who were not yet registered.[83] Increasingly, medical authorities acknowledged that prostitutes remained infectious well after the visible symptoms of primary or secondary syphilis had disappeared.[84]

Recent breakthroughs in the diagnosis of gonorrhea also challenged the accuracy of clinical examination. Using the new techniques of microbiology, Neisser was able to isolate the causative agent for gonorrhea in 1879. This led to the identification of untreated chronic gonorrhea as the frequent cause of sterility and inflammatory pelvic disorders in women. As a result, doctors began to regard gonorrhea in women as a much more common and serious ailment than they had previously assumed.[85]

In Britain, these new findings served to undermine medical confidence in regulation by the early 1880s. At the 1881 Select Committee, two medical witnesses testified that it "is now generally acknowledged" that gonorrhea was a "specific" disease.[86] They also agreed that the new medical understanding of gonorrhea and syphilis had repudiated the older, "flawed" pathology underlying the acts: "When those Acts were introduced it was generally [erroneously] supposed that by inspection a surgeon could tell whether a patient was

230

infectious or not, and it was upon that idea that the Contagious Diseases acts originally were founded, both abroad and here."[87]

Contagious Diseases Acts authorities stubbornly clung to the older pathology and defended their sanitary program against all criticism. They rationalized the increase in secondary syphilis and gonorrhea in a number of ways. During the early seventies, they ascribed any temporary increase in V.D. to the incompetence and open sabotage of the civilian surgeons and to the successful resistance campaign waged by repealers. Later they blamed the increase on the army's policy of depriving soldiers of their pay when interned in the hospital for V.D. and on the ability of women to move freely in and out of the subjected districts. Through it all, they stood confident in their policy of selective cure and quarantine; they did not seriously question the efficacy of examining only one sex or the adequacy of available diagnostic and therapeutic procedures.[88]

Admiralty and hospital authorities anticipated a dramatic increase in venereal disease after the suspension of the compulsory clauses of the acts, so that "the common sense of the Nation would consent at the end of the year to see the clauses reimposed."[89] Indeed, Dr. Aldridge of Southampton reported a marked increase in syphilis among prostitutes in 1883: whereas previously there had been twice as many cases of gonorrhea than syphilis, the number were now equal.[90] Edward St. Aubyn, chairman of the managing committee of the Royal Albert after Woollcombe's death, wrote discouragingly to the Admiralty in 1888 about the operation of the "voluntary system" of medical care for prostitutes (even after the acts had been repealed, the Admiralty continued to subsidize the lock wards in both Devonport and Portsmouth). According to St. Aubyn, lock-ward cases once more followed a seasonal pattern, similar to Sloggett's reports in the early sixties. During the summer and fall of 1887 "fine weather" and the "money going around due to the Jubilee year" kept the prostitutes out. However, as winter progressed, the wards "got fuller." This would "faze [sic] off in summer," although they expected more cases than the previous year. Finally he cautioned against the increase in "the malignant forms" of V.D. among lock patients. "Quack doctors and chemists are doing a roaring trade. . . . Beastly advertisements from the former are posted on every wall and gate post within 10 miles of the towns."[91]

As Admiralty officials noted, the women had reverted to their old habits of waiting to enter the hospital until they were totally incapacitated from carrying on their business. Yet reports on the increased virulence and incidence of venereal disease had become a self-fulfilling

231

prophecy. Authorities saw what they expected to see. Furthermore, they made no attempt to remove the stigma from the treatment of venereal disease – the lock wards were open only to prostitutes, who were then isolated from other patients, placed under strict surveillance, and not permitted to return to the hospital if they left without prior authorization. As such, the lock wards of the Royal Albert Hospital, as a structure of confinement and social discipline, would persist in Devonport until the second decade of the twentieth century.[92]

12 *The local repeal campaign, 1874–86*

By 1874, repeal work in the subjected districts had reached a virtual standstill, in part a reflection of the general state of discouragement that pervaded the national movement. In Plymouth, Littleton and Marshall were involved in a "holding action" and frequently turned their attention to defending indigent women in court who were charged with offenses unrelated to the C.D. acts. In that year, James Stansfeld tried to revive agitation in the dock and garrison towns through the organization of the Subjected Districts League and a new emphasis on "rescue and defense" work among the inscribed women. Beginning in 1874, but reaching a climax in 1876, deputations were once again sent down to the Three Towns, local committees were reactivated, and large public meetings were planned. In conjuction with this new agitation, the *Shield* carried extensive coverage of C.D. acts trials with the hope of creating another *cause célèbre* akin to the 1875 Percy case in Aldershot.[1]

Although similar attempts were made to revive interest in Southampton, plans for large public meetings and rescue efforts found meager local support. Reports by national agents sent to stir up the Southampton district were discouraging; in 1875, Mr. Bligh was so disheartened by the local response that Henry Wilson of Sheffield offered to spend a day there "for the purpose of calling upon influential friends."[2]

The new wave of agitation was more successful in Plymouth than Southampton, probably because the old leaders and spokesmen for repeal were willing to join in the fray again. The National Association, nonetheless, treated the Devonport district with extreme caution, recognizing that supporters of the acts attended repeal meetings and regularly challenged criticism of the acts.[3]

To revive local interest in repeal, the National Association and the LNA planned separate meetings for men and women to be held "consecutive with the Church Congress"[4] scheduled in Plymouth for early October 1876. At the National Association's conference, James Stans-

233

feld and F. C. Banks, the association's national secretary, looked back to the past glories of the local repeal crusade in 1870 and reflected on its present state. Banks recalled the fourteen public meetings held there in 1870 when "resolutions denouncing these Acts were carried with applause . . ." Since then "the matter had remained dormant in that neighborhood" but "sympathy with Repeal was not dead, but only sleeping."[5] He also praised the rescue work conducted in the district: ". . . since the year 1870 the Association had had an office in Plymouth which had been devoted exclusively to the rescue of children who had been persecuted by the police engaged to carry out these Acts (Hisses.)."[6] Banks and Stansfeld both called upon their audience again to combine repeal activity with rescue work among subjected women.[7]

The October meetings revived local interest in repeal. By the end of 1876 the gentlemen's and ladies' committees had been reactivated, as well as the workingmen's association. Rescue efforts greatly benefited from this excitement. The *Shield* reported that "many friendless, struggling industrious orphan girls and many poor women, hunted by the spy police" had been aided. "These applications have been more numerous since the publicity [alerted] ignorant and timid girls and others whom the police frequently try to terrify into signing the voluntary submission."[8]

Soon after the October meetings, the Plymouth and Devonport League for the Repeal of the C.D. acts was formed, with Alfred Balkwill as its honorary secretary *pro tem.*[9] One of the first activities of the new league was to sponsor a public meeting in Devonport for February 1877. A circular signed by fourteen clergymen and ministers had been distributed to advertise the event. Both the February 13 meeting, which was adjourned in chaos, and the subsequent meeting on February 20 were unmitigated disasters for the repeal cause. On both occasions proponents of the acts were able to take over the meetings and pass amendments in favor of the acts. They were supported, according to the *Devonport Independent,* by "an organized band of disturbers who had placed themselves under the gallery, and who prevented the speakers being fairly heard."[10] These disturbances were orchestrated by notable supporters of the acts, like Christopher Bulteel, Mr. Groser (editor of the *Western Morning News*), and Dr. May (magistrate and former mayor of Devonport).[11]

At the second meeting, William Littleton condemned the presumption of the "necessity of vice" underlying the acts as a "monstrous assertion." When he called prostitution "the violation of natural law," so that "disease necessarily followed its practice," he was frequently interrupted and booed by pro-acts forces.[12] Alfred Balkwill tried to take a broader social view of the issues but fared no better. He tried to connect the C.D. acts with inequities in the marriage laws that made divorce among the poor impossible, and with the unfair regulations that enforced celibacy on soldiers. He too was "interrupted" by Mr. Hicks, who disparaged his remarks and contended that the meeting was called to consider the C.D. acts and "not the Marriage Laws."[13]

A heated discussion over the reclaiming effects of the acts followed, with Christopher Bulteel praising the rescue efforts of the police and hospital personnel, and Sedley Wolferstan, former house surgeon to the Royal Albert, charging officials of the acts with falsifying records to make them appear more favorable. Finally, when Mr. Swan tried to compare the record of the Royal Albert to the National Association's Plymouth Refuge home, "an uproar commenced." Mr. Groser called him a "paid agent" and objected to his taking up so much time, "contending that in as much as he was not a Plymouth man, and that this was a meeting convened to hear the opinions of the men of Plymouth on the subject, he was out of order in addressing the audience." An appeal was made to Dr. May to use his influence to quiet the mob, but he coyly refused on the grounds that he was a "simple auditor." A scuffle then broke out between Marshall and May. One more advocate of repeal was permitted to speak, and then "the meeting refused to hear any more." The chairman lost control of the assemblage, and an amendment in favor of the acts was passed.[14]

For the first time the *Shield* had to confront a serious defeat in public. How was it to explain the triumph of this "disgraceful riotous opposition" at a repeal meeting? It reminded its readers that twenty previous meetings had been held in the Three Towns, all strongly for repeal. It also stressed the local character of the meeting, with only local, inexperienced men as speakers.[15] Finally, it characterized most of the noisy disrupters as "educated and respectable young roughs," that is, middle-class rakes, who had cried "Morals be blowed; think of our health and constitutions."[16] By emphasizing the middle-class background of the young rowdies, repealers sought to expose the class bias of the opposition and to dispel any impression that they had lost the support of the local working class.

These disavowals notwithstanding, repealers had been badly burned by the experience. When Mr. Swan reported in March 1877 that the workingmen's committee wanted him to lecture as soon as possible in Devonport, he was instructed "not to speak in public there for the time being."[17] The National Association sought to recoup their losses more subtly. They tried to enlist the help of the women's group to salvage repeal efforts in Greater Plymouth. The executive committee

235

called upon Mrs. Butler and the LNA to consider organizing a Plymouth mission to help "counteract the effect of the two meetings recently held at Plymouth."[18] In a letter to Joseph Edmondson, Mrs. Butler discussed the possibility of such a mission modeled on the recent success of the Bristol mission: "Some of our veteran ladies hold themselves ready to go elsewhere, where they may seem to be called and they have, with courageous hearts, suggested to me that the next place should be Plymouth where our opponents have been achieving victories in meetings."[19] She hoped that the "women's work" would be succeeded "by a visit from some of our best speakers from all parts, who should hold, not one, but a series of meetings, making a regular assault upon the place." In fact, there was never a follow-through campaign, although she had asked Mr. Stansfeld to "stir up" the National Association to this idea.[20]

The ladies went it alone in the Three Towns. Seven meetings—one public and six in drawing rooms—were sponsored by the LNA in April 1877. Mrs. Lucas, Mrs. Tanner, and Mrs. Steward, all prominent members of the executive board of the national LNA, along with Mrs. Goulder, a paid agent of the LNA, formed a deputation to Plymouth. The *Shield* reprinted the *Western Morning News'* disgruntled comments on the gatherings: "A series of meetings 'for women only' are about to be held at which there will be no check of misstatements, no fear of opposing arguments, and from whose wholly one-sided gatherings petitions may be sent to Parliament as the voice of 'the women of Plymouth.' "[21]

Increasingly, however, repeal efforts in Plymouth shifted away from political agitation to rescue work. In 1877 local members of the LNA responded enthusiastically to Stansfeld's appeal that they take a more active role in ameliorating the condition of subjected women. As mentioned earlier, the national leadership of the LNA had first encouraged Stansfeld's plans, but it soon grew concerned that the new rescue impulse would divert energies from political activity.[22]

Nowhere were these fears more fully realized than in the Three Towns. The latter history of the repeal campaign in Plymouth was a history of seduction and cooption by Ellice Hopkins's social-purity movement. The motives for this realignment were mixed. Local repealers wanted to expand the limited repeal platform still insisted upon by the national groups and also wanted to ameliorate the condition of fallen women. Some were also eager to approach the problem of prostitution in a nonpolitical and noncontroversial context.

This new emphasis on rescue work well suited the local mood in Plymouth in the late seventies. Beginning in 1877 religious revivals

236

were capturing local attention. Especially popular among poor women, these revivals excited a tremendous amount of sexual prurience as well as heightened religious and class tension.[23] The national repeal groups, although not entirely approving of the crass emotionalism and prejudices of the revivals, still tried to rechannel the popular excitement thus generated to their own cause.

Over the decade, the burden of rescue work fell on John Marshall and his wife, with assistance and guidance from William Littleton. Since 1870 a room had been fitted up in the National Association office as a haven for young girls trying to elude the police. Marshall and his wife resided there and oversaw the rescue operations, screening "unfortunates" for the Rescue Society of London. Marshall was to become the male martyr figure of the campaign, constantly harassed by the police, who periodically stormed into his house, intimidated his wife, and also accosted him on the street. With roots in the working-class community, he was able to establish an effective intelligence network among the poor.[24]

In their outreach program, Marshall and Littleton sought out special types of women.[25] The *Shield* characterized most cases as involving "friendless, struggling industrious orphan girls."[26] Marshall and Littleton seemed to seek out "domesticated" fallen women, as William Acton described the women of the London Lock Asylum – women not likely to earn their livings on the streets for very long.[27] In part the tales of "industrious orphan girls" were also a propagandist device and an attempt to pacify the national executive committee. Littleton and Marshall sometimes vouched for the "respectability" of the couples accused of harboring a diseased prostitute, although subsequent investigation showed a number of such defendants to be of dubious character.[28]

By 1875, Marshall seemed aware of the futility of his rescue efforts. Asked to explain the decrease in the number of women who had applied to him for help (seventy-nine in 1875 as against ninety-one in 1875), he stated that "the women become degraded by the examination and believe so long as the law remains they must submit."[29] For others, the notoriety of the examination had rendered them outcasts, causing their friends to shun them and their landladies to turn them "out of doors." Marshall could not offer them a viable alternative outside of a stay in a rescue home in London and a future career as a domestic servant. The problems of poverty were much more than he could cope with: many of those who came to him were "women and children" coming for "warmth and food," not "common women" but simply friendless. For "financial reasons," the women were not assisted as much as "they or we desire" and they "were soon afterwards found walking the streets having all the appearance of 'registered' women . . ."[30]

The difficulty of rescue work among subjected women was only part of the problem. Marshall had serious disputes with the ladies' committee that was set up to work with him. In 1877, the LNA annual report announced that a "Rescue Committee of Ladies had been formed during the past year which meets at the house of Mr. Marshall, agent of the National Association." A midnight mission was also formed in that year, with nine members of the LNA participating. On that occasion, the executive committee of the National Association thanked the ladies "for organizing such valuable work . . . in connection with the agent of the National Association."[31]

Nonetheless, the Ladies' Rescue Committee began to assume an independent status, quite distinct from Marshall and from repeal operations. This was precipitated in part by the death of William Littleton in 1877, leaving Marchall alone to direct rescue efforts. The ladies did not like taking their orders from a workingman, nor was Marshall equipped to assume leadership by himself. In February 1879, he wrote the executive committee and expressed discouragement at "the isolated position he holds at present, no one offering to help him or advise him, like the late Mr. Littleton was in the habit of doing."[32]

During the early part of November 1879 Marshall was away on a speaking engagement before workingmen's groups in the south of England. He reported that during his absence a midnight mission had been held "at the close [of which] five girls were taken to his house, and put in Mrs. Marshall's care, by a man believed to be Mr. Groser of the *Western Morning News*." He queried the committee as to what should be done, and he was told to ascertain "if indeed it was Mr. Groser."[33] It was.

That incident presaged further subversive efforts. In November 1879, Ellice Hopkins, a leading light in the new social-purity movement, came to Plymouth to promote the establishment of an industrial school for girls. Like Butler, Hopkins was a female pioneer in moral reform whose example helped to legitimize women's role in rescue work. She too attacked the double standard and called for a radical change in male behavior. Unlike Butler, however, Hopkins did not connect prostitution to larger feminist issues, particularly to the economic and political disabilities of woman. However independent her own career, she preached adherence to women's traditional role to others; according to her biographer, she believed that "home duties should take the first place in a woman's life" and that it was "the Divine order that the man is the head of the woman."[34]

238

Hopkins's moral reform efforts were concentrated in three main areas: the establishment of preventive homes for friendless girls not yet "fallen" from virtue; lectures to working-class mothers on how to avoid incest and immorality in their overcrowded homes; and, her favorite project, the founding of men's chastity leagues.[35] These activities represent the new preventive thrust of moral reform in the late Victorian period: a concentration on adolescent rather than adult sexuality and a massive propagandist assault on the double standard and the sexual habits of the poor.

In Plymouth, Hopkins found a receptive audience for all her programs. According to a repeal agent's report, she had "many private interviews and small meetings with ladies and seemed thoroughly to rouse many to a sense of their duty in relation to the fallen."[36] She also met with influential community leaders to discuss her plans for preventive work among friendless girls. She presented them with her new scheme, soon to be enacted in the Industrial School Amendment Act of 1880. The act would enable police to remove children summarily from brothels and place them in industrial schools. Hopkins noted the direct relevance of the proposed legislation to the Three Towns, where, she had been informed, one hundred and fifty children were living in brothels. Her message was quite explicit: social salvation necessitated the uprooting of old evil habits.[37]

The pro–C.D. acts people – the guardians, hospital authorities, many of the magistrates – loved her. That was the kind of social-purity message they had been waiting for. They quickly banded together to form a rescue society of their own. Their Plymouth Friendless Girls' Association later merged with the Social Purity Society and received the professional assistance of the metropolitan police, who helped them track down juvenile girls on the brink of dissipation. Alarmed, the National Association wrote to Miss Hopkins to apprise her of this collusion.[38]

The new rescue effort also won over almost all the members of the ladies' committee attached to Marshall's rescue home. Moral uplift was now divorced from questions of venereal disease and class legislation. Partly "on the advice of Miss Hopkins," the ladies had decided to dissolve the earlier committee. Their reasons, according to Mr. Swan, the repeal agent, were that "during Marshall's absence there was no proper control, or surveillance of the girls; and that during the day they been known to go into objectionable places and mix with unsuitable company." The ladies did not like the relaxed regime of Marshall's home. They further objected to "two young men," Marshall's nephews, "who lived in the house." "Both are

239

quiet and respectable; and nothing was hinted at improper; save the fact that it did not seem right to have young men living in a Rescue home."[39]

In vain, the National Association tried to impress on the Plymouth ladies the political damage done the repeal cause by their actions. Mr. Swan, who arrived after the committee had been dissolved, reported:

> At first I tried to save the Members of the Committee from throw-
> ing themselves into an untried association which would not do
> Rescue work on Repeal lines, but help to bolster up Anniss and
> Co., and I pointed out the difference in the mode of doing the work
> between the London Rescue Society and the Penitentiary system. I
> believe Mrs. Richardson and others have had their minds so opened
> that they will be on their guard against any attempt to gain advant-
> age for the Acts party, and they resolutely say they will not take
> any money from Government funds.[40]

In the face of this debacle, Marshall was instructed to close up the office. Significantly, Miss Priestman and Mrs. Tanner of the national LNA came to his defense, praising his past zeal and dismissing allegations of impropriety. Mrs. Tanner said that she thought "much importance ought not be attached to the present attacks on Mr. Marshall which has [sic] arisen out of the fact that our Repeal friends had amalgamated with Miss Hopkins' party for rescue work, which included many pro-Acts men and women."[41] But their pleas were to no avail. Marshall and his wife left town in 1880, and he was ultimately sent on the repeal lecture circuit to speak at working-class gatherings. His political efforts took on a decidedly evangelical cast, as he frequently spoke at open-air meetings of the Salvation Army. After repeal in 1886 he announced his intentions to embark on a career as an "assistant preacher in connexion with a body of Christians in Kettering before long."[42]

Josephine Butler and the LNA, however, would not give up on Plymouth. In 1880 the LNA annual report announced that contact had been made with the ladies' committee of the Friendless Girls' Association, and a number of ladies had agreed to help in the repeal movement.[43] In 1882 Butler suggested a new mission to Plymouth that would coincide with the excitement generated by Moody and Sankey's revivalist meetings there.

> I have read with interest mixed with pain, the reports of this – of
> the crowds of men, gentlemen, soldiers, sailors, etc., who came to
> the "Penitent Form" conferring their sins and miseries and of not a
> few of the poor women of the Towns, *sinners,* tho' I doubt if
> Anniss' drilled women found their way there.[44]

Although she questioned the sincerity of these conversions, she thought that the revivalist atmosphere could be turned to good use: ". . . I have sometimes observed that hearts are more easily reached in behalf of some practical reform and some real outward conflict with evil, after such a religious movement." She hoped to launch a full-fledged campaign by capturing the current popular enthusiasm, at the same time drawing attention to recent local criticism of Anniss's testimony before the 1882 Select Committee, where he took full credit for recent improvements of the streets. Paid agents would attend to the details of organization whereas "educated ladies, unpaid workers" would then be free to do the serious work of propaganda.[45]

Nonetheless, the reports of the LNA deputations in the 1880s were generally discouraging. Alice Bewicke, visiting the district in December 1881, spoke at a series of drawing-room meetings and mothers' meetings there. Her time between meetings was taken up "by calls upon the different persons indicated as carrying weight in the town." But all "people could talk about was the *reclamation* of poor misguided girls." She "found them grossly impertinent to myself."[46] Her estrangement and bewilderment at the local scene carried over to her work among poor women: "It is a kind of work I do not the least understand. The mothers look so poor; there are such lines of care and labour and sorrow on their faces."[47] She interpreted the local debates in the newspapers over the conditions of the streets, "juvenile depravity," and overcrowded living conditions as symptoms of a general demoralization that had infected all classes: "Plymouth cannot make a stand by itself against the Acts, being slowly ruined by them."[48]

The general mood of Plymouth repealers was one of conciliation and rapprochement with their former antagonists. In January 1882, a meeting between pro- and anti-acts advocates was held to consider alternative sanitary measures to the C.D. acts. James Stuart of Cambridge spoke of the need for voluntary lock hospitals to care for diseased men and women. Alfred Balkwill observed that opponents and supporters shared the "general desire . . . for the improvement morally and physically of society" but differed on "the means of attaining the end in view." Repealers "objected to the contract between the State and the prostitute; the instincts of women spoke out more distinctly than those of men in opposition to the acts, and they were entitled to consideration." Although Christopher Bulteel insisted that the "voluntary system had failed" during the eighteen months it had been tried in the Three Towns, Frederick Row, another prominent regulationist, was more conciliatory. He agreed that repealers and advocates shared a common interest, and saw no reason why a volun-

241

tary system, using the same institutions and with the same financial backing, should not be a satisfactory alternative.[49]

Both sides met again to hear Ellice Hopkins on her return to Plymouth in August 1883, after the acts had been suspended. Hopkins told her audience that she did not want to discuss the merits or demerits of the acts, "but she wanted them to consider what could best be done at the present juncture." Her program included a social-purity movement for young men, coupled with legal and institutional measures to suppress working-class "immorality." Like her program, Hopkins's language was a curious mixture—an extravagant blend of military, revolutionary, and bureaucratic rhetoric. She began with an exhortation to revolutionary idealism: "Unless the men and women would give their life-blood this evil would go on. Without shedding of blood there was no remission of sins." The incendiary spirit she called forth was best epitomized by the Nihilists of Russia: "Why should not their young men in warehouses be banded together in some kind of organizations such as the Nihilists have exhibited in their circles and through which they have leavened the whole society of Russia?" The new millennium would be ushered in by the White Cross Army, "a society for the promotion of social purity, for the purpose of banding men together to respect their own purity, not to do or suffer injury to be done to women, and to endeavour to spread principles of purity among their friends and neighbors." Educational efforts were not enough; coercive measures were necessary as well. She hoped that the "company" to be formed out of that meeting would commit itself to "take into custody every man and woman who were found publicly soliciting in the streets." Because they were fighting against an "organized evil," they must "turn the full force of their educational, compulsory and reformatory machinery upon it instead of leaving it to breed amongst the children . . ." This revolution in social habits could be attained by the implementation of existing legislation. The Industrial Schools Amendment Act, the Artisans Dwelling Act, the Glasgow Police Act, and the Criminal Law Amendment Act would prohibit public solicitation and facilitate police intervention into the private lives of poor women and children.[50]

Both repealers and supporters of the acts praised her plans. When, however, Reverend Marle, a local repealer, tried to put forth an amendment condemning any legislation that would sanction vice, he was opposed by Reverend Wilkinson of Plymouth on the grounds that such a resolution would "divide them." A precarious and inherently unstable balance had been reached.[51]

A vigilance committee was soon formed to implement Hopkins's three-pronged attack on vice. Regulationists and repealers alike embraced social purity as an alternative to the now-suspended Contagious Diseases Acts. In fact, some of the activities of the vigilance committee, particularly the night patrols, constituted an informal continuation of certain provisions of the acts. The nocturnal patrols of the new society drew heavy criticism in the local press. The *Western Figaro* condemned the actions of the "New Inquisitorial Society,"[52] whereas the *Western Daily Mercury* expressed dismay over the "demoralizing" "spectacle of respectable ladies perambulating the town from twilight to midnight . . . for the purpose of tracking young persons of both sexes whom they happen to observe about the streets of Plymouth after dark."[53] The editors also deplored the use of former metropolitan policemen as rescue agents, for this continued "the system of espionage" that was "the most repellent feature" of the C.D. acts. At least under the regulation system, women had legal recourse against the police, who were "responsible for the mistakes they made." This informal use of spies "by a small confederation of citizens" offered no such protection and constituted a "repulsive conspiracy" that could "sap the morals of a neighborhood."[54]

The local application of social-purity legislation initially met with the same mixed response. In 1885, when landlords in East Stonehouse were threatened with prosecution under the Criminal Law Amendment Act, they summarily evicted ninety prostitutes from their premises. Homeless, the women were compelled to wander the streets day and night. Two were subsequently found lying in a pigsty in Devonport and were charged with vagrancy. Public officials did not know what to do with the women and soon permitted them to return to their former abodes.[55] For the next twenty years local police informally administered a policy of segregation, permitting prostitutes to remain undisturbed in a restricted locality. This policy was only curtailed in 1904 when, under pressure from a newly constituted vigilance committee, police were forced to crack down on brothels and streetwalkers in the notorious Octagon area.[56]

Local purity advocates also tried to follow through on the preventive and educational measures suggested by Hopkins. These activities were integrated into a general assault on traditional lower-class sexual mores. Purity groups sought to educate the working class on the value of chastity and sexual repression through lectures and the distribution of tracts. Their propaganda campaign was complemented by institutional and legal measures against public immorality.

The controversy over the bazaar known as the Fancy Fair in 1886 united many of the repressive forces active at the time. In March of

243

that year, concerned citizens met to consider the "suppression" of the Fancy Fair on Phoenix Street, East Stonehouse. Sergeant-Major Young, a staunch regulationist, complained that numbers "of young girls were being ruined in that place every week, and afterwards bringing contamination into the homes of the well-to-do as nurse girls and servants." Mr. Brutton, the chief constable in Stonehouse, further estimated that forty-five to fifty girls had come to their ruin by attending the "Fancy Fair." "Out of those forty or fifty girls, nineteen had been in the Albert Hospital."[57]

The disappearance of Emily Robertson, last seen at the Fancy Fair, further darkened suspicions. On April 3, 1886, Henry Greenslade, a "migratory fiddler" with a long history of brothel-keeping offenses, was prosecuted under the new provisions of the Criminal Law Amendment Act for unlawfully detaining Emily, seventeen, "against the will of her lawful guardians." Mrs. Robertson described the steady downfall of her daughter's character: "The girl used to frequent the 'Fancy Fair' and it was to that place that the witness attributed her daughter's position." The subsequent discussion at the trial was devoted entirely to the immoral influence of the fair. A traditional form of working-class entertainment, the fair represented easy social intercourse between the sexes[58] and defiance of work and time discipline. As such, it increasingly came under official attack in the late nineteenth century as efforts were made to provide a more structured and separate social life for working men and women. The Girls' Evening Home Movement, with its reading, music drill, and cooking lessons, advertised itself as an alternative to the "aimless street saunters" of working girls who find "their way in crowds to such places as the fancy fair."[59]

Ellice Hopkins and the vigilance committee represented one of the strands of social purity that arrived on the scene in Plymouth. The Salvation Army was the other. It also set up a rescue home in Plymouth in 1886. It had been active there since 1882, and its open-air meetings and rowdy processions had excited much public opposition. Alfred Balkwill welcomed them, and quickly came to their defense. For the Salvation Army had somehow colonized the unrespectable poor: "The complaint of the rough character of the crowd shows its success . . . . How much better to attract them to the out-door service – to the march – and to have them crowding into the meeting than for them to be sitting in the public-house ruining body and soul."[60] In its vigorous "disregard of form and convention," [61] in the violence of its revivalist enthusiasm, the Salvation Army seemed to have penetrated the residuum in a way that both repealers and bourgeois purity advocates had failed to do.

244

The local repeal campaign

Similar developments occurred in Southampton, although they were not part of an organized purity crusade. One by one, the traditional fairs were abolished by order of the town council in the late seventies. The Above-Bar Fair was "wiped out" on account of its "moral delinquencies" and "customary orgies," and the Trinity Fair was limited to only one day.[62] In the early eighties, the *Weekly Hampshire Independent* complained of the "bearishness" of girls and boys perambulating on High Street; it also announced plans for a lodging house and cooking classes for working girls under the auspices of the Y.W.C.A.[63] Also appearing on the scene was the Salvation Army, with its "hysterical form of religion." As in Plymouth, the "hallelujah lasses" promised to "open fire" on the residuum. Their first meeting was a great success, although the newspaper account grumbled about the "admixture of stinks going on from such an assemblage."[64]

Thus, by the time the Contagious Diseases Acts were suspended in 1883, something of the new social and political conditions under which subjected women were to live had become apparent. Local officials, who "deplored the condition of the streets," at first tried to lobby against their suspension. Local deputations and petitions were sent to the Home Secretary from Southampton and Plymouth, with the hope that a "strong expression of feeling by inhabitants of towns like Plymouth" would "cause them [the House of Commons] to reconsider its decision to suspend the compulsory clauses."[65] Public officials also pleaded for the retention of the acts on the basis of "local option."[66] Repealers countered with a wave of activity among the local groups: the Three Towns ladies' committee met fourteen times during the year 1883, and was active in petition and propagandist work.[67]

But with repeal of the acts imminent, military and local authorities scurried around looking for substitute legislation, arranging for the enforced detention of diseased prostitutes in the workhouse, and lobbying for various Detention-in-Hospital bills.[68] The Admirality continued to pay for the confinement of prostitutes in civil hospitals, even after repeal.[69] Police continued a policy of segregation for prostitutes, and social-purity organizations endeavored to compel the rest of the poor to adhere to a more rigid standard of sexual respectability. In Plymouth, repealers and regulationists collaborated in the new purity campaigns that offered moralistic goals in a noncontroversial and nonpolitical framework. In the transition to social purity, moral concerns had been disconnected from larger feminist issues, and the feminist context of the repeal movement had been subverted.

245

Epilog

Everything that happened in Plymouth and Southampton was reproduced at the national level with the same intensity and drama. Throughout the country, preventive approaches to moral reform rapidly superseded the more limited efforts to reform and rescue the experienced prostitute. The 1880s witnessed the proliferation of clubs and armies to train the young and innocent in sexual repression. As in the Three Towns, these voluntary and propagandist efforts were complemented by repressive public measures against unrespectable sexual activity. Compared to mid-Victorian moral-reform movements, this new social-purity crusade was more oriented to a male audience, more hostile to working-class culture, and readier to use the instruments of state to enforce a repressive sexual code.

Social purity especially focused on youthful sexuality as a dangerous form of sexual activity. The desire to protect the young, particularly young females, from sexual abuse was not new, nor did it fully eclipse public anxiety over "illicit" sexual activity between adults. But it is noteworthy that the cultural image of the female victim in the 1880s was several years younger than her popular stereotype in earlier decades.

W. T. Stead's exposé of child prostitution in London epitomized this new preoccupation with childhood sexuality. Appearing in the *Pall Mall Gazette* in the summer of 1885, "The Maiden Tribute to Modern Babylon" proved to be one of the most successful pieces of scandal journalism published in Britain during the nineteenth century.[1] In lurid and prurient detail, it documented the sale of "five pound" virgins to aristocratic old rakes. The series had an electric effect on public opinion: "The crowds [in London] and the days remind me of revolution days in Paris," exclaimed Josephine Butler.[2] An enormous public demonstration (estimated at 250,000) was held in Hyde Park[3] to demand the passage of legislation raising the age of consent for girls from thirteen to sixteen. Reformers of all shades were represented on the dozen or so demonstration platforms, including representatives from the various factions within the repeal camp. For one brief moment, feminists and personal-rights advocates joined with Anglican bishops and Socialists to protest the corruption by aristocrats of young innocents.[4]

The white-slavery and child-prostitution scandals had all the symptoms of a cultural paranoia overtaking Britain in the late nineteenth century, as its industrial preeminence was seriously challenged by the United States and other new industrial nations, its military position and imperial holdings by Germany, and its domestic peace and class structure by the spread of labor unrest and the growth of socialism.[5] In fact, the evidence for widespread involuntary prostitution of British girls at home or abroad is slim. During the 1870s and 1880s officials and reformers were able to uncover a small traffic in women between Britain and the Continent, although the women enticed into licensed brothels in Antwerp and Brussels were by no means the young innocents depicted in the sensational stories. Similarly, there undoubtedly were some child prostitutes on the streets of London, Liverpool, and elsewhere; here too, their numbers were grossly exaggerated by the purity propaganda. Nor were most of these young girls victims of false entrapment, as the vignettes in "The Maiden Tribute" would suggest.[6]

Whatever the discrepancy between perception and reality, "The Maiden Tribute" succeeded in its immediate goal; it forced the passage of the Criminal Law Amendment Act of 1885, which raised the age of consent for girls to sixteen. "How wonderfully the protection of girls' bill passed last night on the top of this wave of popular anger: We are now working to strike out all the police clauses in committee!" exclaimed Butler.[7] And here, of course, was the historical irony. For the Criminal Law Amendment Act, even in its diluted final form, gave police far greater summary jurisdiction over poor workingwomen and children—a trend that Butler and her circle had always opposed.[8]

This irony was not lost on foreign observers at the time. Yves Guyot, a French abolitionist, condemned the new bill out of hand as "outrageously unequal and unjust" toward workingwomen. Besides raising the age of consent, "The Act gives power for the *suppression* of all houses in which women, whose relations with the other sex lack the sanction of priest or registrar, find shelter." He could well appreciate why religious fanatics were behind the bill, but he was at a loss to comprehend how it could be supported by men "who most frequently urged the claims of women to be regarded by the law as responsible human beings." "It is no less strange," he remarked, "that many of the very women who have braved insult and calumny in demanding these rights were among the first and loudest supporters of the measure for their furthest restriction."[9]

Epilog

The modern observer is forced to pose the same question. Why did male and female repealers, who were advocates of personal rights, antistatist in their political ideology, and even knowledgeable of the realities of working-class prostitution, permit themselves to be swept up in a movement with such repressive political implications?

Let us review abolitionist involvement in the events leading up to the publication of "The Maiden Tribute." Repeal ties to the white-slavery crusade were even stronger than to the social-purity movement as a whole. In 1880 Alfred Dyer, a Quaker and prominent repealer, published a pamphlet on the entrapment and enforced detention of young British girls in the licensed brothels of Brussels. His exposé, *The European Slave Trade in English Girls,* led to the formation of the London Committee for Suppressing the Traffic in British Girls. The committee was chaired by Benjamin Scott, another leading abolitionist, and its members included Josephine Butler, William Shaen, and others. The committee's findings in turn stimulated the appointment of a committee in the House of Lords "to inquire into the protection of young girls from artifices to induce them to lead a corrupt life, and into the means of amending the same." W. T. Snagge, the Lords' committee's chief investigator, was able to document a small international traffic in British girls. His report heavily implicated Belgian officials in this criminal activity and castigated British police and diplomatic authorities for their complacency and indifference.[10]

Most of the testimony before the Lords' committee focused on juvenile prostitution at home rather than on white slavery abroad. The recommendations of the committee reflected this double interest: they included increased sanctions against procurers and international traffickers and procurers, but they also recommended raising the age of consent to sixteen.[11]

White slavery and child prostitution proved to be an explosive combination. The subsequent efforts of the London committee reflected the continued intertwining of these two issues. Its members soon realized that "all that goes on in Brussels and Paris also goes on in London."[12] During its investigations of the foreign traffic in young women, the committee acquired information on the sale of virgins to aristocratic rakes in West End brothels that led to the prosecution of a fashionable procuress, Mrs. Jeffries. The Jeffries trial caused a public sensation, as it exposed "the complicity of royal aristocratic personages with this infamous trafficker in flesh and blood."[13] Nonetheless, in 1884 Parliament still balked at passing a bill that would raise the age of consent and punish traffickers in vice. Faced with this impasse,

Butler and Catherine Booth of the Salvation Army turned to W. T. Stead for assistance. The result was "The Maiden Tribute."[14]

Repealers' motives for taking up the issues of white slavery and child prostitution were mixed. A certain amount of political opportunism undoubtedly played a part. In his early pamphlet, Dyer had explicitly connected the traffic in British girls with the need to fill the licensed brothels of Europe.[15] Later on, repealers hoped that the excitement over Stead's revelations would rekindle popular enthusiasm for repeal. Their hopes were soon realized. Throughout the country local correspondents reported that "the revelations of July" had "revolutionized" repeal work. "From every side, fresh help has come . . . " Interest in repeal work " . . . had deepened and widened with the noble impetus given to all Social Purity work by Stead's heroic denunciations."[16]

Feminists and personal-rights advocates within the repeal camp also tended to share the same feelings of guilt and anxiety over youthful sexuality as other members of the middle class. These conflicting emotions of fear and guilt operated both consciously and unconsciously. Defenders of the age-of-consent legislation tried to depict girls as the passive victims of male sexual abuse and not responsible for their sexual activity. Their formal denial of girlhood sexuality reflected a "transitional" view of childhood and adolescence as stages in life marked by dependency but not by any specific psychosexual development. Accordingly, reformers only rarely made reference to the actual sexual development of the girls they were seeking to protect.[17] Nonetheless, anxiety over the sexual precocity of working-class girls existed just beneath the surface. We have seen, in the case of Plymouth and Southampton, how the closing of fairs and the establishment of "girls' evening homes" were linked to mounting public concern over the easy social and sexual intercourse between working girls and boys. Sometimes this secret obsession with young girls as sexual objects found a more perverse expression, as the brisk commerce in Victorian child pornography and Stead's own prurient exposés amply demonstrate.[18]

Butlerites, of course, repudiated these obviously repressive and perverse manifestations. As ladies and gentlemen, they felt obliged to redress the sexual wrongs done to working-class girls by men of a superior class, but they registered the same feelings of repugnance and ambivalence toward incorrigible girls as they had earlier toward unrepentant prostitutes. For them as well as for more repressive moralists, the desire to protect young girls thinly masked coercive impulses to control their voluntary sexual responses.

Feminists and republicans were also attracted to the radical political message in Stead's exposé of aristocratic vice and governmental corruption.[19] The disreputable performance of M.P.s during the debates over the age of consent simply confirmed their worst suspicions about "the vicious upper classes." During the debates, old rakes like Cavendish Bentinck treated prostitution as a necessary and inevitable evil, whereas others openly defended sexual access to working-class girls as a time-honored prerogative of gentlemen. One member of the House of Lords acknowledged that "very few of their Lordships . . . had not when young men, been guilty of immorality. He hoped they would pause before passing a clause within the range of which their sons might come."[20]

Both the white-slavery and child-prostitution crusades served to assuage middle-class guilt without really implicating members of the bourgeoisie in the sexual oppression of working-class women and girls. As a myth of international conspiracy, white slavery encouraged the belief that the sinister forces exploiting women existed outside society, and were not fundamental to its basic social and economic arrangements. Likewise, Stead's exposés blamed the corruption of innocents on superannuated aristocrats, and devoted scant attention to the economic exploitation of women under capitalism that would lead them to take up prostitution on a voluntary basis. This antiaristocratic bias may also have prompted the inclusion of a clause in the 1885 act against homosexuality, another "perversion" associated with the corruption of youth by upper-class profligates.[21]

Although they generally opposed protective legislation, repealers were able to rationalize state intervention to protect children from sexual abuse on the grounds that they were attacking "crime," not "vice." It had always been their policy to "*let individuals alone,* not to pursue them by any outward punishments . . . but to attack *organized prostitution . . .* a third party."[22] In the case of child prostitution, "They believed in the equality of men and women; but they had never believed in the equality of children with them," declared James Stansfeld in Parliament.[23]

Not all defenders of the proposed legislation troubled themselves with such fine distinctions. For rigid moralists like Catherine Booth, "Vice [was] crime."[24] It was these more repressive forces that eventually won the day and subsequently utilized the new legislation to attack "vice" as well as "crime."

Despite the public outcry against corrupt aristocrats and international traffickers, the clauses of the new bill were mainly enforced against members of the working class, not their social betters or "foreigners." This was no historical accident. The passage of the Criminal Law Amendment Act of 1885 coincided with a new interventionist approach to working-class culture. The 1880s had reawakened older fears of the dangerous classes as a threat to the social and political order. Respectable citizens were gripped by a fear of "Outcast London," a vast, unsupervised, and estranged underclass that could be readily mobilized into the revolutionary ranks of the new Socialist movement.[25] This fear spread throughout the country, and was reproduced on the local level in newspaper series on "Outcast Southampton," "Outcast Liverpool," and the like.[26]

One cultural and political response to this threat was a radical effort to remake working-class culture and to root out the traditional social and sexual habits of the poor. The social-purity movement, emerging in the late seventies and gaining momentum after "The Maiden Tribute," reflected the new spirit of liberalism and liberal reform, which, according to Gareth Stedman Jones, exposed a "more coercive, interventionist policy toward the 'residuum.' "[27] The old voluntary methods of highly individualist charities and reform groups gave way to a more interventionist model, as men like Charles Booth and Alfred Marshall suggested a combination of welfare programs and labor camps to promote social efficiency and isolate the unrespectable poor from the rest of the working class. Although social-purity advocates still used the older rhetoric of liberal reform and stressed voluntary efforts, they were much readier to use the instruments of the state to enforce their code than earlier moral-reform efforts.[28]

Control of children was the key to this radical transformation. Only by disciplining and training children at an early age could one truly transform the character of a class. Control over children also afforded authorities and reformers enormous leverage over other members of the working-class household and community. We have already seen how the Industrial School Amendment Act of 1880 was applied in this regard.[29] In similar fashion, the Criminal Law Amendment Act, which was supposed to raise the age of consent, was mainly enforced to control adult sexual behavior.[30]

The popular emotion excited by the white-slavery scandals fed the flames of the most prurient social-purity elements. In the "wake of Stead's shocking revelations," the National Vigilance Association (not to be confused with the feminist Vigilance Association) was formed.[31] Its initial purpose was to ensure the local enforcement of the Criminal Law Amendment Act, although it later turned its attention to burning "obscene" books and attacking music halls, theaters, and bogus registry offices, as well as setting up rescue homes.[32]

Under pressure from local vigilance associations, police officials mainly applied the new act against prostitutes and brothel keepers, rather than white slavers and the seducers of children. Between 1885 and 1914, an average of 1,200 brothels were prosecuted in England and Wales each year, fourteen times the annual average of prosecutions in the ten years preceding 1885. This crackdown coincided with similar drives against streetwalking in the capital and major provincial cities.[33]

Thus reformist energies were channeled into a conservative, morally repressive movement.[34] To what extent were repealers implicated in this trend? In a moment of enthusiasm, practically everyone associated with the repeal cause jumped on the purity and vigilance bandwagon. Local chapters of the LNA helped to found vigilance committees in their districts, and two regional repeal groups, the Southwest Counties League and the Midland Counties Electoral League, eventually amalgamated with the National Vigilance Association after 1886, when the C.D. acts were abolished.[35]

Repeal leaders of all persuasions initially filled many of the committee positions of the National Vigilance Association. However, this collaboration was short-lived for Butler and her friends on the LNA executive, as well as for most of the personal-rights advocates in the National Association. Most of these persons resigned when the prurient and repressive direction of the National Vigilance Association became apparent.[36]

Throughout the 1880s and the 1890s, the journal of the feminist vigilance association (now calling itself the Personal Rights Association) condemned the methods of the National Vigilance Association and accused it of persecuting "the poorest, most helpless and most forlorn of womankind."[37] Butler also publicly aired her disapproval of the social-purity movement. In 1897 she explicitly warned her workers against "the soundness of principle of those engaged in social purity work."

> It may surprise and shock some who read those lines that I should say (yet I must say it), beware of purity workers in our warfare. Beware of "Purity Societies" which seek affiliation with our Society.... We have learned that it is not unusual for men and women to discourse eloquently in public, of the home, of conjugal life, of the divinity of womanhood . . . and yet to be ready to accept and endorse any amount of coercive and degrading treatment of their fellow creatures, in the fatuous belief that you can oblige human beings to be moral by force, and in so doing that you may in some way promote social purity![38]

Her warnings came too late. The new social-purity movement had passed her by, while absorbing a goodly number of the LNA rank and file.[39]

252

Epilog

Conclusion

What then was the legacy of the repeal campaign for the three groups who have been the focus of our attention: the working class, feminists, and doctors? Let us begin with the working class. As mentioned earlier, the acts and the subsequent public policy that followed their repeal drastically altered the structure of prostitution and the character of prostitutes' relationship with the larger working-class community. The social isolation of prostitutes was largely imposed from above, but it received the passive acquiescence of the poor themselves.

There is some evidence that certain segments of the working class had also internalized the values of social purity in the late nineteenth century. Thousands of respectable workingmen were recruited into white-cross armies throughout the nation and dedicated themselves to promoting the single standard of chastity and attacking public and private vice.[40] The prescriptive literature distributed by social-purity groups also seems to have influenced the child-rearing practices of the time. Edwardian working-class parents were notable for their strict schedules, puritanical treatment of masturbation, and for the severe restrictions they placed on their teenage daughters' social and sexual behavior.[41] The general decline in venereal disease throughout the late nineteenth century and early part of the twentieth century may partially have reflected a new standard of chastity (as well as cleanliness) among most classes of society.[42]

The repeal of the acts also forced doctors to explore alternative strategies to control the spread of venereal disease. After the 1880s, doctors and regulationists were recruited into the new social-purity movement, although some continued to defend regulation. In towns where the acts had formerly been enforced, purity crusades against brothel keeping and street solicitation invariably stimulated renewed demands for the reintroduction of the acts. Doctors and churchmen spearheaded these clean-up campaigns, and took the occasion to blame the present "state of the streets" and juvenile depravity on the repeal of the acts.[43] During the 1904 purity crusade in Plymouth, for example, Dr. Paul Swain, an old regulationist and senior surgeon of the Royal Albert, deplored the disgraceful "rowdyism" of boys and girls on the streets at night. In contrast,

> The streets of Plymouth have never been so free and quiet from immorality since the repeal of the C.D. Acts. Under these Acts the number of immoral women was materially diminished, many of the younger ones were reclaimed, juvenile vice was abolished and many

253

a young girl was prevented from going on the streets. The repeal of the Acts was in my opinion one of the most wicked things ever done by a weak government at the beck and call of ignorant and infatuated faddists.[44]

Outside these garrison towns, many doctors had grown resigned to the repeal of the acts and to the unlikelihood of their reintroduction in Britain in the face of hostile public opinion. Some even acknowledged that the acts had been sanitary failures. The continuing decline of venereal disease among British troops well after 1886 undermined the sanitary argument for regulation.[45] Later venereologists also came to recognize the practical futility of regulation, inasmuch as most prostitutes had already contracted gonorrhea and syphilis early in their career, prior to their public registration. It had also become an accepted fact that young clandestine prostitutes or "amateurs" were the most active disseminators of gonorrhea and syphilis.[46]

Medical specialists also came to regard the Contagious Diseases Acts as institutional incarnations of a flawed and discredited pathology. Doctors gained a new appreciation of the long-term consequences of both gonorrhea and syphilis, after Noegerrath and Neisser (1872 and 1879) identified untreated chronic gonorrhea as the frequent cause of sterility and inflammatory pelvic ailments of women and after Fournier (1894) established tabes dorsalis (neurosyphilis of the spinal cord) and general paralysis of the insane as tertiary complications of syphilis.[47] These new findings caused medical specialists to doubt the accuracy of clinical diagnosis and to question their own ability to cure venereal complaints in men and women.[48]

Until Salvarsan came into general use during World War I, doctors looked to changing social and sexual mores, rather than to medical intervention, to bring about the control of venereal disease. As one doctor commented, "Twenty years ago most doctors in this country believed that state regulation was the only path of success; today there is reason to believe that we in England are no worse off without regulation than our friends are with it."[49] Dr. Ernest Lane, a staunch regulationist of the old days, voiced a similar sentiment at an international conference in 1904. He had "been amongst the Cassandra-like prophets of the evil that would happen on repeal. The facts . . . [of] the past eighteen years had therefore been a surprise to him, but he was now convinced that there were other and better means of dealing with the question than the old C.D. Acts."[50]

Increasingly, medical reformers joined with purity advocates in a concerted effort to educate the population to the values of chastity as the best prophylaxis against V.D. Out of this medico-moral coalition, the social-hygiene movement of the early twentieth century was born. The "task of social hygiene," with its scientific approach to the moral and medical issues of eugenics, venereal disease, and birth control, united the medical profession and the social-purity forces at last. The Plymouth Vigilance Society had merely given early expression to this emerging alliance.[51]

Finally, what were the implications of the repeal campaign for the feminist movement? The campaign against the acts provided later feminists with an important lesson in militancy and with a stirring example of feminist political leadership. Edwardian suffragists took note of the militant by-election tactics of the campaign, of the effectiveness of repealers' extraparliamentary activities, and of the need for feminists to operate outside both political parties.[52] Constitutionalists as well as militants came to treasure Butler as a great founding mother of modern feminism. Her portrait was regularly sold at suffrage meetings, and all the suffragist newspapers periodically recounted her heroic actions in Colchester and Pontefract.[53]

To later feminists, the LNA and its mission also embodied an ideal of sisterhood and female solidarity that transcended class barriers. In 1914 the Socialist feminist Sylvia Pankhurst reminded her working-class followers that Butler's propaganda had "aroused the greatest sympathy amongst the working people of Colchester, especially the women by whom the C.D. Acts were always referred to as 'those blackguard Acts.' "[54]

Besides providing an important political example, the repeal campaign firmly committed later feminists to an attack on the double standard and "male vice." The sixteen-year campaign against state regulation ingrained the theme of the sexual wrongs perpetrated against women by men on later feminist consciousness. After repeal, the "women's revolt" became "a revolt that is Puritan and not Bohemian. It is an uprising against the tyranny of organized intemperance, impurity, mammonism, and selfish motives."[55]

This intense anger at male sexual license undoubtedly contributed to the militancy of the Edwardian suffragists. The violent extraparliamentary activities of the Women's Social and Political Union reflected not only frustration at women's limited political gains over the past forty-five years between 1865 and 1910 or even the "irrational" character of the politics of the time.[56] The acts of arson, window breaking, and tearing up of golf links were part of a real sex war, whose explicit political precedent may be traced to the campaign against the C.D. acts. Indeed the official response to feminist activities – in particular the forced feeding of militant suffragists in prison – carried the same perverse overtones of sexual violence and outrage as had the speculum examination in the 1870s and 1880s.[57]

The fuller knowledge of the devastating effects of venereal disease reinforced feminist indignation against male vice and the complicity of the regular medical profession. The new findings on the extent and seriousness of syphilis and gonorrhea demonstrated that male sexual license not only ruined and degraded some women, but led to disease that was the hidden cause off the widespread ill health of married women. Following the lead of reforming doctors, feminists castigated the rest of the medical profession for protecting transgressing husbands while keeping wives in ignorance of the true nature and origin of their disorder.[58]

Thus there is a strong continuity between Josephine Butler's assertion that all men suffered from venereal disease at some time in their lives and the attack on male vice mounted by Christabel Pankhurst in her pamphlet *The Great Scourge* (1913). Both used sensational and misleading statistics that were largely propagated by the medical profession. Both interpreted V.D. as divine punishment for male profligates and sexual supremacists. Both held the medical profession responsible for encouraging men in sexual promiscuity. Finally, both called for a single standard of sexual conduct, based on the female ideal of chastity. Pankhurst's slogan of "Votes for Women and Chastity for Men" reechoed the older radical refusal to cater sexually to men so long as women remained subordinates.

Nonetheless this attack on patriarchy and male vice involved no positive assertion of female sexuality. It was still couched within the terms of a "separate sphere" ideology and assumed that women were essentially moral, "spiritual" creatures who needed to be protected from essentially animalistic, "carnal" men. Moreover, the obsession with male vice again sidetracked early-twentieth-century feminists into crusades against white slavery, while obscuring the economic basis of prostitution. It even prompted the most progressive women of the day to advocate raising the age of consent to twenty-one. Finally, it led to repressive public policies. Commenting on the enforcement of the White Slavery Act of 1912, Sylvia Pankhurst remarked, "It is a strange thing that the latest Criminal Amendment Act, which was passed ostensibly to protect women, is being used almost exclusively to punish women."[59] As late as 1914, feminists were rediscovering once again that the state "protection" of young women inevitably led to coercive and repressive measures against those same women.

Notes

ABBREVIATIONS

B.J.V.D. *British Journal of Venereal Disease*
B.M.J.   *British Medical Journal* ·
D.I.   *Devonport Independent and Stonehouse Gazette* (Plymouth)
J.S.S.   *Journal of the Statistical Society of London* ·
LNA   Ladies' National Association
M.T.G.   *Medical Times and Gazette* (London)
NA   National Association
N.L.J.   *National League Journal* (London)
P.P.   *Parliamentary Papers*
P.R.O.   Public Record Office
W.D.M.   *Western Daily Mercury* (Plymouth)
W.H.I.   *Weekly Hampshire Independent* (Southampton)
W.M.N.   *Western Morning News* (Plymouth)

INTRODUCTION

1. Cecil Woodham-Smith, *Florence Nightingale, 1820–1910* (New York, 1951), p. 267.
2. An M.P. to Josephine Butler, quoted in *Josephine Butler: An Autobiographical Memoir*, eds. George W. Johnson and Lucy Johnson (London, 1909), p. 90.
3. An Act for the Prevention of Contagious Diseases at Certain Naval and Military Stations, 27 and 28 Vict. c. 85; An Act for the Better Prevention of Contagious Diseases at Certain Naval and Military Stations, 29 and 30 Vict. c. 96; An Act to Amend the Contagious Diseases Acts, 1866, 32 and 33 Vict. c. 86.
4. See, for example, Richard L. Bianco, "The Attempted Control of Venereal Disease in the Army of Mid-Victorian England," *Journal of the Society for Army Historical Research* 45 (Winter 1967), 234–41.
5. Keith Thomas, "The Double Standard," *Journal of the History of Ideas* 20 (1959), 199; Eric Trudgill, *Madonnas and Magdalens: The Origins and Development of Victorian Sexual Attitudes* (New York, 1976), pp. 191–3.

257

6. Judith R. Walkowitz, "Notes on the History of Victorian Prostitution," *Feminist Studies* 1 (Spring 1972), 105–14; Gertrude Himmelfarb, "Mayhew's Poor: A Problem of Identity," *Victorian Studies* 14 (March 1971), 307–20; Leonore Davidoff, "Class and Gender in Victorian England: The Diaries of Arthur J. Munby and Hannah Cullwick," *Feminist Studies* 5 (Spring 1979), 88–92.
7. Davidoff, "Class and Gender," 88.
8. Brian Harrison, "Underneath the Victorians," *Victorian Studies* 10 (March 1967), 257; Eugene L. Rasor, *Reform in the Royal Navy; A Social History of the Lower Deck 1850 to 1889* (London, 1955), pp. 98, 99.
9. Michel Foucault, *The History of Sexuality. Volume I: An Introduction,* trans. R. Hurley (New York, 1978); Jeffrey Weeks, *Coming Out: Homosexual Politics in Britain from the Nineteenth Century to the Present* (London, 1977).
10. Carroll Smith-Rosenberg, "Bodies, Boundaries and Invasion: Prostitution and the Family in Antebellum America." Presented at New York University, 10 May 1979.
11. Davidoff, "Class and Gender," 88, 90. Studies that focus on this single repressive code of sexualtiy include Steven Marcus, *The Other Victorians: A Study of Sexuality and Pornography in Mid-Nineteenth Century England* (New York, 1966); Peter T. Cominos, "Late-Victorian Sexual Respectability and the Social System," *International Review of Social History* 8 (1963), 18–48, 216–50; Ben Barker-Benfield, *The Horrors of the Half-Known Life: Male Attitudes Toward Women and Sexuality in Nineteenth-Century America* (New York, 1976).
12. Harrison, "Underneath," p. 250; Charles Rosenberg, "Sexuality, Class, and Role," *American Quarterly* 25 (May 1973), 131–53; Carroll Smith-Rosenberg, "Sex as Symbol in Victorian Purity: An Ethno-historical Analysis of Jacksonian America," in *Turning Points: Historical and Sociological Essays on the Family,* eds. John Demos and Sarane S. Boocock, *American Journal of Sociology* 84 (1978), supplement; F. B. Smith, "Sexuality in Britain, 1800–1900: Some Suggested Revisions," in *A Widening Sphere: Changing Roles of Victorian Women,* ed. Martha Vicinus (Bloomington, 1977), 182–98.
13. Raymond Williams, *Marxism and Literature* (Oxford, 1977), p. 113.
14. Ray Strachey, *The Cause: A Short History of the Women's Movement in Great Britain* (London, 1928). ch. 10; Josephine Kamm, *Rapiers and Battleaxes: The Women's Movement and Its Aftermath* (London, 1966), ch. 6.
15. See, for example, Harold Perkin, *The Origins of Modern English Society, 1780–1880* (London, 1969), p. 444.
16. Brian Harrison, *Drink and the Victorians: The Temperance Question in England 1815–1872* (London, 1971), pp. 174, 175, 224, 371, 378, 381; "State Intervention and Moral Reform," in *Pressure from Without in Early Victorian England,* ed. Patricia Hollis (London, 1974), pp. 319, 321.

17. Paul McHugh, "The Campaign to Repeal the Contagious Diseases Acts: Some Organizational Questions" (Ph.D. diss., Oxford Univ., 1976). McHugh carefully analyzes the structure and political tactics of the numerous repeal organizations that proliferated over the course of the nineteenth century.
18. See Mary Ryan, "The Power of Women's Networks: A Case Study of Female Moral Reform in Antebellum America," *Feminist Studies* 5 (Spring 1979), 66–86.
19. Myrna Trustram, "State Regulation of Vice–Colchester and the Contagious Diseases Acts, 1864, 1866, 1869" (B.A. thesis, Univ. of Essex, 1977).
20. Reverend Gledstone, *Shield* (London), 14 April 1877.
21. Judith R. Walkowitz and Daniel J. Walkowitz, " 'We Are Not Beasts of the Field': Prostitution and the Poor in Plymouth and Southampton Under the Contagious Diseases Acts," *Feminist Studies* 1 (Winter 1973), 73–106; Judith R. Walkowitz, "The Making of an Outcast Group: Prostitutes and Working Women in Nineteenth Century Plymouth and Southampton," in *A Widening Sphere*, pp. 72–93.
22. For a recent study of prostitution that demonstrates the virtues as well as the drawbacks of relying on local sources of this sort, see Frances Finnegan, *Poverty and Prostitution: A Study of Victorian Prostitutes in York* (Cambridge, 1979).

1. THE COMMON PROSTITUTE IN VICTORIAN BRITAIN

1. William Acton, *Prostitution* [1870], ed. Peter Fryer (New York, 1968), p. 24.
2. Ibid.
3. Reverend William Tuckniss, "The Agencies at Present in Operation Within the Metropolis for the Suppression of Vice and Crime," in *London Labour and the London Poor*, ed. Henry Mayhew (4 vols., London, 1861–2; rpt., New York, 1968), IV, 30–8.
4. See Leon Radzinowicz, *History of English Criminal Law and Its Administration from 1750* (4 vols., London 1948–68), I, 2.
5. These observations were particularly frequent during the "hungry" forties. See, for example, Henry Mayhew's interviews with destitute needlewomen in *The Unknown Mayhew*, eds. E. P. Thompson and Eileen Yeo (New York, 1972), pp. 168–80.
6. Daniel Cooper, testimony before the House of Commons Select Committee on the Administration, Operation, and Effects of the Contagious Diseases Acts of 1866–9, *P.P.*, 1882 (340), IX, Q. 3928, 3930, 4067. In his responses Cooper raised the problem of what constituted a "professional" prostitute and denied that many prostitutes were simultaneously able to carry on a respectable "business" like dressmaking during the day. See, for example, Q. 4069: "Many women are in business, and

increase their earnings by sly prostitution; but they are so few that I can scarcely bring them within comparison."

7. Joan Scott and Louise Tilly, "Women's Work and the Family in Nineteenth Century Europe," *Comparative Studies in History and Society* 16 (Winter 1975), 57.

8. Arthur Engel, "Immoral Intentions: The University of Oxford and the Problem of Prostitution, 1827–1914," *Victorian Studies* 23 (1979) 79–107; *Lock Hospital Reports, 1846–1871*, Royal College of Surgeons, London; William Tait, *Magdalenism: An Inquiry into the Extent, Causes, and Consequences of Prostitution* (Edinburgh, 1840), p. 25; P.R.O., Admiralty Papers, Adm. 1/6122, 3 February 1869; Frances Finnegan, *Poverty and Prostitution: A Study of Victorian Prostitutes in York* (Cambridge, 1979), p. 71.

9. The majority of prostitutes in the London Lock Hospital in the 1840s and 1850s listed themselves as Anglicans, although the chaplain would tend to put down Anglican if there were any doubt or vagueness. See *Lock Hospital Reports, 1846–1871*. Most inmates of the Rescue Society of London had attended Sunday school and most could read and write "tolerably well." *Rescue Society Reports, 1877–1882*. Butler Collection, Fawcett Library, London. In a conversation, Gareth Stedman Jones noted that prostitutes were active in "Church and King" type riots against ritualist missionaries in the East End during the 1850s. For prostitutes' response to militarism and the Boer War, see Emma K. Smith (pseud.), *A Cornish Waif's Story* (New York, 1956), p. 65.

10. *P.P.*, 1882 (340), IX, App. B; Reverend G. Merrick, *Work Among the Fallen, as Seen in the Prison Cells* (London, 1890); A. Maude Royden, foreword, *Downward Paths: An Inquiry into the Causes Which Contribute to the Making of the Prostitute* (London, 1913); Gladys Mary Hall, *Prostitution: A Survey and a Challenge* (London, 1933), p. 31; H. Llewellyn Smith, ed., *The New Survey of London and Labour* (London, 1932), pp. 341, 342; Tait, *Magdalenism*, p. 24.

11. Abraham Flexner, *Prostitution in Europe* (New York, 1914), p. 6.

12. Merrick, *Work Among the Fallen,* pp. 26, 27.

13. *Eighth Annual Report of the Homes of Hope, 1868* (London, 1869), pp. 16, 17. *Lock Hospital Reports, 1857–1863; Rescue Society Reports, 1877–1882, 1883–1885*. The *Lock Hospital Report* for 1858, for example, stated (p. 15) that the "larger part of women have been in service." Between 1874 and 1877, 82 percent (1,080 out of 1,310 cases) of the inmates of the Rescue Society homes had been domestic servants. *Twenty-fifth Annual Report of the Rescue Society, 1877,* p. 14.

14. Father Nugent, testimony before the Select Committee of the House of Lords Appointed to Inquire into the State of the Law Related to the Protection of Young Girls, *P.P.,* 1882 (344), XIII, Q. 112, 113; *P.P.,* 1882 (340), IX, App. 9.

15. These new jobs in the "tertiary" sector had many of the social disabilities

associated with domestic service. Royden, *Downward Paths,* pp. 15, 18; Llewellyn Smith, *New Survey,* p. 342.

16. Derek Hudson, ed., *Munby, Man of Two Worlds: The Life and Diaries of Arthur J. Munby, 1828–1910* (London, 1972), p. 46.

17. Scott and Tilly, "Women's Work," 41–3.

18. For example, half or full orphans constituted 64 percent of the female lock patients in the London Lock Hospital in 1849; 69 percent of the inmates in the Glasgow Magdalen Institution in 1870; 78 percent of the prostitute prisoners in Clerkenwell Jail in 1882; 67 percent of Merrick's sample of Millbank prostitutes; 90 percent in the House of Mercy at Bovey Tracey in 1874; 68.4 percent of the female inmates of Rescue Society homes between 1877 and 1881; 76 percent of the inmates of the London Female Preventive and Reformatory Institution in 1910–11. See "Report of the London Hospital, 1849," p. 11; William Logan, *The Great Social Evil; Its Causes, Extent, Results and Remedies* (London, 1871); *P.P.,* 1882 (340), IX, App. 9; Merrick, *Work Among the Fallen,* p. 31; *Rescue Society Reports,* 1877–82; Flexner, *Prostitution,* p. 76; P.R.O., Admiralty Papers, Adm. 2/6179, 29 August 1870.

19. Michael Anderson, *Family Life in Nineteenth Lancashire* (Cambridge, 1971) p. 148. The proportion of half orphans among prostitutes in institutions was roughly comparable to the percentage of orphans among the unmarried mothers applying to the Foundling Hospital in London, from 1830 to 1900. Thanks to John Gillis for this latter information.

20. Bracebridge Hemyng, "Prostitution in London," in *London Labour,* p. 215.

21. "Abstract of the Case Book," in *Twenty-sixth Annual Report of the Rescue Society, . . . 1878,* pp. 22–41.

22. Merrick, *Work Among the Fallen,* p. 33. Until 1885 the age of consent was 13. Hence prostitutes did not arbitrarily select that age to protect clients or male friends from legal prosecution. After 1885 the age of consent was raised to 16, but prostitutes still continued to report the same age of sexual initiation.

23. *Eighteenth Annual Report of the Rescue Society, . . . 1870,* p. 17.

24. Ibid.

25. See W. T. Stead, *The Maiden Tribute of Modern Babylon (The Report of the "Pall Mall Gazette's" Secret Commission)* (London, 1885).

26. J. B. Nevins, "Enquiry into the Condition of Prostitution," *Medical Enquirer* 2 (1876–7), 17–28, Finnegan, *Poverty and Prostitution,* p. 81.

27. *Lock Hospital Reports, 1849–1863.*

28. *Thirteenth Annual Report of the Rescue Society, . . . 1882,* p. 39.

29. "Abstract of the Case Book," in *Twenty-sixth Annual Report, . . . 1878,* pp. 22–41.

30. Merrick, *Work Among the Fallen,* p. 40.

31. "Juvenile Prostitution in London," in *Twenty-fifth Annual Report of the Rescue Society, . . . 1877,* p. 61.

32. "Abstract of the Case Book," in *Twenty-sixth Annual Report of the Rescue Society, . . . 1878*, pp. 22–41; Royden, *Downward Paths*, p. 16.

33. *Lock Hospital Reports, 1857–1863;* Frederick W. Lowndes, *Prostitution and Syphilis in Liverpool, and the Working of the Contagious Diseases Acts at Aldershot, Chatham, Plymouth, and Devonport* (London, 1876), p. 12; Alexander Patterson, "Statistics of Glasgow Lock Hospital Since Its Foundation in 1805—With Remarks on the Contagious Diseases Acts, and on Syphilis" (1882), 318; (1882) 411. Reprinted from *Glasgow Medical Journal* 18 (1882).

34. Patterson, *Statistics;* M. Berkeley Hill, *"Illustrations of the Workings of the Contagious Diseases Acts," B.M.J.* 2 (1867), 563.

35. For example, between 1857 and 1863, only 191 out of 1,432 (or 13.3 percent) single female lock patients in the London Lock Hospital were 26 years and older. *Lock Hospital Reports, 1857–63.* Prostitutes imprisoned for drunkenness and disorderly behavior were somewhat older. Reverend J. W. Horsley, a Clerkenwell prison chaplain, noted in *Jottings from Jail* (London, 1887), p. 8, that few prostitutes in prison were over 40 and that ages 20 to 30 were usually "the worst decade." According to James Greenwood, *The Seven Curses of London* (Boston, 1869), p. 25, Curragh "Wrens" ranged from 17 to 25. Women registered under the Contagious Diseases Acts were also heavily concentrated in this age category. "Report of the Assistant Commissioner of Metropolitan Police on the Operation of the Contagious Diseases Acts" (1881), *P.P.,* 1882, LII. See also William Acton, testimony before the Select Committee of the House of Lords Appointed to Consider the Contagious Diseases Acts (1867–8), *P.P.,* 1871, VIII, Q. 972, 973, 1060; Finnegan, *Poverty and Prostitution,* p. 81.

36. Daniel Cooper, testimony before the Select Committee on the Best Means of Protecting Infants Put Out to Nurse, *P.P.,* 1871 (372), VII, Q. 2624.

37. William Acton, "Observations on Illegitimacy in the London Parishes of St. Marylebone, St. Pancras, and St. George's Southwark, During the year 1857; Deduced from the Returns of the Registrar General," *J.S.S.* (December 1859), 491–505; John Gillis, "Servants, Sexual Relations, and the Risk of Illegitimacy in London, 1801–1900" (unpublished) p. 6.

38. Henry Mayhew reported that costermongers paired off into quasi-monogamous relations in their mid-teens, without evidence of early pregnancy. *London Labour and the London Poor, I, 21;* Peter Laslett, "The Age of Sexual Maturity," in *Family Life and Illicit Love in Earlier Generations* (Cambridge, 1977), p. 230; Finnegan, *Poverty and Prostitution,* pp. 83, 84.

39. Merrick, *Work Among the Fallen,* p. 33; Royden, *Downward Paths,* p. 31.

40. "Report of the Local Government Inspector," *P.R.O.,* Home Office Papers, H. O. 45/9547/59343L.

41. Charles Drysdale, quoted in *B.M.J.* 1 (1866), 184.

42. Today it is estimated that sterility results in more than 10 percent of

untreated cases of gonorrhea. For prostitutes who contracted syphilis the rate of miscarriage, stillbirth, and sickly infants would have been very high during the first five years of the infection. R. S. Morton, *Venereal Diseases* (London, 1966), p. 55; "Report of the Royal Commission on Venereal Diseases," *P.P.*, 1916 (Cd. 8190), XVI, app. I.

43. P.R.O., Home Office Papers, H.O. 45/9547/59443L.

44. Commentators generally agreed that the rigors of streetwalking discouraged most women from pursuing the "gay life" for very long; many probably left the streets within a few days or weeks; most of the rest remained in prostitution less than two years. Only a small proportion remained beyond their mid-twenties. Daniel Cooper, testimony before the 1882 Select Committee on the C.D. acts, *P.P.*, 1882, IX, Q. 4067; P.R.O., Adm. 1/6148, 1875; Finnegan, *Poverty and Prostitution*, p. 83.

45. For example, the *Thirty-first Annual Report of the Rescue Society, . . . 1883*, p. 27: "May God have mercy on the destroyers of these children—*sometimes their own.*" In the 1950s Kinsey reported that 6 percent of the 8,000 white middle-class women surveyed had had sexual contact with an adult relative during childhood. For a critical summary of the sociological literature on incest, see Judith Iterman and Lisa Hirschman, "Father-Daughter Incest," *Signs* 2 (Summer 1977), 735–56.

46. See "Insubordination of Children," *Twenty-eighth Annual Report of the Rescue Society, . . . 1877*, pp. 55, 56; Royden, *Downward Paths*, p. 20.

47. Robert Roberts, *The Classic Slum* (Manchester, 1971), p. 33; Louise Ermy, *The Memoirs of a Working Woman* (Norwich, 1934), p. 31; Laura Oren, "The Welfare of Women in Laboring Families: England 1860–1950," in *Clio's Consciousness Raised: New Perspectives on the History of Women*, eds. Mary S. Hartman and Lois Banner (New York, 1974), pp. 226–44; Sheila Ryan Johanssen, "Sex and Death in Victorian England: An Examination of Age- and Sex-Specific Death Rates, 1840–1910," in *A Widening Sphere: Changing Roles of Victorian Women*, ed. Martha Vicinus (Bloomington, 1977), pp. 163–81.

48. Mrs. Layton, "Memories of Seventy Years," in *Life as We Have Known it*, ed. Margaret Lleywelyn Davies [1931] (New York, 1975), p. 26. None of the surveys on prostitutes' family backgrounds indicate a preponderance of motherless over fatherless women.

49. *Thirty-third Report of the Rescue Society, . . . 1885*, p. 53.

50. Merrick, *Work Among the Fallen*, p. 39. Forty-two percent of the women in Reverend Horsley's sample also went on the street "as a matter of choice." *PP.*, 1882, IX, App. 9.

51. A brothel keeper, quoted in *Maiden Tribute*, p. 8.

52. Royden, *Downward Paths*, p. 45.

53. James Hammick, "On the Judicial Statistics of England, with Special Reference to the Recent Returns Relating to Crime," *J.S.S.* 30 (1867), 391, 392; *P.P.*, 1867–8, LXVII.

54. "Report of the Royal Commission on Venereal Disease," *P.P.*, 1916 (8190), XVI, App. I. Alan Dawley, "Prostitution and the Reproduction of Sexual Relations in Nineteenth Century America," paper presented before the Davis Center Seminar, Princeton University, 7 April 1978. Dawley (p. 19) cites statistics of "syphilis rejection rate of army recruits" that (with the exception of middle-class death rates) roughly correspond with the distribution of syphilitic death rates cited above. One must add a cautionary note to these statistics, however, as they were based only on imperfect clinical diagnosis and not on serological tests.

55. Tait, *Magdalenism*, p. 25. Wages for female textile workers varied significantly between skilled and unskilled workers and according to regions—for example, between Glasgow and Lancashire.

56. Hudson, *Munby*, p. 69.

57. A. E. Chesterton, *In Darkest London* (London, 1926), p. 77.

58. Engel, "Prostitution in Nineteenth-Century Oxford."

59. Merrick, *Work Among the Fallen*, p. 19.

60. A soldier's woman, quoted in Hemyng, "Prostitution in London," p. 235.

61. Tait, *Magdalenism*, p. 30; Acton, *Prostitution* (1870), p. 4; Hemyng, "Prostitution in London," pp. 240–359; Finnegan, *Poverty and Prostitution*, chs. 2, 4; Nevins, "Enquiry into Prostitutiion," pp. 17–28. In Hull, for example, 88.5 percent of prostitutes were listed as residing in third-class brothels, catering to operatives, apprentices, farm workers, soldiers, and sailors (Nevins, "Enquiry," p. 22). The police returns of 1857 and 1869 identified two-thirds of London prostitutes as residing in "low neighborhoods in low lodgings," to distinguish them from the "well-dressed prostitutes" who walked the streets or remained in brothels. Some of these streetwalkers left their neighborhood to conduct their business in more prosperous quarters, but, in general, they seem to have stayed within their neighborhood and catered to a clientele appropriate to the neighborhood.

62. Hudson, *Munby*, pp. 40, 41.

63. William Logan, *An Exposure from Personal Observation of Female Prostitution in London, Leeds, and Rochdale, and Especially in the City of Glasgow, with Remarks on the Cause, Extent, and Remedy of the Evil* (Glasgow, 1843), p. 72; testimony of Mr. Bond, surgeon to the metropolitan police, before the Royal Commission on the Administration and Operation of the Contagious Diseases Acts, 1868–69 (1871), *P.P.*, 1871 (C. 408-I), XIX, Q. 15040; Acton, *Prostitution Considered in Its Moral, Social, and Sanitary Aspects in London and Other Large Cities; with Proposals for the Mitigation and Prevention of Its Attendant Evil* (London, 1870), p. 81; Hemyng, "Prostitution in London," p. 240. During the 1840s, women in third-class brothels in Leeds, Manchester, and Glasgow averaged twenty to thirty shillings a week, at a shilling per

customer. This was a substantial sum at the time, but in these explicit brothels they had to pay a major part of their takings to the brothel keeper. In the sixties and seventies, a shilling continued to be the going price for a soldier's woman in London and elsewhere, many of whom did not average the same number of customers as brothel inmates. Nor were soldiers' prostitutes at the rock bottom of the pay scale. They could afford to be more selective than the park women, who, according to Hemyng, (p. 243) "give themselves up to disgusting practices," or the old worn-out prostitutes who "retire for prostitution into dirty low courts . . . with shop boys, errand lads, petty thieves, and labouring men, for a few paltry coppers."

64. Hemyng, "Prostitution in London," p. 240; F. W. Lowndes, "The Liverpool Lock Hospital and the Prevalence and Severity of Constitutional Syphilis in Liverpool," *B.M.J.* 1 (1880), 727.
65. Hemyng, "Prostitution in London," p. 223.
66. Ibid., p. 235.
67. Ibid., p. 220.
68. Acton, *Prostitution* (1870, Fryer ed.), pp. 36, 37. The number of explicit brothels in London had declined to two by 1868.
69. Nevins, "Enquiry into Prostitution," p. 22. Finnegan, *Poverty and Prostitution*, pp. 69, 70, also notes a decline in known prostitutes and in houses of ill-fame in mid-Victorian York, but she offers no explanation.
70. Nevins, "Enquiry into Prostitution," p. 22; C. A. Pearl, *The Girl with the Swansdown Seat* (New York, 1955), pp. 190, 191.
71. Acton, *Prostitution Considered in Its Moral, Social, and Sanitary Aspects in London and Other Large Cities; with Proposals for the Mitigation and Prevention of its Attendant Evil* (London, 1857), p. 121; Engel, "Immoral Intentions"; see Chapter 10.
72. Reverend J. E. Mercer, *The Conditions of Life in Angel Meadow*, paper read before the Manchester Statistical Society, 28 April 1897 (Manchester, 1897); Robert D. Storch, "Police Control of Street Prostitution in Victorian London: A Study in the Contexts of Police Acton," in *Police and Society*, ed. David H. Bayley (Beverly Hills, Calif., 1977); p. 66; Finnegan, *Poverty and Prostitution*, p. 35.
73. Tait, *Magdalenism*, p. 76; Acton, *Prostitution* (1870, Fryer ed.), p. 56.
74. Frederick Rodgers, *Labour, Life, and Literature* (London, 1913), pp. 3, 4.
75. Hemyng, "Prostitution in London," p. 253; John Binny, "Thieves and Swindlers," in Henry Mayhew, ed., *London Labour and the London Poor*, IV, 365. According to Frederick Wreford, police chief of Plymouth, it "would be only a thief prostitute who would keep a crimp"; this "would not be done in an ordinary brothel." *P.P.*, 1882, IX, Q. 162.
76. Reverend J. E. Mercer, *The Conditions of Life*, p. 173. Mercer remarked that rescue workers found "a more vicious state of affairs [here] than even in the worst parts of Whitechapel. For in London they said, it is

chiefly women who gather together other women in houses of ill-fame, whereas in Angel Meadow it is frequently young men who hold girls in their power, and who pass idle dissolute lives on the earnings of their poor slaves."

77. For literary images of prostitution, see Françoise Basch, *Relative Creatures: Victorian Women in Society and the Novel* (New York, 1974), section 3, "Fallen Women."

78. Ronald Pearsall, *The Worm in the Bud: The World of Victorian Sexuality* (Toronto, 1969), p. 283.

79. Roberts, *The Classic Slum,* p. 24.

80. P.R.O., H.O., 45/6628, 17 March 1858.

81. James Greenwood, *In Strange Company: The Notebook of a Roving Correspondent* (London, 1873), pp. 131, 132.

82. Mary Higgs, "Three Nights in Women's Lodging Houses," in *Into Unknown England 1866–1913: Selections from the Social Explorers,* ed. Peter Keating (Glasgow, 1976), p. 277.

83. Mary Higgs, *Glimpse into the Abyss* (London, 1906), p. 214.

84. Ibid., p. 213; Hudson, *Munby,* p. 50.

85. Cecil Bishop, *Women and Crime* (London, 1931), p. 69.

86. Greenwood, *Seven Curses,* pp. 217, 218.

87. Andrew Cluer, *Plymouth and Plymouthians* (Plymouth, 1974).

88. Higgs, "Three Nights," p. 285.

89. *P.P.,* 1882 (344), XIII, Q. 139.

90. Acton, *Prostitution* (1870), p. 23.

91. Tait, *Magdalenism,* p. 76.

92. Henry Courtenay, letter to the Home Office, P.R.O., H.O. 45/9547/59343L/3, 14 October 1885. Report of Superintendent of "P" Division, Metropolitan Police, Metropolitan Police Papers, P.R.O., Mepol., 2/355, 18 August 1904.

93. Sarah Robinson, *The Soldier's Friend: A Pioneer's Record* (London, 1913), p. 49.

94. Ibid.

95. P.R.O., H.O. 45/6628, 17 March 1856.

96. Hemyng, "Prostitution," p. 230.

97. Finnegan, *Poverty and Prostitution,* p. 53. Although prostitutes lived among the Irish poor in Plymouth, Irish girls were in fact *underrepresented* among registered prostitutes. See 1871 Census Schedule, P.R.O., R.G. 10/2120; P.R.O., Admiralty Papers, Adm. 1/6122, 3 February 1869.

98. Acton, *Prostitution* (1870), p. 23.

99. Ibid., p. 24.

100. Elwyn Jones and John Lloyd, eds., *The Ripper File* (London, 1976), p. 73.

101. Rodgers, *Labour,* pp. 3, 4; "Petition to the Queen," *Reynolds Newspaper* (London), 28 October 1888.

2. SOCIAL SCIENCE AND THE GREAT SOCIAL EVIL

1. See Helen Ware, "Prostitution and the State: The Recruitment, Regulation and Role of Prostitution in the Nineteenth and Twentieth Century" (Univ. of London, Ph.D. diss., 1969).
2. William Gladstone, *The Gladstone Diaries*, eds. M. R. D. Foot and H. G. G. Matthew (4 vols., Oxford, 1974), III, xlviii; Derek Hudson, ed., *Munby, Man of Two Worlds: The Life and Diaries of Arthur J. Munby, 1828–1910* (London, 1972).
3. William Bevan, *Prostitution in the Borough of Liverpool* (Liverpool, 1843); Ralph Wardlaw, *Lectures on Female Prostitution,* (Glasgow, 1842); Robert Vaughan, *The Age of Great Cities* (London, 1843); William Logan, *An Exposure from Personal Observation of Female Prostitution in London, Leeds and Rochdale, and Especially in the City of Glasgow; with Remarks on the Cause, Extent, Results and Remedy of the Evil* (Glasgow, 1843); J. D. Talbot, *The Miseries of Prostitution* (London, 1844); Michael Ryan, *Prostitution in London, with a Comparative View of That of Paris, and New York* (London, 1839); William Tait, *Magdalenism: An Inquiry into the Extent, Causes, and Consequences of Prostitution* (Edinburgh, 1840).
4. Barbara Taylor, "Socialism, Marriage and the Working Class" (unpublished).
5. Sarah Stickney Ellis, *The Woman of England, Their Social Duties, and Domestic Habits* (Philadelphia, 1841), chs. 7–11.
6. Michael Ryan, *The Philosophy of Marriage in Its Social, Moral, and Physical Relations* (London, 1839), p. 42.
7. Ibid.
8. See Lawrence Stone, *The Family, Sex, and Marriage in England 1500–1800* (New York, 1977); E. P. Thompson, "Patrician Society, Plebeian Culture," *Journal of Social History* 7 (Summer 1974), 368; Rayna Rapp and Ellen Ross, "Sex and Society: A Research Note from Social History and Anthropology" (unpublished, 1979). By the early Victorian period, production had been largely removed from the household, and masters no longer had the same personal ties to their employees. Evangelical writers interpreted the presence of public women on the streets, as well as the growing estrangement between classes, as symptomatic of the breakdown of cohesive social authority in the "age of the great cities."
9. Bevan, *Prostitution*, p. 5.
10. Tait, *Magdalenism*, p. 176.
11. A. J. B. Parent-Duchâtelet, quoted in Wardlaw, *Lectures*, pp. 16, 17.
12. Ryan, *Philosophy*, pp. 17–19; Tait, *Magdalenism*, pp. 96–7.
13. Tait, *Magdalenism*, p. x.
14. Ryan, *Philosophy*, pp. 17–19; Tait, *Magdalenism*, p. 254.
15. "Your Fellow-Workman, a Socialist," to the Editor, *New Moral World*

(1837), 406. Special thanks to Barbara Taylor for the following references to Owenite and Chartist journals.

16. Allen Davenport, *Life of Thomas Spence* (1839), p. 22.
17. "The British Female Penitent Refuge," *New Moral World* (1841), 54.
18. Barbara Taylor, "Socialism, Marriage"; Keith Thomas, "The Double Standard," *Journal of the History of Ideas* 20 (1959), 195–216.
19. Wardlaw, *Lectures,* pp. 14, 15.
20. Taylor, "Socialism, Marriage," p. 18.
21. Wardlaw, *Lectures,* p. 10.
22. Quoted in Taylor, "Socialism, Marriage," p. 17.
23. Tait, *Magdalenism,* x.
24. A. J. B. Parent-Duchâtelet, *De la prostitution dans la ville de Paris, considérée sous le rapport de l'hygiène publique de la morale et de l'administration* (2 vols., Paris, 1857), I, 18.
25. Henry Milton, "Paris, Its Dangerous Classes," *Quarterly Review* 70 (1842), 20.
26. The women were overwhelmingly between the ages of 20 and 26. Parent-Duchâtelet, *De la prostitution,* I, 83, 84.
27. Only 25 percent of the women were illegitimate. However, a striking proportion were orphans and homeless.
28. Parent-Duchâtelet, *De la prostitution,* I, 83, 84.
29. Michael Cullen, *The Statistical Movement in Early Victorian Britain* (New York, 1975), p. 62.
30. Philip Abrams, *The Origins of British Sociology 1834–1914* (Chicago, 1968), p. 39.
31. Cullen, *Statistical Movement,* p. 110.
32. Tait, *Magdalenism,* p. 26.
33. Ibid., pp. 2–4.
34. Ibid., p. 25. Bevan, *Prostitution,* p. 8, observed the same influx of factory girls into Liverpool for purposes of prostitution during times of distress.
35. Tait, *Magdalenism,* p. 80.
36. Abrams, *Origins,* p. 40.
37. See Charles A. Valentine, *Culture and Poverty: Critique and Counter-Proposals* (Chicago, 1967).
38. Tait, *Magdalenism,* p. 143.
39. Talbot, *Miseries,* p. 43.
40. Tait, *Magdalenism,* pp. 35, 155; Wardlaw, *Lectures,* pp. 39, 41.
41. Parent-Duchâtelet, quoted in Tait, *Magdalenism,* p. 236.
42. Wardlaw, *Lectures,* p. 150.
43. *First Report of the Associate Institute for Improving and Enforcing Laws for the Protection of Women* (London, 1846), p. 34.
44. Ibid., p. 10.
45. Ibid., p. 40.

46. See J. A. Banks and Olive Banks, *Feminism and Family Planning* (New York, 1964), ch. 3.
47. See Cott, *Bonds of Womanhood,* ch. 4; Whitney R. Cross, *The Burned-Over District: The Social and Intellectual History of Enthusiastic Religion of Western New York 1800–1850* (Ithaca, 1950), bks. IV and V; Kathleen Heasman, *Evangelicals in Action: An Appraisal of their Social Work in the Victorian Era* (London, 1962), pp. 26–8.; Edward J. Bristow, *Vice and Vigilance: Purity Movements in Britain Since 1700* (Dublin, 1977).
48. James Miller, *Prostitution Considered in Relation to Its Cause* (Edinburgh, 1859), p. 7.
49. Abrams, *Origins,* p. 45.
50. Heasman, *Evangelicals,* pp. 153–6; "Woman's Work in the Reformatory Cause," *Reformatory and Refuge Union Journal* (1862), 39.
51. Quoted in Keith Nield, introduction, *Prostitution in the Victorian Age: Debate on the Issues from Nineteenth-Century Critical Journals* (Westmead, 1973).
52. See the exchange between a Mr. Rowley and the Commander of the "K" division of the metropolitan police, P.R.O., Home Office Papers, H.O. 45/6628, 17 March 1858.
53. See Chapter 4.
54. Nield, *Prostitution,* introduction.
55. [W. R. Greg], "Prostitution," *Westminster Review* 53 (1850), 481.
56. Ibid., 484.
57. Ibid., 486, 487.
58. See Charles Drysdale, a Neo-Malthusian, to the editor, *Medical Press and Circular* (1869), 413, and the angry responses (1869), 449.
59. Greg, "Prostitution," 454.
60. Ibid., 493.
61. Ibid., 491.
62. Steven Marcus, *The Other Victorians: A Study of Sexuality and Pornography in Mid-Nineteenth-Century England* (New York, 1966), p. 2.
63. Acton, *Prostitution* (1870, Fryer ed.) (New York, 1968), p. 24.
64. William Acton, *The Functions and Disorders of the Reproductive Organs in Childhood, Youth, Adult Age, and Advanced Life Considered in Their Physiological, Social, and Moral Relations,* 6th ed. (London, 1875), p. 200.
65. Acton, *Prostitution* (1870, Fryer ed.), p. 59.
66. Ibid. (1857), p. 121.
67. Ibid. (1870, Fryer ed.), p. 26.

3. VENEREAL DISEASE

1. Like judicial statistics, medical statistics of the Victorian period have to be used cautiously. First, medical statistics were based on flawed diag-

noses. Second, classification and nomenclature changed over the course of the nineteenth century. For example, in army returns, primary and secondary syphilis were first listed separately only in 1879; moreover, chancroid and syphilis were not distinguished in military returns until 1905. Nineteenth-century death rates for syphilis did not include mortality for parasyphilitic diseases, although deaths from aneurysm paralleled the decline of deaths attributed to syphilis. It would be fair to argue, then, that military medical statistics and civilian death rates for syphilis are rough indicators of the long-range change in incidence and virulence in syphilis and gonorrhea. For a discussion of venereal-disease statistics, see C. H. Melville, "The History and Epidemiology of Syphilis in the More Important Armies," in *A System of Syphilis,* eds. D'Arcy Power and J. K. Murphy (6 vols. London, 1910), VI, 28; Christopher Lloyd and Jack L. S. Coulter, *Keevil's Medicine and the Navy, 1200–1900,* (4 vols., Edinburgh, 1963) IV, 266–71.

2. William Sloggett, "History and Operations of the Contagious Diseases Acts in the Home Ports," P.R.O., Adm. 1/6418, 10 April 1873, p. 2.

3. William Acton, "Observations on Venereal Diseases in the United Kingdom: From Statistical Reports in the Army, Navy, and Merchant Service, with Remarks on the Mortality from Syphilis in the Metropolis, Compiled from the Official Returns of the Registrar-General," *Lancet* 2 (1846), 370, 371.

4. *Lancet* 1 (1846), 279.

5. William Acton, *Prostitution, Considered in Its Moral, Social, and Sanitary Aspects, in London and Other Large Cities and Garrison Towns; with Proposals for the Control and Prevention of Its Attendant Evils* (London, 1870), pp. 53, 54.

6. Ibid., p. 55; J. B. Curgenven, *The Contagious Diseases Act of 1866, and Its Extension to the Civilian Population* (London, 1868), p. 12.

7. Acton, *Prostitution,* p. 55.

8. Sir John Simon, "Eleventh Report of the Medical Officer of the Privy Council," *P.P.,* 1868–69 (4127), XXXII; *Lancet* 2 (1869), 410, 411.

9. "Report of the Royal Commission on Venereal Diseases," *P.P.,* 1916 (Cd. 8190), p. 23, especially as follows: "While we have been unable to arrive at any positive figures, the evidence we have received leads us to the conclusion that the number of persons who have been infected with syphilis, acquired or congenital, cannot fall below 10 percent of the whole population in the large cities, and the percentage affected with gonorrhea must greatly exceed this proportion." Although this estimate was hotly debated at the time, it was not out of line with the estimated numbers of syphilitics among other European urban populations at the time. See David Newman, "The History and Prevention of Venereal Diseases," *Glasgow Medical Journal* 81 (1914), 88–100. For the distribution of syphilitic and parasyphilitic deaths, see App. 1 of the 1916 "Report." Ironically, while public concern over syphilis was mounting in

the early 1860s, the incidence of syphilis among enlisted men had just peaked and had begun to decline. *P.P.,* 1916, XVI, pp. 7–9 and App. 1.

10. Newman, "History," p. 95.
11. Mid-Victorian clinical diagnosis of the first two stages of syphilis roughly corresponded to contemporary medical diagnosis, although the disabling effects of tertiary syphilis on the cardiovascular and central nervous system were not fully recognized until later. Today acquired syphilis is characterized clinically as follows: "The primary lesion usually appears about 3 weeks after exposure as a papule at the site of the initial invasion; after erosion, it presents a variety of forms, the most distinctive, although not the most frequent, being an indurated chancre; invasion of blood precedes the initial lesion, and a firm, non-fluctuant, painless satellite bubo commonly follows. Infection without chancre is frequent. After 4 to 6 weeks even without specific treatment, the chancre begins to involute and a generalized secondary eruption may appear, often accompanied by mild constitutional symptoms. Secondary manifestations disappear spontaneously within weeks to years. In the early years latency may be interrupted by recurrence of infectious lesions of the skin and mucous membrane or developing lesions of the eye and central nervous system; in later (5 to 20) years, by destructive non-infectious lesions of skin, viscera, bone, and mucosal surfaces. Latency sometimes continues through life and sometimes spontaneous recovery occurs. In other instances, and unpredictably, late disabling manifestations occur in cardiovascular, central nervous or other systems. Actual fatality rates cannot be accurately estimated; prenatal infection is frequently fatal before birth or in infancy. Early acquired syphilis does not result in death or serious disability; late manifestations shorten life, impair health and limit occupational efficiency." Abraham Berenson, ed., *Control of Communicable Diseases in Man,* 12th ed. (Washington, D.C., 1975), p. 315. Doctors are still uncertain about the period of communicability for cases of syphilis. It is accepted that syphilis is infectious during the primary and secondary stages, and also during recurrent lesions of the skin and mucous membranes. However, the extent of communicability during the latency period, when no visible symptoms are present, "is not established; inapparent lesions make this stage potentially infectious." Ibid., p. 316.
12. *P.P.,* 1867–8, XXXVII, p. xiii.
13. Ibid.
14. T. Wyke, "Hospital Facilities for and Diagnosis of Venereal Disease in England 1800–1870," *B.J.V.D.* 49 (1973), 80.
15. M. Berkeley Hill, *Syphilis and Local Contagious Disorders* (London, 1868), p. 24.
16. Ibid.
17. *P.P.,* 1867–8, XXXVII, p. 2.
18. Hill, *Syphilis,* p. 24.

19. John Chapman, "Prostitution in Relation to National Health," *Westminster Review* 36 (1869), 208, 209.
20. Frederick Hollick, *A Popular Treatise on Venereal Disease* . . . (New York, 1852), p. 298: Hill, *Syphilis,* p. 261.
21. Chapman, "Prostitution," p. 231.
22. John S. Haller and Robin Haller, *The Physician and Sexuality in Victorian America* (Urbana, 1974), p. 262.
23. Etienne Lancereaux, *A Treatise on Syphilis,* trans. C. Whitley (2 vols., London, 1868–9), I, 280.
24. Ibid., I, 281.
25. Charles Rosenberg, "The Therapeutic Revolution: Medicine, Meaning and Social Change in Nineteenth-Century America," *Perspectives in Biology and Medicine* (1977), 490. Owsei Temkin, "Therapeutic Trends and the Treatment of Syphilis Before 1900," *Bulletin of the History of Medicine,* 39 (1955), 309–16.
26. Ibid.
27. Temkin, "Trends," p. 313.
28. A. G. Miller, "Four and a Half Years Experience in the Lock Wards of the Edinburgh Lock Infirmary," *Edinburgh Medical Journal* 28 (1882), 400.
29. Ibid.; John Ward Cousins, "Analysis of One Hundred and Eighty-Two Cases Treated in the Lock Wards of the Royal Portsmouth, Portsea and Gosport Hospital," *M.T.G.* (1871), 524.
30. Chapman, "Prostitution," pp. 205, 206.
31. Leonard J. Goldwater, *Mercury: A History of Quicksilver* (Baltimore, 1972), p. 215.
32. *P.P.,* 1867–8, p. xviii.
33. L. W. Harrison, "Some Lessons Learnt in Fifty Years Practice in Venereology," *B.J.V.D.* 30 (1954), 185.
34. Louis Lasagna, *The V.D. Epidemic: How It Started, Where It's Going and What to Do About It* (Philadelphia, 1957), pp. 65, 66.
35. Ibid., pp. 67, 68.
36. Goldwater, *Mercury,* pp. 224–8.
37. Philippe Ricord, quoted in Ernst Finger, *Gonorrhea: Being a Translation of the Sexual Organs and Its Complications* (New York, 1924), p. 11.
38. The contemporary clinical diagnosis of gonorrhea in males generally corresponds with the mid-Victorian diagnosis, but the modern understanding of the signs, incidence, and seriousness of gonorrhea in adult females has changed drastically. Today, as in 1860, it is recognized that acute gonorrhea in males and females is an infection of the mucous membranes. In males "a purulent discharge from the anterior urethra appears usually 2 to 9 days or later after an infecting exposure. The infection is often self-limited, by may extend to the posterior urethra where it may produce epididymitis and prostatitis, and result in a chronic carrier state. Asymptomatic urethral carriage also may occur."

Berenson, *Communicable Diseases,* p. 131. In females, a few days after exposure an infection of the urethra or endocervix occurs; the symptoms are often so mild as to pass unnoticed. "In some [females] there is pelvic invasion at the first, second, or later menstrual period, with mild or severe symptoms of salpingitis [pelvic inflammatory disease] or pelvic peritonitis" (ibid.) Salpingitis often results in sterility. Although death is rare, complications for women are frequent and may be disabling. If untreated, the period of communicability, particularly in females, may extend for months or years. Contemporary authorities seriously doubt whether the cauterization and irrigations administered to male or female patients in the nineteenth and early twentieth centuries "cured" them of gonorrhea or rendered them noninfectious.

39. Oliver Wendell Holmes, quoted in Lasagna, *V.D. Epidemic,* p. 17.
40. Finger, *Gonorrhea,* p. 13.
41. In 1869, Sir John Simon declared that gonorrhea was not "even temporarily of much importance to women," Although the *Lancet,* representing a minority view, argued that gonorrhea could cause "internal inflammation and permanent barrenness." *Lancet* 2 (1869), 410, 411.
42. Acton, *Prostitution,* p. 86.
43. *P.P.,* 1867–68, XXXVII, p. vii.
44. Henry Lee, quoted in William Sinclair, *On Gonorrheal Infection in Women* (London, 1888), p. 3.
45. Acton, *Prostitution,* p. 81.
46. L. W. Harrison, *The Diagnosis and Treatment of Venereal Diseases in General Practice,* 2nd ed. (Oxford, 1919), p. 209; A. W. McLachlan, *Handbook of Diagnosis and Treatment of Venereal Diseases* (Baltimore, 1947), pp. 231–3.
47. Office of Health Economics, *The Venereal Diseases* (London, 1963).
48. Goldwater, *Mercury,* p. 227.
49. Newman, "History," p. 95.
50. Diday, quoted in Sinclair, *Gonorrheal Infection,* p. 5. Sinclair commented: "This is surgery fit for satyrs."
51. J. Lane, quoted in Acton, *Prostitution,* p. 86.
52. See Carroll Smith-Rosenberg, "Puberty to Menopause: The Cycle of Femininity in Nineteenth Century America," in *Clio's Consciousness Raised: New Perspectives on the History of Women,* eds. Mary S. Hartman and Lois W. Banner (New York, 1974), p. 33.
53. *Lancet* 1 (1850), 701.
54. Quoted in William Acton, *A Practical Treatise on Diseases of the Urinary and Generative Organs* (London, 1851), pp. 298–300.
55. *Lancet* 1 (1850), 661, 701, 723; *B.M.J.* (1857), 443, 458, 513, 700; *M.T.G.* 23 (1851), 190, 196, 248.
56. For a general discussion of the two-tiered system of hospital care, see B. Abel-Smith, *The Hospitals 1800–1948; A Study in Social Administration* (London, 1964); J. Bristowe and T. Holmes, "The Hospitals of the

United Kingdom," in "Sixth Report of the Medical Officer of the Privy Council, 1863," *P.P.,* 1864, XVIII, App. 15.

57. F. W. Lowndes, *Lock Hospitals and Lock Wards in General Hospitals* (London, 1882), pp. 22, 23.
58. Bristowe, "The Hospitals."
59. John Woodward, *To Do the Sick No Harm: A Study of the British Voluntary Hospital System to 1875* (London, 1974), p. 49.
60. For a discussion of American hospitals see Charles E. Rosenberg, "And Heal the Sick: The Hospital and the Patient in the Nineteenth Century America," *Journal of Social History* 10 (1976–7), 428–47.
61. Bristowe, "The Hospitals."
62. Ibid.
63. Lowndes, "The Liverpool Lock Hospital and the Prevalence of Severity of Constitutional Syphilis in Liverpool," *B.M.J.* 1 (1880), 728.
64. "Minutes of the Hospital House Committee, 1862–1872." London Lock Hospital Papers, H. 32, Royal College of Surgeons.
65. W. S. C. Copeman, "The Royal Hospitals Before 1700," in *The Evolution of Hospitals in Britain,* ed. F. N. J. Poynter (London, 1964), p. 34.
66. Abel-Smith, *The Hospitals,* p. 22.
67. Michel Foucault, *Madness and Civilization: A History of Insanity in the Age of Reason,* trans. R. Howard (New York, 1965), p. 7.
68. Acton, *Prostitution* (1857 ed.), p. 134.
69. There is a fascinating medical continuity here. Theodor Rosebury maintains that these two diseases were generally confused until the fifteenth century. According to his view, syphilis, as distinguished from leprosy, was the child of the scientific revolution, thanks to the more precise diagnostic skills developed at that time. Theodor Rosebury, *Microbes and Morals: The Strange Story of Venereal Disease* (New York, 1971), p. 63.
70. T. J. Wyke, "Manchester and Salford Lock Hospital 1818–1917," *Medical History* 19 (1975), 73.
71. Robert Lees, "The 'Lock Wards' of Edinburgh Royal Infirmary," *B.J.V.D.* 37 (1961), 188; "Annual Report of the London Lock Hospital, 1854," in *Lock Hospital Reports, 1846–1871,* p. 5, Lock Hospital Papers.
72. Wyke, "Manchester and Salford Lock Hospital," p. 80.
73. "Annual Report of the London Lock Hospital, 1851," pp. 10, 11.
74. "Centenary Report of Lock Hospital and Asylum, 1846," p. 1.
75. "Annual Report of the London Lock Hospital, 1849," p. 5.
76. "Annual Report of the London Lock Hospital, 1863," p. 9. Medical statistics on lock-hospital patients were occasionally printed in medical journals.
77. Lees, "Lock Wards," p. 186; conversation with Prof. M. Jeanne Peterson of Indiana University.
78. Abel-Smith, *The Hospitals,* ch. 2.
79. "Annual Report of the London Lock Hospital, 1854," p. 9.

80. Bristowe, "The Hospitals."
81. Lees, "Lock Wards," p. 187.
82. Acton, *Prostitution*, p. 81.
83. "Prostitution: Its Medical Aspects," *Lancet* 2 (1858), 198.
84. Lees, "Lock Wards," p. 188; *An Abstract of Rules and Orders Made at a General Court of Governors of the Lock Hospital, Held November 28, 1754, and Confirmed with Additions and Alterations by the General Court, Held April 21, 1814* (London, 1814), p. 4.
85. Abel-Smith, *The Hospitals*, pp. 12, 13.
86. "Annual Report of the London Lock Hospital, 1867," p. 5.
87. Ibid.
88. Acton, *Prostitution* (1870, Fryer ed.) (New York, 1968), p. 193.
89. Ibid.
90. F. W. Lowndes, *The Extension of the Contagious Diseases Acts to Liverpool and Other Seaports, Considered Practically* (Liverpool, 1876), p. 75.
91. Acton, *Prostitution* (Fryer ed.), p. 194.
92. James R. Lane, quoted in Lowndes, "Liverpool Lock Hospital," 727.
93. Ibid.
94. Age statistics of female lock patients in lock hospitals and lock wards in Glasgow, Liverpool, and Edinburgh were taken from the following sources: J. B. Talbot, *The Miseries of Prostitution* (London, 1844), pp. 29, 30; Hill, *Syphilis*, pp. 33–6; *Lock Hospital Reports*, 1849–63; Miller, "Four and a Half Years," p. 387; F. W. Lowndes, *Prostitution and Syphilis in Liverpool and the Working of the Contagious Diseases Acts . . .* (London, 1876), p. 12; Alexander Patterson, "Statistics of Glasgow Lock Hospital Since Its Foundation in 1805 – With Remarks on the Contagious Diseases Acts, and on Syphilis," *Glasgow Medical Journal* 18 (1882), 411; William Tait, *Magdalenism: An Inquiry into the Extent, Causes, and Consequences of Prostitution in Edinburgh* (Edinburgh, 1840), p. 24.
95. Hill, "Illustrations of the Working of the Contagious Diseases Acts," *B.M.J.* (1867), 583; Abraham Flexner, *Prostitution in Europe* (New York, 1914), pp. 174, 175.
96. These statistics were compiled from the Lock Hospital Reports from 1857 to 1863.
97. "Report of the Lock Hospital, 1856," p. 13.
98. Patterson, *P.P.*, 1882, IX, Q. 2891.
99. Lowndes, "Liverpool Lock Hospital," p. 727.
100. Miller, "Four and a Half Years," pp. 385, 398.
101. Hill, *Syphilis*, p. 55.
102. Hill, *Lancet* 1 (1868), 130.
103. Dr. James Lane, quoted in Acton, *Prostitution*, p. 88.
104. Ambrose King and Claude Nichol, *Venereal Disease* (London, 1969), p. 204.
105. *Lancet* 2 (1869), 443.
106. Sinclair, *On Gonorrheal Infection*, ch. 6.

4. THE CONTAGIOUS DISEASES ACTS AND THEIR ADVOCATES

1. Eugene L. Rasor, *Reform in the Royal Navy; A Social History of the Lower Deck 1850 to 1880* (Hamden, Conn., 1976), p. 89; E. M. Sigsworth and T. H. Wyke, "A Study of Victorian Prostitution and Venereal Disease," in Martha Vicinus, ed., *Suffer and Be Still: Women in the Victorian Age* (Bloomington, 1973), p. 77. Repealers ascribed a more sinister motive to these vague titles: they argued that the titles deliberately obscured the intention and purpose of the Acts. See, for example, Josephine Butler, *Reminiscences of a Great Crusade* (London, 1911), p. 2.
2. Keith Thomas, "The Double Standard," *Journal of the History of Ideas* 20 (1959), 199.
3. Deborah Gorham, "The 'Maiden Tribute of Modern Babylon,' Reexamined: Child Prostitution and the Idea of Childhood in Late-Victorian England," *Victorian Studies* 21 (Spring 1978), 353–79.
4. Quoted in Gordon Haight, "Male Chastity in the Nineteenth Century," *Contemporary Review* 219 (1971), 252.
5. See Chapter 2.
6. Ben Barker-Benfield, "The Spermatic Economy: A Nineteenth-Century View of Sexuality," *Feminist Studies* 1 (1972), 45–74.
7. "Report of the Royal Commission on the Administration and Operation of the Contagious Diseases Acts 1866–69 (1871)," *P.P.*, 1871 (C. 408), XIX.
8. "Controlment of Syphilis," *Lancet* 2 (1846), 510–11.
9. C. W. Shirley Deakin, *The Contagious Diseases Acts, 1864, 1866, 1868 (Ireland) and 1869. From a Sanitary and Economic Point of View* (London, 1872), p. 31.
10. J. Bristowe and T. Holmes, "The Hospitals of the United Kingdom," in "Sixth Report of the Medical Officer of the Privy Council, 1863," *P.P.*, 1864, XVIII, App. 15.
11. O. R. Macdonagh, "Nineteenth Century Revolution in Government: A Reappraisal," *Historical Journal* 1(1958), 58, 59.
12. Philip Abrams, *Origins of British Sociology 1834–1914* (Chicago, 1968), p. 38.
13. Sir John Simon, "Eleventh Report of the Medical Officer of the Privy Council," *P.P.*, 1868–9 (4127), XXXII, p. 8.
14. Brian Bond, "The Late-Victorian Army," *History Today* 11 (September 1961), 616–24; Rasor, *Reform in the Royal Navy*, passim; Cecil Woodham-Smith, *Florence Nightingale 1820–1910* (New York, 1951), pp. 267, 288.
15. Brian Harrison, "Underneath the Victorians," *Victorian Studies* 10 (March 1967), 257.
16. Bond, "The Late-Victorian Army," p. 628.

276

17. "Report of the Royal Commission on the Health of the Army," *P.P.*, 1857, XVIII, p. xv.
18. Ibid., pp. vi–xii. See also Woodham-Smith, *Florence Nightingale*, p. 206.
19. Christopher Lloyd, *Keevil's Medicine and the Navy 1200–1900* (4 vols., Edinburgh, 1963), IV, 268.
20. See Bryson's obituary in G. H. Brown, ed., *Lives of the Fellows of the Royal College of Physicians 1826–1925* (London, 1955), IV, 126, 127. Here Bryson is described as a military Gradgrind type, a grimly over-bearing presence: his "preoccupation with statistics and lack of hospital experience combined with his blunt manner and want of humanity unfit-ted him for the responsibilities of his high office." Bryson continued to be a strong supporter of the regulationist cause.
21. F. B. Smith, "Ethics and Disease in the Later Nineteenth Century: The Contagious Diseases Acts," *Historical Studies* 15 (October 1971), 122.
22. William Sloggett, "History and Operations of the Contagious Diseases Acts in the Home Ports," P.R.O., Adm. 1/6418, 10 April 1873, 2.
23. Ibid.
24. Ibid.
25. Ibid.
26. Ibid., p. 4.
27. Woodham-Smith, *Florence Nightingale*, p. 267.
28. "Report of the Committee to Inquire into the Prevalence of Venereal Disease in the Army and Navy," P.R.O., War Office Papers, W.O. 33/12, 1862.
29. Ibid.
30. Ibid.
31. Woodham-Smith, *Florence Nightingale*, p. 267.
32. A number of the parliamentary supporters of this bill, like Lyon Playfair and Sir John Pakington, were also active social and medical reformers. Still, they did not try to arouse public support for the act as a far-reach-ing social reform.
33. For the activities of local officials in Plymouth and Southampton, see Chapter 8.
34. The dockyard police and naval patrol were first organized in 1860: Rasor, *Reform*, p. 74.
35. Charles H. Melville, "History of Preventive Measures in the British Army," in *A System of Syphilis*, eds. D'Arcy Power and J.K. Murphy. (6 vols., London, 1910), VI, 85.
36. E. T. Cook, *The Life of Florence Nightingale* (2 vols., London, 1914), I, 74, 75.
37. "A Correspondent," to the editor, *Times*, 22 August 1863.
38. Ibid. See also the *Times*: 25 August 1863; 27 August 1863; 28 August 1863; 31 August 1863; 1 September 1863; 2 September 1863; 3 Sep-tember 1863; 4 September 1863; 5 September 1863; 7 September 1863.

39. Martineau was fed information about the continental system by Florence Nightingale. Cook, *The Life,* I, 74, 75.

40. "Legislation for Prostitution," *B.M.J.* 2 (1864), 42.

41. "Pseudo-cures for a Social Evil," *B.M.J.* 2 (1863), 425.

42. *B.M.J.* 2 (1864), 42, 94, 103.

43. Sloggett, "History and Operations," p. 15.

44. Ibid., p. 8.

45. Ibid., p. 7.

46. Macdonagh, "Nineteenth Century Revolution in Government," pp. 57, 58.

47. An Act for the Better Prevention of Contagious Diseases at Certain Naval and Military Stations, 29 and 30 Vict. c. 96.

48. *P.P.,* 1867–8 (4031), XXXVII, p. XXIX.

49. Sloggett, "History and Operations," p. 7.

50. See Deakin, *Contagious Diseases Acts,* p. 31.

51. Sloggett, "History and Operations," p. 9.

52. See Sloggett's testimony before the House of Commons Select Committee on the Contagious Diseases Act, *P.P.,* 1868–9 (306), VII, Q. 55–119.

53. Harveian Medical Society of London, *Report of the Committee for the Prevention of Venereal Diseases, Read Before and Adopted by the Society, 1 July 1867* (London, 1867).

54. Sloggett, "History and Operations."

55. For example, see *B.M.J.* 1 (1868), 21, 87, 139, 494; 2 (1868), 16, 313, 489. Also, *Lancet* 2 (1868), 417; 1 (1869), 23; 1 (1869), 754, 765; 1 (1870), 168.

56. Sloggett, "History and Operations," noted: " . . . an association was formed in London, which included among its members the heads of all the great medical corporate bodies, in addition to the most eminent physicians and surgeons, a large number of the clergy, including many of the higher ranks of the Church, and many other persons eminent as statesmen and philanthropists." George Butler was shouted down when he tried to read a paper critical of the acts at a church congress in 1871. Josephine Butler, *Personal Reminiscences of a Great Crusade* (London, 1896), p. 55. By the 1880s, most Protestant denominations, as well as the Catholic Church (in the person of Cardinal Manning), had sided with repealers. In contrast, no official body of the Church of England formally opposed the acts.

57. *B.M.J.* 2 (1868), 489.

58. See the correspondence between a Mr. Rowley and the commander of the "K" division of the metropolitan police, Home Office Papers, P.R.O., H.O. 45/6628, 17 March 1858.

59. William Harris, Assistant Commissioner of Metropolitan Police, quoted in William Acton, *Prostitution* (1870, ed. Fryer) (New York, 1968), p. 153.

60. Ibid., pp. 155, 156.

61. "Ex-Constable of the Devonport Division," *The Social Evil with Sugges-*

tions for Its Suppression and Revelations of the Working of the Contagious Diseases Acts (Bristol, 1882), p. 6.

62. Ibid., p. 13.

63. According to Paul McHugh, 70 percent of the supporters of regulation in Parliament voted against the Women's Disabilities Bill in 1876. "The Campaign Against the Contagious Diseases Acts: Some Organizational Aspects" (Ph.D. diss., Oxford Univ., 1976), p. 237.

64. George Drysdale, Physical, Sexual and Natural Religion (London, 1855), p. 270.

65. Charles Drysdale, to the editor, Medical Press and Circular (1870), 153.

66. For the status hierarchy in the medical profession, see M. Jeanne Peterson, The Medical Profession in Mid-Victorian London (Berkeley, 1978).

67. Fryer, introduction to Prostitution, p. 8. For Hill and Drysdale, see the following entries in G. V. Plarr, Plarr's Lives of the Fellows of the Royal College of Surgeons of England (2 vols., London, 1939): "Matthew Berkeley Hill," I, 537, 538; "C. R. Drysdale," I, 306.

68. F. W. Lowndes was house surgeon at the Liverpool Lock Hospital; James Barr, James Lane, and Berkeley Hill were all attached to the London Lock Hospital; Acton was trained at St. Bartholomew's; and Drysdale was surgeon to the Rescue Society of London. Frederick Lowndes, The Extension of the Contagious Diseases Acts to Liverpool and Other Seaports, Considered Practically (Liverpool, 1876); Plarr, Lives, I, 306, 537, and vol. II, 675; Fryer, introduction to Prostitution, p. 8.

69. "Working Classes and the Doctors," Lancet 2 (1871), 619. William Acton reiterated much the same sentiment in his 1857 proposal for the establishment of a "self-supporting sanitary society" for prostitutes: Acton, Prostitution Considered in Its Moral, Social, and Sanitary Aspects in London and Other Large Cities; with Proposals for the Mitigation and Prevention of Its Attendant Evil (London, 1857), p. 157.

70. See, for example, the report of the meeting of the Reading Pathological Society, B.M.J. 2 (1868), 313; Berkeley Hill, "Statistical Results of the Contagious Diseases Acts," J.S.S. 33 (1870), 435–85. In the subjected districts, advocates of the acts defended their operation at meetings of local scientific and literary societies. See, for example, Philip Hopgood, "On the Successful Operation of the Contagious Diseases Acts," read before the Portsea Island Society for the Culture of Society and Literature, as reported in the Portsmouth Times and Naval Gazette (Portsmouth), 30 March 1872.

71. Abrams (Origins, p. 45) argues that this "orientation towards consensus" flourished in a period when the "party system had collapsed."

72. Brian Harrison, "Francis W. Newman," Dictionary of British Temperance Biography (Sheffield, 1973), pp. 90–2; "Matthew Berkeley Hill," Plarr's Lives, I, 537, 538; Deborah Gorham, "The Hills of Birmingham: Victorian Reform as a Family Business" in The Victorian Family: Structure and Stresses, ed. Anthony S. Wohl (New York, 1978), pp. 119–47.

73. Gorham, "The Hills," p. 129.
74. Harrison, "Francis W. Newman," pp. 91–2.
75. M. D. Hill, *Eton and Elsewhere* (London, 1928), pp. 18–31; Gorham, "The Hills," p. 143.
76. S. J. Tanner, *Suffrage Movement in Bristol: How the Women's Suffrage Movement Began in Bristol Fifty Years Ago* (Bristol, 1918).
77. Hill, "Illustrations," pp. 21, 22. In this article Hill recommends the use of plainclothesmen: "To require a woman to walk through the public streets accompanied by an officer in uniform makes her occupation at once notorious to all who can see her."
78. *D.I.* (Plymouth), 12 November 1870.
79. The following biographical details are drawn from Curgenven's obituary in *B.M.J.* (1903), 1104, 1105.
80. Peterson, *Medical Profession,* p. 125, estimates that a sizeable proportion of doctors had military experience. She also observes that the military did not have the reputation of attracting the "ablest and best students."
81. Acton, quoted in Brian Harrison, *Drink and the Victorians: The Temperance Question in England 1815–1872* (London, 1971), p. 358.
82. See the discussion of Berkeley Hill's paper, "Should the Principle of the Contagious Diseases Act Be Applied to the Civil Population?" *Transactions of the National Association for the Promotion of Social Science* (London, 1869), pp. 448–50.
83. *Lancet* 2 (1846), 573.
84. Acton, *Prostitution* (1870), p. 157.
85. Acton, speech before the Medical Officers of Health, quoted in *B.M.J.* 1 (1870), 35.
86. Simon, "Eleventh Report," pp. 3–13.
87. Sheldon Amos, *A Comparative Survey of Laws in Force for the Prohibition, Regulation and Licencing of Vice in England and Other Countries* (London, 1877), pp. 467, 470.
88. Sloggett, "History and Operations," p. 12.
89. An Act to Amend the Contagious Diseases Acts, 1866. 32 and 33 Vict. c. 86.
90. William Acton, "Shall the Contagious Diseases Act Be Extended to the Civil Population?" Speech before the Medical Officers of Health (18 December 1869), p. 8.
91. Ibid.
92. Leon Radzinowicz, *History of English Criminal Law and Its Administration from 1750* (6 vols., London, 1948–68), I, 19; Michel Foucault, *Madness and Civilization: A History of Insanity in the Age of Reason,* trans. R. Howard (New York, 1965), ch. 2.
93. J. J. Garth Wilkinson, *The Forcible Introspection of Women for the Army and Navy by the Oligarchy Considered Physically* (London, 1870), p. 15.

94. A phrase coined by the *Saturday Review.* See J. A. Banks and Olive Banks, *Feminism and Family Planning in Victorian England* (New York, 1972), pp. 94–7.
95. Deakin, *The Contagious Diseases Acts,* p. 27.
96. Speech of Mr. Hanbury in the House of Commons, quoted in Banks and Banks, *Feminism and Family Planning,* p. 96.
97. William Acton, *A Practical Treatise on Diseases of the Urinary and Generative Organs* (London, 1875), pp. 214, 215.

5. THE REPEAL CAMPAIGN

1. Joseph Rowntree to Henry J. Wilson, 17 November 1883. Henry J. Wilson papers, box 79, Fawcett Library, London.
2. See T. William Heyck, "British Radicals and Radicalism, 1874–1895: A Social Analysis," in *Modern European Social History,* ed. Robert J. Bezucha (Lexington, Ky., 1972), pp. 28–57.
3. As early as 1860, Florence Nightingale had privately communicated with various officials and statesmen over proposals to introduce a regulation system in England; her intervention led to the appointment of the 1862 Committee to Inquire into the Prevalence of Venereal Disease in the Army and Navy. At Nightingale's instigation Harriet Martineau also wrote a series of letters to the *Times,* attacking the "continental" system on moral and sanitary grounds. However, these individual efforts failed to sway government officials or to stir up public opinion on the subject. See Cecil Woodham-Smith, *Florence Nightingale 1820–1910* (New York, 1951), p. 267; E. T. Cook, *The Life of Florence Nightingale* (2 vols., London, 1914), I, pp. 74–5.
4. See Brian Harrison, *Drink and the Victorians: The Temperance Question in England 1815–1872* (London, 1971), p. 232: "The fluidity of the political situation in these years was accentuated in 1867 by franchise extension, which presented great opportunities to a militant reforming movement backed by nonconformist and middle class and working class support."
5. R. B. Williams, "Origin of the Repeal Movement," *Shield* (London), 5 June 1886.
6. Daniel Cooper, quoted in Josephine Butler, *Personal Reminiscences of a Great Crusade* (London, 1911), p. 5.
7. Williams, "Origins."
8. J. L. Hammond and Barbara Hammond, *James Stansfeld: A Victorian Champion of Sex Equality* (London, 1972) pp. 141, 142.
9. M. Berkeley Hill, "Should the Principle of the Contagious Diseases Act Be Applied to the Civil Population?" *Transactions of the National Association for the Promotion of Social Science* (London, 1869), pp. 428–38; *Bristol Times and Mirror* (Bristol), 11 October 1869; *Western Daily Press* (Bristol), 5 October 1869.
10. "National Association for the Repeal of the Contagious Diseases Acts,"

unpublished archival summary, Butler Collection, Fawcett Library, London.

11. "National Association"; Brian Harrison, "State Intervention and Moral Reform," in *Pressure from Without in Early Victorian England,* ed. Patricia Hollis (London, 1974), pp. 319, 321.

12. Josephine E. Butler, *An Autobiographical Memoir,* ed. George W. Johnson and Lucy A. Johnson (Bristol, 1909), p. 231.

13. "Women's Protest," quoted in Butler, *Personal Reminiscences,* pp. 9, 10.

14. Daniel Cooper, quoted in ibid., p. 6.

15. *Spectator* (8 January 1870), 39.

16. "The Shrieking Sisterhood," *Saturday Review* (19 March 1870), 391.

17. John Morley, "Short Letter to Some Ladies," *Fortnightly Review* 7 (1870), 378.

18. "First Annual Report of the Ladies' National Association for the Repeal of the Contagious Diseases Acts, 1870," *LNA Reports, 1870–1886,* Fawcett Library, London, p. 6.

19. In 1882 the annual income of repeal groups was estimated at £5,000, a rather small sum in comparison with the incomes of temperance groups and later social-purity organizations like the National Vigilance Association. Subscribers to middle-class groups rarely contributed less than two shilling sixpence, whereas the Working Men's National League, which claimed a membership of 22,000 in 1879, set its dues lower, at sixpence. For the most part, repeal groups depended heavily on a few wealthy donors, most of them Quakers. As a consequence, their annual income could be significantly affected by the death of a principal benefactor, like Edward Backhouse, as well as by the fluctuating state of popular enthusiasm. See "History of the English Repeal Movement," n.d., box 285, Wilson Papers, Fawcett Library; Maurice Gregory, "Some Notes on the Financial Relations Between 'Friends' and the Association for Moral and Social Hygiene and Its Predecessors," n.d., Social Purity Collection, Friends Library, London.

20. See, for example, "NA Minutes," 3 (11 December 1876), no. 1087; 3 (30 April 1876), no. 1216; 4 (21 June 1880), no. 2389; 5 (7 July 1884), no. 4130; 6 (27 April 1885), no. 4411. See also the Butler correspondence: Elizabeth Wolstenholme to Henry J. Wilson, 19 June 1873, no. 3286; Josephine Butler to Mary Priestman, 12 August 1874, no. 3332 Although the LNA shared premises with the National Association in London, most of the business of the LNA was conducted from Liverpool, where Josephine Butler lived, and from Bristol, where Margaret Tanner, the treasurer of the LNA, lived. Executive board-meetings were held in the various towns where board members resided.

21. "Report from the Royal Commission on the Administration and Operation of the Contagious Diseases Acts 1866–69 (1871), *P.P.,* 1871 (C. 408), XIX.

22. A. J. Mundella and F. D. Maurice, quoted in Hammond and Hammond, *James Stansfeld,* p. 156.
23. Hammond and Hammond, *James Stansfeld,* p. 160.
24. Ibid, pp. 167–9.
25. Mr. Bruce, quoted in Josephine Butler, *A Letter on the Subject of Mr. Bruce's Bill Addressed to the Repealers of the Contagious Diseases Acts* (Liverpool, 1872).
26. "First Annual Report of the Ladies' National Association . . . , 1870."
27. A. J. Mundella to Henry J. Wilson, 29 December 1872, M.D. 6008, Wilson Collection, Sheffield Public Library.
28. Josephine Butler to Henry Wilson, 1872, Butler Collection.
29. On 26 February 1870 Butler wrote to the *Dover News:* "Our appeal is to the provincial papers, as a 'consipiracy of silence' exists against us on the part of the London press—a conspiracy which is a confession of weakness."
30. Hammond and Hammond, *James Stansfeld,* p. 206.
31. "Fifth Annual Report of the Ladies' National Association . . . , 1875."
32. Josephine Butler to Henry J. Wilson, 18 March 1875, no. 3364, Butler Collection. Butler's continental tour, and later Wilson's trip to the U.S. in 1876, helped to spark abolitionist and social-purity movements in the countries visited.
33. *Times,* quoted in Hammond and Hammond, *James Stansfeld,* p. 190.
34. James Stansfeld to Josephine Butler, 21 October 1874, no. 3240, Butler Collection.
35. Josephine Butler to her niece, Edith Leopold, April, 1875, no. 3829; Butler to Charlotte Wilson, 2 April 1875, no. 3842; Butler to H. J. Wilson, 19 or 26 April 1875, no. 3852, Butler Collection.
36. Hammond and Hammond, *James Stansfeld,* p. 191.
37. On the question of medical care for syphilitics, Stansfeld disagreed with many repeal leaders who opposed specialized lock hospitals subsidized by the government. Stansfeld argued for a less punitive attitude toward venereal-disease sufferers. As a former president of the Local Government Board, he believed that the Poor Law could adequately handle the problem of indigent or vagrant venereal-disease sufferers. He also believed that prostitutes would be legally considered eligible for medical treatment under the Poor Law. See Hammond and Hammond, *James Stansfeld,* pp. 202, 203.
38. "Report of the House of Commons Select Committee on the Administration, Operation and Effects of the Contagious Diseases Acts of 1866–69," *P.P.,* 1878–9 (323), VIII; *P.P.,* 1880 (114), VIII; *P.P., 1881 (351), VIII; P.P.,* 1882 (340), IX.
39. Hammond and Hammond, *James Stansfeld,* p. 220.
40. James Stuart wrote to Henry Wilson that the majority report "grounds itself on the effect of the Acts in Devonport." 12 October 1882. Wilson Collection, box 79, Fawcett Library.

41. Heyck, "British Radicals," pp. 38–41.
42. Samuel H. Beer, *Modern British Politics: A Study of Parties and Pressure Groups* (London, 1965), p. 53.
43. Josephine Butler, General Circular to LNA Executive, 8 December 1882. Wilson Collection, box 79, Fawcett Library.
44. The *N.L.J.* regularly carried reports of meetings in the East End. See "Public Meeting in East London," 1 July 1882; "Great Meeting of Men in East London," 1 March 1883; "Women's Meeting in London," 1 March 1883.
45. "History of the English Repeal Movement," p. 7.
46. Hammond and Hammond, *James Stansfeld,* p. 229.
47. James Stuart, *Reminiscences* (London, 1912), p. 217.
48. Josephine Butler to Miss Priestman, 25 April 1883, Butler Collection.
49. *Lancet* 1 (1884), 857.
50. W. T. Stead, *The Maiden Tribute of Modern Babylon (The Report the "Pall Mall Gazette's" Secret Commission)* (London, 1885); Michael Pearson, *The Age of Consent: Victorian Prostitution and Its Enemies* (Newton Abbott, 1972); Josephine Butler to Miss Priestman, 5 June 1885, Butler Collection.
51. In a letter to her son Stanley, Butler reported that "A member of Parliament whom we met at Cambridge told us that the amount of pressure brought to bear at this moment by the country was, he thought, 'unprecedented in the history of any agitation.' " Butler, *Autobiographical Memoir,* p. 173. For charges of 'obscenity" against repeal literature, see C. W. Shirley Deakin, *The Contagious Diseases Acts: The Contagious Diseases Acts, 1864, '66, '68 (Ireland), '69. From a Sanitary and Economic Point of View,* read before the Medical Society of University College, London, 30 November 1871 (London, 1872).
52. "History of the English Repeal Movement," p. 18; W. A. Coote, ed., *A Romance of Philanthropy: Being a Record of Some of the Principal Incidents Connected with the Exceptionally Successful Thirty Years' Work of the National Vigilance Association* (London, 1916), p. 120. In 1890, a British committee was established to agitate against regulation in the colonies. See Henry J. Wilson, *Copy of a Rough Record of Events and Incidents connected with the Repeal of the Contagious Diseases Acts, 1868–69* (Sheffield, 1906).
53. See Harrison, *Drink,* ch. 6; Harrison, "State Intervention"; R. D. French, *Anti-Vivisection and Medical Science in Victorian Society* (Princeton, 1975).
54. This biographical profile is based on Heyck, "British Radicals"; W. S. Fowler, *A Study in Radicalism and Dissent: The Life and Times of Henry Joseph Wilson, 1833–1914* (London, 1961); and the Wilson papers in the Fawcett Library and Sheffield Public Library.
55. A. J. Mundella, quoted in Paul McHugh, "The Campaign Against the Contagious Diseases Acts: Some Organizational Aspects" (Ph. D. diss., Oxford Univ. 1976), p. 75.

56. In 1872, Wilson had become embroiled in a characteristic dispute with a working-class agent named Hardy. Joseph Edmondson, one of his co-workers in the Northern Counties League, had permitted Hardy to give a public speech and permitted him access to the blue books. Wilson warned that Edmondson had kindled in Hardy a dangerous insurrectionary spirit. "He says you want him to have & carry about the Blue Book of Evidence. He says he could have explained the Acts & Bruce's Bill as well as you did, if he had been in possession of the Acts!!! Impudence!" Henry J. Wilson to Joseph Edmondson, 11 November 1872, no. 3198. Butler Collection.
57. Heyck, "British Radicals," p. 35.
58. Henry J. Wilson to the Executive Committee of the Northern Counties League, 19 July 1875. Butler Collection.
59. McHugh, "Campaign Against the Contagious Diseases Acts," p. 103.
60. This biographical profile is based on Eugene Rasor, "William Shaen," (unpublished, 1979) and Margaret Josephine Shaen, *William Shaen: A Brief Sketch* (London, 1912).
61. Jessie Herbert to Henry J. Wilson, 1 October 1882. Butler Collection.
62. See Chapters 6 and 7.
63. See the discussion of F. W. Newman in Gertrude Himmelfarb, "The Victorian Angst," *Victorian Minds: A Study of Intellectuals in Crises and of Ideologies in Transition* (New York, 1952), pp. 300–13.
64. Paul Thompson, *Socialists, Liberals, and Labour: The Struggle for London, 1885–1914* (Toronto, 1967), ch. 5.
65. George Dyer, quoted in *Eastern Post and City Chronicle* (London), 16 April 1881.
66. Thompson, "Socialists, Liberals, and Labour," ch. 5. F. A. Ford visited 26 Radical clubs in 1884, some with as many as 600 to 700 members. "NA Minutes" 5 (13 October 1884) 4187; 5 (27 October 1884) 4201. Ford's expenses were paid by the National Association.
67. "NA Minutes" 2 (2 November 1872), no. 525; 3 (18 December 1875), no. 768, Butler Collection. In 1877, 1,600 officeholders in trade unions, clubs, and friendly societies were members of the Working Men's National League. *N.L.J.*, 1 September 1877.
68. Robert Applegarth to Henry J. Wilson, 19 February 1907, Butler Collection. A. W. Humphrey, *Robert Applegarth: Trade Unionist, Educationist, Reformer* (London, 1913), p. 255, reported that Applegarth requested that they interview subjected women on three separate occasions. Finally, a subcommittee was sent down to the military hospitals. After a perfunctory walk through Aldershot hospital, his colleagues headed back for lunch, when he turned back. "Where are you going?" he was asked. "I am going back." "Because," he answered, "I left behind all I came to get – information."
69. See Applegarth's questioning, Royal Commission of 1871, *P.P.*, 1871 (C. 408-I), Minutes of Evidence, Q. 12684-9.

70. "NA Minutes," 2 (24 February 1872), no. 696; 3 (11 December 1876), no. 1087; 6 (15 March 1886), no. 475; Josephine Butler to H. J. Wilson, 7 April 1873, no. 3250, Butler Collection.
71. Heyck, "British Radicals," pp. 42, 43.
72. See, for example, "First Annual Report of the LNA . . . , 1870"; "Summary of Action in the Subjected Districts," *Shield* 13 April 1878.
73. Charlottee Wilson, "Memoir of Mrs. Henry J. Wilson," n.d., M.D. 2469-17, Wilson Collection, Sheffield Public Library; W. T. Stead, *Josephine Butler: A Life Sketch* (London, 1887), pp. 42, 43.
74. Butler, *Personal Reminiscences*, p. 23.
75. See, for example, the meetings held in Plymouth in spring 1870. *Shield*, 23 May 1870; 20 June 1870.
76. *Shield*, 20 January 1877.
77. Ibid.
78. Ibid.
79. Lucraft ran as a temperance, repeal, and workingman's candidate. *N.L.J.*, 1 September 1879; 1 November 1879; 1 December 1879.
80. *N.L.J.*, 1 December 1879.
81. *N.L.J.*, 1 November 1879.
82. *N.L.J.*, 1 September 1879. The great Covent Garden Bazaar for the Anti-Corn Law League was cited as a precedent.
83. The most successful deputation was that of the workingmen's in 1872. *Shield*, 3 August 1872.
84. *Shield*, 4 May 1872.
85. These by-election challenges occurred early in the campaign, in Newark and Colchester in 1870 and in Pontefract in 1872. During the mid-seventies active intervention in parliamentary elections by repeal groups declined. Many repealers placed their loyalty to the Liberal Party above the repeal cause, especially when the proposed candidate came from working-class ranks.
86. Hammond and Hammond, *James Stansfeld*, p. 151. The government wanted Storks for a post in the War Office.
87. Myrna Trustram, "State Regulation of Vice–Colchester and the Contagious Diseases Acts 1864, 1866, 1869." (B.A. thesis, Univ. of Essex, 1977), pp. 24, 25.
88. Stead, *Josephine Butler*, p. 53.
89. Butler, *Personal Reminiscences*, p. 49.
90. Ibid., pp. 26–8. As Butler pointed out, "The battle was a severe one, for those were the days of hustings, harangues, and open voting."
91. "To the Electors of the Borough of Colchester." Broadsides on "King Stork," Wilson Collection, box 285, Fawcett Library.
92. Butler, *Personal Reminiscences*, p. 33.
93. Ibid., p. 31. The mobilization of brothel keepers against repeal resembled the violent and effective organization of publicans against the Alliance's Permissive bill. See Harrison, *Drink and the Victorians*, p. 244.

94. Butler, *Personal Reminiscences,* pp. 48, 49.
95. In Pontefract repealers were opposing Mr. Childers, First Lord of the Admiralty, who won the by-election by a much smaller margin than expected. Butler remarked in *Personal Reminiscences* (p. 46), "Personally . . . Mr. Childers never seemed to me a very devoted adherent to the evil system." Childers later supported repeal bills.
96. Josephine Butler to Joseph Edmondson, 28 April 1872, no. 3136: "I trust you will warn Mr. Stansfeld against the encroachments of these terrible aristocratic doctors . . . no words can tell what I and other women suffer at the sight of this *violent desire* on the *part* of *certain powerful* men to legislate by one means or another *this hideous personal outrage.*" Butler Collection.
97. In *An Appeal to the People of England on the Recognition and Superintendence of Prostitution by Governments* (Nottingham, 1870), p. 30, Butler threatened a "servile rebellion of an unusual and awkward kind." She further conjured up the image of "popular rebellions, when the mob proceeds to acts of violence" and "women rioters should take their chance of being shot down with men."
98. Josephine Butler, quoted in *W.D.M.,* 13 June 1870.
99. J. J. Garth Wilkinson, *The Forcible Introspection of Women for the Oligarchy Considered Physically* (London, 1870), p. 15.
100. Josephine Butler, "The Garrison Towns of Kent," *Shield,* 25 April 1870; 2 May 1870; 9 May 1870.
101. A soldier's woman, quoted in ibid., 2 May 1870.
102. "To the Electors," Wilson Collection, Fawcett Library.
103. Josephine Butler to Charlotte Wilson, 26 August [1872], no. 3175, Butler Collection.
104. A registered woman, quoted in a letter from Josephine Butler to J. J. Garth Wilkinson; reprinted in *The Forcible Introspection,* p. 33.
105. These letters were originally collected by Butler to be presented to the Royal Commission of 1871, as evidence of respectable working-class opinion. When the commission refused to consider them, they were published by repealers instead.
106. Thomas Gibson, *Vox Populi,* p. 18.
107. William Gilliver, ibid., p. 20.
108. Josephine Butler to her niece, Edith Leopold, April 1875, no. 3839, Butler Collection.
109. Reverend Arthur, quoted in *Transactions,* pp. 448, 449.
110. See, for instance, *The Royal Commission as a Court of Justice: Being an Examination of the Declaration of the Commissioners that "The Police Are Not Chargeable with Any Abuse of Their Authority"* (London, 1871).
111. Managers of the Metropolitan Female Reformatories, *An Exposure of the False Statistics of the Contagious Diseases Acts (Women) Contained in Parliamentary Paper, No. 149, on the Return of the Assistant Com-*

missioner of the Metropolitan Police (London, 1873). Instead, argued the *Exposure* (pp. 8–10), there was "no actual reduction of brothels but . . . their character was merely changed." Similarly, "fallen" women did not decrease but "found other abodes." As to juvenile prostitutes, the report maintained that the earlier estimates of juvenile prostitutes before compulsory inspection had exaggerated the numbers of "suspected and unregistered girls." In subsequent reports, police deliberately chose "*not to register* and, therefore, to exclude from their comparative statements young girls found in an evil course of life." Moreover, whatever improvements had occurred in the public order of subjected districts was largely due to local police efforts to enforce the new licensing laws.

112. Birkbeck Nevins, *Statement on the Grounds upon Which the C. D. Acts Are Opposed* (Liverpool, 1874). Nevins argument may be summarized as follows. First, a decline in the incidence of syphilis was evident even before the acts became operative. Second, an actual increase in both gonorrhea and secondary syphilis had taken place among enlisted men while the acts were in force. The earlier decline in primary syphilis had been illusory, a consequence of concealment. Finally, prostitutes were interned in the hospital for gonorrhea, not syphilis, presumably simply to keep beds filled.

113. F. C. Banks to James Stansfeld, 22 May 1884. "National Association Letter Book," Butler Collection.

114. Josephine Butler, General Circular to LNA Executive Board, 4 December 1882, Wilson Collection, box 79, Fawcett Library.

115. Josephine Butler, General Circular to LNA Executive Board, 11 January 1879, Butler Collection.

6. THE LEADERSHIP OF THE LADIES' NATIONAL ASSOCIATION

1. "First Annual Report of the Ladies National Association for the Repeal of the Contagious Diseases Acts, 1870," *LNA Annual Reports,* 1870–86. Josephine Butler Collection, Fawcett Library, London.

2. Mary Priestman to George Butler, 21 February 1901, Butler Collection.

3. This group also includes Elizabeth Wolstenholme, who had been a member of the General Committee in 1870. The social profile of the LNA leadership has been culled from a variety of printed and archival sources. The most important archival sources include the "Dictionary of Quaker Biography," Friends Library, London, and the local-history archives of Newcastle, Bristol, Manchester, Belfast, and Liverpool. Printed sources include the obituaries in the *Shield* (London) and the *Annual Monitor* (London). The associational life of LNA leaders has been traced through the *Women's Suffrage Journal, Vigilance Journal,* and *Personal Rights Review.* The membership and subscription lists of the following organizations and institutions have also been consulted: Ladies' National

Association; Vigilance Association; Social Purity Association; Old Park Lock Hospital.

4. Mary Priestman, on the role of Josephine Butler and the LNA, n. d., Butler Collection.

5. Margaret Tanner to Charlotte Wilson, 23 May 1875, no. 3487, Butler Collection.

6. Peter Rylands, quoted in *Josephine E. Butler: An Autobiographical Memoir,* eds. George W. Johnson and Lucy A. Johnson (London, 1909), p. 112.

7. When John Addington Symonds encountered Butler in Oxford he underwent a traumatic sexual experience: "his reproductive equipment swelled." Quoted in Glen Petrie, *A Singular Iniquity: The Campaigns of Josephine Butler* (New York, 1971), p. 90.

8. There have been numerous biographies of Butler, but none that was adequately grounded in the social history of the repeal campaign. See her own admirable memoir, *Personal Reminiscences of a Great Crusade* (London, 1911). Also by Butler: *Memoir of John Grey of Dilston* (Edinburgh, 1869); *Recollections of George Butler* (Bristol, 1892), and *Autobiographical Memoir.* Biographies of her include W. T. Stead, *Josephine Butler: A Life Sketch* (London, 1887); Millicent Fawcett and E. M. Turner, *Josephine Butler: Her Work, Principles and Their Meaning for the Twentieth Century* (London, 1927); E. Moberly Bell, *Josephine Butler: Flame of Fire* (London, 1962), and Petrie, *A Singular Iniquity.*

9. Stead, *Josephine Butler,* p. 3.

10. Josephine Butler, quoted in Bell, *Flame of Fire,* p. 105.

11. Petrie, *Singular Iniquity,* p. 27.

12. Kathleen Heasmen, *Evangelicals in Action: An Appraisal of their Social Work in the Victorian Era* (London, 1962), p. 167.

13. Petrie, *Singular Iniquity,* p. 24.

14. Ibid., p. 36.

15. Josephine Kamm, *Rapiers and Battleaxes: The Women's Movement and Its Aftermath* (London, 1966), p. 113.

16. Petrie, *Singular Iniquity,* p. 33.

17. Josephine Butler, quoted in Petrie, *Singular Iniquity,* p. 44.

18. A G. Butler to G. G. Butler, 4 January 1901, Butler Collection; Butler, *Autobiographical Memoir,* p. 58.

19. Butler, *Recollection,* p. 184; *Autobiographical Memoir,* pp. 60, 64; Maurice Gregory, *The Suppression of the White Slave Traffic: Historical Sketch of the English Section of the Movement* (London, 1908), p. 4.

20. Kamm, *Rapiers,* p. 114; Butler, *Autobiographical Memoir,* pp. 81–3.

21. Stead, *Josephine Butler,* p. 18.

22. Thanks to Professor Carroll Smith-Rosenberg for these observations.

23. Butler, quoted in Bell, *Flame of Fire,* p. 103.

24. *LNA Annual Reports,* 1870–86.

25. Eliza Wigham, for example, spent many years nursing an ailing step-

mother. "The Woman at Home," Scrapbook Collection, July 1895, vol. AA/105, Friends Library.

26. *Annual Monitor* (1906), 140. Contrast this with Charlotte Wilson's report of her early marriage to Henry Wilson: "For some years after my marriage, I was too much occupied with my children to undertake outside work. . . . We never had more than two servants and moreover we had other domestic duties to perform as well. I was head nurse myself and I always had the children with me." Mrs. Wilson had her last child in 1876 and with some difficulty participated publicly in the campaign. Letter to Miss Soltan, 28 September 1903, M.D. 2469-10; a notice of golden anniversary, September 1909, M.D. 2469-11, Wilson Collection. Sheffield Public Library, Sheffield.

27. Henry J. B. Heath, *Margaret Bright Lucas* (London, 1890), p. 16.

28. "Report of the Annual Meeting held at Hull, Oct. 19, 1876," in "Sixth Annual Report of the LNA . . . 1876."

29. Stead, *Josephine Butler,* p. 31.

30. E. F. Richards, introduction to *Mazzini's Letters to an English Family,* ed. E. F. Richards (London, 1920–2), I, 23.

31. Their own Quaker home had exposed them to total abstinence and abolitionism. See Brian Harrison, *Dictionary of British Temperance Biography* (Sheffield, 1973), p. 100.

32. Petrie, *Singular Iniquity,* p. 142. Because of his repeal work, Stansfeld lost his standing as a major Radical leader in the late 1870s and was denied a position in Gladstone's cabinet in 1880.

33. Josephine Butler, quoted in "Interesting Reminiscences: A Talk with Mrs. Josephine Butler," *Woman's Signal* 2 (13 September 1894). Only one woman, Lydia Becker, was constitutionally unable to get on with men. Becker's unprepossessing appearance was used to caricature feminists as ugly bluestockings. Josephine Kamm, *Rapiers and Battleaxes: The Woman's Movement and Its Aftermath* (London, 1966), p. 134.

34. Margaret Bright Lucas, quoted in Heath, *Margaret Bright Lucas,* p. 14.

35. Butler, *Personal Reminiscences,* p. 104.

36. Charles Finney, quoted in Heasman, *Evangelicals,* p. 25.

37. Josephine Butler to a "Friend," 24.121, no. 99, Mary Estlin Collection, Dr. Williams' Library, University of London.

38. *Shield,* May 1891.

39. Josephine Butler, quoted in *Shield,* August 1900.

40. Josephine Butler to Mary Priestman, 20 November 1882, Butler Collection.

41. Sylvia Pankhurst, *The Suffragette Movement: An Intimate Account of Persons and Ideals* (New York, 1931), pp. 32, 33. See J. Whitwell Wilson's response: "It is a trying affair, shows me afresh that after all it is *religious* people who are the real strength of our movement." J. Whitwell Wilson to Henry J. Wilson, 20 December 1875, no. 3829, Butler Collection.

42. "William Henry Ashurst," *Dictionary of National Biography,* (London, 1885), II, 182, 183; E. F. Richards, introduction, *Mazzini's Letters,* pp. 23–6; Emilie Venturi to Joseph Cowen, 4 December 1871, B. 114, A. 921, Cowen Collection, Newcastle-upon-Tyne Central Library.

43. *Shield,* December 1899.

44. Edith Hurwitz, *Politics and the Public Conscience: Slave Emancipation and the Abolitionist Movement in Britain* (London, 1973), pp. 92, 93.

45. See Elizabeth Cady Stanton, *Eighty Years and More: Reminiscences of Elizabeth Cady Stanton* (London, 1898), ch. 22.

46. J. A. Banks and Olive Banks, *Feminism and Family Planning in Victorian England* (New York, 1964), pp. 33, 39; Helen Blackburn, *Women's Suffrage: A Record of the Women's Suffrage Movement in the British Isles with Biographical Sketches of Miss Becker* (London, 1922), p. 127.

47. Blackburn, *Women's Suffrage,* p. 127.

48. *W.D.M.,* 11 September 1872.

49. See Helen Blackburn, *A Hand-book for Women Engaged in Social and Political Work* (Bristol, 1881); S. J. Tanner, *Suffrage Movement in Bristol: How the Women's Suffrage Movement Began in Bristol Fifty Years Ago* (Bristol, 1918).

50. Françoise Basch, *Relative Creatures: Victorian Women in Society and the Novel* (New York, 1974), ch. 1; Anna Jameson, *Sisters of Charity, Catholic and Protestant; and the Community of Labor* (Boston, 1857), p. 163.

51. Josephine Butler to Mary Priestman, 4 May 1874, no. 3327, Butler Collection. For a discussion of these themes see Butler, *Women's Work.* Repeal was less of an abiding concern for many of the men. There was, at times, a willingness to subordinate repeal to other issues. The "interchangeability" of reform issues was reflected in the correspondence between Henry J. Wilson and J. Thomby, an active Sheffield Liberal: if it was not possible to rouse Sheffield on the Permissive bill (permitting local option for prohibition), Thomby maintained, "well then go in for a furor on the Repeal of the Contagious Diseases Acts, Church and State, or something else." December 1872, M.D. 6010, Wilson Collection.

52. Mary Hume-Rothery, *A Letter Addressed to the Right Hon. W. E. Gladstone, M.P., and the Other Members of Her Majesty's Government and of Both Houses of Parliament, Touching the Contagious Diseases Acts of 1866 and 1869, and Their Proposed Extension to the Civil Population of This Kingdom* (Manchester, 1870), p. 18.

53. Keith Thomas, "The Double Standard," *Journal of the History of Ideas* 20 (1959), 213.

54. *Shield,* 9 May 1870.

55. Josephine Butler to Miss Priestman, 18 November 1883, no. 3315, Butler Collection.

56. Josephine Butler to Charlotte Wilson, 12 November 1883, no. 3313, Butler Collection.

57. Butler, *Personal Reminiscences,* p. 44.
58. The Vigilance Association for the Defense of Personal Rights was most closely associated with the LNA in Manchester and Bristol. Sometimes these joint ventures became a problem. See, for example, Elizabeth Wolstenholme to Henry J. Wilson, 19 June 1873, no. 3286, Butler Collection.
59. Josephine Butler to Joseph Edmondson, 28 April 1872, no. 3139, Butler Collection; F. W. Newman, *The Political Side of the Vaccination Question* (London, 1879); R. D. French, *Anti-Vivisection and Medical Science in Victorian Society* (Princeton, 1975); Mary Hume-Rothery, *Women and Doctors: Or Medical Despotism in England* (London, 1871).
60. Hume-Rothery, *Letter to Gladstone.* Repealers accepted the prevailing view of the uterus as the site of female mysteries: "God has implanted in women an instinct which impels them as strongly as possible to conceal the organs of generation from the sight and touch of men. He has enabled them to give effect to this instinct by framing their bodies in such a manner as to completely shelter those organs, and to bring their whole muscular strength to bear on their defense in case of attack." Thomas Markby, quoted in Isabella Hooker, *Womenhood: Its Sanctities and Fidelities* (Boston, 1888), p. 78.
61. Josephine Butler to J. J. Garth Wilkinson, reprinted in J. J. Garth Wilkinson, *The Forcible Introspection of Women for the Army and Navy by the Oligarchy Considered Physically* (London, 1870), p. 25. Doctors active in the repeal campaign, like C. B. Taylor, did not share Butler's sentiments regarding the internal examination; they distinguished between examinations administered voluntarily to private patients and the compulsory examination of registered prostitutes.
62. Hume-Rothery, *Letter to Gladstone.*
63. John Morley, "Short Letter to Some Ladies," *Fortnightly Review* 7 (1870), 375; Josephine Butler, "Garrison Towns of Kent," *Shield,* 25 April 1870.
64. See Chapter 3.
65. Josephine Butler to Vernon Lushington, P.R.O., Admiralty Papers, Adm.1/6148, 12 January 1870.
66. Thomas Worth, *A Second Letter to the Hon. William Gladstone* (Nottingham, 1870).
67. Josephine Butler to Vernon Lushington, P.R.O., Adm. 1/6148, 12 January 1870.
68. *Seventh Annual Report of the Bristol Old Park Lock Hospital for Women Only, 1877* (Bristol, 1878).
69. "Eighth Annual Report of the LNA, . . . 1877."
70. "Fifteenth Annual Report of the LNA, . . . 1884."
71. Ibid.
72. Josephine Butler to J. J. Garth Wilkinson, reprinted in *Forcible Introspection,* p. 25. Butler was here referring to the small House of Rest she

earlier ran in Liverpool; as an antivaccinationist and homeopathist she continued her opposition to the medical profession.

73. Reverend William Tuckniss, "The Agencies at Present in Operation Within the Metropolis, for the Suppression of Crime," in *London Labour and the London Poor,* ed. Henry Mayhew (rpt., New York, 1968), 34.

74. Mary Ryan, "The Power of Women's Networks: Female Moral Reform in Utica, New York," *Feminist Studies* 5 (Spring 1979), 66–89; Carroll Smith-Rosenberg, "Beauty, the Beast, and the Militant Woman," *American Quarterly* 23 (1971), 562–84; Nancy F. Cott, "Passionlessness: An Interpretation of Victorian Sexual Ideology, 1790–1851," *Signs* 4 (1979), 219–36; Barbara J. Berg, *The Remembered Gate. Origins of American Feminism: The Woman and the City, 1800–1860* (New York, 1978).

75. Josephine Butler, quoted in Fawcett, *Josephine Butler,* p. 72.

76. "Letter from the Right Hon. James Stansfeld, M.P., to the Ladies' National Association and the Other Repeal Associations throughout the Kingdom, 1875," *LNA Reports.*

77. See the local correspondents' reports in the "Tenth Annual Report of the LNA, . . . 1879."

78. "Fifteenth Annual Report of the LNA, . . . 1884."

79. "Eighth Annual Report of the LNA, . . . 1878."

80. Josephine Butler, *On the Moral Reclaimability of Prostitutes* (London, 1870).

81. In 1870–1, LNA income totaled £1,007; in 1875, £953; and in 1884, £726. See *LNA Annual Reports, 1870–1886.*

82. Bristol, Edinburgh, Liverpool, Leeds, Newcastle, and London numbered among the ten branches with the largest subscriptions and donations in 1870, 1875, or 1884. Bristol, York, Newcastle, Liverpool, Edinburgh, Leeds, and London were among the ten branches with the largest number of individual subscribers in 1870, 1875, and 1884. Thanks to Rachel Bernstein for compiling these statistics.

83. Stead, *Josephine Butler,* p. 42.

84. Charlotte Wilson, "Memoir of Mrs. Henry J. Wilson," n.d., M.D. 2469–17, Wilson Collection, Sheffield Public Library.

85. Mary Priestman, "Ladies' Branch Associations," *N.L.J.,* 1 December 1881.

86. Gertrude Wilson to Henry J. Wilson, 15 January 1870, M.D. 2547–5, Wilson Collection, Sheffield Public Library.

87. Charlotte Wilson, "Memoir."

88. J. Whitwell Wilson to Henry J. Wilson, 2 September 1875, no. 3845; Josephine Butler, circular to LNA Executive, 11 December 1877, Butler Collection.

89. There were 74 LNA subscribers from Bristol in 1870; 58 in 1875; and 73 in 1884.

7. CLASS AND GENDER CONFLICT

1. "Second Annual Report of the LNA, . . . 1871," *LNA Reports, 1870–1886,* Butler Collection, Fawcett Library, London.
2. Josephine Butler, *Personal Reminiscence of a Great Crusade* (London, 1911), p. 31.
3. Josephine Butler to Mr. Childers, 12 February 1873, Henry J. Wilson Papers, Fawcett Library, London.
4. Glen Petrie, *A Singular Iniquity: The Campaigns of Josephine Butler* (New York, 1971), p. 139.
5. See Chapter 9.
6. *Shield,* 28 October 1876; 4 November 1876.
7. "Eighth Annual Report of the LNA, . . . 1878."
8. Josephine Butler, n.d. [1872], no address, no. 3187. Butler Collection.
9. Josephine Butler, circular to the LNA Executive, 1877. Butler Collection.
10. Josephine Butler to the LNA Executive, 11 October 1877. Butler Collection.
11. Ibid.
12. Josephine Butler to Maurice Gregory, 15 April 1899: Butler Collection. Wilson's private letters to his wife Charlotte, who was active in the LNA, and his daughter Helen (whom he constantly belittled in his correspondence) bear out this characterization. See his response to the women of the Moral Education Society during his trip to America in 1876. Henry J. Wilson to Charlotte Wilson, May 1876, M.D. 6043, Wilson Collection, Sheffield Public Library.
13. Henry J. Wilson to Charlotte Wilson, 14 May 1876, M.D. 6028, Wilson Collection, Sheffield Public Library.
14. Henry J. Wilson to Gertrude Wilson, 5 Jan, 1870. M.D. 2547–2, Wilson Collection. Wilson indicated that he strongly objected to clauses three to seven in the Women's Protest, which stressed their objection to the double standard and the violation of the constitutional rights of workingwomen.
15. Butler, "Industrial School Amendment Act."
16. James Stuart to Henry J. Wilson, 4 September 1875, Butler Collection. Butler responded that "she had foreseen that probably before her death this sway of the pendulum would begin towards punishment, but she is startled to find it has began so soon."
17. Charlotte Wilson to Josephine Butler, 7 March 1883, Butler Collection.
18. Josephine Butler to Charlotte Wilson, 26 August [1872], no. 3175, Butler Collection.
19. "Second Annual Report of the LNA, . . . 1871."
20. "Working Men!" LNA poster displayed during the Colchester by-election of 1870, Wilson Collection, Fawcett Library.
21. "Seventh Annual Report of the LNA, . . . 1876."
22. Ibid.
23. "Fifteenth Annual Report of the LNA, . . . 1884."

24. Josephine Butler to Henry J. Wilson, 22 April 1875, no. 3380. See also H. J. Hanham, "Liberal Organizations for Working Men, 1860–1914," *Bulletin of the Society for the Study of Labour History,* no. 7 (Autumn 1963), 5–7.
25. See the interchange between Robert Applegarth and Josephine Butler, Royal Commission of 1871, *P.P.* (C. 408–1), Minutes of Evidence, Q. 12115. See also the *Bee-Hive* editorials against women's employment and women's suffrage: "Men and Women," 17 April 1875; "Women's Work," 19 April 1873; "Women's Suffrage," 3 May 1873; "Women's Protective and Provident League," 6 December 1876.
26. *Second Annual Report of the Vigilance Society . . . , 1873.*
27. Josephine Butler to Mary Priestman, 5 December 1876, Butler Collection.
28. For example, see the "Ninth Annual Report of the LNA, . . . 1878."
29. See, for example, a report of a "working women's association" in the *Shield,* 20 February 1873; "Ninth Annual Report of the LNA, . . . , 1878"; Josephine Butler to Mary Priestman, 26 October 1872, no. 3193, Butler Collection.
30. Josephine Butler, *A Letter to the Members of the Ladies' National Association* (Liverpool, 1875), Butler Collection.
31. Isabella Stuart, "To the Women of Britain [1872]," *Abolitionist Flysheets,* Butler Collection.
32. Butler, *Personal Reminiscences,* p. 31.
33. Ibid., p. 28. Butler further remarked, "This incident did not represent exactly the kind of influence which we had entreated the working women to use with their husbands who had votes, but I confess it cheered me not a little."
34. Dorothy Thompson, "Women and Nineteenth-Century Radical Politics: A Lost Dimension," in *The Rights and Wrongs of Women,* eds., Juliet Mitchell and Ann Oakley (Harmondsworth, 1976), pp. 121, 122. See Chapter 3.
35. Ibid., pp. 136–8.
36. Thanks to Professors Martha Vicinus and Carroll Smith-Rosenberg for these observations.

8. PLYMOUTH AND SOUTHAMPTON

1. "Report of the House of Commons Select Committee on the Administration, Operation, and Effects of the Contagious Diseases Acts of 1866–69," 1882 (340), IX, XXVI.
2. "Deputation from Plymouth, Devonport, etc. to the Home Secretary," *D.I.,* 26 May 1883; *W.D.M.,* 26 June 1883.
3. *Shield,* 2 May 1870.
4. A. P. Balkwill to Henry J. Wilson, 17 February 1902, Butler Collection, Fawcett Library, London.

5. After a period of extreme economic depression following the Napoleonic Wars, Plymouth's growth was spurred by the construction of the Plymouth breakwater, which made it a much safer port, and facilitated the docking of warships, liners, and merchant ships. See G. W. Hoskins, *Devon* (London, 1964), pp. 162–75.

6. As Eric Hobsbawm has remarked, before 1889 "waterside labour was not seriously or permanently organized" nationally. The presence of such an omnipotent employer as the Admiralty would tend to have inhibited union activity in any case. Furthermore, Devonport dockers, despite government cutbacks, were afforded steadier employment than their counterparts in commercial ports. Eric Hobsbawm, "National Unions on the Waterside," in *Labouring Men: Studies in the History of Labour* (London, 1954), p. 204. Dock laborers and seamen did try to organize in Southampton in 1872 and 1874. *W.H.I.*, 15 June 1872, 8 June 1874.

7. Census (1871), *P.P.*, 1873, LXXXI, pt. 1, A. P. Prowse, "Pauperism," *W.D.M.*, 1 April 1870; P.R.O., Poor Law Correspondence, M.H. 12/2429, 11 May 1861; M.H. 12/2430, 23 July 1861.

8. Gareth Stedman Jones, *Outcast London: A Study in the Relationship Between Classes in Victorian Society* (Oxford, 1971), p. 48. The statistics of registered single women living alone in lodgings was based on a 10 percent sampling of all single women aged 15 to 29 and residing in lodgings in Plymouth. P.R.O., 1871 Manuscript Census, R.G. 10/2112–24. For further details, see Chapter 9. Given the movement of women on and off the register, the proportion of women in lodgings who had been on the register over the course of the year was undoubtedly higher than 40 percent.

9. Hoskins, *Devon,* p. 122. Devonport was created as a political entity in 1813 out of these new imperatives. East Stonehouse, on the other hand, never achieved municipal status in the nineteenth century. Lacking the necessary municipal institutions, it was a much less orderly town. Whereas Plymouth and Devonport were able to enact by-laws under the Towns Police Clause Act of 1847 to control streetwalking and "disorderly houses," East Stonehouse, as an unincorporated town, was not. As a consequence, brothel keepers prosecuted in Plymouth frequently moved into East Stonehouse.

10. See, for example, Towns Police Clause Act, 1847 (10 and 11 Vict. c. 89); Wine and Beerhouse Act, 1869–70 (32 and 33 Vict. c. 27, and 33 and 34 Vict. c. 29); and Licensing Act 1872 (35 and 36 Vict. c. 94).

11. Andrew Cluer, *Plymouth and Plymouthians* (Plymouth, 1974).

12. Henry Whitfeld, *Plymouth and Devonport in Times of War and Peace* (Plymouth, 1900), pp. 402, 405.

13. 1851 Manuscript Census Schedule, P.R.O., H.O. 107/1879.

14. Sam Hugill, *Sailortown* (London, 1967), p. 76.

15. Sam Hugill, *Shanties and Sailors' Songs* (London, 1969) p. 160. More likely than not Jack would catch his "dose" from one of the "Judies" or

"Mary Ellens" of Castle Street. In 1828, a list was compiled of 18 women from the Castle Street taverns who entered the Plymouth workhouse with venereal disease. W362/92/2, 1828, Devon County Record Office, Plymouth.

16. This public disorder distressed poor residents as much as their social superiors. In 1828, 10 female inhabitants of Lambayhill complained of the disgusting language and attitudes of local prostitutes and called for their removal from "hence for the sake of the children, the sight of these witches is enough to contaminate the morals of any female, leaving children out of the question." W362/92/2, 1828, Devon County Record Office, Plymouth.

17. Inspector Anniss, testimony before the Royal Commission of 1871, *P.P.,* 1871, IX, Q. 729-732; "Report of the House of Commons Select Committee on the Administration, Operation, and Effects of the Contagious Diseases Acts of 1866–69," *P.P.,* 1882 (340), IX, Apps. 1–4. Plymouth authorities reported (App. 1) that on Licensing Day, 1869, 32 public houses and beershops used as brothels were closed; in the three ensuing years, 22 more "such houses were closed in like manner." Devonport and East Stonehouse authorities reported a similar trend.

18. Mr. F. Wreford, testimony before the Royal Commision of 1871, *P.P.,* 1871, IX, Q. 8791–93.

19. See Chapter 10.

20. A. Temple Patterson, *A History of Southampton. Vol. 2: The Beginnings of Modern Southampton 1836–1867* (Southampton, 1971), pp. 92–4.

21. "First Report of the Royal Commission on the Liquor Licensing Laws," *P.P.,* 1897 (Cd. 8355), XXXIV, Q. 8312, 8754, 17473, 17586. Prostitutes also used back alleys and brought men back to their rooms.

22. Whitfield, *Plymouth and Devonport,* p. 399.

23. Cluer, *Plymouth and Plymouthians.*

24. *Shield,* 19 April 1873. See also the case of Mary Charters (*W.D.M.,* 3 May 1870), who was brought up on a drunk and disorderly charge: "She had formerly been in the workhouse which she left as she was made to wash, and she said she would rather go to prison than go there again."

25. See Emma Jones's letter to the Poor Law Board, P.R.O., Poor Law Correspondence, M.H. 12/2434, 26 June 1870 and 1 July 1870.

26. In 1844, Francis Cooper, the surgeon to the Southampton workhouse, protested to the board of guardians that two venereal patients were made to share the same bed so that each party "was exposed by contingent juxtaposition under the same covering to the offensive and purulent discharges which are generated by the various forms of the complaint under which the respective parties labour." Quoted in A. Fessler, "Venereal Disease and Prostitution in the Reports of the Poor Law Commissioners, 1834–1850," *B.J.V.D.* (1951), 154, 155.

27. Agnes Weston, *My Life Among the Bluejackets* (London, 1909), p. 10.

28. *W.D.M.,* 23 November 1870; John W. Elvins, *Directory of Plymouth, Stonehouse, Devonport, Stoke and Morice Town* (Plymouth, 1862). The style of rescue and preventive work in South Devon followed the general historical development in Great Britain. Old-fashioned penitentiaries like the Devon and Exeter Penitentiary and the Plymouth Female Penitentiary were founded in the early nineteenth century and maintained a grim, repressive regime. An 1870 Admiralty report of the latter institution described it as only wanting "real penitents," and subjecting new inmates to solitary confinement and head shaving. The House of Mercy at Bovey Tracey and the Barley House of Mercy in Plymouth were established by high church sisterhoods in the 1850s and 1860s. The Plymouth Female Home was established in 1860 as a protest against the harsh management of the penitentiary. There were no outreach until 1870, when national repeal associations conducted midnight missions and employed working-class agents to seek out registered prostitutes at the examination house and in their neighborhoods. P.R.O., Adm. 1/6179, 1870; *W.D.M.,* 11 January 1871.
29. Patterson, *Southampton,* II, 132.
30. W. T. Swan to the editor, *N.L.J.,* 1 February 1878.
31. William Sloggett, "History and Operations of the Contagious Diseases Acts in the Home Ports," P.R.O., Adm. 1/6418, 1 April 1873.
32. Ibid.
33. Ibid.
34. *D.I.,* 5 December 1874.
35. Whitfeld, *Plymouth and Devonport,* pp. 543, 544.
36. William Luscombe, Testimony Before the Royal Commission of 1871, *P.P.,* 1871, IX, Q. 4649.
37. Ibid., Q. 5156.
38. See, for example, P.R.O., Home Office Papers, H.O.45/9 April 1870; *Shield,* 14 October 1870, 4 November 1871; *P.P.,* 1882, IX, Q. 54, pp. 481–3.
39. James Stuart commented that the majority report of the 1882 Select Committe "grounds itself on the effect of the Acts in Devonport." James Stuart to Henry J. Wilson, 12 October 1882, Wilson Collection, box 79, Fawcett Library.
40. M. Berkeley Hill, "Illustrations of the Workings of the Contagious Diseases Act," *B.M.J.* 1 (1868), 21.
41. P.R.O., Adm. 1/6122, 3 February 1869.
42. Ibid., 1 March 1869.
43. P.R.O., Adm. 1/6064, August 1868.
44. "Report of the House of Commons Select Committee on the Contagious Diseases Act," *P.P.,* 1868–9 (306), VII: Minutes of Evidence, Q. 914.
45. *A Letter to the Lords of the Admiralty from the Surgeons in Charge of the Lock Wards of the Royal Albert Hospital, Devonport: Including Results of Treatment and Comments on Evidence Lately Given Before a*

Select Committee of the House of Commons on the Contagious Diseases Act, 1866 and Suggestions for the Future Management of the Lock Wards (London, 1869).

46. P.R.O., Adm. 1/6123, 6 September 1869.
47. Vernon Lushington, P.R.O., Adm. 1/6123, 15 October 1869.
48. Thomas Woollcombe, ibid.
49. Alfred Balkwill remarked in his 1907 memoir: "To show the length the supporters would go, the house surgeon assured me that the figures in the books of the hospital were erased and altered so as to make them appear favorable to the Acts." Balkwill to Henry J. Wilson, 17 February 1902, Butler Collection.
50. P.R.O., Adm. 1/6123, 23 November 1869.
51. Ibid., 26 November 1869.
52. Ibid.
53. P.R.O., Adm. 1/6179, 17 December 1869.
54. See the cases of Harriet Hicks, Ann Lambert, and Elizabeth Bond, where the "bias" of the sitting Devonport magistrates was noted. P.R.O., Adm. 1/6143, 19 July 1870; Adm. 1/6144, 9 August 1870.
55. "Memorial of Magistrates and Other Leading Persons in Plymouth, Devonport, Stonehouse and Dartmouth, in Favor of the Contagious Diseases Acts," reprinted in the Royal Commission of 1871, *P.P.*, 1871, IX, App. D.
56. John Ryder, testimony before the Royal Commission of 1871, *P.P.*, 1871, IX, Q. 8269.
57. *P.P.*, 1875, LXI. In contrast, Plymouth magistrates included no physicians, although physicians were still influential members of the community.
58. "The Memorial of the Undersigned Magistrates, Clergy, Medical Practitioners, and Others in the Borough of Plymouth and Devonport, and Township of Stonehouse," *P.P.*, 1882 (356), LIII; Association for Promoting the Extension of the Contagious Diseases Acts, *Sixth Report on the Operation of the Contagious Diseases Acts* (London, 1875).
59. Elvins, *Directory* (1873).
60. P.R.O., Metropolitan Dockyard Correspondence, Mepol. 1/58, 25 January 1860.
61. "Religion in the Examination Rooms," *Shield*, 17 January 1874. Superintendent Wakeford, in charge of the Devonport district of the metropolitan police, was an active temperance man.
62. P.R.O., Mepol. 1/58, 1867.
63. *Twentieth Annual Report of the Rescue Society of London for the Year Ending 1872*, (London, 1873), p. 29. It should be noted that these "middle-aged men . . . from London," as Admiralty officials characterized them, were in reality local men who had worked as dockyard police previous to their new assignment under the acts. As a consequence they had extensive personal associations with the local population.
64. P.R.O., Home Office Papers, H.O. 45/9615/A11468, 1881.

65. James Crouch, quoted in *A Collection of Opinion on English, Colonial, and Continental Towns, and Police Regulation, for the Sanitary Supervision of Vice* (n.p., n.d.).
66. A. P. Balkwill to Henry J. Wilson, 17 February 1902, Butler Collection.
67. *LNA Annual Reports*, 1870–86, Butler Collection.
68. Caroline Nicholson, "What I Saw at the Royal Albert Hospital," *Abolitionist Flysheets*, Butler Collection; "The Withdrawal of Registered Women from Moral Influences," *Shield*, 21 January 1871.
69. Caroline Nicholson, "Abolition of Slavery on the Gold Coast: Is it Consistent with the Establishment of Slavery at Home?" *Abolitionist Flysheets*, Butler Collection.
70. There were also "closet" sympathizers like Alfred Rooker, who correctly felt that his public espousal of the cause would hurt his political career. "Minutes of the National Association for the Repeal of the Contagious Diseases Acts" 2 (13 November 1871), no. 111, Butler Collection. Subscription lists of the LNA and N.A., as well as local newspaper accounts of branch meetings, were used to identify the members of the ladies' and gentlemen's committees. Active members of the local branches substantially exceeded the number of Plymouth subscribers to the LNA and the N.A.
71. *W.D.M.*, 15 June 1914.
72. "Mr. W. S. Littleton of Devonport," *Shield*, 19 May 1877.
73. *Shield*, 3 March 1877.
74. Inspector Sloggett to Vernon Lushington, P.R.O., Adm. 1/6179, 1 June 1870; Adm. 1/6206, 31 January 1871.
75. *W.H.I.*, 24 February 1874; *Women's Suffrage Journal* (Manchester, 1870). p. 76.
76. *W.H.I.*, 1870–4, passim; Dr. Hearne frequently clashed with Dr. Aldridge on the subject of compulsory vaccination. See, for example, *W.H.I.*, 3 June 1876.
77. Mrs. Edmund Kell, testimony before the Royal Commission of 1872, *P.P.*, IX, Q. 16, 870–900.
78. *W.H.I.*, 28 January 1871; "Meeting of the Land and Labour League, *W.H.I.*, 15 October 1870; 27 May 1871.
79. *W.H.I.*, 4 June 1870; *Shield*, 20 June 1870.
80. *W.H.I.*, 21 November 1874. Dr. Aldridge was also a member of a nonconformist temperance society. *W.H.I.*, 2 February 1876.
81. P.R.O., *Ind.* 18, 187, 1875. See also, "Our Portrait Gallery; James S. Pearce, Esq.," *Southern Reformer: A Political, Social, and Critical Review for the Southern Counties*, 3 July 1880.
82. *Shield*, 16 May 1870.
83. P.R.O., Adm. 1/6253, 16 September 1872.
84. O. R. Macdonagh, "Nineteenth-Century Revolution in Government: A Reappraisal," *Historical Journal* 1 (1958), 52–67.
85. *W.H.I.*, 26 February 1870.
86. Ibid., 26 November 1870.

9. THE REPEAL CAMPAIGN IN PLYMOUTH AND SOUTHAMPTON

1. *Shield,* 8 August 1870; *W.D.M.,* 29 July 1870, 3 August 1870.
2. "Women of Plymouth and Devonport Suffering Under the Contagious Diseases Acts!" *Abolitionist Flysheets,* Butler Collection, Fawcett Library, London.
3. *Shield,* 3 August 1870.
4. "The Death of a Naval Surgeon in a House of Ill-Fame," *D.I.* 16 August 1869.
5. *W.D.M.,* 29 July 1870; 3 August 1870.
6. *Shield,* 8 August 1870.
7. E. M. King, *Rational Dress; or the Dress of Women and Savages* (London, 1882). In this pamphlet (p. 17), King referred to herself as a "dress doctor." See also King's article, "Co-operative Housekeeping," *Contemporary Review* 23 (December 1873), 66–91.
8. E. M. King to the editor, *Shield,* 15 August 1870.
9. Letter from E. M. King to "Electors of the Borough of Colchester," reprinted in *Shield,* 5 November 1870; E. M. King to Dear Friend, 28 December 1870, Butler Collection. At the 1872 annual meeting of the Social Science Congress in Plymouth, Mrs. King read a paper on "Work of an International Peace Society and Women's Place in It," *Women's Suffrage Journal,* 1 October 1872, p. 137. During the 1870s King was a member of the executive board of the National Association. "Minutes of the National Association for the Repeal of the Contagious Diseases Acts" (2–6), 1870–86, Butler Collection.
10. In 1869 Cooper circulated a pamphlet, entitled *A Remedy Worse Than Death,* to M.P.s. See "Origin of the Repeal Movement," letter to the editor by "Honour to Whom Honour Is Due," *Shield,* 17 April 1886.
11. See, for example, "Rules and Regulations," in *Twenty-fifth Annual Report of the Rescue Society, 1877* (London, 1878), p. 5. in *Rescue Society Reports, 1877–1898,* Butler Collection.
12. *Shield,* August 1900.
13. *Shield,* 2 May 1870.
14. "The Contagious Diseases Acts: Opponents of the Acts Interfering with the Metropolitan Police," *W.D.M.,* 29 July 1870.
15. In covering the trial, the *Shield,* with its teetotaling readership, omitted mention of Dennaford's profession. "Prosecution of the Opponents of the Acts by the Admiralty – Protracted Proceedings," *Shield,* 8 August 1870.
16. P.R.O., Adm. 1/6180, 4 August 1870.
17. *Shield,* 8 August 1870.
18. *D.I.,* quoted in *Shield,* 15 August 1870.
19. William Sloggett, "A History and Sketch of the Operation of the Contagious Diseases Acts in the Home Ports," P.R.O., Adm. 1/6418, 10 April 1873.

20. Benjamin Scott, *A State Iniquity, Its Rise, Extension, and, Overthrow* (London, 1894), p. 120.
21. Ibid.
22. Mrs. Lewis, testimony before the Royal Commission on the Administration and Operation of the Contagious Diseases Acts 1866–69 (1871), *P.P.*, 1871, XIX, Q.12573.
23. Christopher Bulteel to the editor, *W.D.M.*, 17 June 1870.
24. The workingmen's petition complained of the intimidation and publicity attendant upon registration; the debasing influence of the examination process; the broad discretionary powers given to the police; the prejudicial character of the acts as class and sex legislation; and the false presumption underlying the acts that prostitution was a necessity, rather than an eradicable evil. *Shield*, 23 May 1870.
25. *Shield*, 20 June 1870.
26. *Shield*, 10 September 1870.
27. Ibid.
28. "Meeting of Women in Plymouth," *W.D.M.*, 8 June 1870.
29. "Medicamentarius" to the editor, *W.D.M.*, 25 April 1870.
30. "Fair Play" to the editor, *W.D.M.*, 10 May 1870.
31. "Medicamentarius" to the editor, *W.D.M.*, 4 June 1870.
32. A. R. R. Preston to the editor, *W.D.M.*, 28 May 1870. See Helen Ware's remarks on the conflicting analysis of William Tait, "Prostitution and the State: The Recruitment, Regulation and Role of Prostitution in the Nineteenth and Twentieth Century" (Ph.D. diss., Univ. of London 1969), p. 17.
33. A. R. R. Preston to the editor, *W.D.M.*, 20 July 1870.
34. Christopher Bulteel to the editor, *W.D.M.*, 30 May 1870, 22 June 1870, 6 July 1870; "The Contagious Diseases Acts: Noisy Meeting at Plymouth," *W.D.M.*, 13 June 1870.
35. Their critique would form the basis of an influential report published in 1871 jointly by the "Managers of the Metropolitan Female Reformatories" entitled *An Exposure of the False Statistics of the Contagious Diseases Acts* (London, 1871).
36. *W.D.M.*, 20 June 1870, and *Shield*, 10 September 1870, 17 September 1870, 15 July 1871.
37. The *Western Daily Mercury*, for example, congratulated the ladies of Teignmouth for preferring the "privacy and duty of domestic life to stumping about the country with foolish virgins of unattractive aspect who seek in the unhealthy excitement of rant compensation for the absence of husband, children and home." *W.D.M.*, 23 August 1871.
38. Reverend H. A. Greaves, quoted in "Crowded and Excited Meeting in Plymouth," *W.D.M.*, 23 April 1870.
39. See *W.D.M.*, 2 July 1870, 22 July 1870, 25 July 1871, 27 July 1871.
40. *W.D.M.*, 8 June 1870.
41. "A Friend to Women" to the editor, *W.D.M.*, 7 July 1870.

42. A. R. R. Preston to the editor, *W.D.M.*, 24 June 1870.
43. Mary Hume-Rothery to the editor, *W.D.M.*, 20 July 1870.
44. Josephine Butler to the editor, *W.D.M.*, 18 July 1870.
45. Inspector Sloggett, P.R.O., Adm. 1/6253, 29 March 1877.
46. King, "Women of Plymouth and Devonport."
47. Mary Hume-Rothery to the editor, *Shield*, 15 August 1870.
48. "Illegal Detention of a Woman at the Royal Albert Hospital, Devonport," *Abolitionist Flysheets*, Butler Collection.
49. Thomas Woollcombe to Vernon Lushington, P.R.O., Adm. 1/6143, 19 July 1870.
50. Admiral Codrington to Vernon Lushington, P.R.O., Adm. 1/6143, 19 July 1870.
51. "Report of the Assistant Commissioner of Police of the Metropolis on the Operation of the Contagious Diseases Acts" (1881), *P.P.*, 1882 (29), LIII; Sloggett, "History and Sketch."
52. *The Royal Commission as a Court of Justice: Being an Examination of the Declaration of the Commissioners that "the Police Are Not Chargeable with Any Abuse of Their Authority"* (Nottingham, 1871); " Report of Messrs. Shaen and Roscoe upon the Working of the C. D. Acts in Canterbury" (unpublished report, n.d.), Henry J. Wilson Collection, Fawcett Library, London.
53. *Shield*, 28 October 1870.
54. *Shield*, 1 August 1870.
55. Josephine Butler, *On the Moral Reclaimability of Prostitutes* (London, 1870).
56. Sloggett, "History and Sketch."
57. "NA Minutes" 2 (10 November 1873), no. 1012; 2 (24 November 1873), no. 1032, Butler Collection.
58. E. M. King to the editor, *Shield*, 15 August 1870.
59. Mrs. Hampson, private letter reprinted in *Shield*, 1 October 1870.
60. "First Annual Report of the LNA, . . . 1870–71," *LNA Reports*, 1870–86.
61. Josephine Butler, speech before annual meeting of the LNA in Plymouth. Quoted in *W.D.M.*, 16 September 1872. Elizabeth Wolstenholme voiced similar indignation at the sight of "clean, well-fed, fairly well-dressed and tolerably decorous prostitutes" in the Three Towns who lived "in the midst of this smooth, easy, half-conscious vice." "The Moral Effects of the Acts in Plymouth," *Shield*, 15 October 1872.
62. "Which Shall Prevail?" (1872), *Abolitionist Flysheets*, Butler Collection, Fawcett Library, London.
63. "Tactics at Plymouth," *Shield*, 27 May 1870, complained that the *Western Morning News* refused to publish letters to the editors in response to abusive letters.
64. "Summary of Action in the Subjected Districts," *Shield*, 13 April 1878. Anniss's statistics were further repudiated by local magistrates and police

authorities before the Royal Commission of 1871 and the Select Committee of 1882. The debate was widely covered by repealers, who reproduced thousands of copies of the interchange of letters between the Devonport town council and the Home Office.

65. It was also felt that William Littleton's influence in Devonport might have encouraged the Devonport town council to take a stand, whereas the Plymouth town council did not. Further, the district in which the Three Towns were situated was known as the Devonport district, and thus Mr. Bruce's speech gave Devonport a particularly bad name.

66. William Sloggett, P.R.O., Adm. 1/6253, 17 June 1872.

67. Sloggett, "History and Sketch," P.R.O., Adm. 1/6418, 10 April 1873.

68. "M.D." to the editor, *W.H.I.,* 19 February 1870.

69. *W.H.I.,* 26 February 1870.

70. Sloggett, P.R.O., Adm. 1/6179, 1 June 1870; Adm. 1/6206, 31 January 1871.

71. "Memorial from the Southampton Branch of the National Anti-Contagious Diseases Acts Association, Asking That the Operation of the Act Within the Borough May Be Suspended Till Its Provisions Are Discussed in Parliament." P.R.O., Adm. 1/6178, 15 March 1870. "Memorial from the Southampton Corporation," Adm. 1/6178, 1 April 1870.

72. "Report of the Assistant Commissioner," *P.P.,* 1882, LIII.

73. *Shield,* 1 June 1872. Butler also reported, "Girls told me of conversations which pass *begun* by the spy, who appears to solicit, who talks lightly to the poor girl, and uses many arts in order to entrap her into betraying her real character—if she be a prostitute. Those whom I saw resembled 'fast men' in appearance and gait, dressed rather showily, with a good deal of gold chain and ornament. A girl said to me, 'They come up and speak so free to you; any poor girl would think it was a *gentleman* who wanted her to go with him.' " "Garrison Towns of Kent," *Shield,* 9 May 1870.

74. P.R.O., Adm. 1/6206, 31 January 1871.

75. *Shield,* 3 December 1870.

76. "The Anti-Contagious Diseases Act Agitation," *W.H.I.,* 11 June 1870.

77. *Hampshire Independent* (Southampton), reprinted in *Shield,* 25 February 1871.

78. Dr. Hearne to the editor, *W.H.I.,* 18 February 1871.

79. Mrs. Kell, testimony before the Royal Commission of 1871, *P.P.,* 1871, XIX, Q. 16, 870–900.

80. Sloggett, "History and Sketch."

81. "NA Minutes" 2 (13 May 1872), no. 336; 2 (27 May 1872), no. 362.

82. Reverend Edmund Kell to the editor, *Shield,* 18 January 1873.

83. "Report of the Assistant Commissioner," *P.P.,* 1882, LIII.

84. Inspector Sloggett to Mr. Bruce, Home Secretary, P.R.O., Home Office Papers, H.O. 45/1, 10 February 1873.

10. THE MAKING OF AN OUTCAST GROUP

1. See Chapter 8.
2. A. J. B. Parent-Duchâtelet, *De la prostitution dans la ville de Paris, Considérée sous le rapport de l'hygiene publique de la morale, et de l'administration* (2 vols., Paris, 1857); William Sanger, *History of Prostitution: Its Extent, Causes and Effects Throughout the World* (New York, 1897).
3. "Report of the Assistant Commissioner of Police of the Metropolis on the Operation of the Contagious Diseases Acts (1881)," *P.P.,* 1882 (291), LIII.
4. According to the 1871 manuscript census schedules, women interned in the lock wards of the Royal Albert Hospital, Devonport, averaged 21.8 years; in the Royal Portsmouth, Gosport, and Portsea Hospital, where Southampton women were interned, they averaged 21.2 years. Manuscript census schedules, P.R.O., R.G. 10/2133; R.G. 10/1127. Metropolitan police statistics also confirm this age concentration. *P.P.,* 1882, LIII.
5. According to police returns ("Report of the House of Commons Select Committee on the Administration, Operation, and Effects of the Contagious Diseases Acts of 1866–69," *P.P.,* 1882, IX, App.), all 503 women in the greater Plymouth district were listed as residing in brothels– private lodgings where the women brought men home. Of this number, it has been calculated that 220 women were single, aged 15 to 29, and residing in Plymouth. They constituted 39.1 percent of all single women, aged 15 to 29, residing in lodgings in Plymouth in spring 1871, as based on a 10 percent sampling of single women in Plymouth. P.R.O., R.G. 10/2112-2124. In addition, 80 percent of the brothels under surveillance in Plymouth catered to a working-class clientele. "Report from the Royal Commission on the Administration and Operation of the Contagious Diseases Acts 1866–69 (1871)," *P.P., 1871* (C. 408-1), XIX, Q.331.
6. According to the manuscript census of 1871, 33 of the 77, or 42.9 percent, of the women interned in the Royal Albert Hospital were born in Greater Plymouth, whereas 37 out of 77, or 48.0 percent, were born in the rest of Devon and Cornwall. Earlier hospital reports identified the women as indigenous to the region, although a larger proportion were from the nearby countryside. P.R.O., R.G. 10/2123; Adm. 1/6122, 3 February 1869. Of the 31 women identified as prostitutes residing on three notorious streets in Plymouth, 15, or 48.3 percent, came from the surrounding countryside. P.R.O., R.G. 10/2120. Fifty-two percent of the single women residing in lodgings on these streets were from the surrounding countryside. Registered women lived throughout this immediate neighborhood, and any single woman living alone in lodgings there would automaticallly have been suspect to the metropolitan police and forced to register as a prostitute. See also John Saville, *Rural Depopulation in England and Wales 1851–1951, Studies in Rural Sociology.*

(London, 1957) pp. 31, 32. Between 1863 and 1870 90 percent of the women sent to the Devon House of Mercy from the lock wards of the Royal Albert were half or full orphans. P.R.O., Admiralty Papers, Adm. 1/6179, 29 August 1870.

7. For example, Mr. Luscombe, a Plymouth magistrate, stated: "We are unfortunately situated in this way, we are close to Cornwall, and when a poor woman is asked the question, 'Do you belong to the town?' she says 'No.' 'Where did you come from?' and then we find, I am sorry to say, almost four out of five of the young women before us are girls from Cornwall." *P.P.,* 1871, XIX, Q. 5155.

8. "Report of the Assistant Commissioner of Police of the Metropolis on the Operation of the Contagious Diseases Acts (1874)," *P.P.,* 1875, LXI; *P.P.,* 1876, LXI.

9. See Chapter 1.

10. See, for example, *Shield* (London), 25 April 1870, 1 April 1871, 29 June 1871, 15 July 1871; P.R.O., Adm. 1/6418, 30 October 1873 and 5 November 1873; "Report of the House of Commons Select Committee on the Administration, Operation and Effects of the Contagious Diseases Acts of 1866–69," *P.P.,* 1881, VIII, Q. 4130.

11. Illegitimacy rates in southeastern and southwestern England were lower than for England and Wales as a whole, although reporters for the *Morning Chronicle* in the 1840s noted the entrenched tradition of premarital sexuality among the "Methodist" fishermen, miners, and agricultural workers of the south. The bastardy register for the Southampton workhouse in the early nineteenth century reveals that mothers of illegitimate offspring confined there were generally upper servants "seduced" by male servants or artisans. Albert Leffingwell, *Illegitimacy and the Influence of Season upon Conduct; Two Studies in Demography* (New York, 1892), p. 15; P. E. Razzell and R. W. Wainwright, eds., *The Victorian Working Class: Selections from Letters to the Morning Chronicle* (London, 1973), pp. 29, 33, 34.

12. *P.P.,* 1871, XIX, Q. 8442, 8443.

13. Ibid., Q. 10677.

14. These data were compiled from the manuscript census of 1871, P.R.O., R.G. 10/2120. See also Judith R. Walkowitz, "We Are Not Beasts of the Field: Prostitution and the Campaign Against the Contagious Diseases Acts" (Ph.D. diss. Univ. of Rochester, 1974), ch. 7.

15. A Series Entitled, " 'Our House' and Its Tenants; Being Sketches of Working Class Life; in a Basement and Eight Stories," appeared in *D.I.* 1883 and contained detailed description of women's wages. *D.I.,* 19 May 1883; 26 May 1883; 2 June 1883; 9 June 1883; 16 June 1883; 23 June 1883; 20 June 1883; 7 July 1883; 14 July 1883. See also "Orchard Lane Style Service," *W.H.I.,* 3 April 1878; testimony of Mr. Bignold, factory inspector for Devon and Cornwall, before the Commission of Labor, *P.P.,* 1892, XXV, Q. 10, 127–30, 288.

16. Brian Harrison, *Drink and the Victorians*, p. 47.
17. P.R.O., Poor Law Correspondence, M. H. 12/11007, 31 October 1874.
    See also Sheila Johansson, "Sex and Death in Victorian England: An
    Examination of Age- and Sex-Specific Death Rates, 1840–1910," in *A
    Widening Sphere: Changing Roles of Victorian Women,* ed. Martha
    Vicinus (Bloomington, 1977), pp. 163–81. Prostitutes were more likely
    to contract venereal disease than laundresses to contract tuberculosis.
    Still, prostitutes and the poor regarded V.D. as a secondary health haz-
    ard and were generally unaware of the long-term consequences of syphi-
    lis as well as chronic gonorrhea in women.
    In fact, contemporary medical opinion regards syphilis as debilitating
    and fatal for only a portion of untreated female sufferers. Early acquired
    syphilis, for instance, "does not result in death or serious disability."
    Abraham Berenson, *Control of Communicable Diseases in Man,* 12th
    ed. (Washington, D.C., 1975), p. 315. Moreover, a study of the medical
    records of untreated syphilitics living at the turn of the century revealed
    that 60 to 70 percent of the sample of 473 men and women underwent
    "spontanteous cure," whereas only 10 percent ultimately died from terti-
    ary complications. Mortality rates due to tertiary complications were
    twice as high for males as for females. Also, "nonfatal but debilitating
    effects of late complications affected males in the same ratio." William J.
    Brown et al., *Syphilis and Other Venereal Diseases* (Cambridge, Mass.
    1970), pp. 17–20, 104.
    Likewise, alcoholism was an occupational hazard for prostitutes, but
    they were not the only women in their neighborhood addicted to drink.
    For the drinking habits of the women in the notorious districts in Plym-
    outh, see Rev. G. R. Prynne, *Thirty-Five Years of Mission Work in a
    Garrison and Seaport Town* (Plymouth, 1883), pp. 14–15.
18. The living standard among streetwalkers in Plymouth and Southampton
    varied. See J. Walkowitz, "We Are Not Beasts" (dissertation), pp. 235,
    240, 242. On the whole, however, Plymouth and Southampton prosti-
    tutes in the 1870s seem to have been more prosperous than their coun-
    terparts in mid-Victorian York, who catered to soldiers and laborers
    rather than sailors. See Frances Finnegan, *Poverty and Prostitution: A
    Study of Victorian Prostitutes in York* (Cambridge, 1979). The destitu-
    tion of soldiers' women may partially explain the high proportion in
    Finnegan's sample who entered rescue homes.
19. Reports from Kent emphasized the seasonality of prostitution among
    hop pickers, who moved into garrison towns when regiments arrived.
    P.P., 1871, XIX, Q. 12289, 15628, 17009. The increase in numbers was
    generally associated with increased disorderly behavior and rates of ve-
    nereal disease. *P.P.,* 1881, VIII, Q. 4130.
20. *P.P.,* 1881, VIII, App. 12. According to this appendix, registered women
    in Greater Plymouth averaged 23 years of age in 1871 and 19 years in
    1866. They would average 26 years in 1881. The 1866 figure should be

used cautiously, as a formal register of all known prostitutes was not established until 1868, so that this figure represents Anniss's informal survey.

21. *P.P.,* 1882, LIII. In 1868, 38 percent of the registered women in the Devonport district were under 21, so that the Southampton figure for 1871 is quite appropriate.
22. *P.P.,* 1882, LIII.
23. *P.P.,* 1871, XIX, Q. 7500, 10292-295, 11199.
24. Bracebridge Hemyng, "Prostitution in London," in *London Labour and the London Poor,* ed., Henry Mayhew rpt., (New York, 1968), IV, 226–32; P.R.O., Home Office Papers, H.O. 45/6628, 17 March 1858.
25. *P.P.,* 1871, XIX, Q. 20209.
26 Andrew Cluer, *Plymouth and Plymouthians* (Plymouth, 1974).
27. *W.D.M.,* 26 April 1872.
28. Even within the category of the very poor there was a tremendous range: for example, police constable John Brown and his family resided in a lodging house at 14 Summerland Place, Plymouth, next door to Thomas Kneebone, a well-known brothel keeper. This geographic and social proximity made Admiralty officials wary of relying on the local police constable to enforce the Contagious Diseases Acts or to apprehend deserters. A man like John Brown, as one naval doctor remarked, would have had a "natural" reluctance to turn in his neighbors. *W.D.M.,* 11 February 1870, 12 November 1870; *P.P.,* 1868–9, VII, Q. 210. When Reverend Prynne, the local parish priest, was asked to describe the character of the inhabitants of Plymouth's Octagon neighborhood, he spoke of them as a laboring, manufacturing, and seafaring population: "There are also a good many small shopkeepers, old clothes sellers, rag and bone storekeepers, costermongers, 'chandlers,' who sell anything, from 'ladies' brass and farthing dips; small public-house keepers, lodging-house keepers for travellers, i.e. tramps, and also, I grieve to say, keepers of a much worse description." Reverend G. R. Prynne, *Thirty-five Years of Mission Work,* p. 13.
29. On the three Plymouth streets 68.0 percent of single women aged 15 to 29 resided in lodgings. In the poor working-class Octagon district surrounding and including the three streets, 43.7 percent of the 309 single women, aged 15 to 29, lived independent of their families, relatives, or employers (R.G. 10/2120). Registered women lived throughout this immediate neighborhood, and any single woman living alone in lodgings there would have been counted as a prostitute by the metropolitan police. In contrast, only 8.2 percent of single women, aged 15 to 29, resided in lodgings in Plymouth generally. P.R.O., R.G. 10/2112, 2124. For a more detailed statistical study of the notorious streets, see Judith Walkowitz and Daniel Walkowitz, " 'We Are Not Beasts of the Field,' Prostitution and the Poor Under the Contagious Diseases Acts," *Feminist Studies* 1 (Winter 1973), 73–106.

30. P.R.O., M.H. 12/2422, 17 June 1851; M.H. 12/2434, 26 June 1870, 1 July 1870; *W.D.M.*, 26 January 1872.

31. *W.D.M.*, 22 September 1871. Social isolation among the poor is conveyed in a remarkable autobiography of a woman who lived on King Street, Plymouth, near the Octagon neighborhood around the turn of the century. See "Emma Smith" (pseud.), *A Cornish Waif's Tale: An Autobiography* (New York, 1956), ch. 2, "Life in a Plymouth Slum." For the seasonal geographic and occupational mobility among prostitutes and the Southampton and Plymouth poor, see the testimony of Tom McCarthy before the Royal Commission on Labour, *P.P.*, 1892, XXXVI, pt. 2 Q. 12, 275; Smith, ch. 4, "An Elopement Minus the Romance," *W.H.I.*, 13 August 1870; P.R.O., Adm. 1/6069, 31 October 1868.

32. *W.H.I.*, 18 November 1874. Plymouth prostitutes accounted for one out of three petty session offenses committed by women in the 1870s and 1880s. Most were charged with being drunk and disorderly; only 6.7 percent of the charges brought against prostitutes between 1870 and 1881 involved theft. *P.P.*, 1882, IX, Apps. 1 and 4; *W.D.M.*, 4 November 1871; *W.M.N.*, October 1886. This contrasts sharply with Finnegan's argument for extensive (rather than occasional) predatory behavior and criminality among York's prostitutes. Finnegan, *Poverty and Prostitution*, ch. 4.

33. *W.H.I.*, 26 October 1878.

34. A lady visitor, quoted in Prynne, *Mission Work*, pp. 14, 15.

35. Ibid., p. 15.

36. Walkowitz and Walkowitz, "We Are Not Beasts," p. 204.

37. Police returns for Plymouth confirm the virtual absence of bullies or crimps there. Also, they listed only 76 children living with the 503 registered women in the district in 1871. The returns listed 236 children "belonging to" the 198 brothel keepers of the district. *P.P.*, 1881, VIII, App. 12.

38. Despite the sensational literature on white slavery in the late nineteenth century, it is unclear how many recruits were the victims of coercion and false entrapment. Some sources argued that although prostitutes often acted as decoys for young women, their motives appeared largely disinterested, particularly as competition for customers was already fierce. Rather, from what they could gather, these prostitutes saw themselves as performing a kindness to young women down on their luck, although they might also have been eager for others to become "outcasts" like themselves. See, for example, *Downward Paths: An Inquiry into the Causes Which Contribute to the Making of the Prostitute*, with a foreword by A. Maude Royden (London, 1913), p. 55.

39. "Report of Messrs. Roscoe and Shaen."

40. *P.P.*, 1871, XIX, Q. 8429.

41. *Shield*, 17 December 1870.

42. Ibid., 26 May 1871.
43. Quoted in Josephine Butler, "The Garrison Towns of Kent," *Shield,* 25 April 1870.
44. J. J. Garth Wilkinson, *The Forcible Introspection of Women for the Army and Navy by the Oligarchy Considered Physically* (London, 1870), p. 15.
45. *P.P.,* 1871, XIX, Q. 20297.
46. Ibid., Q. 7206, 10548.
47. Ibid., Q. 12631.
48. "Illegal Detention of a Woman at the Royal Albert Hospital," *Abolitionist Flysheets,* Butler Collection, Fawcett Library, London.
49. *W.D.M.,* 19 December 1871, 25 March 1872, 21 August 1872, 28 February 1874; *W.M.N.,* 4 May 1874.
50. *W.D.M.,* 6 April 1886.
51. *P.P.,* 1871, XIX, Q. 20297.
52. Ibid., Q. 8303.
53. Ibid.
54. Ibid., Q. 19,558.
55. *P.P.,* 1882, IX, App. 26.
56. *P.P.,* 1881, VIII, Q. 3296; *D.I.,* 19 September 1874; *W.D.M.,* 7 August 1871.
57. *P.P.,* 1882, LIII.
58. *Shield,* 4 July 1870.
59. Ibid., 28 February 1871.
60. *D.I.,* 7 and 14 October 1876.
61. *D.I.,* 22 October 1883. See also the case of Maria Barnett, who was hidden by her brothel keeper from the police. Admiralty Papers, P.R.O., Adm. 1/6418, 30 October 1873 and 5 November 1873.
62. Ellice Hopkins, *Work in Brighton, or Women's Mission to Women* (London, 1877), p. 91.
63. *Shield,* 10 February 1877.
64. Ibid., 15 July 1871. Salvation Army rescue workers reported the same kind of cooperation from lodging-house keepers in Woolwich, who permitted them to "hold meetings in their kitchens regularly" and to "go in and out amongst the girls without interfering at all." *Saved in Time: Annual Report of the Women's Social Work for 1892–3* (London, 1893), p. 8.
65. Ibid., 1 July 1871.
66. P.R.O., Adm. 1/6202, 23 September 1871; *Shield,* 20 September 1873.
67. *W.H.I.,* 3 December 1870; *W.D.M.,* 11 February 1871; P.R.O., Adm. 1/6202, 23 September 1871.
68. *W.D.M.,* 12 April 1870, 17 October 1870; *Shield,* 15 July 1871, 8 April 1873.
69. *W.H.I.,* 3 December 1870.
70. *Shield,* 12 November 1870.

71. Ibid., 9 June 1877.
72. *P.P.*, 1871, XIX, Q. 17350.
73. Ibid., Q. 17342.
74. Ibid., Q. 17351.
75. Ibid., Q. 12644.
76. *Shield,* 4 April 1870. This woman subsequently became a paid agent for the repealers.
77. *W.D.M.*, 7 August 1870; *W.H.I.,* 2 September 1872, 2 May 1874; *P.P.,* XIX, Q. 8429.
78. P.R.O., Adm. 1/6428, 30 October 1873. At Barnett's trial, Thomas Inch testified that Anniss had asked him, "Do you know what she is?" "And I replied I did." "He then said she was a prostitute and I was a fool to marry her." The town clerk asked Inch if he would presently marry Barnett, as she would be likely to go with other men while he was at sea. Inch responded at first jocularly, "What the eye doesn't see, the heart don't feel," and then more seriously, "But I don't think you ought to say that, Sir; I believe that she would reform if I married her." *Shield,* 20 September 1873.
79. *P.P.,* 1881, VIII, App. 18.
80. *P.P.,* 1882, LIII; *Eighth Annual Report of the Royal Albert Hospital, 1870–1; Fourteenth Annual Report of the Royal Albert Hospital, 1876–7;* Devonport Hospital, Devonport.
81. This trend was noted and debated as early as 1873. See, for example, *Shield,* 6 November 1873; Birkbeck Nevins, *Statement on the Grounds on Which the C. D. Acts Are Opposed* (Liverpool, 1874); P.R.O., Adm. 1/6418, 6 February 1875.
82. V. A. C. Gatrell and T. B. Hadden, "Criminal Statistics and Their Interpretation," in E. A. Wrigley, ed., *Nineteenth-Century Society: Essays in the Use of Quantitative Methods and Study of Social Data* (Cambridge, 1972), pp. 353, 356, 364.
83. "Houses of Ill-Fame at Plymouth," *W.D.M.,* 24 March 1904. The article reported on the chief constable's visit to Portsmouth, Cardiff, Manchester, Liverpool, and Leeds. In Portsmouth, he reported, "The condition of things is somewhat similar to that which exists in Plymouth, in the sense that the houses are allowed to remain undisturbed in a comparatively limited area . . . . " In the other towns, a policy of segregation had already given way to repression. See also Edward Bristow, *Vice and Vigilance: Purity Movements in Britain Since 1700* (Dublin, 1978), p. 162.
84. See Ellice Hopkins's speech on the Proposed Industrial Schools Amendment Act, quoted in "Proposed Industrial School for Girls," *W.M.N.,* 25 November 1879. In some places, the "kidnapping" of brothel keepers' children provoked a community resistance akin to the response to the C.D. acts. The attempt by an officer of the Reformatory and Refuge Union to enforce the act in Woolwich met with the following response:

"In taking these children to the police station, I went first with the elder girl, and was followed by about 300 people and had to encounter a heavy shower of flowerpots and other missiles." Quoted in Ellice Hopkins, *Drawn unto Death: A Plea for the Children Coming Under the Industrial Schools Act Amendment Act, 1880* (London, 1884). The act soon had the effect of forcing lodging-house keepers to send their children away or to refuse to rent to prostitutes. Bristow, *Vice*, p. 155; Robert R. Dolling, *Ten Years in a Portsmouth Slum* (London, 1896), pp. 64, 65.

85. Abraham Flexner, *Prostitution in Europe* (New York, 1914), pp. 74, 241–3; Sir William Nott Bower, *Fifty-Two Years a Policeman* (London, 1926), pp. 141–4; *Liverpool Review*, 28 January 1893; "Report of the Royal Commission on the Duties of the Metropolitan Police," *P.P.*, 1908, L, Q. 39644, 39647, 39785, 40300; P.R.O., Home Office Papers, H.O. 45/9678/A47459; H.O. 45/9964/X15663; H.O. 45/9740/A55536; H.O. 45/10123, B13517.

86. A. Temple Patterson, *A History of Southampton, 1700–1914* (Southampton, 1975), pp. 106–13. Patterson notes that, as had happened in London, the dockers' strike in Southampton in 1890 focused attention on "Outcast Southampton." The Simnel Street area was identified as the worst slum district of all. The result of the campaign was the "clearing" of the Simnel Street area. See "The Exceeding Bitter Cry of Outcast Southampton," *W.H.I.*, 8 November 1890; "In Darkest Southampton," 20 December 1890. A similar strike occurred in Plymouth earlier that year but did not result in a clearing out of the prostitute area. In the midst of the general strike, organizers from the Gas Workers Union took note of the low wages paid to women and their relationship to the number of fallen women in the district. "May Day Demonstrations at Plymouth," *W.D.M.*, 5 May 1890. A full-scale crusade against open prostitution did not occur until 1904, when the National Vigilance Association assisted local agitators. Devon Record Office, Plymouth, Minutes of the Vigilance Society, Acc. 94/Q., *W.D.M.*, 22 January 1904, 2 February 1904, 18 February 1904, 20 February 1904; *Vigilance Record* (London), March 1904.

87. *P.P.*, 1908, L, Q. 40300; Flexner, *Prostitution*, pp. 241–4.

88. P.R.O., H.O. 45/9745/A56729/4, 21 February 1895; H.O. 45/10430/A55693/19, 26 October 1907.

89. *Downward Paths*, p. 48.

90. Police official, quoted in Bristow, *Vice*, p. 169.

91. P.R.O., H.O. 45/140266/15, 16 August 1916; "Vice and the Law; Difficulties of Police Action," *Times*, 28 February 1917; "Out of the Depths," *Herald*, 20 July 1918; H. Llewellyn Smith, ed., *The New Survey of London Life and Labour* (London, 1932), pp. 91, 297–9, 323, 324, 341.

92. Gareth Stedman Jones, *Outcast London: A Study in the Relationship*

between Classes in Victorian Society (Oxford, 1971), p. 348; E. H. Phelps Brown, *The Growth of British Industrial Relations: A Study from the Standpoint of 1906–14* (London, 1965), pp. 19–46, 65, 66, 84.

93. B. L. Hutchins, *Women in Modern Industry* (London, 1915), p. 232; A. L. Bowley, *Wages and Incomes in the United Kingdom Since 1860* (Cambridge, 1937), p. 15.

94. See Raphael Samuel, "Comers and Goers," in *The Victorian City,* eds., H. J. Dyos and Michael Wolff (London, 1973), I, 123–60.

11. THE HOSPITALS

1. Admiralty Papers, Adm. 1/6292, 8 January 1873.
2. Ibid.
3. P.R.O., Adm. 1/6236, 16 September 1872.
4. P.R.O., Adm. 1/6292, 28 January 1873.
5. The full title of the Portsmouth Hospital was the Royal Portsmouth, Portsea and Gosport Hospital. Portsmouth had operated lock wards under the Admiralty since 1858; the Royal Albert since 1863.
6. "Sixth Annual Report of the Medical Officer of the Privy Council," *P.P., 1864* (3416), XXVIII.
7. P.R.O., Adm. I/6291, 3 June 1873.
8. P.R.O., Adm. 1/6292, 12 July 1873.
9. Ibid.
10. Ibid.
11. Ibid., 19 July 1873.
12. P.R.O., Adm. 1/6498, 16 January 1879.
13. *Illustrated London News,* 5 July 1862; *P.P.,* 1864, XXVIII.
14. P.R.O., Adm. 1/6122, 1 March 1869; 5 April 1869.
15. *First Annual Report of the Royal Albert Hospital, Devonport, 1863–64* (Devonport, 1864); Devonport Hospital, Devonport.
16. *Eighth Annual Report . . . Royal Albert Hospital, 1870–71.*
17. *First Annual Report . . . Royal Albert Hospital; Eighth Annual Report . . . Royal Albert Hospital.*
18. The Admiralty and War Office contributed a total of £25,645 toward the building of the "Lock Hospital at Devonport." The Admiralty also provided an annual subsidy of £30 per bed. By 1869 169 beds were available for diseased prostitutes at the Royal Albert and 120 at Portsmouth. William Sloggett, "History and Operations of the Contagious Diseases Acts in the Home Ports," P.R.O., Adm. 1/6418, 10 April 1873: *Eighth Annual Report . . . Royal Albert Hospital; Ninth Annual Report . . . Royal Albert Hospital, 1871–72.*
19. *Ninth Annual Report . . . Royal Albert Hospital.*
20. Reverend Binns, quoted in "The Royal Albert Hospital, Devonport," *W.D.M.,* 30 November 1870; Frederick Row, *idem.* The newspaper arti-

cle was reprinted as a fly sheet by repealers, *Abolitionist Flysheets,* Butler Collection, Fawcett Library, London.

21. Thomas Woollcombe, P.R.O., Adm. 1/6365, 25 August 1875.
22. P.R.O., Adm. 1/6365, November 1875.
23. Thomas Woollcombe, P.R.O., Adm. 1/6122, 16 January 1869.
24. *First Annual Report . . . Royal Albert Hospital.*
25. P.R.O., Adm. 1/6179, 17 May 1870; Adm. 1/6418, 6 February 1875; "Annual Meeting of the Royal Albert Hospital," *W.D.M.,* 27 November 1872.
26. P.R.O., Adm. 1/6179, 22 January 1870.
27. A. E. Chesterton, *In Darkest London* (London, 1926), p. 79.
28. See, for example, Mary Priestman, E. M. King, and Isabella Henley, "Charity at Other People's Expense," *Shield,* 17 September 1870; William Littleton, testimony before the Royal Commission on the Administration and Operation of the Contagious Diseases Acts 1866–69 (1871), *P.P.,* 1871 (C. 408-I), XIX, Q. 1347–53.
29. As Reverend Hawker, the chaplain of the Royal Albert, explained, matrons "are what one terms approaching [i.e. almost] ladies, such as would know how to conduct themselves, and be a pattern and an example to the inmates." *P.P.,* 1871, XIX, Q. 7367.
30. *P.P.,* 1871, XIX, Q. 1347–53.
31. The *Shield* (15 August 1870) complained that this usurpation placed "women at the will of a young man."
32. Josephine Butler, "The Garrison Towns of Kent," *Shield,* 2 May 1870.
33. Lucy Bull, testimony before the Royal Commission of 1871, *P.P.,* 1871, XIX, Q. 7794.
34. P.R.O., Adm. 1/6401, 9 April 1876.
35. William Acton, "Shall the Contagious Diseases Act Be Extended to the Civilian Population?" speech before the Medical Officers of Health, 18 December 1869 (London 1869).
36. P.R.O., Adm. 1/6418, May 1873. In prisons, little toys and "what nots" made as presents for the matron were confiscated and destroyed as part of a systematic effort to undermine the self-respect and identity of female convicts. "Petting and Fretting of Female Convicts," *Meliora* 6 (1864), 49.
37. P.R.O. Adm. 1/6418, May 1873.
38. P.R.O. Adm. 1/6292, 23 January 1872.
39. William Acton, *Prostitution,* ed. Peter Fryer (New York, 1968), p. 95.
40. For example, for the year 1870–1, there were 1,033 lock cases involving 935 individual women; in 1875–6, 517 cases involving 296 women; and in 1876–7, 477 cases involving 195 women. *Eighth Annual Report . . . Royal Albert Hospital; Thirteenth Annual Report . . . Royal Albert Hospital; Fourteenth Annual Report . . . Royal Albert Hospital.*
41. *Eighth Annual Report . . . Royal Albert Hospital.*
42. *Shield,* 5 November 1870; *P.P.,* 1871, XIX, App. C.

43. "Petting and Fretting," p. 49.
44. *P.P.*, 1871, XIX, Q. 11834.
45. *The Royal Commission as a Court of Justice: Being an Examination of the Declaration of the Commissioners that "The Police Are Not Chargeable with Any Abuse of their Authority"* (Nottingham, 1871).
46. See the case of Elizabeth Cotzibitch below, *Shield,* 11 March 1876.
47. P.R.O., Adm. 1/6122, 16 January 1869; Adm. 1/6123, 1 March 1869; Adm. 1/6418, 26 September 1872; Adm. 1/6417, 15, 16 March 1876, and 18 April 1876.
48. P.R.O., Adm. 1/6123, 5 April 1869; Adm. 1/6418, 26 September 1872; and 1/6418, 15, 16, 17 June 1873.
49. "Unconstitutional and Cruel Tyranny at the Royal Albert," *Shield,* 11 March 1876.
50. P.R.O., Adm. 1/6401, 28 March 1876.
51. Ibid., 5 April 1876; 20 April 1876.
52. Ibid., 9 April 1876.
53. "The Escape of Hospital Patients at Devonport," 17 May 1883.
54. An enigmatic notation exists in the 1883 index of the Admiralty papers, on this point: "Inspector of Devonport Police Recommends Anniss for Promotion–approved–afterwards cancelled." P.R.O., IND. 18, 332.
55. "Escape of Hospital Patients."
56. P.R.O., IND. 18, 349 (1884).
57. Sloggett, Adm. 1/6736, 1884.
58. See Chapter 3.
59. P.R.O., R.G. 10/2133; R.G. 10/1127.
60. M. Berkeley Hill, "Illustrations of the Workings of the Contagious Diseases Acts," *B.M.J.* 2 (1867), 583.
61. Minority Report, *P.P.,* 1882 (390), IX, p. l–lxxxvii. Hill, "Illustrations," noted that in the early years young girls were constantly in and out of the Portsmouth Hospital with recent cases of syphilis and chancroid.
62. *P.P.,* 1871, XIX, Q. 3293.
63. *Royal Commission as a Court of Justice.*
64. *Medical Enquirer* (Liverpool) 4 (1878), 18.
65. Ibid. L. B. Taylor, *Reply to Mr. W. Paul Swain's Defense of the Act* (Nottingham, 1870).
66. "M.D." to the editor, *Shield,* 16 September 1884.
67. Charles Drysdale, testimony before the House of Commons Select Committee on the Administration, Operation and Effects of the Contagious Diseases Acts of 1866–69, *P.P.,* 1881 (351), VIII, Q. 472.
68. *P.P.,* 1871, XIX, Q. 4560. Sloggett assumed that these items were placed in the cavity to absorb uterine discharge, but they also may have served as primitive contraceptive devices.
69. *Shield,* 6 September 1884.
70. *P.P.,* 1881, VIII, Q. 2400.
71. *P.P.,* 1871, XIX, Q. 2696. Although based on a false premise, Moore

and Sloggett's argument was in some sense correct. "Uterine" discharge (as opposed to vaginal discharge) is a symptom of gonorrheal infection, and was probably more common among prostitutes than among "virtuous" married women.

72. *The Royal Commission as a Court of Justice.*
73. *Shield,* 5 November 1870.
74. *A Letter to the Lords of the Admiralty from the Surgeons in Charge of the Lock Wards of the Royal Albert Hospital, Devonport: Including Results of Treatment, Comments on Evidence Lately Given Before a Select Committee of the House of Commons, on the Contagious Diseases Act, 1866, and Suggestions for the Future Management of the Lock Wards* (London, 1869).
75. Ibid.
76. P.R.O., Adm. 1/6123, 19 October 1869.
77. *P.P.,* 1871, XIX, Q. 4130.
78. R. S. Morton, *Venereal Diseases* (London, 1966), p. 28. Josephine Butler's report on the women in the garrison towns of Kent: "One has not been long at home [from the lock hospital], and says she came back much worse than she went. She thinks her hands have been poisoned; they have broken out in such sores (there is plenty of evidence of mercurial treatment)." *Shield,* 25 April 1870.
79. *Medical Enquirer* 5 (1883), 2.
80. Taylor, *Reply to Mr. W. Paul Swain.*
81. Dr. May, Mayor of Plymouth, quoted in *Twelfth Annual Report . . . Royal Albert Hospital, 1874–75.*
82. C. H. Melville, "The History and Epidemiology of Syphilis in the More Important Armies," in *A System of Syphilis,* ed. D'Arcy Power and J. K. Murphy (6 vols., London, 1910), VI, 96–8; Birkbeck Nevins, *Statement On the Grounds upon Which the C. D. Acts Are Opposed* (1874) and *What Public Measures Can with Benefit Be Adopted for the Diminution of Venereal Diseases?* (1880); P.R.O., Adm. 1/6418; February 1875; Adm. 1/6365, 12 October 1875; Adm. 1/6439, 8 June 1877; IND. 18, 283; "Retribution for Plymouth," *Shield,* 10 August 1878.
83. "Facts and Arguments About the C. D. Acts," *Shield,* 16 September 1871.
84. Henry Lee, 1881, VIII, Q. 781, remarked on the "almost universal opinion of medical men at this day . . . that syphilis may be communicated by the secretions of persons who have long passed the stage of primary syphilis."
85. William Sinclair, *On Gonorrheal Infection in Women* (London, 1888), p. 22.
86. *P.P.,* 1881, VIII, Q. 102.
87. *P.P.,* 1881, VIII, Q. 776. None of the witnesses before the 1881 committee mentioned the new findings on the close correlation between syphilis and general paresis.

88. P.R.O., Adm. 1/6418, 6 February 1875; Adm. 1/6365, 12 October 1875.
89. P.R.O., Adm. 1/6287, 8 May 1883.
90. P.R.O., IND. 18, 832 (1883).
91. Edward St. Aubyn, P.R.O., Adm. 1/6287, 30 April 1888.
92. *The Royal Albert Hospital, Devonport: An Epitome* (Plymouth, 1922).

12. LOCAL REPEAL CAMPAIGN, 1874–86

1. See, for example, their coverage of the Anniss trial (*Shield,* 28 October 1876) and the Charles Turner case, "An Englishman's Castle Is His Home," (1877), *Abolitionist Flysheets,* Butler Collection, Fawcett Library, London.
2. "Minutes of the National Association for the Repeal of the Contagious Diseases Acts" 3 (11 January 1875), no. 366, Butler Collection.
3. Ibid. (3 May 1875), no. 522.
4. Ibid. (16 October 1876), no. 1032.
5. F. C. Banks, quoted in "Crowded Meetings at Plymouth During the Sittings of the Church Congress," *Shield,* 21 October 1876.
6. Ibid.
7. Ibid.
8. *Shield,* 20 January 1877.
9. "NA Minutes" 3 (6 November 1876) no. 1052.
10. *D.I.,* quoted in *Shield,* 24 February 1877. Interestingly, the *Shield* (31 March 1877) carried a story of "rowdyism" in Plymouth streets and tried to connect this instance of juvenile delinquency with the earlier meetings.
11. *Shield,* 20 March 1877.
12. William Littleton, quoted in "The Adjourned Meeting in Plymouth: An Amendment in Favour of the Acts Carried," *D.I.,* reprinted in *Shield,* 3 March 1877. The *Shield* noted Mr. Bulteel's personal resentment against repealers: "Mr. Bulteel will not have forgotten his old antagonists, the managers of the Rescue Society [who had disparaged his rescue efforts in Plymouth]."
13. A. P. Balkwill, quoted in ibid.
14. Ibid.
15. "Defeats at Plymouth and Devonport: Our Opponents at Bay," *Shield,* 3 March 1877.
16. Ibid., 31 March 1877.
17. "NA Minutes" 3 (5 March 1877), no. 1160.
18. Ibid. (26 February 1877), no. 1154.
19. Josephine Butler to Joseph Edmondson, 6 March 1877, Butler Collection.
20. Ibid.
21. *W.M.N.,* 14 April 1877.
22. See Chapter 6.

23. *D.I.,* 15 November 1877, 17 November 1877, and "The Confessional Unmasked," *Reynolds News,* 5 May 1872.
24. "Letter from the Right Hon. James Stansfeld, M.P., to the Ladies' National Association and the Other Repeal Associations Throughout the Kingdom, 1875," *LNA Reports, 1870–1886,* Butler Collection, Fawcett Library.
25. Ibid. Marshall and Littleton periodically cropped up in the police columns of the local newspapers, appearing at trials unrelated to the C. D. acts. Their presence stood out in Plymouth courts. They were the only interested third parties who supported indigent women in legal distress. See "Value of a Rescue Society," *W.D.M.,* 17 January 1872. See also ibid., 26 October 1872, and *D. I.,* 19 September 1874.
26. *Shield,* 9 June 1877.
27. William Acton, *Prostitution,* ed. Peter Fryer (London, 1967), p. 194.
28. See, for example, "NA Minutes," for the Norris case, 2 (2 December 1872), no. 572; Gunn case, 2 (10 November 1873), no. 1012; Hallett case, 4 (21 April 1879), no. 1966.
29. John Marshall, quoted in Stansfeld, "Letter."
30. *Shield,* 20 January 1877.
31. "NA Minutes" 3 (5 November 1877), no. 1369.
32. Ibid. 4 (24 February 1879), no. 1908.
33. Ibid. (10 November 1879), no. 2153.
34. Rosa Barrett, *Ellice Hopkins, A Memoir,* p. 21.
35. Hopkins viewed Butler's works as remedial, her own as preventive. Barrett, *Ellice Hopkins,* p. 111; Edward J. Bristow, *Vice and Vigilance: Purity Movements in Britain Since 1700* (Dublin, 1977), pp. 4–6, 129–31.
36. "NA Minutes" 4 (23 February 1880), no. 2248.
37. "Proposed Industrial School for Girls," *W.M.N.,* 25 November 1879.
38. "NA Minutes" 4 (23 February 1880), no. 2248.
39. Ibid. (15 December 1879), no. 2184.
40. Ibid. Significantly, Mr. and Mrs. Balkwill and Mrs. Bishop refused to join the new committee.
41. Ibid., 4 (12 January 1880), no. 2201.
42. Ibid. (8 December 1879), no. 2174; 4 (12 January 1880), no. 2201; 4 (23 February 1880), no. 2248; 4 (24 February 1879) 1908, 6 (12 January 1885), no. 4271; 6 (27 April 1885), no. 4411; 6 (11 May 1885), no. 4434; 6 (12 October 1885), no. 4566; 6 (15 March 1886), no. 4751.
43. "Eleventh Annual Report . . . LNA, 1880."
44. Josephine Butler to Joseph Edmondson, 30 October 1882, Butler Collection.
45. Ibid.
46. Alice Bewicke, "Meetings at Plymouth," *N.L.J.,* January 1881.
47. Alice Bewicke to the editor, *Shield,* 25 February 1882.
48. Bewicke, "Meetings at Plymouth."

49. "Conference in Plymouth," *Shield,* 7 January 1882.
50. "Public Meeting at Plymouth: The Partial Suspension of the Acts. A Suggested Alternative Measure," *N.L.J.,* August 1883.
51. *Shield,* 7 July 1883.
52. *Western Figaro* (Plymouth), 14 December 1883.
53. *W.D.M.,* quoted in *Shield,* 2 February 1884.
54. Ibid.
55. Yves Guyot, *English and French Morality from a Frenchman's Point of View* (London, 1885), p. 85.
56. "Houses of Ill-Fame at Plymouth," *W.D.M.,* 24 March 1904.
57. "The Suppression of the Fancy Fair," *D.I.,* 20 March 1885.
58. Ibid., 3 April 1886.
59. "A Girls' Movement or Girls' Evening Homes," *W.M.N.,* 18 October 1886.
60. "Is There Not a Cause?" Alfred Balkwill to the editor, *W.D.M.,* 22 June 1883.
61. "Great Demonstrations," ibid., 15 January 1883.
62. *W.H.I.,* 14 June 1876; 19 June 1876; 24 June 1876.
63. Ibid., 7 December 1881.
64. Ibid., 26 November 1881.
65. "Deputation from Plymouth, Devonport, etc. to the Home Secretary," *D.I.,* 26 May 1883. See also P.R.O., Adm. 1/6278, 8 May 1883; Adm. 1/6287, 1884; Adm. 1/6718, 15 September 1884.
66. *W.D.M.,* 26 June 1883.
67. "Fourteenth Annual Report . . . LNA, 1883."
68. See, for example, the editorial on Lord Hartington's Detention in Hospital bill, *W.D.M.,* 9 July 1883.
69. See, for example, P.R.O., Adm. 1/6287, 30 April 1888; 19 October 1888.

EPILOG

1. W. T. Stead, *The Maiden Tribute of Modern Babylon (The Report of the "Pall Mall Gazette's" Secret Commission)* (London, 1885).
2. Josephine Butler to Henry J. Wilson, 10 July 1885, M.D. 2545–15, Wilson Collection, Sheffield Public Library, Sheffield.
3. Edward J. Bristow, *Vice and Vigilance: Purity Movements in Britain Since 1700* (Dublin, 1977), p. 113.
4. Ibid.; *Justice: The Organ of Social Democracy,* 11 July 1885, 5 September 1885.
5. Gareth Stedman Jones, *Outcast London: A Study in the Relationship Between Classes in Victorian Society* (Oxford, 1971), ch. 18; Bernard Semmel, *Imperialism and Social Reform* (Garden City, 1960), passim. Although the relationship needs to be explored further, it was perhaps more than coincidence that 1885 witnessed massive socialist gatherings

in the East End as well as the Hyde Park demonstration to denounce criminal vice. See "Monster Socialist Demonstration," *Reynolds Newspaper,* 4 October 1885.

6. P.R.O., Home Office Papers, H.O. 45/9546/59343; H.O. 45/9575/ 593435; H.O. 45/9599/98018; Bristow, *Vice,* pp. 88–91; Deborah Gorham, "The 'Maiden Tribute of Modern Babylon' Re-Examined: Child Prostitution and the Idea of Childhood in Late-Victorian England," *Victorian Studies* 21 (Spring 1978), 358, 359.

7. Josephine Butler to Mary Priestman, 10 July 1885, Butler Collection, Fawcett Library, London.

8. Michael Pearson, *The Age of Consent: Victorian Prostitution and Its Enemies* (Newton Abbott, 1972), pp. 164, 165; Kellow Chesney, *The Anti-Society: An Account of the Victorian Underworld* (Boston, 1970), p. 364.

9. Yves Guyot, *English and French Morality from a Frenchman's Point of View* (London, 1885), p. 66.

10. *Six Years' Labour and Sorrow: Being the Fourth Report of the London Committee for Suppressing the Traffic in British Girls for the Purpose of Continental Prostitution* (London, 1885).

11. Snagge's report appears as an appendix to the "Report of the Select Committee (H.L.) on the Law Relating to the Protection of Young Girls from Artifices to Induce Them to Lead a Corrupt Life," *P.P.,* 1881, IX.

12. Josephine Butler to Miss Priestman, 5 June 1885, Butler Collection.

13. *Sentinel* (London), June 1885.

14. Bristow, *Vice,* pp. 118–21.

15. *Six Years' Labour.*

16. "Sixteenth Annual Report of the LNA, . . . 1885," *LNA Annual Reports, 1870–1886,* Butler Collection.

17. Gorham, "Maiden Tribute," pp. 369–70.

18. See Ronald Pearsall, *The Worm in the Bud: The World of Victorian Sexuality* (Toronto, 1969), pp. 350–63.

19. Even *Reynolds News* (12 July 1885), a popular republican newspaper, referred to Stead as an "insurgent against the corrupt government."

20. A member of the House of Lords, quoted in Gorham, "Maiden Tribute," p. 366.

21. Jeffrey Weeks, *Coming Out: Homosexual Politics in Britain from the Nineteenth Century to the Present* (London, 1977), pp. 18–20.

22. Josephine Butler, quoted in Bristow, *Vice,* p. 155.

23. *Hansard Parliamentary Debates* (Commons), 3rd ser., 30 (6 August 1885), col. 1345.

24. Catherine Booth, quoted in Guyot, *Morality,* p. 37.

25. See Jones, *Outcast London, passim.*

26. See, for example, "The Exceeding Bitter Cry of Outcast Southampton," *W.H.I.,* 8 November 1890.

27. Jones, *Outcast London,* p. 303.

28. One of the major proponents of labor colonies was General Booth of the Salvation Army; see Jones, *Outcast London,* pp. 303–312.
29. See Chapters 10 and 12.
30. Weeks, *Coming Out;* pp. 16–19.
31. W. A. Coote, *A Romance of Philanthropy: Being a Record of Some of the Principal Incidents Connected with the Exceptionally Successful Thirty Years of the National Vigilance Association* (London, 1916), p. 4.
32. Ibid., chs. 2–9.
33. Bristow, *Vice,* p. 154.
34. For an interpretation of the American social purity movement, see David Pivar, *Purity Crusade: Sexual Morality and Social Control, 1868–1900* (Westport, 1973).
35. Coote, *Romance of Philanthropy,* p. 120.
36. Bristow, *Vice,* p. 117.
37. *Personal Rights Journal,* January 1889.
38. Josephine Butler, quoted in Jessie Higson, *The Story of a Beginning* (London, 1955), pp. 35, 36.
39. See "Sixteenth Annual Report of the LNA, . . . 1885"; Bristow, *Vice,* p. 117.
40. Bristow, *Vice,* pp. 103–6.
41. Robert Roberts, *The Classic Slum: Salford Life in the First Quarter of the Century* (Bungay, 1971), ch. 3; Bristow, *Vice,* p. 130; Paul Thompson, *The Edwardians* (London, 1975), ch. 5.
42. Abraham Flexner, *Prostitution in Europe* (New York, 1914), p. 41, n. 2. Scientific studies indicate that washing with soap and water before and after intercourse is moderately effective protection against venereal disease. William Darrow, "Personal Prophylaxis for Venereal Disease," *Journal of the American Medical Association* 233 (1975), 444–6.
43. P.R.O., H.O. 45/9740/A55536.
44. Dr. Paul Swain, quoted in "Plymouth by Night," *W.M.N.,* 26 January 1904.
45. "Report of the Royal Commission on Venereal Diseases," *P.P.,* 1916 (col. 8190), XVI, p. 9.
46. *Shield,* December, 1899.
47. J. E. Moore, "Public Health Measures for the Control of Syphilis," *Lancet* 1 (1951), 699.
48. William Sinclair, *On Gonorrheal Infection in Women* (London, 1888), p. 22; Flexner, *Prostitution in Europe,* pp. 174, 175.
49. Dr. White, quoted in *The Dangers of Syphilis and the Question of State Control: Report of a Discussion at the Seventeenth International Congress of Medicine* (London, 1914).
50. "Notes by the Way," *W.D.M.,* 18 February 1904.
51. See Havelock Ellis, *The Task of Social Hygiene* (Boston, 1915); Bristow, *Vice,* ch. 6.
52. "The Lesson of the Great Crusade," *Common Cause,* 19 May 1910.

53. *Common Cause,* 2 June 1910; "Beware the C. D. Acts," *Woman's Dreadnought* 17 October 1914; "The Contagious Diseases Acts: Past and Present," *Vote,* 19 April 1918.
54. "Josephine Butler," *Woman's Dreadnought,* 24 October 1914.
55. "The New Woman," *Woman's Signal,* 29 November 1894.
56. George Dangerfield, *The Strange Death of Liberal England* (New York, 1935); Constance Rover, *Women's Suffrage and Party Politics in Britain, 1866–1914* (London, 1967).
57. It is interesting that both the Socialist and feminist press decried the plans to impose the periodical examination on prostitutes during World War I in the same outraged tone as the mid-Victorian feminists. See, for example, *Herald* (London), 8 November 1918, 16 April 1918; *Common Cause* 1, November 1918.
58. Louise Creighton, *The Social Disease and How to Fight It* (London, 1914); Christabel Pankhurst, *The Great Scourge and How to End It* (London, 1913).
59. "Protecting Women?" *Woman's Dreadnought,* 19 December 1914.

Selected bibliography

ARCHIVAL SOURCES

London. Dr. Williams' Library. University of London.
    Mary Estlin Collection.
London. Fawcett Library:
    Henry J. Wilson Collection.
    Josephine Butler Collection.
    Autograph Collection:
    "Letter Book of the Executive of the National Association for the Repeal of the Contagious Diseases Acts." August 1883–June 1886.
    "Minutes of the Executive Committee of the Ladies' National Association." 1875–80.
    "Minutes of the London Committee of the Ladies' National Association." November 1880–January 1884.
    "Minutes of the National Association for the Repeal of the Contagious Diseases Acts." Vols. 2–6, 1870–86.
    National Vigilance Association Collection.
London. Public Record Office:
    Admiralty Papers, Adm. 1.
    Home Office Papers, H.O. 45.
    Manuscript Census, 1851 and 1871.
    Metropolitan Dockyard Correspondence, Mepol. 1.
    Metropolitan Police Papers, Mepol. 2.
    Poor Law Correspondence, M.H. 12.
    War Office Papers, W.O. 33.
Newcastle-upon-Tyne. Newcastle-upon-Tyne Central Library:
    Cowen Collection.
Plymouth. Devon Records Office:
    "Devonport: Quarter Sessions and Finance Committee Minute Book. 2 vols. 1851–97."
    "Devonport: Registry of Summary Convictions, Midsummer, 1875 to Easter, 1892."
    "Minutes of the Vigilance Society, 1904–5."
Plymouth. Swarthmore Meeting House:
    "Minutes of the Plymouth Friends' Meeting." 1872–80.

323

Selected Bibliography

Sheffield. Sheffield Public Library:
Henry J. Wilson Collection.

UNPUBLISHED THESES AND PAPERS

Ayers, Gwendolyn M. "The Origins and Development of England's First State Hospitals with Special Reference to the Services Provided by the Metropolitan Asylums Board for the Patients with Infectious Diseases." Ph.D. diss. Univ. of London, 1967.

Dawley, Alan. "Prostitution and the Reproduction of Sexual Relations in Nineteenth-Century America," paper presented before the Davis Center Seminar, Princeton Univ., 7 April 1978.

McHugh, Paul. "The Campaign to Repeal the Contagious Diseases Acts: Some Organizational Aspects." Ph.D. diss. Oxford Univ., 1976.

Rapp, Rayna, and Ross, Ellen. "Sex and Social Structures," paper presented at the Sexuality and Power Conference, New York Univ., New York, 1 April 1978.

Trustram, Myrna. "State Regulation of Vice – Colchester and the Contagious Diseases Acts 1864, 1866, 1869." B.A. thesis. Univ. of Essex, 1977.

Walkowitz, Judith R. " 'We Are Not Beasts of the Field': Prostitution and the Campaign Against the Contagious Diseases Acts." Ph.D. diss. Univ. of Rochester, 1974.

Ware, Helen. "Prostitution and the State: The Recruitment, Regulation, and Role of Prostitution in the Nineteenth and Twentieth Century." Ph.D. diss. Univ. of London, 1969.

ANNUAL REPORTS

Ladies' National Association for the Repeal of the Contagious Diseases Acts. *Annual Reports, 1870–1886.*

Lock Hospital Reports, 1846–1871.

Northern Counties League for the Repeal of the Contagious Diseases Acts. *Annual Reports, 1873–1883.*

Rescue Society Reports, 1877–1898.

Royal Albert Hospital, Devonport. *Annual Reports, 1863–1886.*

Vigilance Society for the Defense of Personal Rights and for the Amendment of the Law in Points Wherein It Is Injurious to Women. *Annual Reports. 1871–1885.*

NEWSPAPERS AND PERIODICALS

Annual Monitor. London: 1881, 1888, 1895, 1896, 1899, 1906, 1909, 1916.

Anti-Vaccinator and Public Health Journal. London: 1872–3.

British Medical Journal. London: 1857, 1863–70, 1880, 1903.

Common Cause. London: 1910, 1918.

The Daily Post. Liverpool: 1872, 1876.

Selected Bibliography

Devon and Cornwall Temperance Journal: Advocate of the Permissive Bill. Plymouth: 1872.

Devonport Independent and Stonehouse Gazette (weekly). 1869, 1870, 1874, 1876, 1877, 1880–3, 1886.

Eastern Post and City Chronicle. London: 1879, 1881.

Englishwoman's Review. London: 1870.

Female's Friend. London: 1846.

Herald. London: 1918.

Justice: The Organ of Social Democracy. London: 1885.

Lancet. London: 1840, 1846, 1850, 1853, 1858, 1859, 1868–78, 1884.

Liverpool Review. 1893.

Liverpool Weekly Mercury. 1872.

Medical Enquirer: A Monthly Journal. Liverpool: 1875–8, 1883.

Medical Press and Circular. London: 1869, 1870.

Medical Times and Gazette London: 1851, 1871.

Meliora, A Quarterly Review of Social Sciences in Its Ethical, Economical, Political and Ameliorative Aspects. London: 1859–69.

National League Journal. London: 1877–83.

National Reformer: Secular Advocate and Free Thought Journal. London: 1869–71, 1880, 1884, 1885.

Penny Bee-Hive. London: 1870. Later *The Bee-Hive,* 1871–6; *Industrial Review,* 1877, 1878.

Portsmouth Times and Naval Gazette. London: 1862–9.

Reformatory and Refuge Journal. London: 1862–9.

Republican: An Advocate and Record of Republican and Democratic Principles and Movements. London: 1870–2.

Reynolds Newspaper (weekly). London: 1871, 1872, 1880, 1883, 1885, 1888.

Saturday Review. London: 1864–70.

Sentinel. London: 1882–6.

Shield. London: 1870–86, 1899, 1900.

Spectator. London: 1870.

The Times. London: 1863, 1917.

Vigilance Journal. London: 1882–5. Later *Personal Rights Review.* London: 1889–1900.

Vote. London: 1918.

War Cry and Official Gazette of the Salvation Army. London: 1886.

Weekly Hampshire Independent. Southampton: 1870–4, 1876, 1878, 1890.

Western Daily Mercury. Plymouth: 1870–4, 1876, 1878–83, 1886, 1887, 1890, 1904, 1914.

Western Daily Press. Bristol: 1869.

Western Morning News. Plymouth: 1874, 1877, 1879, 1880, 1883, 1886.

The Woman's Dreadnought. London: 1914.

The Woman's Signal. London: 1894.

Women's Suffrage Journal. Manchester: 1870, 1872.

Selected Bibliography

PUBLIC DOCUMENTS

Great Britain. "Sixth Annual Report of the Medical Officer of the Privy Council, 1863." *P.P.,* 1864 (3416), XXVIII.

"Report of the House of Commons Select Committee to Inquire into the Pathology and Treatment of the Venereal Disease, with a View to Diminish Its Injurious Effects on the Men of the Army and Navy (1864)." *P.P.,* 1867–8 (4031), XXXVII.

"Report of the House of Commons Select Committee on the Contagious Diseases Act." *P.P.,* 1868–9 (306), VII.

"Report from the Royal Commission on the Administration and Operation of the Contagious Diseases Acts 1866–9 (1871)." *P.P.,* 1871 (C.408–I), XIX.

"Copy of Memorial to the Home Department in Favour of the Contagious Diseases Acts, Signed by Members of the Medical Profession Resident in London." *P.P.,* 1872, XLVII.

"Report of the House of Commons Select Committee on the Administration, Operation, and Effects of the Contagious Diseases Acts of 1866–69." *P.P.,* 1878–9 (323), VIII; *P.P.,* 1880 (114), VIII; *P.P.,* 1880 (301), VIII; *P.P.,* 1881 (351), VIII; *P.P.,* 1882 (340), IX.

"Report from the Select Committee on Poor Removal Together with the Proceeding of the Committee and Minutes of Evidence." *P.P.,* 1878–9 (282), XII.

"Report of the Assistant Commissioner of Police of the Metropolis on the Operation of These Acts (1881)." *P.P.,* 1882 (291), LIII.

"Report of the Select Committee of the House of Lords Appointed to Inquiry into the State of the Law Related to the Protection of Young Girls." *P.P.,* 1882 (344), XIII.

"The Memorial of the Undersigned Magistrates, Clergy, Medical Practitioners, and Others, in the Borough of Plymouth and Devonport, and Township of Stonehouse." *P.P.,* 1882 (356), LIII.

"Judicial Statistics (England and Wales) for 1884." *P.P.,* 1884–5, (C. 4518) LXXXVI.

Hansard Parliamentary Debates (Commons), 3rd ser., 30 (6 August 1885), col. 1345.

"Judicial Statistics (England and Wales) for 1886." *P.P.,* 1887 (C. 5155), XL.

"First Report of the Royal Commission on the Liquor Licensing Laws." *P.P.,* 1897 (C. 8355), XXXIV.

"Report of the Royal Commission on the Duties of the Metropolitan Police." *P.P.,* 1908, L.

"Report of the Royal Commission on Veneral Diseases." *P.P.,* 1916 (Cd. 8190), XVI.

"Report of the House of Commons Street Offences Committee." *P.P.,* 1928–9 (Cmd. 3231), IX.

Selected Bibliography

"Report of the Committee on Homosexual Offences and Prostitution."
P.P., 1956–7 (Cmd. 247), XIV.

PRINTED SOURCES PUBLISHED BEFORE 1918

Acton, William. "Prostitution." *Transactions of the National Association for the Promotion of Social Sciences* 1 (1857), 605–8.
  Prostitution. 1870. Edited by Peter Fryer. New York, 1968.
  Prostitution Considered in Its Moral, Social, and Sanitary Aspects in London and Other Large Cities; with Proposals for the Mitigation and Prevention of Its Attendant Evil. London, 1857.
  The Functions and Disorders of the Reproductive Organs in Youth, in Adult Age, and in Advanced Life: Considered in Their Physiological, Social, and Moral Relations. London, 1857.
Alison, Archibald. *The Principle of Population.* Edinburgh, 1840.
Amos, Sheldon. *Laws in Force for the Prohibition, Regulation and Licensing of Vice in England and Other Countries.* London, 1877.
Association for Extending the Contagious Diseases Act. *The Effects of the Contagious Diseases Acts in Diminishing Disease in the Army and Navy and Among the Civil Population.* Being an Examination of a Paper Read Before the Statistical Society of London by the Right Hon. James Stansfeld, M.P. London, 1876.
Bevan, William. *Prostitution in the Borough of Liverpool.* Liverpool, 1843.
Birmingham Anti-Contagious Diseases Acts Association. *Report of Deputation to Plymouth, with Summary of Results of Cases Investigated, and Short-Hand Notes of Enquiry by Referees as to the Case of Maria Bennett.* Birmingham, 1870.
Blackburn, Helen. *Women's Suffrage: A Record of the Women's Suffrage Movement in the British Isles, with Biographical Sketches of Miss Becker.* London, 1902.
Butler, Josephine. *Address Delivered at Croydon, July 3, 1871.* London, 1871.
  Address Delivered in Craigie Hall, Edinburgh, Feb. 24, 1871. Manchester, 1871.
  An Appeal to My Countrymen. 1870.
  An Appeal to the People of England on the Recognition and Superintendance of Prostitution by Government. 1870.
  An Autobiographical Memoir. Edited by G. W. Johnson and L. A. Johnson. Bristol, 1928.
  A Letter on the Subject of Mr. Bruce's Bill Addressed to the Repealers of the Contagious Diseases Acts. Liverpool, 1872.
  A Letter to the Members of the Ladies' National Association. Liverpool, 1875.
  Memoir of John Grey of Dilston. Edinburgh, 1869.
  New Era: Containing a Retrospect of the History of the Regulation System in Berlin of the Repeated Opposition Directed Against the

327

System There . . . and of the Source Whence Hope Arises for the Future. Liverpool, 1872.

Personal Reminiscences of a Great Crusade. London, 1911.

Recollections of George Butler. Bristol, 1892.

Social Purity. An Address Given at Cambridge, in May 1879. London, 1879.

Sursum Corda; Annual Address to the Ladies' National Association. Liverpool, 1871.

The Constitution Violated. Edinburgh, 1871.

ed. *Vox Populi.* Liverpool, 1871.

ed. *Women's Work and Women's Culture.* London, 1869.

Chapman, John. "Prostitution and Government Efforts in Controlling It," *Westminster Review* 93 (1900), 119–79.

Colquhoun, Patrick. *Treatise on the Police of the Metropolis.* London, 1797.

Compston, H. F. B. *The Magdalen Hospital: The Story of a Great Charity.* London, 1917.

Coote, W. A. *A Romance of Philanthropy. Being a Record of Some of the Principal Incidents Connected with the Exceptionally Successful Thirty Years' Work of the National Vigilance Association.* London, 1916.

Cousins, John Ward. "Analysis of One Hundred and Eighty-Two Cases Treated in the Lock Wards of the Royal Portsmouth, Portsea and Gosport Hospital," *M.T.G.* (1871), 469, 470, 524.

Curgenven, J. B. *The Contagious Diseases Act of 1866 and Its Extension to the Civil Population of the United Kingdom.* Paper read at the meeting of the health department of the National Association for the Promotion of the Social Sciences, March 30, 1868. London, 1868.

Deakin, C. W. Shirley. *The Contagious Diseases Acts: The Contagious Acts, 1864, '66, '68 (Ireland), '69. From a Sanitary and Economic Point of View.* Read before the Medical Society of University College, London, November 30, 1871. London, 1872.

Dolling, Robert R. *Ten Years in a Portsmouth Slum.* London, 1896.

Downward Paths: An Inquiry into the Causes Which Contribute to the Making of the Prostitute, with a foreword by A. Maude Royden. London, 1913.

Ellis, Havelock. *The Task of Social Hygiene.* Boston, 1915.

Flexner, Abraham. *Prostitution in Europe.* New York, 1914.

[Greg, W. R.] "Prostitution," *Westminster Review* 53 (1850), 448–506.

Gregory, Maurice. *A Short Summary of the Parliamentary History of State-Regulated Vice in the United Kingdom.* London, 1900.

Some Notes on the Financial Relations Between "Friends" and the Association for Moral and Social Hygiene and Its Predecessors. N.p., n.d.

The Suppression of the White Slave Traffic: Historical Sketch of the English Section of the Movement. London, 1908.

Selected Bibliography

Hill, M. Berkeley. "Illustrations of the Workings of the Contagious Diseases Acts," *B.M.J.* (1867), 583, 585.

"Statistical Results of the Contagious Diseases Acts," *J.S.S.* 33 (1870), 435–85.

Syphilis and Local Contagious Disorders. London, 1868.

Hopkins, Jane Ellice. *Drawn unto Death.* London, 1882.

Hume-Rothery, Mary. *A Letter Addressed to the Right Hon. W. E. Gladstone, M.P. and the Other Members of Her Majesty's Government and of Both Houses of Parliament, Touching the Contagious Diseases Acts of 1866 and 1869, and Their Proposed Extension to the Civil Population of This Kingdom.* Manchester, 1870.

Ingestre, Viscount. *Meliora: Or Better Things to Come.* 2nd ed. London, 1852.

Lancereaux, Etienne. *A Treatise on Syphilis,* trans. C. Whitley. 2 vols. London, 1868–9.

Leffingwell, Albert. *Illegitimacy and the Influence of Season upon Conduct; Two Studies in Demography.* New York, 1892.

Logan, William. *An Exposure from Personal Observation of Female Prostitution in London, Leeds, and Rochdale, and Especially in the City of Glasgow; with Remarks on the Cause, Extent, Results and Remedy of the Evil.* Glasgow, 1843.

Lowndes, F. W. "The Liverpool Lock Hospital and the Prevalence and Severity of Constitutional Syphilis in Liverpool," *B.M.J.* 1 (1880), 727–9.

Prostitution and Syphilis in Liverpool, and the Working of the Contagious Diseases Acts, at Aldershot, Chatham, Plymouth, and Devonport. London, 1876.

Managers of Metropolitan Female Reformatories. *An Exposure of the False Statistics of the Contagious Diseases Acts.* London, 1871.

Mayhew, Henry, ed. *London Labour and the London Poor.* 4 vols. London, 1861–2; reprint, New York, 1968.

Melville, C. H. "The History and Epidemiology of Syphilis in the More Important Armies" in *A System of Syphilis,* Ed. D'Arcy Power and J. K. Murphy. 6 vols. London, 1910.

Merrick, Rev. G. *Work Among the Fallen, as Seen in the Prison Cells.* London, 1890.

Miller, A. G. "Four and a Half Years Experience in the Lock Wards of the Edinburgh Lock Infirmary," *Edinburgh Medical Journal* 28 (1882), 385–403.

Miller, James. *Prostitution Considered in Relation to Its Cause.* Edinburgh, 1859.

National Association for the Repeal of the Contagious Diseases Acts. *Condition of the Subjected Districts Since the Suspension of Compulsory Periodical Examination.* London, 1884.

Nevins, J. B. "Enquiry into the Condition of Prostitution," *Medical Enquirer* 2 (1876–7), 17–28.

Selected Bibliography

Statement on the Grounds upon Which the C. D. Acts Are Opposed. London, 1874.

What Public Measures Can with Benefit Be Adopted for the Diminution of Veneral Diseases? London, 1880.

Newman, David. "The History and Prevention of Veneral Diseases," *Glasgow Medical Journal* 81 (1914), 88–100.

Pankhurst, Christabel. *The Great Scourge and How to End It.* London, 1913.

Parent-Duchâtelet, A. J. B. *De la prostitution dans la ville de Paris considérée sous le rapport de l'hygiène publique, de la morale, et de l'administration.* 2nd ed. 2 vols. Paris, 1857.

Prynne, Rev. G. R. *Thirty-five Years of Mission Work in a Garrison and Seaport Town.* Plymouth, 1883.

Robinson, F. W. [A Prison Matron]. *Female Life in Prison.* 2 vols. London, 1862.

The Royal Commission as a Court of Justice: Being an Examination of the Declaration of the Commissioners That "the Police Are Not Chargeable with Any Abuse of Their Authority." Nottingham, 1871.

Sanger, William W. *History of Prostitution: Its Extent, Causes and Effects Throughout the World.* New York, 1897.

Scott, Benjamin. *A State Iniquity, Its Rise, Extension, and Overthrow.* London, 1894.

Simon, John. *Report on the Contagious Diseases Act, Showing the Expense In Policy, and General Inutility of Its Proposed Extension to the Civil Population.* London, 1871.

Sinclair, William. *On Gonorrheal Infection in Women.* London, 1888.

Six Years' Labour and Sorrow: Being the Fourth Report of the London Committee for Suppressing the Traffic in British Girls for the Purpose of Continental Prostitution. London, 1885.

Stead, W. T. *Josephine Butler: A Life Sketch.* London, 1887.

The Maiden Tribute of Modern Babylon (The Report of the "Pall Mall Gazette's" Secret Commission). London, 1885.

Tait, William. *Magdalenism: An Inquiry into the Extent, Causes and Consequences of Prostitution.* Edinburgh, 1840.

Talbot, J. B. *The Miseries of Prostitution.* London, 1844.

Three Towns Directory. Plymouth, 1873.

Wardlaw, Richard. *Lectures on Female Prostitution.* Glasgow, 1842.

Weston, Agnes. *My Life Among the Bluejackets.* London, 1909.

Whitfeld, Henry. *Plymouth and Devonport in Times of War and Peace.* Plymouth, 1900.

Wilkinson, J. J. Garth. *The Forcible Introspection of Women for the Army and Navy by the Oligarchy Considered Physically.* London, 1870.

Wilson, J. H. *Copy of a Rough Record of Events and Incidents Connected with the Repeal of the Contagious Diseases Acts, 1864–6–9.* Sheffield, 1906.

Selected Bibliography

PRINTED SOURCES PUBLISHED AFTER 1918

Abel-Smith, B. *The Hospitals 1800–1948: A Study in Social Administration.* London, 1964.

Abrams, Philip. *Origins of British Sociology 1834–1914.* Chicago, 1968.

Ackerknecht, Edward. "Hygiene in France, 1815–48," *Bulletin of the History of Medicine* 22 (1948), 117–55.

Anderson, Michael. *Family Life in Nineteenth-Century Lancashire.* Cambridge, 1971.

Anderson, Mosa. *H. J. Wilson: Fighter for Freedom, 1833–1914.* London, 1953.

Ariès, Philippe. *Centuries of Childhood: A Social History of Family Life,* trans. Robert Baldick. New York, 1962.

Banks, J. A., and Banks, Olive. *Feminism and Family Planning in Victorian England.* New York, 1964.

Barker-Benfield, Ben. "The Spermatic Economy," in *The American Family in Social-Historical Perspective,* ed. Michael Gordon. New York, 1973.

Basch, Françoise. *Relative Creatures: Victorian Women in Society and the Novel.* New York, 1974.

Bianco, Richard L. "The Attempted Control of Venereal Disease in the Army of Mid-Victorian England," *Journal of the Society for Army Historical Research* 45 (Winter 1967), 234–41.

Booth, Charles. *Charles Booth's London.* Edited by Albert Fried and Richard Elman. London, 1969.

Bower, Sir William Nott. *Fifty-Two Years a Policeman.* London, 1926.

Briggs, Asa. "Cholera and Society in the Nineteenth Century," *Past and Present* 19 (April 1961), 76–96.

Bristow, Edward. *Vice and Vigilance: Purity Movements in Britain Since 1700.* Dublin, 1977.

Brown, E. G. Phelps. *The Growth of British Industrial Relations: A Study from the Standpoint of 1906–1914.* London, 1965.

Brown, G. H., ed. *Lives of the Fellows of the Royal College of Physicians 1826–1925.* 4 vols. London, 1955.

Butler, A. S. G. *Portrait of Josephine Butler.* London, 1954.

Chesney, Kellow. *The Anti-Society: An Account of the Victorian Underworld.* Boston, 1970.

Chevalier, Louis. *Dangerous Classes and Laboring Classes in Paris During the First Half of the Nineteenth Century,* trans. Frank Jellinek. New York, 1973.

Cluer, Andrew. *Plymouth and Plymouthians.* Plymouth, 1974.

Comfort, Alex. *The Anxiety Makers: Some Curious Preoccupations of the Medical Profession.* Bristol, 1967.

Cominos, Peter L. "Late-Victorian Sexual Respectability and the Social System," *International Review of Social History* 8 (1963), 18–48, 216–50.

331

Selected Bibliography

Cott, Nancy F. "Passionlessness: An Interpretation of Victorian Sexual Ideology, 1790–1851," *Signs* 4 (1979), 219–36.

Dangerfield, George. *The Strange Death of Liberal England.* New York, 1935.

Davidoff, Leonore. "Class and Gender in Victorian England: The Diaries of Arthur J. Munby and Hannah Cullwick," *Feminist Studies* 5 (Spring 1979), 87–141.

Engel, Arthur, "Immoral Intentions: The University of Oxford and the Problem of Prostitution, 1827–1914," *Victorian Studies* 23 (1979), 79–107.

Erikson, Kai. *Wayward Puritans: A Study in the Sociology of Deviance.* New York, 1966.

Fawcett, Millicent, and Turner, E. M. *Josephine Butler: Her Work, Principles and Their Meaning for the Twentieth Century.* London, 1927.

Fessler, Arnold. "Advertisements on the Treatment of Venereal Disease and the Social History of Veneral Disease," *B.J.V.D.* 25 (1949), 84–7.

"Venereal Disease and Prostitution in the Reports of the Poor Law Commissioners, 1834–1850," *B.J.V.D.* 27 (1951), 154–7.

Finnegan, Frances. *Poverty and Prostitution: A Study of Victorian Prostitutes in York.* Cambridge, 1979.

Foucault, Michel. *The History of Sexuality. Volume I: An Introduction,* trans. R. Hurley. New York, 1978.

Madness and Civilization: A History of Insanity in the Age of Reason, trans. R. Howard. New York, 1965.

Fowler, W. S. *A Study in Radicalism and Dissent: The Life and Times of Henry Joseph Wilson 1833–1914.* London, 1961.

French, R. D. *Anti-Vivisection and Medical Science in Victorian Society.* Princeton, 1975.

Gatrell, V. A. C, and Hadden, T. B. "Criminal Statistics and Their Interpretation," in *Nineteenth-Century Society: Essays in the Use of Quantitative Methods and Study of Social Data.* Cambridge, 1972.

Gillis, John R. "Servants, Sexual Relations and the Risks of Illegitimacy in London, 1801–1900," *Feminist Studies* 5 (Spring 1979), 142–73.

Gorham, Deborah. "The 'Maiden Tribute of Modern Babylon' Re-examined: Child Prostitution and the Idea of Childhood in Late-Victorian England," *Victorian Studies* 21 (Spring 1978), 353–79.

Hall, Gladys Mary. *Prostitution: A Survey and a Challenge.* London, 1933.

Haller, John S., and Haller, Robin. *The Physician and Sexuality in Victorian America.* Urbana, 1974.

Hammond, J. L., and Hammond, Barbara. *James Stansfeld: A Victorian Champion of Sex Equality.* London, 1932.

Harrison, Brian. *Drink and the Victorians: The Temperance Question in England, 1815–1872.* London, 1971.

"State Intervention and Moral Reform," in *Pressure from Without in Early Victorian England,* ed. Patricia Hollis. London, 1974.

Selected Bibliography

"Underneath the Victorians," *Victorian Studies* 10 (March 1967), 239–62.

ed. *Dictionary of British Temperance Biography*. Sheffield, 1973.

Hartman, Mary S., and Banner, Lois, eds. *Clio's Consciousness Raised: New Perspectives on the History of Women*. New York, 1974.

Heasman, Kathleen. *Evangelicals in Action: An Appraisal of Their Social Work in the Victorian Era*. London, 1962.

Heyck, T. William, "British Radicals and Radicalism, 1874–1895: A Social Analysis," in *Modern European Social History*, ed. Robert J. Bezucha. Lexington, Ky., 1972.

Himmelfarb, Gertrude. "Mayhew's Poor: A Problem of Identity," *Victorian Studies* 14 (March 1971), 307–20.

Hoskins, G. W. *Devon*. London, 1964.

Hudson, Derek, ed. *Munby, Man of Two Worlds: The Life and Diaries of Arthur J. Munby, 1828–1910*. London, 1972.

Hugill, Sam. *Sailortown*. London, 1967.

Shanties and Sailor's Songs. London, 1969.

Jones, Gareth Stedman. *Outcast London: A Study in the Relationship Between Classes in Victorian Society*. Oxford, 1971.

Kamm, Josephine. *Rapiers and Battleaxes: The Women's Movement and Its Aftermath*. London, 1966.

Keating, Peter, ed. *Into Unknown England 1866–1913: Selections from the Social Explorers*. Glasgow, 1976.

Lasagna, Louis. *The V.D. Epidemic: How It Started, Where It's Going and What to Do About It*. Philadelphia, 1975.

Laslett, Peter, *Family Life and Illicit Love in Earlier Generations*. Cambridge, 1977.

L'Esperance, Jean. "The Work of the Ladies' National Association for the Repeal of the Contagious Diseases Acts," *Bulletin of the Society for the Study of Labour History* (Spring 1973), 14–16.

Lloyd, Christopher. *Keevil's Medicine and the Navy, 1200–1900*. 4 vols. Edinburgh, 1963.

Macdonagh, O. R. "Nineteenth-Century Revolution in Government: A Reappraisal," *Historical Journal* 1 (1958), 52–67.

McLaren, Angus. *Birth Control in Nineteenth-Century England*. New York, 1978.

McLeod, R. M. "Law, Medicine and Public Opinion: The Resistance to Compulsory Health Legislation 1870–1901," *Public Law* (1967), 189–211.

Marcus, Steven. *The Other Victorians: A Study of Sexuality and Pornography in Mid-Nineteenth-Century England*. New York, 1966.

Moore, J. E. "Public Health Measures for the Control of Syphilis," *Lancet* 1 (1951), 699–713.

Morton, R. S. *Venereal Diseases*. London, 1966.

Nield, Keith, ed. *Prostitution in the Victorian Age: Debate on the Issues from Nineteenth-Century Critical Journals*. Westmead, 1973.

Selected Bibliography

Owen, David. *English Philanthropy 1660–1960.* Cambridge, Mass., 1964.

Patterson, A. Temple. *A History of Southampton. Vol. 2: The Beginnings of Modern Southampton 1836–1867.* Southampton, 1971.

A History of Southampton, 1700–1914. Southampton, 1975.

Pearson, Michael. *The Age of Consent: Victorian Prostitution and Its Enemies.* Newton Abbot, 1972.

Perkin, Harold, *The Origins of Modern English Society, 1780–1880.* London, 1969.

Peterson, M. Jeanne. *The Medical Profession in Mid-Victorian London.* Berkeley, 1978.

Petrie, Glen. *A Singular Iniquity: The Campaigns of Josephine Butler.* New York, 1971.

Pivar, David. *Purity Crusade: Sexual Morality and Social Control 1868–1900.* Westport, Conn., 1973.

Plarr, G. V. *Plarr's Lives of the Fellows of the Royal College of Surgeons of England.* 2 vols. London, 1930.

Rasor, Eugene L. *Reform in the Royal Navy; A Social History of the Lower Deck 1850 to 1889.* Hamden, Conn., 1976.

Rolph, C. A., ed. *Women of the Streets: A Sociological Study of the Common Prostitute.* London, 1955.

Rosebury, Theodor. *Microbes and Morals: The Strange Story of Venereal Disease.* New York, 1971.

Rosen, George. *Madness in Society: Chapters in the Historical Sociology of Mental Illness.* Chicago, 1971.

Rosenberg, Charles. "And Heal the Sick: The Hospital and the Patient in the Nineteenth Century America," *Journal of Social History* 10 (1976–7), 428–47.

"Sexuality, Class and Role in Nineteenth Century America," *American Quarterly* 24 (1973), 131–53.

"The Therapeutic Revolution: Medicine, Meaning and Social Change in Nineteenth-Century America," *Perspectives in Biology and Medicine* 20 (1977), 485–506.

Rover, Constance. *Women's Suffrage and Party Politics in Britain, 1866–1914.* London, 1967.

Ryan, Mary. "The Power of Women's Networks: A Case Study of Female Moral Reform in Antebellum America," *Feminist Studies* 5 (Spring 1979), 66–89.

Samuel, Raphael. "Comers and Goers," in *The Victorian City: Images and Realities,* ed. H. J. Dyos and Michael Wolff. New York, 1973.

Saville, John. *Rural Depopulation in England and Wales 1851–1951: Studies in Rural Sociology.* London, 1957.

Semmel, Bernard. *Imperialism and Social Reform.* Garden City, N.Y., 1960.

Shelley, Alan Ramsay. *The Victorian Army at Home.* London, 1977.

Sigsworth, E. M., and Wyke, T. J. "A Study of Victorian Prostitution and

Venereal Disease," in *Suffer and Be Still: Women in the Victorian Age,* ed. Martha Vicinus. Bloomington, 1972.

Smith, F. B. "Ethics and Disease in the Later Nineteenth Century: The Contagious Diseases Acts," *Historical Studies* 15 (October 1971), 118–35.

Smith, Llewellyn, ed. *The New Survey of London and Labour.* London, 1932.

Smith-Rosenberg, Carroll. "Beauty and the Beast and the Militant Woman: A Case Study in Sex Roles and Social Stress in Jacksonian America," *American Quarterly* 23 (October 1971), 562–84.

Stearns, Peter N. "Working-Class Women in Britain, 1890–1914," in *Suffer and Be Still: Women in the Victorian Age,* ed. Martha vicinus. Bloomington, 1972.

Storch, Robert D. "Police Control of Street Prostitution in Victorian London: A Study in the Contexts of Police Action," in *Police and Society,* ed. David H. Bayley. Beverly Hills, Calif., 1977.

Strachey, Ray. *The Cause: A Short History of the Women's Movement in Great Britain.* London, 1928.

Temkin, Owsei. "Therapeutic Trends and the Treatment of Syphilis Before 1900," *Bulletin of the History of Medicine* 39 (1955), 309–16.

Thomas, Keith. "The Double Standard," *Journal of the History of Ideas* 20 (1959), 195–216.

Thompson, E. P. *The Making of the English Working Class.* New York, 1963.
and Yeo, Eileen, eds. *The Unknown Mayhew.* New York, 1972.

Thompson, Paul. *Socialists, Liberals, and Labour: The Struggle for London, 1885–1914.* Toronto, 1967.

Tobias, J. J. *Crime and Industrial Society in the Nineteenth Century.* New York, 1967.

Trudgill, Eric. *Madonnas and Magdalens: The Origins and Development of Victorian Sexual Attitudes.* New York, 1976.

Vicinus, Martha, ed. *A Widening Sphere: Changing Roles of Victorian Women.* Bloomington, 1977.

Walkowitz, Judith R., and Walkowitz, Daniel J. " 'We Are Not Beasts of the Field': Prostitution and the Poor in Plymouth and Southampton Under the Contagious Diseases Acts," *Feminist Studies* 1 (Winter 1973), 73–106.

Weeks, Jeffrey. *Coming Out: Homosexual Politics in Britain from the Nineteenth Century to the Present.* London, 1977.

Williams, Raymond. *Marxism and Literature.* Oxford, 1977.

Woodham-Smith, Cecil. *Florence Nightingale, 1820–1910.* London, 1951.

Wyke, T. J. "Hospital Facilities for and Diagnosis of Venereal Disease in England 1800–1870," *B.J.V.D.* 49 (1973), 78–85.
"Manchester and Salford Lock Hospital 1818–1917," *Medical History* 19 (1975), 73–90.

335

Index

Index

338

Index

thorities, repeal movement, medical support for; syphilis, venereal disease
domestic service, *see* women's work, domestic service
double standard, 3, 6, 43, 48, 70, 71, 90, 93, 128, 141, 142, 238, 239, 255, 256, 294 n14
  see also sex prejudice; sexual behavior; sexual ideology
dress, 13, 26, 195, 208
  reform of, 129
dressmakers, *see* women's work, clothing trades
Drysdale, Charles, 81, 82
Drysdale, George, 81
Dyer, Alfred, 248, 249
  The European Slave Trade in English Girls, 248
Dyer, George, 102

Edinburgh, 23, 37, 39, 63, 64, 125, 133, 142
Edinburgh Society for the Protection of Young Girls, 39
Edmondson, Joseph, 141, 285 n56
Elmy, Elizabeth Wolstenholme, 82, 93, 120, 123
Estlin, Mary, 114, 121, 126, 175

family
  evangelical concept of, 33–4
  and marriage, feminist views of, 125, 128
  working-class, 145, 251
  see also sexual behavior; sexual ideology; women's sphere
Fawcett, Millicent, 125
female subculture, *see* women's networks
feminism, 5, 81, 82, 91, 119, 131, 132, 146, 165, 166, 172, 238
  higher education, 6, 117, 125
  and individual rights, 88, 93
  and marriage, 125, 128
  property rights, 6, 125
  and sex, 255–6
  suffrage, 6, 83, 88, 91, 125, 129, 134, 162, 255
  see also individual rights; *separate*

reform movements and associations; women's public and political activities
feminists, 1, 85, 111, 112, 113, 128, 130, 178, 202, 245, 247, 249, 253
Finsbury Radical Clubs, 102
Flexner, Abraham, 15
Foucault, Michel, 4, 5, 59
Fournier, Alfred, 230, 254
Fowler, William, 95

Gladstone, William, 1, 32, 76, 96, 128, 130
Glasgow, 16, 63, 133
Glasgow Police Act, 242
gonorrhea, 2, 18, 49, 50, 55, 56, 64, 65, 183, 226, 227, 230, 254, 288 n112
  medical theory of, 53–4, 227, 228, 272 n38
  medical treatment of, 54, 254
  and pelvic infections, 54
  and sterility in women, 54
Greater Plymouth, 7, 8, 152, 153, 154, 157, 162, 163, 176, 179, 188, 193, 197, 205, 235
Greenwich, 25
Greenwood, James, 26, 27
Greg, W. R., 42, 43, 44, 45, 46, 71
Grey, Hannah, 115
Grey, Harriet, 115
Grey, John, 115
Grey, Margaretta, 115
Groser, A., 234, 235, 238

Hampshire, 198
Hampson, Mrs. R., 144, 186, 191
Harcourt, Vernon, 99
Harris, William, 80, 81
Harrison, Brian, 6
  Drink and the Victorians, 6
Hartington, Lord, 99
Harveian Medical Society of London, 79, 81
Hearne, Edwin, 168, 190
Hemyng, Bracebridge, 17, 22, 23, 29
Hicks, Harriet, 181–4, 185, 203, 204, 299 n54

339

Index

Index

Land and Labour League, 101, 168
Lane, James, 62, 63, 64
Langley, Baxter, 106
laundresses, *see* women's work,
   laundering
Leeds, 133, 134, 135, 140, 142, 143
leprosy, 59, 274 n69
Lewis, Mrs., 175, 181
Liberal Party, 95, 96, 98, 99, 100,
   106, 152, 162, 166, 168, 169,
   186 n85
   Radicals, 74, 90, 94, 96, 98, 100,
      104, 106, 113, 169
Liddell, John, 76
Littleton, William, 176, 190, 233,
   234, 237, 238, 318 n25
Liverpool, 16, 27, 63, 94, 106, 116,
   134, 143, 186, 211, 247, 251
lock asylums, *see* lock hospitals
lock hospitals, 2, 18, 57, 65, 75,
   131, 133, 136, 181, 197, 209,
   241
   admissions to, 58, 61
   conditions in, 214–15, 224
   disturbances in, 214, 217, 223–4,
      226
   finances of, 59, 60, 218–20, 227,
      313 n18
   functions of, 57, 59–60, 61, 62,
      159, 215, 220, 222–3
   hierarchy in, 221
   moral and social training in, 216,
      220–1, 222, 224
   patients, 57, 61, 63, 159, 216
      ages, 63, 262 n35
      origins, 63–4, 260 n9, 305 n6
lock wards, *see* lock hospitals
lodging house keepers, 21, 26, 28,
   106, 138, 147, 163, 198, 200,
   205, 206, 211, 251, 286 n93
   relations with prostitutes, 28, 198,
      200, 206
lodging houses, 21, 24, 25, 28, 30,
   45, 46, 76, 103, 111, 159, 172,
   193, 203, 204, 239, 252, 265
   n76, 287 n111, 305 n5, 308 n39
Logan, William, 33
London
   East End prostitutes, 13–14, 22,
      23, 29–30

extension of C.D. acts, 80, 82, 86
hierarchy of prostitutes, 23
proportion of venereal patients
   among the sick poor, 50
repeal of C.D. acts, 92, 99
West End prostitutes, 22, 23, 42
London Committee for Suppressing
   the Traffic in British Girls, 248
London Society for the Protection of
   Young Girls and the Suppres-
   sion of Juvenile Prostitution
   (London Rescue Society), 17–
   18, 39–40, 91, 101, 176, 190,
   206, 237, 240
Lowndes, F. W., 64
Lucas, Margaret Bright, 119, 121, 236
Lucraft, Benjamin, 105
Lushington, Vernon, 161

McLaren, Duncan, 120
magistrates, 7, 128, 138, 163, 168,
   174, 190, 204, 224, 239
Malta, 78, 106
Manchester, 25, 49, 63, 105, 125
Manning, Cardinal, 278 n56
Marshall, John, 103, 132, 166, 167,
   175, 184, 190, 233, 235, 237,
   239, 240, 218 n25
Martineau, Harriet, 77, 126, 281 n3
masturbation, 45, 100
Maurice, F.D., 95
Mayhew, Henry, *London Labour
   and the London Poor,* 179
Mazzini, Giuseppe, 101, 123
mechanics' institutes, 104, 176
medical profession, 59, 60, 86, 97,
   129, 254, 255, 256
   authorities, 2, 78, 92
   elite, 82, 88
   see also doctors
Medical Officers of Health, 87
medical reform, 125, 129–31, 173,
   254
metropolitan police, *see* police
middle class, provincial, 115
   *See also different categories of re-
      form; separate reform move-
      ments and associations;* sexual
      behavior; sexual ideology;
      women's sphere

341

Index

Midland's Electoral League, 94, 113, 252
military, 48, 72, 73, 74, 75, 80, 129, 162, 169, 230
reform, 173
Miller, James, 41
Moore, M. M., 182, 288
moral reform, 40, 61, 70, 72, 116, 125, 131, 139, 162, 170, 173, 222, 246, 251, 298 n28
see also repeal movement; separate reform movements and associations; social purity
moral reformers, 20, 33, 34, 85, 152, 203, 205
see also Ladies' National Association; repealers; social purity
Moral Reform Union, 101
Munby, A. J., 16, 22, 23, 32
Mundella, A. J., 95, 100, 143

National Association for the Promotion of Social Science, 82, 92, 124
National Association for the Repeal of the Contagious Diseases Acts (National Association) 2, 92, 103, 106, 129, 138, 140, 252
activities in Greater Plymouth, 152, 166–7, 180, 186, 233, 234, 235, 237, 240
ineffectiveness of, 96, 98, 100, 101, 111, 137
leadership, 92, 99–101
and women, 93
National Education League, 99, 162
National Liberal Federation, 98
National Medical Association, 97
National Vigilance Association, 99, 251, 252
navy, see Admiralty
needleworkers, see women's work, clothing trades
Neisser, Albert, 230, 254
Nevins, Birkbeck, 111
Newcastle, 49, 134
Newman, F. W., 82, 83, 84
Newman, John Henry, 83
Nichol, Elizabeth Pease, 124
Nicholson, Caroline, 165, 221

Nightingale, Florence, 1, 75, 76, 77, 120, 281 n3
Noegerrath, Emil, 254
Nonconformity, see religion, Nonconformist
Northbrook, Lord, 99
Northern Counties League, 94, 96, 100, 113, 140–1
North of England Council for Promoting the Higher Education of Women, 117
Northumberland, 115
Nottingham, 91
nurses, 221, 222, 224

Oldham, 26
orphanages, 157
Owenite Socialism, 35, 36
Oxford, 22, 116

Pankhurst, Christabel, The Great Scourge and How to End It, 256
Pankhurst, Sylvia, 255
Parent-Duchâtelet, A. J. B., 36, 37, 38, 43, 44, 46, 193
De la prostitution dans la ville de Paris, 36
Parliament, 1, 2, 72, 74, 76, 79, 98, 110, 111, 117, 248
House of Commons, 70, 96, 100, 245
House of Lords, 40, 80, 86, 248, 250
Select Committee of 1869, 86
of 1881, 230
of 1882, 241
Percy case, 110, 143, 233
personal rights, see individual rights
Personal Rights Association, see Vigilance Association
pimps, 25, 45, 159, 211, 212
Plymouth, 30, 124, 132, 133, 147
composition of population, 29
concentrated areas of prostitution, 25, 155, 159, 203, 206
economic conditions in, 154, 195, 212

Index

Index

sex prejudice, 23, 55, 56, 65, 71, 81, 140, 176, 221
  see also repeal movement, sexual divisions; sexual behavior; sexual ideology
sexual behavior
  female, 43, 45, 71, 81, 84, 123, 147, 178, 203, 256
  male, 42, 44, 45, 53, 70, 71, 81, 100, 110, 146, 256
  middle-class, 45, 53, 81, 123
  working-class, 199, 239, 243, 245, 251, 253
  youthful, 239, 246, 249
sexual harassment, 34, 39, 46, 108
sexual ideology, 3, 4, 5, 7, 19, 33, 35, 55, 56, 57, 60, 69, 70, 72, 85, 128, 130, 141, 142, 183, 249, 254, 292 n60
  middle-class, 5, 33, 35, 45, 56, 141, 249
  working-class, 200, 203, 204–5, 210
Shaen, William, 101, 248
Sheffield, 96, 100, 129, 135, 253
Shield, 92, 109, 152, 176, 189, 234, 235, 237
Simmons, Ebenezer, 181, 182, 183
Simon, John, 50, 85
Sloggett, William, 160, 161, 180, 187, 191, 214, 215, 216, 219, 223, 225, 226, 228, 229, 231
Snagge, W. T., 248
social hygiene, 255
social investigation, 32, 37, 124
socialism, 35, 247, 251, 255, 319–320 n5
social purity, 100, 133, 139, 166, 211, 236, 242–5, 251, 252, 253, 254, 255
  origins in Plymouth, 238–40
  and working class, 237, 246, 311–12 n84
Social Purity Association, 101, 127, 239
Society for the Suppression of Vice, 42
soldiers, 23, 24, 159
Southampton, 30, 130, 133, 147
  compared to nearby towns, 169–70; crime in, 154

economic conditions in, 154, 195, 212
  as key subjected town, 7
  legal resistance in, 205
  prostitutes in, 9, 192–201, 210, 231
  repeal in, 167–9, 188–91, 233
  social purity in, 245
Southampton Female Asylum, 157
Southampton Women's Suffrage Society, 168
Southwest Counties League, 252
speculum and speculum examination, 56, 57, 93, 95, 108, 130, 146, 169, 205, 221, 229, 292 n61, 322 n57
  as "instrumental rape," 109, 110, 114, 129, 170, 201–2, 256
Stansfeld, James, 6, 96, 97, 98, 101, 103, 104, 120, 132, 139, 233, 234, 236, 250, 283 n37
Stanton, Elizabeth Cady, 124
state intervention, 3, 71, 72, 128, 140, 246, 250, 251, 255, 256
Stead, W. T. 21, 99, 117, 120, 134, 250, 251
  "Maiden Tribute of Modern Babylon," 246, 247, 248–9, 251
Steward, Mary, 127, 129, 236
Storks, Henry, 106
Stuart, James, 241
Subjected Districts League, 233
Swain, Paul, 92, 253
Swan, W. T., 103, 157, 235, 239, 240
syphilis, 2, 18, 22, 44, 48, 49, 51, 55, 63, 64, 65, 85, 111, 130, 158, 177, 182, 183, 195, 223, 226, 227, 230, 231, 254, 264 n54, 270 n9, 288 n112
  medical theory of, 50–1, 229, 254, 271 n11, 307 n17
  medical treatment of, 51–2, 283 n37
  mercury treatment of, 52–3, 55, 59, 229, 326 n78

Tait, William, 25, 33, 36, 37, 38, 39, 41, 43, 46, 47

345

Index

Talbot, J. B., 33, 39
Tanner, Margaret, 93, 114, 119, 120, 121, 122, 127, 175, 236, 240
Taylor, Charles Bell, 91, 92, 292 n61
temperance, 33, 41, 123, 124, 162, 165, 167
Thomas, Keith, 70
Thomasson, J. P., 121
Thompson, Dorothy, 145
Three Towns, see Greater Plymouth
Tilly, Louise, 16
Tod, Isabella, 124
tuberculosis, 195
Tyler, Wat, 108

United Kingdom Alliance, 99, 103
uterus, 57, 292 n60

Vaccination Acts, 71, 108, 129
  antivaccination movement, 99, 179
venereal disease, 3, 19, 42, 48, 60, 73, 75, 152, 156, 159, 161, 171, 184, 195, 215, 230, 253, 254, 307 n17
  medical theory of, 49, 183, 230
  medical treatment for, 48, 50, 64, 65, 232, 253, 254
  in men, 54, 55, 56, 58, 59, 229, 237
  preventive care of, 63, 65
  repealers' view of, 93, 97, 111, 130, 179, 234, 256
  see also chancroid; gonorrhea; lock hospitals; syphilis
Venturi, Emily Ashurst, 101, 120, 123
Vigilance Association, 129, 251, 252, 292 n58
vigilance committees, 212, 252

Walker, Lucy, 127, 133
Wardlaw, Ralph, 33, 35, 36, 37, 43
War Office, 2, 72, 76
Western Daily Mercury, 162
Western Morning News, 162, 236, 238

Weston, Agnes, 157
white slavery, 17, 247, 248–52, 256, 309 n38
White Slavery Act of 1912, 256
Wigham, Elizabeth, 122, 123
Wilkinson, J. J. Garth, *The Forcible Introspection of the Women for the Army and Navy by the Oligarchy Considered Physically*, 108
Williams, Raymond, 5
Williams, R. B., 91, 176, 206
Wilson, Charlotte, 108, 129, 134, 135, 290 n26
Wilson, Gertrude, 135, 140
Wilson, H. J., 96, 98, 100–1, 104, 135, 137, 140, 141, 143, 233, 285 n56, 291 n51, 294 n12
Windsor, 78
Wolferstan, Sedley, 161, 235
Wolstenholme, Elizabeth, see Elmy, Elizabeth Wolstenholme
women reformers, *see separate reform movements and associations;* women's public and political activities
women's networks
  between classes, 6, 9, 131, 136, 138, 176, 180, 222, 255
  between prostitutes, 201
  middle-class, 113
  working-class, 26, 27, 31, 206
women's public and political activities, 3, 88, 93, 121, 131, 134, 135, 139, 144, 178, 238, 302 n37
  see also separate reform movements and associations
Women's Social and Political Union, 255
women's sphere, 7, 117, 131, 178, 238, 256
women's suffrage, *see feminism*
women's work, 22, 32, 46, 62, 117, 119, 143, 145, 154, 194, 213, 264 n55
  clothing trades, 14, 15, 24, 34, 38, 62, 195, 209, 222, 226
  domestic service, 15, 16, 62, 63, 119, 157, 165, 194, 195, 223, 237

346

Index